THE
FamilyCircle
CHRISTMAS TREASURY

Other Books by Family Circle:

THE BEST OF FAMILY CIRCLE COOKBOOK
1986 FAMILY CIRCLE COOKBOOK
ABZ'S OF COOKING
RECIPES AMERICA LOVES BEST
FAMILY CIRCLE HINTS BOOK
DELICIOUS DESSERTS
GREAT MEALS ON A TIGHT BUDGET
PERFECT POULTRY
GREAT MEALS IN ONE DISH

To order **FamilyCircle** books, write to Special Projects Dept., Family Circle, 488 Madison Avenue, New York, NY 10022.

To subscribe to **FamilyCircle** magazine, write to Family Circle Subscriptions, 488 Madison Avenue, New York, NY 10022.

Project Staff

Project Editor—Ceri E. Hadda
Copy Editor—Wallace A. Kunukau, Jr.
Book Design—Bessen & Tully, Inc.
Typesetting—Vickie Almquist, Helen Russell
Assistant—Gwen Buckley
Illustrations—Lauren Jarrett

Family Circle Staff

Project Manager—Margie Chan-Yip
Project Coordinators—Joanne Hajdu, Marty Heebner
How-to Editor—Anna Marie Doherty
Associate—Arlene Gise; Assistant—Kathy Rubenstein
Great Ideas Editor—Marie T. Walsh
Production Manager—Michael Golden
Photocomposition Manager—Wendy Hylfelt

Cover Photo—Bill McGinn
Photographers—Jules Alexander, Glen Allison, Tito Barbaris, Ralph Bogertman,
John Galluzzi, Maris/Semel, Bill McGinn, Rudy Muller, Leonard Nones,
Bradley Olman, Bruno Pellegrini, Ron Schwerin, Gordon E. Smith, Bob Stoller,
Bob Strode, Theo, René Velez, Ken Whitmore
How-to Illustrations—William J. Meyerriecks

Published by The Family Circle, Inc.
488 Madison Avenue, New York, NY 10022

Copyright ©1986 by The Family Circle, Inc.

Manufactured in the United States of America

10 9 8 7 6

Library of Congress Cataloging in Publication Data
Main entry under title:

The Family circle christmas treasury.
Includes index.
1. Christmas decorations   2. Christmas cookery.
I. Family Circle, Inc.   II. Title: Christmas treasury.
TT900. C4F36   1986   745.594'1   86-11598
ISBN O-933585-02-0

THE

FamilyCircle

CHRISTMAS TREASURY

TABLE OF CONTENTS

I. HOLIDAY PLANNER 6

II. DECK THE HALLS—OUTSIDE AND IN 20
Outdoor Decorations 22
Decorative Door Trims 29
Window Treatments 34
Entryway Ideas 37
Stockings to Stuff 39
Wreaths 43
Centerpieces 50

III. YULETIDE TREE TRIMMINGS—FROM THE TOP DOWN 58
Tree Toppers 61
Ornaments 68
Garlands 75
Tree Skirts 80

IV. THEMES TO SET THE MOOD 84
Christmas, Victorian-Style 87
The Natural Touch 93
Country Casual 97
With Kids in Mind 101

V. FILLING THE GIFT LIST 106
For Grandma and Grandpa 108
For Him, For Her 116
From Tots to Teens 129
For Kids to Make 145

The Gift Bazaar 148

Last-Minute Gifts 154

Wrapping It Up 158

VI. THE HOLIDAY SPREAD 162

Traditional Christmas Dinner (for 8) 164

Danish Open House Buffet (for 24) 174

Christmas Morning Brunch (for 10) 184

International Feast (for 12) 192

Dinner on the Light Side (for 10) 204

Holiday Entertaining Guide 214

VII. GIFTS FROM THE KITCHEN 230

Preserves and Condiments 232

Breads and Fruitcakes 238

The Christmas Cookie Jar 252

Savory Delights 270

Super-Quick Goodies 274

Food Wrap-Ups 277

Packing and Shipping Food 277

VIII. CRAFT BASICS AND ABBREVIATIONS 278

IX. MATERIALS SHOPPING GUIDE 292

INDEX 294

INTRODUCTION

A *Christmas Treasury—because Christmas is a time to treasure… a time to be with loved ones and exchange gestures of caring. With the joy comes a lot of work, too. You want to select gifts that will please everyone. You want to prepare your home so it will be festive, decorative and warm. And you want your holiday food to be tasty and special.*

The Family Circle Christmas Treasury will help you create the Christmas of your dreams.

We start you off with a "Holiday Planner" to help you organize all your seasonal activities, like gift shopping, cookie baking and buying your tree. Then, you'll find cheery decorating ideas for your entire home, from the lawn and front door to the entryway and all through the house. Projects that are especially quick or inexpensive are marked with symbols (see below).

Because Christmas is also a time to share, you'll want to choose from our menagerie of gifts, like easy-to-make stocking-stuffers and colorful quilts and sweaters. Even if you're a novice—not to worry. Our how-to primer (pages 278-291) will show you the basics of knitting, crocheting and embroidery. And to make your holiday planning even more family-oriented, we've included some projects and recipes the kids can help with.

What's Christmas without a holiday spread? We've included five delectable meals to satisfy virtually every taste and preference. For a casual air, try our "Danish Open House Buffet." With our "Dinner on the Light Side," waist-watchers can indulge without guilt. Or, just be "Traditional" with a glazed ham and all the trimmings! For hassle-free preparation, we give you complete countdowns so all of your courses will be perfectly timed. We've also labeled each recipe to let you know whether it's Low-Cost, Quick and Easy, Make-Ahead or Low-Calorie. If you enjoy receiving food gifts, why not give some of your own? Our chapter of sweet and savory treats will inspire you.

Fill your home with Christmas splendor this year, and every year. Let The Family Circle Christmas Treasury be your guide to creating delicious holiday treats, sure-to-please personalized gifts and decorations to spark everyone's holiday spirits!

A NOTE ON SYMBOLS USED IN THIS BOOK

*Throughout the Christmas Treasury, we've included symbols to help you
identify projects and recipes that suit your skill level and preferences.*

💲 Low-Cost   ⚡ Quick and Easy   ◀◀ Make-Ahead   🎚 Low-Calorie

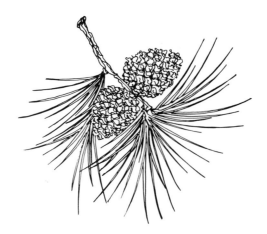

THE
HOLIDAY
PLANNER

There are so many things to keep track of during the holiday season—shopping, gift making, gift wrapping, holiday baking... the list goes on and on. That's why organization is a must! Our helpful holiday guidelines are designed to make your Christmas planning a joyful process now and always.

We start you off in late summer with gift planning and your big craft projects, and see you all the way through leaving a snack for Santa on Christmas Eve. Flip to our lists (beginning on page 10) and start making notes to yourself. You'll never be frantic during the Christmas rush again!

LATE SUMMER

- Start your gift list (see page 12) by thinking about people's talents, travel and hobbies. To cut down on returns, update clothing sizes for everyone on your gift list. (Remember that babies will be almost five months bigger by Christmas time!)
- Consider planning a holiday bazaar at your local church or school.
- Start making those gifts that take a bit more effort, such as the Trip Around the World and Kentucky Mountain Chain Quilts on page 110; cuddly Twin Stuffed Dolls (page 138); our Mr. and Mrs. Claus outdoor decoration (page 24); a matching Orange Tweed Cardigan and Hat (page 134); and cute Twig Doll Furniture (page 132).

SEPTEMBER

- Send away for holiday mail-order catalogs.
- Put together the items you'll be selling at your bazaar (see ideas in the "Gift Bazaar," page 148).

OCTOBER

- Now's the time to make your more intricate decorations, like the Door Tree (page 29), perky Stockings (page 41) and the Peppermint Candy Wreath (page 48).
- Make a list of the ingredients you'll need for Christmas baking and holiday meals. Check your pantry inventory.

8 WEEKS TILL CHRISTMAS

- It's time to bake the breads, cookies and cakes you plan to freeze. (See pages 191 and 258 for freezing tips.)

7 WEEKS TILL CHRISTMAS

- Mark all special dates for the season on your calendar—school and church concerts, parties, school vacations, etc.

- Start collecting a basketful of inexpensive stocking-stuffers and small gifts for children and unexpected guests.
- Avoid last-minute searching: Gather your favorite holiday recipes and keep them in an envelope. Make a list, with page numbers, of recipes in books. Note which can be made ahead.

6 WEEKS TILL CHRISTMAS

- Order catalog gifts *now*. Most take from 4 to 6 weeks to arrive.
- Buy the Christmas turkey to store in your freezer, if you have space.
- Do any of your cooking utensils, serving dishes, platters, glasses and china place settings need replacing?

Tip Store nonperishable foods to be used during the holidays for one meal in a labeled bag—easy to find when you start cooking.

- Make sure all electrical appliances—including TV, mixer, hot trays—are in working order.
- Decide what additional holiday decorations you're going to make rather than buy (see Chapters II, III and IV).

5 WEEKS TILL CHRISTMAS

- Get some of your gift shopping done early at church bazaars and school fairs.

Tip Start saving boxes in useful sizes for packing presents.

- Polish silver pieces. Store in airtight plastic bags.
- Make edible gifts to give (see Chapter VII).
- Buy Christmas cards and stamps. You should also collect all of your other paper supplies, like napkins, paper cups, wrapping paper and ribbon (or alternative gift-wrapping materials such as fabric, baskets and tins).
- Update your Christmas card list by noting any address or name changes.

4 WEEKS TILL CHRISTMAS

- Mail those Christmas cards.
- Send invitations out for Christmas and holiday parties.
- Make fruitcakes and plum puddings. Store to mellow (see page 248).
- Do you have enough cooking pots and stovetop burner space for the dishes you plan to serve?
- Make and freeze hors d'oeuvres and casseroles.
- Plan menus for Christmas Eve, Christmas Day and for parties. (See "The Holiday Spread," pages 162 to 229, for five menus and countdowns.)
- Special-order goose, game or fresh turkey for Christmas dinner.
- Plan time for a special holiday outing or activity with each of your children, perhaps an afternoon of gift making they can be involved in (see page 145).

3 WEEKS TILL CHRISTMAS

- Schedule beauty appointments—haircut, perm, manicure, etc.
- Have your kids help you make a Gingerbread House (see page 55).
- Stock up on canned and frozen foods, crackers and chips for instant snacks.
- Do you have enough paper and cleaning supplies (foil, wax paper, food-storage and garbage bags, dish detergent)?
- Are your holiday outfits in tip-top shape? (Fix hems and loose buttons; make alterations and get clothing dry-cleaned.) Add a dash of excitement to your wardrobe with sequins for Fantasy Fashion Trims (see page 122).
- Make pie shells and freeze.

Tip Wrap and tag presents as you buy them. Tag the children's presents with numbers if you don't want them to guess whom the packages are for!

2 WEEKS TILL CHRISTMAS

- It's time to go to work on those outdoor decorations: Hanging the lights, decorating your door—and setting out the wooden Mr. & Mrs. Claus (see page 24) you've made.
- Take a look at your tablecloths—do you see any burn holes? Stains? Fix, clean and iron now.
- Arrange to exchange baby-sitting time with another mother so each of you will have free shopping hours.
- Are there any items on your mail-order list that haven't arrived yet?
- Devote an evening or two to any last-minute gifts you want to make.
- Buy batteries for presents that need them.

Tip Use some of your homemade goodies as hostess gifts at holiday parties you're attending. (For last-minute edibles to give, see page 274.)
- Find the Christmas stockings! (Unless you've made special new ones for the family, see page 41.)

1 WEEK TILL CHRISTMAS

- Do your indoor decorating. Remember to put holiday towels in the bathroom and decorations in the kitchen and the guest room. (For easy decorating ideas, see Instant Yuletide Windows, page 36, and Jiffy Decorations, page 38.)
- Start stocking up on ice cubes.
- Buy your tree and store it temporarily in a bucket of water in the garage. (See page 60 for other tips on Christmas tree care.)
- Test tree lights. (See page 70 for Christmas tree light safety tips.)
- Do you have graham crackers or cookies for Santa's snack?

COUNTDOWN TO A HOLIDAY PARTY

Use this party planner for any of your holiday parties, whether company's coming just for cocktails or for a sumptuous feast. It will help space out your chores so you aren't too exhausted to enjoy your own get-together!

Once you've decided how many people to invite and have planned your menu, it's time to make lists.

List #1: Food Include everything from snacks—mints and nuts—and "real" food (such as casseroles) to ingredients needed for all recipes. Divide the list into two columns: nonperishables and perishables.

List #2: Beverages Liquor, mixers, juice, soda (have plenty on hand for nondrinkers), coffee, tea.

List #3: Nonfood items Cocktail napkins, plastic glasses, dripless candles, ice, flowers or centerpieces, paper towels, aluminum foil.

One Week Before
1. Order the ice and flowers and check your beverage inventory against your list.
2. Shop for nonperishable foods.
3. Buy everything on List #3, except ice and flowers.

Four Days Before
4. Select the serving dishes you'll use and set them aside in your cupboard. Need more? Ask a friend now.
5. Check tablecloths, napkins, place mats. Wash and press them if you need to.

6. Make sure you have enough silverware, ashtrays, vases, pitchers, etc.

Three Days Before
7. Do the heavy cleaning, such as floors and walls, and tidy up the house. Let the whole family pitch in.
8. Decide where guests' coats will go. If in a closet, have enough hangers on hand.

Two Days Before
9. Buy the perishables on List #1. Wash and trim the vegetables, then refrigerate them.

One Day Before
10. Make extra ice if needed.
11. Prepare the dishes which can be reheated or served cold.

"The" Day
12. Give the house a once-over in the morning. (If your bedroom is the coat room, neaten it now.)
13. Pick up the flowers and the ice.
14. Use "kid power" to help clean. Set out ashtrays and guest soaps.
15. Arrange the flowers, candles and set up the eating areas and bar.
16. Assemble the ingredients for the dishes which must be cooked that day.

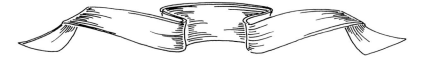

HOLIDAY PLANNING LISTS

To ensure that you'll be super-organized this holiday season, we've included this section of lists designed especially with the Christmas rush in mind. With these helpers at your side, your gift-giving and shopping will be a breeze, and your party will go off without a single hitch—all because you've planned well, and well ahead. Use our lists as style guides for creating your own lists. Or, write directly into the book with a pencil and erase for future use.

CHRISTMAS CARD LIST

Make a list of the people you plan to send cards to this year, then check your supply. Go out and buy any additional cards you'll need. Or, make some yourself with help from the kids (suggestions on page 146). While you're at it, take a trip to the post office for festive holiday stamps. *Note:* We've set up a "received from" column on this list so that you can reciprocate those who remembered *you* during the holidays.

SEND TO　　　　　　　　　　　　　　　　**RECEIVED FROM**

GIFT LIST

Your immediate family and closest friends will obviously head this list, but now is the time to plan for the other special people who sometimes slip through the cracks during the holiday rush—such as your mail carrier, your newspaper boy, your hairdresser. With this list, you'll be sure to include everyone, plus be able to keep track of how much is coming out of your wallet!

NAME	GIFT ITEM	SIZE	COST (Budget/Actual)

GIFT BAZAAR LIST

Get your neighborhood or church friends together and organize a local bazaar. Jot down who'll be involved and what each person will contribute. A bazaar is a great way to make a little extra holiday cash for a local charity or for yourself. You may also find some great items at the bazaar to help fill your own gift shopping list.

PERSON   **CONTRIBUTION**

_____   _____

_____   _____

_____   _____

_____   _____

_____   _____

_____   _____

_____   _____

_____   _____

_____   _____

_____   _____

_____   _____

_____   _____

_____   _____

_____   _____

_____   _____

_____   _____

_____   _____

_____   _____

_____   _____

_____   _____

_____   _____

_____   _____

CRAFTS MATERIALS LIST

Once you've decided which beautiful crafts and decorations you'll make this year—check your supplies. Write down what you'll need to buy in order to complete your projects. Be sure to check our Materials Shopping Guide on page 293 for specific manufacturer's products that are suggested for some of our projects.

CRAFT	MATERIALS NEEDED	MATERIALS TO BUY

GUEST LIST

Whom are you inviting to your holiday gathering, and how many guests will attend? Check off the names as RSVPs come in. Make sure you have extra food and beverages on hand for the few unexpected guests that arrive.

GUEST	YES	NO	Bringing a Friend
	☐	☐	☐
	☐	☐	☐
	☐	☐	☐
	☐	☐	☐
	☐	☐	☐
	☐	☐	☐
	☐	☐	☐
	☐	☐	☐
	☐	☐	☐
	☐	☐	☐
	☐	☐	☐
	☐	☐	☐
	☐	☐	☐
	☐	☐	☐
	☐	☐	☐
	☐	☐	☐
	☐	☐	☐
	☐	☐	☐
	☐	☐	☐
	☐	☐	☐
	☐	☐	☐
	☐	☐	☐
	☐	☐	☐
	☐	☐	☐
	☐	☐	☐
	☐	☐	☐

FOOD AND BEVERAGE LIST

As you go through your recipe file for ideas, make a list of all the foods you'd like to serve. (You can narrow it down later.) If you have to borrow freezer space from a neighbor, jot down what dishes are with whom. A beverage list should include items like tea and coffee, as well as assorted liquors, wines and punches.

FINGER FOODS/
APPETIZERS _____

_____

_____

_____

SALAD _____

_____

_____

_____

_____

MAIN COURSE _____

_____

_____

_____

_____

DESSERT _____

_____

_____

_____

BEVERAGES _____

_____

_____

CHORE LIST

Jot down all the things you must do—shopping, cleaning, food preparation—
when they must be accomplished and who is to help you with the task. Also,
make a special chore list for last-minute reminders on Party Day, and be sure
each helper gets a copy.

CHORE TO BE DONE	BY WHOM	DATE TO BE COMPLETED

PARTY SHOPPING LIST

List the foods you must purchase, and don't forget staples, such as sugar, salt, pepper, butter and assorted condiments. How much should you buy? Try to estimate what you think you will need, then add at least 25% more. (Better to eat leftovers for a week than to see the table go bare just when the festivities are getting into gear!)

ITEMS	BUY	RENT	AMOUNT
	☐	☐	
	☐	☐	
	☐	☐	
	☐	☐	
	☐	☐	
	☐	☐	
	☐	☐	
	☐	☐	
	☐	☐	
	☐	☐	
	☐	☐	
	☐	☐	
	☐	☐	
	☐	☐	
	☐	☐	
	☐	☐	
	☐	☐	
	☐	☐	
	☐	☐	
	☐	☐	
	☐	☐	
	☐	☐	
	☐	☐	
	☐	☐	
	☐	☐	

INVENTORY LIST

Don't be caught short! The following checklist will ensure that nothing is overlooked. Place those items that need to be purchased or rented on your Party Shopping List, page 18.

ITEM	**YES**				
Coat Hangers	☐	Tablecloths	☐	Ice Cubes	☐
Ashtrays	☐	Platters	☐	Records/Tapes	☐
Glassware	☐	Warming Trays	☐	Guest Towels/Soap	☐
Silverware	☐	Corkscrews	☐	Extra Light Bulbs	☐
Dishes	☐	Liquor	☐	First-Aid Supplies	☐
Napkins	☐	Mixers	☐	Film/Blank Video Cassette	☐
Chairs	☐	Coffee/Tea	☐	Miscellaneous	
Decorations	☐	Salt/Pepper/Sugar	☐	_____	
Tables	☐	Catsup/Mustard	☐	_____	
		Other Condiments	☐	_____	

FIX-UP LIST

To avoid embarrassments, like a toilet backing up or chairs that collapse, make those repairs that you've been putting off for so long. Assign some of the responsibilities to members of your family well in advance, and give them a "due date."

REPAIR TO BE DONE	**BY WHOM**	**DATE TO BE COMPLETED**
_____	_____	_____
_____	_____	_____
_____	_____	_____
_____	_____	_____
_____	_____	_____
_____	_____	_____
_____	_____	_____
_____	_____	_____
_____	_____	_____

A felt Santa Door Wreath (page 30) welcomes all who come to visit.

DECK THE HALLS
OUTSIDE AND IN

Open the door to a houseful of Christmas decorating ideas! Start by giving the outside of your home a Yuletide look with colorful decorations that lead from the yard right up to the front door. We include instructions for door treatments such as the perky Santa Door Wreath shown at left (with mantel and stocking-stuffer variations), as well as exciting yard decorations like our handsome Mr. and Mrs. Claus display for the lawn (page 24).

Window trims hint at all the holiday spirit within. Wreaths made from cinnamon sticks or leftover wrapping paper (page 35) are as attractive as they are sturdy. Other decorations can be extra special (sew a pair of holiday curtains from muslin or calico—page 36) or extra quick (try one of our Instant Yuletide Window ideas—page 36).

Of course, no holiday home would be complete without special indoor decorations, too. As your guests come through the door, greet them with an entryway that's filled with the warmth of Christmas. Create this spirit by using flowers, candles, ribbons or a bit of all three (page 38).

If you don't already have a cache of heirloom stockings, create your own family treasures from our mantel of international designs (page 41). Place festive wreaths and garlands all over the house. Display our gold Origami Wreath (page 44) on your table or on a wall. Other projects include a charming Gingerbread House (page 55) the kids can help decorate.

For those pressed for time, Jiffy Decorations (page 38) add a Yuletide air in no time at all!

💲 Low-Cost   ⚡ Quick and Easy   ⫘ Make-Ahead   ⫘ Low-Calorie

OUTDOOR DECORATIONS

Mr. and Mrs. Claus (page 24) are built from exterior-grade plywood, so they'll last for many Christmases to come!

FIG. 1 SANTA PATTERN AND CUTTING DIAGRAM FOR ½ SHEET OF PLYWOOD   1 SQ. = 2″

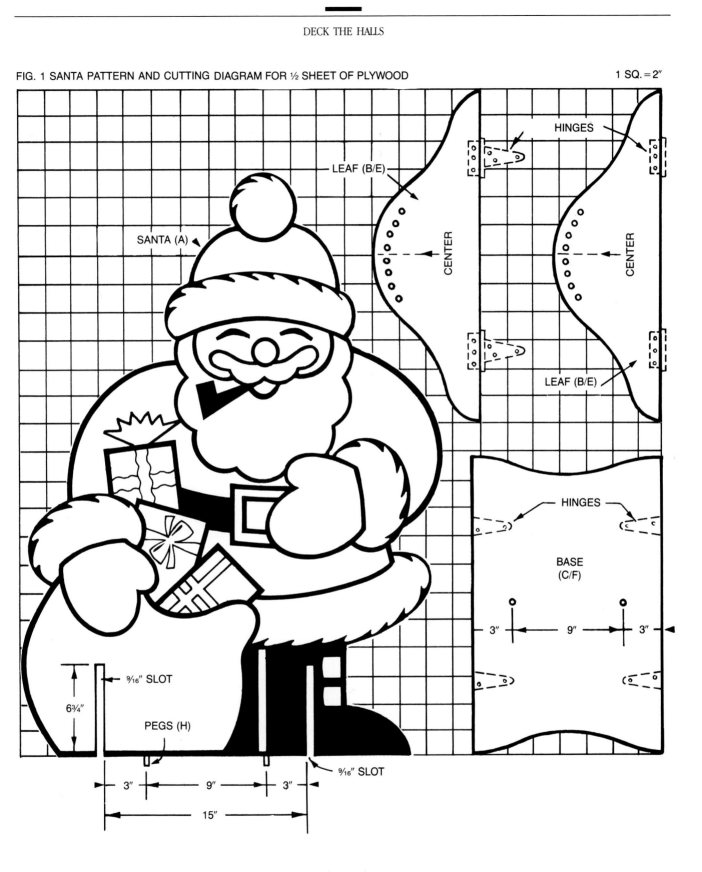

FIG. 2 MRS. CLAUS PATTERN AND
CUTTING DIAGRAM FOR ½ SHEET OF PLYWOOD

1 SQ. = 2″

9/16″ SLOT

CUT BASE AND 2 LEAVES AS IN FIG. 1

PEGS (H)

3   9   3

15

MR. & MRS. CLAUS

AVERAGE: For those with some experience in woodworking.

MATERIALS: Each figure requires one ½″ x 4′ x 4′ piece (one-half sheet) of A-C Ext. APA trademarked plywood; four 2½″ x 4¼″ "T" hinges with ⅜″ Phillips head screws; one ⅜″-dia. x 36″ and one ¼″-dia. x 3″ hardwood dowels; flat clear and flat black polyurethane paint; 18″-wide self-adhesive coverings *(see Materials Shopping Guide, page 293)* in solid colors, except where indicated, as follows:

For Santa—18″ x 88″ black, 18″ x 32″ red, 18″ x 18″ brass, 18″ x 30″ white, 18″ x 12″ blue, 6″ x 7″ candy stripe, 6″ x 6″ yellow, 6″ x 8″ strawberry-green; 6″ x 10″ chrome.

For Mrs. Claus—18″ x 80″ black, 18″ x 30″ white, 18″ x 27″ red, 18″ x 12″ blue, 18″ x 12″ gridworks-red, 6″ x 10″ yellow, 18″ x 12″ brass, 10″ x 12″ chrome.

Tools required: Saber saw; Phillips-head screwdriver; drill with ¼″ and ⅜″ bits; scissors; tracing and carbon paper; rolling pin.

CUTTING DIRECTIONS:

CODE	PIECES	SIZE
A(PLY)	1	½″ x 31″ x 42″ Santa
B(PLY)	2	½″ x 7″ x 23″ Base leaves
C(PLY)	1	½″ x 15″ x 21½″ Base
D(PLY)	1	½″ x 24½″ x 39″ Mrs. Claus
E(PLY)	2	½″ x 7″ x 23″ Base leaves
F(PLY)	1	½″ x 15″ x 21½″ Base
G(DOW)	4	⅜″-dia. x 18″ Braces (2 per figure)
H(DOW)	4	¼″-dia. x 1″ Pegs (2 per figure)

DIRECTIONS:

1. Enlarge the patterns in Figs. 1 and 2 following the directions on page 291.

2. After enlarging the patterns to full

from the ½″ plywood with the saber saw; cut slots in the bottom edge. Sand the edges.

3. Drill ¼″-dia. x 1″-deep holes for pegs (H) in the bottom edge of the figure, 3″ on center from the inside edges of the slots and 9″ apart on center (see Figs. 1 and 2). Apply 2 coats of the flat clear polyurethane to both sides and edges.

4. Apply the black vinyl carefully to the entire front of the figure; press down and roll flat with the rolling pin. (See the manufacturer's general directions.)

5. Return to the enlarged pattern. With a heavy pencil, define the edges of the color sections to create a ¼″ space between all parts (this space will become a black border separating the colored parts when they are applied to the figure).

6. Trace off and transfer the various parts to the appropriate color vinyl (see photo).

7. Start at the top of the figure to apply parts. Check each piece, trim if necessary, then remove the backing and apply that piece to the figure, leaving ¼″ between for the black vinyl to create a "border." Roll flat.

8. The Stand: Drill the ⅜″-dia. holes in the leaves (B/E), starting ½″ on center from each side of the center line, ¾″ on center from the leaf edge and 1″ on center spaces between the holes. Drill ⅜″-dia. holes in the base (C/F), centered front to back, 3″ on center from the side edges, 9″ on center apart (see Figs. 1 and 2).

9. Paint the base leaves (B/E) and the base (C/F) black on all sides. When dry, attach the straight leaf of the hinges to the leaves (B/E), 4″ from each end. Place the base (C/F), bottom up, on the edge of a workbench or table. With the leaf (B/E) hanging down, lightly butt the leaf straight-edge to the edge of the base. Attach the tapered end of the hinges to the underside of the base (C/F).

10. Cut the ⅜″ dowels (G) in half

(18″). Two per figure are required.
11. To erect the figures, raise the leaves (B) upright. Slide the slots in the figure down on the leaves, placing the pegs (H) in the holes in the base. Push a dowel (G) through the holes in the leaves, one in the front of the figure and one at the back. The holes/dowels are placed so the base can be tilted to conform to a sloped ground while the figure remains erect.

QUICK OUTDOOR TRICKS

● *Kids will enjoy this project. Make and hang welcoming "ice panels" outside the house if the weather's freezing. Coil yarn around the bottom of a tin pie pan, with an extra length off the side to use as a hanger. Pour some water in the bottom of the pan; when it's partially frozen, arrange bits of leaves, holly, nuts and stones in a decorative arrangement. When they are frozen in place, gently press the panel out of the pie pan (if it doesn't come out easily, dip the bottom briefly in hot water) and hang it from the branch of a tree or on the front door.*

● *Fill window boxes with spray-painted pinecones and tie an oilcloth "ribbon" around them.*

● *Wind greens around the gatepost and tie with a red oilcloth bow.*

● *Something for the birds: Giant Christmas "balls" that are actually small bags of colored oilcloth filled with nuts and suet. Stitch the bags on one side, keeping the other side open for easy entry, and attach to tree limbs with large bows.*

● *Also for the birds—and for beauty: String cranberry and popcorn garlands on the trees outside your house.*

● *Light the way for guests with home-made lanterns along the walkway to your front door. Fill coffee or vegetable cans with water up to ⅛″ below the rim and put them in the freezer.*

(The ice keeps the can from losing its shape as you work on it.) Then measure a piece of paper (brown paper bagging is good) the size of the can and draw a design. Tape the paper to the can with masking tape and place the can on its side on a folded towel. With a hammer and nail, push along the lines of the pattern, tapping the nail firmly two or three times to make each hole. Melt the ice, drain the can, remove the paper and spray the can with aluminum paint. Secure a short votive candle in the lantern with modeling clay.
(Note: Candles are a fire hazard. Keep the flame below the top of the lanterns, and keep the lanterns out of children's reach.)

● *Replace front door light bulbs with colored ones for a quick festive look.*

● *Use clothespins or wire ties to affix outdoor Christmas lights, if their clips have broken.*

PINE-BRANCH TREE

● *Try using pine branches from your own backyard to create an indoor tree. Start by pushing the ends of the branches into a cone-shaped Styrofoam® form, then spray-paint them green, gold or white. Decorate your "tree" with miniature Christmas balls and garlands.*

● *Greens from your own backyard will look fresh and festive adorning banisters, mantels and outdoor decorations.*

FIG. 3 BIRDS

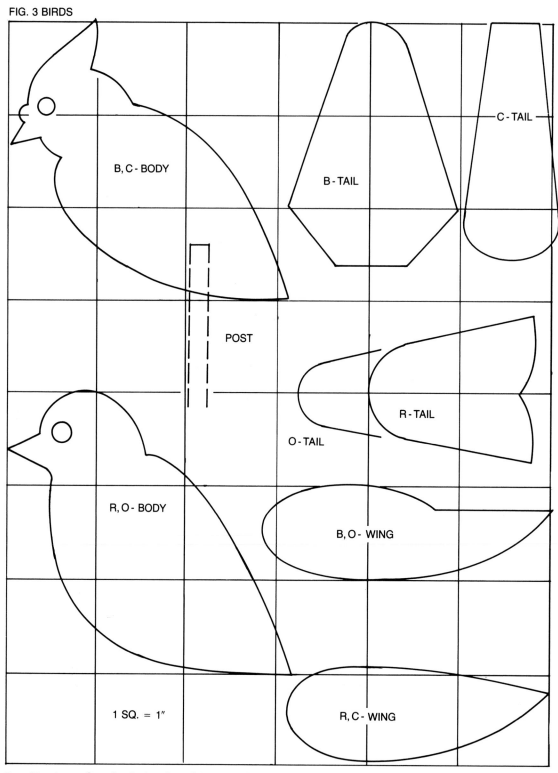

B, C - BODY

B - TAIL

C - TAIL

POST

O - TAIL

R - TAIL

R, O - BODY

B, O - WING

1 SQ. = 1"

R, C - WING

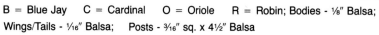

B = Blue Jay   C = Cardinal   O = Oriole   R = Robin; Bodies - 1/8" Balsa;
Wings/Tails - 1/16" Balsa;   Posts - 3/16" sq. x 4 1/2" Balsa

BIRDS 'N' BERRIES WINDOW BOX

AVERAGE: For those with some experience in woodworking.
MATERIALS: Balsa wood; flat polyurethane paints; glue; gingham ribbon bows; real or artificial holly berries; flexible wire.

DIRECTIONS:
1. Enlarge the patterns in Fig. 3 following the directions on page 291.
2. Cut the pattern pieces out of the balsa wood.
3. Paint each part, using the photo as a guide; let dry. Glue these parts together.
4. Wire real or artificial berries to scatter throughout the window box greenery. Attach the ribbon bows to the wire. Insert the berries, bows and birds.

ANOTHER OUTDOOR IDEA

Tie ribbons and rings of juniper and pine around the necks of outdoor terra-cotta animal figurines.

Door Tree

DECORATIVE DOOR TRIMS

POINSETTIAS

As you can see, poinsettias can help you create a very festive entranceway. But if you live in a cooler climate, you should keep them inside. With reasonable care and proper lighting, your Christmas poinsettias can be year-round houseplants, providing brilliant red, white or pink color until spring and delicate green foliage during the other months. Here are some tips to help you keep these beautiful plants healthy and colorful:

Light: *Poinsettias draw vitality from natural light—the more the better. As indoor winter plants, they do best near a window with lots of light. Otherwise, they will tend to shed their leaves prematurely.*

Watering: *Keep your poinsettias moist—never let the soil dry out completely. Test the soil surface with your finger. Add water daily or soak thoroughly at regular intervals. Make sure that drainage is good, too.*

Temperature: *Normal household temperatures—62° to 72°—are ideal for poinsettias in bloom. Night temperatures can drop to 55°. Avoid heated rooms above 75°, temperatures below 50°, chilly drafts and heating systems.*

Humidity: *Humidity above 50% is preferred. Especially low humidity can be very harmful, as the thin leaves are very delicate. Use a plant mister regularly to ensure adequate moisture.*

Feeding: *Poinsettias benefit from regular, constant feeding during the growing season. They prefer a balanced formula fairly high in nitrogen. Reduce the feeding strength by one-half during the winter.*

Insect Control: *Check the plants regularly for signs of infestation. For white flies and mealy bugs, treat plants with an insecticide recommended for this purpose.*

After Christmas: *When Christmas color fades, cut the poinsettias back to about 8". Although this pruning may look severe (and you may feel cruel), new shoots will emerge in the spring. Keep the plants in the house or take them outside for the summer when night temperatures exceed 50°. It is not necessary to repot the poinsettias. Continue to prune or pinch back as desired for shaping during the summer months. Be sure to bring the plants indoors before night temperatures dip below 50°, to ensure healthy-looking leaves.*

ANOTHER SEASON OF BLOOMS

If you leave your poinsettias exposed to normal household lights at night, they will remain year-round foliage plants. To bring them to bloom again, they must be handled in a special way. Poinsettias are short-day, or winter-blooming, plants. They start to bud when nights become 13 hours long, as winter approaches. Any stray light at night at this time interferes with the flowering process. Beginning October 1 until full bloom, probably in early December, poinsettias must have 14 hours of total darkness daily. To achieve this, set the plants in a closet or cover with a large cardboard box every night from 5 P.M. to 7 A.M. Night temperatures during this period should be 62° to 67°; lower temperatures may delay blooming. Provide full natural light during daytime hours. Continue darkness control until the centers are well formed—for about 9 to 10 weeks. Night lights and lowered night temperatures may then be resumed, and your poinsettias will provide another colorful season.

DOOR TREE *(about 7')*

AVERAGE: For those with some crafts experience.
MATERIALS: 2¼ yds. 36"-wide green felt; scraps of colored felt; 5 gold curtain rings; 6 oval tree ornaments for "egg"; 2 dozen clothespins; scraps of ribbon, red and yellow yarn, gold paper, feathers; black and red felt (fine-tip) pens; white glue; about 80 paper fasteners; cord for hangers.

DIRECTIONS:
1. Fold the felt in half lengthwise. Starting about 2' from the bottom, draw a line that tapers to a point at the top of the fold. Cut along the line through both layers (shorten at top to fit the door, if needed).
2. Enlarge the patterns in Figs. 4 and 4A, following directions on page 291.
3. Cut 14 pears, 10 birds in 4 colors (see photo), 7 swans and wings, 11 robes and 12 dresses. Glue wings to swans. Using the bird pieces and photo as a guide, make the following: Add a small circle to partridge head and a large circle to his tail. Decorate 2 calling birds, 3 French hens and 4 turtle doves (see photo). Fold a 5¼" x 32" strip of brown paper into 2"-wide accordion pleats; cut milkmaid (see Fig. 4) through all layers; unfold for the row of 8.
4. For pipes, roll up yellow felt to make 5 tubes graduating from 1½" to 3" long. Fasten them together with a strip of red felt and small sequins (see photo). Make 9.
5. For drums, roll up a 1½" strip of yellow felt to make a drum (about 2" dia.). Glue dark felt to the top and bottom. Glue red yarn in between (see photo). Make 10.
6. For lords, wrap a robe (trimmed as desired) around a clothespin, ☞

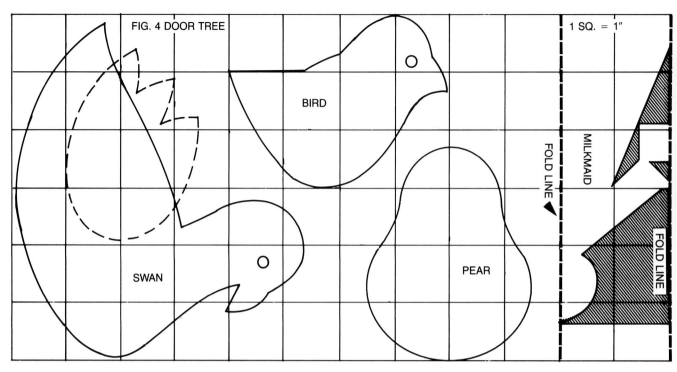

FIG. 4 DOOR TREE

1 SQ. = 1″

BIRD

SWAN

PEAR

MILKMAID

FOLD LINE

FOLD LINE

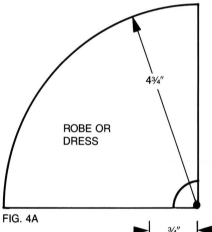

4¾″

ROBE OR
DRESS

FIG. 4A

¾″

back edge and glue. Cut strip of gold paper (notching the upper edge); set it on heads; then lap and glue back edges. Color eyes and mouths with felt pens.

7. For ladies, apply dresses (like robes, above). Wrap yellow yarn "hair" around heads and glue. Color faces, like lords'.

8. Fasten a cord to each ornament (except milkmaids). Arrange them on

the felt tree. Put paper fasteners through the tree above the ornaments (and through the milkmaids). Hang the cords to the "buttons" of the fasteners. Add bows as desired. Fasten the tree to door.

💲

SANTA DOOR WREATH
(page 20) *(26″w.x36″h.)*
MANTEL DECORATION
(13″w. x 18″h.)
AND STOCKING-STUFFER DOLL
(6½″w. x 9″h.)

AVERAGE: For those with some sewing experience.

MATERIALS: For door size, as shown on page 20—26″w. x 36″h.: 30″ x 40″ x ½″ and 22″ x 22″ x ¼″ foam-core boards; 72″-wide felt—⅝ yd. red and ⅜ yd. each of dark, medium and light green and ⅓ yd. each of white and black; two 9″ x 12″ sheets of pale pink felt for face and hands, and 1 sheet each of bright pink for cheeks and gold for belt buckle; 27 red

¾″ buttons with a shank back; glue stick; white glue; clear silicone glue; polyester fiberfill; Scotchgard.

MATERIALS: For mantel size—13″w. x18″h.: 15″ x 20″ x ½″ and 12″ x 12″ x ¼″ foam-core boards; 72″-wide felt—⅓ yd. of red, ⅛ yd. each of dark, medium and light green, ¼ yd. each of white and black; one 9″ x 12″ sheet each of pale pink, bright pink and gold felt; 14 red ½″ buttons with a shank back; clear silicone glue; polyester fiberfill; Scotchgard.

MATERIALS*: For doll size— 6½″w. x 9″h.: 72″-wide felt—¼ yd. of red and ⅛ yd. each of dark, medium and light green; two 9″ x 12″ sheets each of white and black and 1 sheet each of pale pink, bright pink and gold felt; 8 red ⅜″ buttons with a shank back; clear silicone glue; polyester fiberfill; Scotchgard.

*Note: If you are making all 3 sizes, you'll have enough red felt left from the door-size wreath to cut the red portions of the mantel and doll size, too.

FIG. 5 SANTA WREATH - 1 SQ. = 2"   MANTEL - 1 SQ. = 1"   DOLL - 1 SQ. = ½"

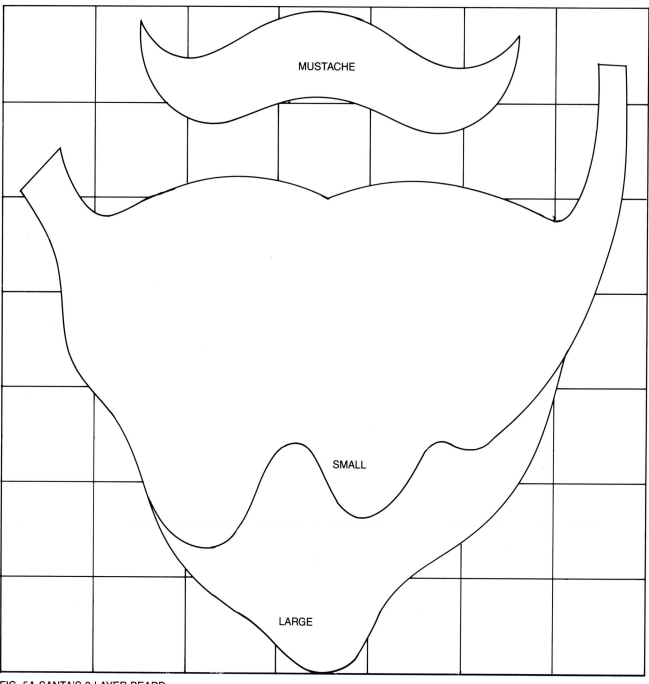

MUSTACHE

SMALL

LARGE

FIG. 5A SANTA'S 3-LAYER BEARD
WREATH - 1 SQ. = 2″
MANTEL - 1 SQ. = 1″
DOLL - 1 SQ. = ½″

DIRECTIONS (for door and mantel sizes):

Read all directions before starting.

1. Trace the actual-size large and small holly leaf patterns separately (see overlay on how-to type; the small leaf is the blank area inside the large one). Cut out leaves in cardboard to make sturdy templates for tracing.

2. Enlarge the Santa pattern in Fig. 5 on a large sheet of brown paper (the pattern is shown without the leaves to make the enlarging easier for you) following the directions on page 291. Also enlarge the mustache and beard pieces in Fig. 5A separately and cut out. From the enlarged pattern, trace off the shapes for the shaded leaf support ring, Santa's belly (extending under the ring), arm, hand, cuff, leg, feet, face, hat, hatband, pompon, nose, cheek, buckle, belt and eyes; cut out the pattern shapes.

3. Cutting (see photo for colors): From the ½″ foam-core board, cut the enlarged Santa pattern (door and/or mantel size) around the outer edges. From the ¼″ board, cut the shaded leaf support ring. From the felt, cut 2 each of mustache/beard pieces, 1 face, 2 eyes, 1 buckle and 1 belt; 30 larger leaf pieces in each color green for door size (14 of each color in small size for mantel Santa). Now cut out the remaining pattern pieces, 1½″ outside the edges all around, to allow room for stuffing with the fiberfill and overlapping board.

4. Holly Leaves: Match the leaves in pairs by color, edges flush. Topstitch close to the edges all around, leaving an opening at the stem end for stuffing. Sew a straight line of stitching down the center, stopping 1″ short of the tip and base (½″ for the smaller leaves). Stuff firmly with fiberfill. Stitch straight across the base to complete; set aside.

For the doll-size wreath, see the separate directions following these.

5. Mustache/Beard: Match the pieces in pairs, edges flush. Topstitch close to the edges, leaving an open-ing at the top; stuff. Stitch the opening closed; set aside.

6. Leaf Support Ring: Cover the ring on one (top) side (around the edges) with the scrap pieces of green or red felt; set aside.

7. Covering the Santa Board (use the photo as a guide): Sew the eyes to the face. Sew the cheeks to the face around the top edges; stuff; sew the bottom edge. Sew the nose with a little stuffing in it. Affix the face to the board with the glue stick.

8. Sew the belt, then the buckle to the red belly piece. Place over the board and glue down the edges, leaving an opening between the legs; stuff with enough fiberfill to make a nice round belly, then bring red felt around the board at the bottom and glue in place on back. (The other rough edges of the red belly piece will be covered with the wreath ring and arm/leg pieces.)

9. Continue to glue/stuff/glue the open edges for all the remaining body pieces, clipping the "seam allowance" where necessary when you overlap the curved board edges; turn under the edges where the felt pieces meet. Do the hat before the brim and pompon; the arms and hands before the cuffs. The top of the boots will be covered by the wreath.

10. Glue the felt-covered leaf ring to the Santa body (see photo), using white glue; let dry.

11. Temporarily put the mustache/beard pieces in place and mark the ring on either side of them. Remove the beard. Sew the red button "berries" to 9 leaves in each color, varying the button placement (see photo). Using clear silicone glue, cover the ring with the leaves (except in beard area), alternating the colors and overlapping the edges to create a full wreath. Make sure the "berries" are evenly distributed. Also, use straight pins to affix the leaf tips to the adjacent leaves.

12. Using silicone, glue the bottom beard, then the middle, then the

mustache in place.

13. Spray the entire wreath with Scotchgard to waterproof the felt. Affix the hanger at the back for door size. Affix a stand at back for mantel size; for the doll, see below.

DOLL-SIZE SANTA WREATH

MATERIALS: See materials for the full-size wreath; you will not need foam-core boards for the doll. Also see note regarding red felt on page 30.

DIRECTIONS:

1. Enlarging and Cutting: Follow Steps 1, 2, 3 above, with these exceptions: Substitute 2 layers of felt in place of the foam-core Santa shape and 2 layers for the ring; do not add extra seam allowance for these 2 shapes; add only ½″ extra seam allowance for all the other shapes requiring it. Cut 8 each of the color felt leaves in the small size.

2. Make only the mustache (see Step 5 above).

3. Match the ring pieces, edges flush, and topstitch around the inner and outer edges.

4. Follow Steps 7 and 8 above, topstitching the face to one of the Santa felt shapes (instead of gluing) and hand-sewing instead of gluing between the legs after stuffing.

5. Follow Steps 9 to 12, sewing by hand and turning under the seam allowances after stuffing; slipstitch the edges for a clean finish. Topstitch or hand-sew the remaining Santa shape to the back of the doll, adding enough stuffing to make it soft and huggable. Spray with Scotchgard to keep it clean a little longer.

DECORATE YOUR FRONT DOOR

like a Christmas package—trim it with wide ribbon, then add a bow, some dried flowers and vines, if you'd like.

WINDOW TREATMENTS

Cinnamon Wreath

💲⚡ CINNAMON WREATH

EASY: Achievable by anyone.
MATERIALS: 8′ heavy (⅛″) wire; tie wire; brown floral tape; #20 wire; 3″ cinnamon sticks; ribbon.

DIRECTIONS:
1. Wire Wreath: Cut the heavy wire in half. Overlap the ends of one piece to make a 15″-dia. circle; fasten the overlap with the tie wire. Repeat; then tape the 2 circles together with the floral tape.
2. Loop a 12″ piece of the #20 wire through each cinnamon stick, twist the ends together and cover with the floral tape.
3. Wire 5 to 6 sticks to make a cluster, then wire the cluster to the wreath. Repeat all around the wreath. Then wrap the wreath with the floral tape.
4. Tie bows and wire them to the wreath about every 8″; tie about 5 bows and wire them to the top.

💲⚡ CINNAMON GARLAND

EASY: Achievable by anyone.
MATERIALS: Thin rope; brown floral tape; #20 wire; 3″ cinnamon sticks; 2½″-wide ribbons; double-faced masking tape.

DIRECTIONS:
1. Cut the rope long enough to drape over the window (see photo, page 34). Cut 2 pieces of the rope for the drop at each side.
2. Wire the cinnamon to the rope (see Steps 2 and 3 above).
3. Tie bows and fasten them (and streamers) to the wall with the double-faced masking tape.

💲⚡ GIFT BOXES WREATH

EASY: Achievable by anyone.
MATERIALS: 10″ square or round of 1″-thick Styrofoam®; gift wrap; 1/16″ ribbon; glue stick; transparent tape; "banker's" pins (1½″ to 2½″ long).

DIRECTIONS:
1. Cut a 1¼″-wide foam wreath with a 10″ outside diameter. Cover with the gift wrap, using the glue stick. Cut small rectangles of foam; wrap them with paper, taping the edges in back and securing the folds at each end with the glue stick. Wrap with the ribbon and tie.
2. Fasten the back of the boxes to the wreath with the glue and pins. Fasten the wreath to the inside of the window with double-faced tape. To dis-guise the back, hang a wreath of greens, the same size, to the ouside of the window.

💲⚡ GIFT BOXES

EASY: Achievable by anyone.
MATERIALS: Boxes; gift wrap; transparent tape; glue stick; ribbon; double-faced tape.

DIRECTIONS:
1. Wrap, tape and glue like the small boxes above.
2. Glue one end of the ribbon to the bottom center of box; bring the ribbon up and over the box; cut the ☞

end and tape it, also, to the bottom center. Repeat at the other two sides.
3. Note: Change the lengths given to suit the ribbon width and box size. Cut ½ yd. of 1½"-wide ribbon. Fold both ends under to overlap at center. Make another loop the same. Place the loops side by side; with the ends even, fold 11" of ribbon over the center of the loops; wrap thin wire (behind bows) around both tails of the 11" ribbon and twist to fasten to form a third pair of bow loops. Fasten the bow to the package with the double-faced tape.

INSTANT YULETIDE WINDOWS

• *Line up a few potted evergreens on the windowsill and add some tinsel, white mini-lights and artificial snow.*
• *Use evergreen garlands to tie back drapes, decorate windowsills and window panes. You can decorate them with Christmas lights, miniature ornaments, ribbon and, of course, pinecones.*
• *Here are some great ways to put your leftover ribbon to good use: Try tucking some colorful bows onto your window panes; hang some as streamers; use it to hang pinecones, holly and decorated Christmas cookies or cookie cutters.*
• *Pin a few shiny Christmas balls to your drapes and valances.*

RUFFLED CURTAINS AND VALANCE

EASY: Achievable by anyone.
MATERIALS: Two 45"-wide fabrics (about 3 yds. printed and 2 yds. striped); 3 curtain rods.

DIRECTIONS:
1. Measure from the curtain rod down to the windowsill for the curtain length. Across the full (45") width of the printed fabric, cut 2 pieces, each 4" shorter than the curtain length. From the striped fabric, cut four 8½" x 45" ruffle strips. Also cut two 14" x 45" valance strips from each fabric.
2. Curtains: Stitch a 1¼" hem at the top (long) edge of the curtain. Seam 2 ruffle strips together at the short ends, then stitch narrow hems at all 4 edges. With the longest machine stitch, sew a gathering row ¾" from a long (top) edge of ruffle. Lap the ruffle 1" over the lower edge of the curtain and pin them together along the gathering row, pulling up the gathers to fit. Topstitch over the gathering row. Repeat for the other curtain.
3. Valance: Seam 2 matching valance strips together at the short ends. Stitch the narrow hem at the lower edge, then the 1¼" hem at the top edge. Repeat for the other valance. Install 2 curtain rods at the top window, one lower than the other, and hang the valances.

ENTRYWAY IDEAS

Silver Foil Mirror and Fan Entryway

SILVER FOIL MIRROR AND FAN ENTRYWAY

EASY: Achievable by anyone.
MATERIALS: 18″-dia.-round un-framed mirror; adjustable plate hanger; cardboard; shiny foil gift wrap; paper clips; staples; glue; tinsel rope; votive candles in glass holders.

DIRECTIONS:
1. Mirror: Hang mirror (in the plate hanger).
2. Trace the mirror to the cardboard. Mark another circle 3½″ outside the drawn circle. Cut out the larger circle, then cut ⅜″ inside the smaller circle. This cardboard ring is a "mat" to hold the foil.
3. Cut the foil paper into 4″-wide strips and fold them into narrow pleats (about ¼″). Staple the inside edge of the strips (with the pleats closed) over the cardboard mat along the inside circle. Glue the rope tinsel over the stapled edges.
4. Push half of a straight pin into the back of the cardboard at the center top, near the inside edge. Place the cardboard over the mirror; bend the upper pin over the mirror to hold the "frame" in place.
5. Fans: Pleat and pinch together the gift wrap; staple together to hold.
6. Use additional gift wrap as a runner. Arrange the fans and candle holders.

OTHER ENTRYWAY IDEAS

● Place a mirrored mat on your entry table. Top with a brightly colored arrangement of candlesticks, votives, baskets and ornaments. Pinks and whites create an especially soft effect.
● Gather a large spray of boxwood with an oversized bow and wire it to your banister. Match it with a wreath of greens looped with the same kind of ribbon and filled with an array of red candles of various heights.
● Intertwine bright red ribbon with some of your Christmas greens. Wrap it around your banister, decorating the spindles with candy canes that you've wired together in pairs and tied with red print ribbon.
● Put your Christmas cards to good use: Punch holes in the cards and thread red ribbon through them, then tie these new "decorations" around banister spindles.
● For a dramatic candle effect on the entry table (be sure to place candles on a metal tray or other flameproof surface), roll an assortment of candles in a hot towel to soften slightly, then quickly roll them in silver or gold glitter and let set. Surround a grouping of these cheery candles with a base of greens.

GOOD SCENTS FOR ENTRYWAYS
To make sure the impression guests get when they enter your home is a sweet one:
● *Set out potpourri in decorative dishes on the table in your entryway.*
● *Light some scented candles on the entry table.*
● *Splash a few drops of perfume or cologne on the light bulbs of your entryway lamps and chandeliers.*
● *Place bars of strong-scented soap in entryway closets and in the drawers of the entry table.*
● *Hang clove-studded oranges in closets to banish mustiness.*

JIFFY DECORATIONS
● *Suspend Christmas balls on ribbon of different lengths and colors from your wall moldings.*
● *Paint a large straw basket red and use it to hold a grouping of plants.*
● *Cover a container with heavy gold foil, then fill it with gold-sprayed leaves, tinsel and pinecones.*
● *For an instant centerpiece, fill a silver or glass platter with a cheery assortment of Christmas balls and strings of miniature white lights.*
● *Tie some bright red ribbon around the necks of vases and lamp shades.*
● *Glue carefully cut pieces of doilies onto the inside of your windows. A helpful hint: Use removable glue, like rubber cement, for easy cleanup.*
● *Weave some ribbon through a wicker basket. Place a plant in it and attach some attractive bows to the plant, using florist's wire.*
● *Decorate a window ledge with holly and ribbon, then stand gingerbread men (real or made from wood) or other tree decorations along the ledge.*
● *Tie a holiday ribbon around glass jars filled with tasty Christmas candy.*

STOCKINGS TO STUFF

Native American Stockings

FIG. 6
STOCKING
1 SQ. = 1″

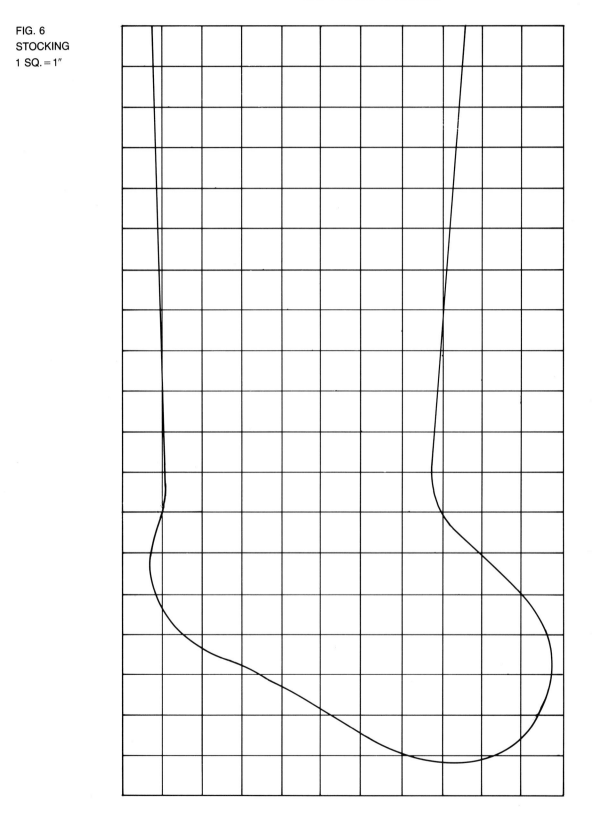

CHRISTMAS STOCKINGS
(about 10' x 18')

AVERAGE: For those with some experience in sewing.

GENERAL DIRECTIONS
Pattern for all stockings: Enlarge the pattern in Fig. 6 on brown paper, following the directions on page 291. The pattern includes a ½″ seam allowance.

MUSICAL AUSTRIA STOCKING

MATERIALS: Remnants of machine-embroidered peasant trims; ⅓ yd. red felt.

DIRECTIONS (see General Directions):
1. Using the pattern, cut 1 back piece from the felt.
2. Edgestitch strips of the trim, row after vertical row until you reach the size of the stocking. Place tape "fabric" on the felt back piece and cut out the stocking shape.
3. With the right side of the tape facing inward, topstitch front to back, ¼″, then ½″ from all edges except the top.
4. Add the ribbon loop inside the top edge at the back seam.

NATIVE AMERICAN STOCKING

MATERIALS: ½ yd. tan and ¼ yd. rust suedecloth; scraps blue and yellow felt; 30″ of strung blue and red caviar beads; 3 dozen ¼″ red, turquoise, yellow and blue craft beads; white glue.

DIRECTIONS (see General Directions):
1. Use the pattern to cut the stocking front and back from the tan suede cloth.
2. Cut the rust suede 1″ x 15½″ and edgestitch lengthwise to the stocking front piece (see photo, page 39).
3. Sew the front and back pieces together with a wide machine-zigzag stitch, ½″ from the edge (leave the top edge open).
4. Cut a 7″-wide x 8″-deep strip for the fringe. Glue the top 1¼″ of the strip to the stocking front, 2″ from the top edge over the vertical strip.
5. Using the photo as a guide, cut small diamond shapes from the 1½″ x 7″ strip of rust suede and glue over the top edge of the fringe band. Glue more felt and rust suede pieces above the band (see photo).
6. With your hand inside the stocking, sew the caviar beads along and around all the rust suede edges.
7. Spread the bottom of the fringe strip flat and cut it into ¼″ strips. Slide the craft beads onto the fringes (see photo).
8. Stitch a 3″ loop of suede inside the top edge at the back seam.

MERRY OLD ENGLAND STOCKING

MATERIALS: ⅓ yd. patchwork fabric or fabric cut from an old quilt in a "crazy quilt" design; ⅓ yd. velvet; ⅓ yd. lining fabric; 8″ of 2½″-wide crocheted lace edging; embroidery floss in a variety of colors.

DIRECTIONS (see General Directions):
1. Using the pattern, cut 1 front from the quilt, 1 back from the velvet and 2 lining pieces.
2. Cover the worn pieces of quilt with strips of lace. Outline each piece with feather stitches; add French knots and lazy daisy stitches where appropriate. (See Stitch Guide, page 290.)
3. With the right sides together, sew the front to the back all around, leaving open at top; clip the toe curve.
4. Repeat Step 3 with the lining pieces.
5. Turn the stocking right side out. Sew the lace trim to the front, 1½″ down from the top edge.
6. Slip the lining into the stocking, wrong sides facing. Turn the stocking ½″ to inside at the top. Turn the lining ⅝″ to inside and pin to the turned-under stocking. Slipstitch the layers together. Fold a 5″ piece of lace in half and sew the inside top edge as a hanger loop.

Hang holiday stockings all around the house—along the mantel, up the staircase, on a towel bar, even on the bathroom shower rod.

STOCKING-STUFFERS FOR GROWN-UPS

You don't have to be a kid to love finding your own stocking on Christmas morning! Here are 13 ideas for filling "big people's" stockings with thoughtful but inexpensive gifts. Use these for starters, as you'll probably come up with many more yourself.

1. For the cook *A bunch of cinnamon sticks tied up with a bright red ribbon; packets of out-of-the-ordinary herbs and spices (like saffron or peppercorns); bouquet garni; cheesecloth; a decorative kitchen timer; a nifty gadget or tool, like a mushroom brush.*

2. For the traveler *A wallet-size currency converter; a tiny foreign language/English dictionary; a travel diary; shoe bags; fold-up slippers for the plane trip; a mini-sewing kit; sample-size beauty and personal-care products, such as toothpaste and deodorant.*

3. For the student *An alarm clock; late-night study treats (popcorn kernels and dried fruit and nuts, for instance); packets of exotic teas or flavored coffees; postcards addressed to home; a colorful wall calendar.*

4. For the athlete/exercise fan *A pedometer; sweatband or wristband; socks (no one ever has too many of these!); muscle-soothing ointment; an exercise cassette; an elastic bandage (just in case!); mini-size shampoo and hair conditioner for the gym.*

5. For the workaholic *A small desk clock or calculator; a pocket diary (with important personal dates—like your birthday—already marked inside); a box of multicolored paper clips; a monogrammed notepad; tickets to a concert or play (even workhorses have to relax!).*

6. For the hostess *Fancy stirrers for drinks; a few scented candles held together with colorful ribbon; a half-dozen napkin rings; paper cocktail napkins and coasters; mini guest soaps; gold and silver markers for writing invitations.*

7. For the gardener *A pair of gardening gloves; miniature tools for indoor gardening; pot wraps (these are pretty "sleeves" to dress up plain plastic pots); a gardening calendar; a hat or visor to shade eyes from the sun.*

8. For the home-sewer *A collection of unique buttons; some fancy trim, such as dainty lace and eye-catching appliqués; a pincushion; a package of needle threaders; a thimble which opens to hold needles or straight pins.*

9. For the visiting long-distance relative *A pocket-size photo album you fill with snapshots of the family; a picture frame for this year's holiday pictures; attractive note cards, a pen and stamps (a gentle reminder to keep in touch!).*

10. For the dieter *A tape measure; a stick-on sign for the refrigerator that says, "Keep Out" or "By Appointment Only"; a pocket calorie counter; a minifood scale; a paperback diet book with really delicious recipes; lots and lots of sugarless gum.*

11. For the bookworm *Two or three paperbacks by his/her favorite author (buy them cheap at a secondhand bookstore); some interesting bookmarks; a set of bookplates; decorative paperback book covers.*

12. For the weekend Picasso *A small sketchbook; miniature set of paints; calligraphy pens or brushes, plus ink; charcoal, pencils, gummed erasers.*

13. For the clotheshorse *Some sweet-smelling sachets and shelf-lining paper to pretty up drawers and closets; the latest style pantyhose; a lace-edged hankie to tuck in her suit pocket or handbag; a subscription to a foreign fashion magazine—this is a splurge, but she'll love it!*

WREATHS

Origami Wreath

💲 ❄ BASIC EVERGREEN WREATH

EASY: Achievable by anyone.
MATERIALS: Various types of evergreen branches, approximately 12″ long (tips are best); florist's wire; wreath form (3- to 4-wire-ring type—not Styrofoam®); wire cutters or heavy scissors; large ribbon bow *(optional)*.

DIRECTIONS:
1. Small Wreaths (less than 17″ in diameter): Begin by winding the end of the florist's wire around 1 wire of the wreath form. Do not cut the florist's wire. Evergreen branches are bound individually to the wreath form with 1 continuous length of florist's wire.
2. Position the branches at a slight angle to the wreath form, alternating the direction of each branch. (This results in a more natural-looking wreath than if the branches were placed all in a straight line.) Continue to bind each branch to the form with the florist's wire until there are no openings in the wreath.
3. Attach the bow with the florist's wire to conceal the stem end of the last branch attached. Or tuck the stem end under the tips of the first pieces attached.
4. Wrap wire on the underside of the wreath form to fasten. Cut off the excess wire.
5. Large Wreath: Instead of working with single branches, bind 3 branches into a bunch with the florist's wire. Follow the directions for small wreaths, treating the bunches in the same way as the branches.

💲 ❄ BASIC ARTIFICIAL WREATH

EASY: Achievable by anyone.
1. Wrap a Styrofoam® wreath form with green floral tape.
2. Insert sprays of greens into the form at a slight angle, covering the top and sides. If it is necessary to divide the greens, cut #16 wire into 7″ lengths, bend into a hairpin shape and use them to secure the greenery to the wreath.

💲 ❄ BASIC BOWS AND STREAMERS

Note: All wrapping is done with thin flexible wire.
Bows: Cut ribbon into 18″ lengths, unless otherwise indicated. Fold the ribbon into loops so the ends meet at center back. Wrap 2 or 3 looped ribbons together at a time, gradually enlarging the loops until the desired bow is achieved.
Assembling: Cut 5″ lengths of #16 wire for each bow and streamer, and tape the bow and streamers to them. Wire-wrap a bow and streamer together, and insert into the wreath.
Streamers: Cut lengths of ribbon and fold the lengths in half; wrap together with wire.

ORIGAMI WREATH *(16″-dia.)*

AVERAGE: For those with some experience with origami.
MATERIALS: 16″-dia. Basic Artificial Wreath (left); 4′ #16 wire; wire cutters; decorative gold "sequins" (we used stars, leaves, paillettes, snowflakes).
For each bow: Three widths (3 yds. each) of gold novelty ribbon (see photo); gold foil wrapping paper (or gold origami paper) for birds.

DIRECTIONS:
1. Assemble the wreath, following directions for the Basic Artificial Wreath. Glue the sequins to the greens.
2. Birds: Cut a 6″ square of gold foil for each bird. Fold the paper in half to form a rectangle. Fold in half again to form a square, unfold and continue folding as directed (see Fig. 7, A to 0). When bird is complete, inflate by blowing into the small hole in the stomach. Repeat for 7 more birds.
Note: The key to producing origami is careful, sharp creasing and perfectly matched edges and corners. See diagrams.
3. Cut the #16 wire into eight 4″ lengths and tape to the bottom of the birds. Spacing evenly, insert the birds into the wreath.
4. Bows and Streamers: Using 3 widths and varying lengths of the gold ribbon, follow the directions for Basic Bows and Streamers (left).

BIRD FIG. 7, A TO O

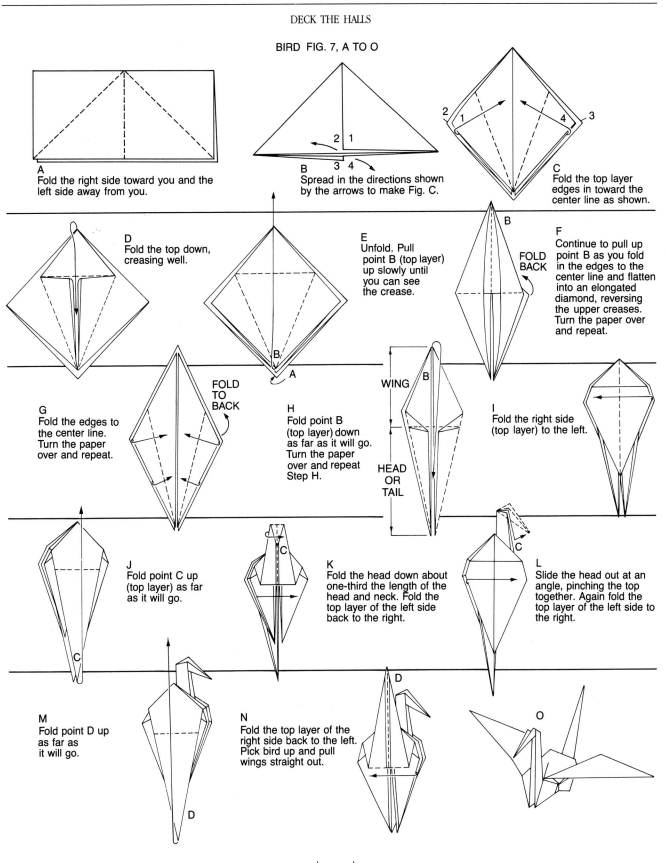

A
Fold the right side toward you and the left side away from you.

B
Spread in the directions shown by the arrows to make Fig. C.

C
Fold the top layer edges in toward the center line as shown.

D
Fold the top down, creasing well.

E
Unfold. Pull point B (top layer) up slowly until you can see the crease.

F
Continue to pull up point B as you fold in the edges to the center line and flatten into an elongated diamond, reversing the upper creases. Turn the paper over and repeat.

FOLD BACK

G
Fold the edges to the center line. Turn the paper over and repeat.

FOLD TO BACK

H
Fold point B (top layer) down as far as it will go. Turn the paper over and repeat Step H.

WING

HEAD OR TAIL

I
Fold the right side (top layer) to the left.

J
Fold point C up (top layer) as far as it will go.

K
Fold the head down about one-third the length of the head and neck. Fold the top layer of the left side back to the right.

L
Slide the head out at an angle, pinching the top together. Again fold the top layer of the left side to the right.

M
Fold point D up as far as it will go.

N
Fold the top layer of the right side back to the left. Pick bird up and pull wings straight out.

O

Poinsettia Wreath

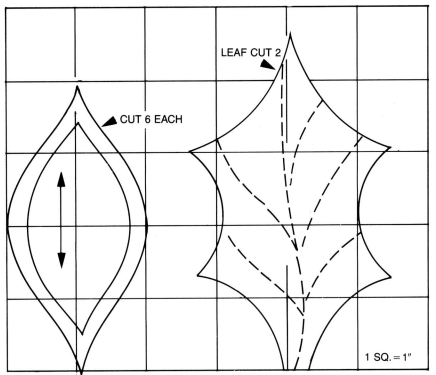

CUT 6 EACH

LEAF CUT 2

1 SQ. = 1"

FIG. 8 POINSETTIAS

POINSETTIA WREATH

EASY: Achievable by anyone.

MATERIALS: Large Basic Evergreen or Artificial Wreath (see page 44); 14 Poinsettias and 28 Leaves (see below—use ½ yd. of 45" wide fabric and 3½ yds. of 3"-wide ribbon; thin, flexible wire; 18" length of wide ribbon).

DIRECTIONS:

1. Assemble wreath, following directions.
2. Make a ribbon bow, following the directions for Basic Bows and Streamers (page 44).
3. Attach the poinsettias, leaves and bow to the wreath.

POINSETTIAS *(about 7"-dia.)*

EASY: Achievable by anyone.

MATERIALS: *(Note:* From ¼ yd. of 45"-wide fabric, you can make 7 poinsettias; from 1¾ yds. of 3"-wide ribbon, you can make 14 leaves.) 45"-wide off-white slipper satin; 3"-wide green velvet floral ribbon; green floral tape; bright pink, red and green glass Christmas beads, ¼" to ⅜" in dia.; green fine-line felt-tip pen; white clear acrylic spray; Alizarin Crimson watercolor paint *(see Materials Shopping Guide, page 293 for items listed above)*; #30-gauge brass wire; 2 small watercolor brushes; dressmakers' carbon; ornament hangers.

DIRECTIONS:

1. Enlarge the patterns in Fig. 8 on paper, following the directions on page 291.
2. **Sizing:** Following the manufacturer's instructions, lightly spray the wrong side of the satin with the clear acrylic; dry; spray again and dry.
3. **Cutting** (for each flower): From the satin, cut 6 each large and small petals; from the green ribbon, cut 2 leaves; from the covered wire, cut 6 each 6" (large) and 5" (small) lengths for the petals; cut two 6½"-long covered wires for the leaves; from the brass wire, cut eight 3" lengths for the beads.
4. **Petals and Leaves:** Stretch the edges of the petals to make them ripple. Starting ½" from the top point of the petal, center the wire lengthwise and glue to the back of the petal. Repeat for the remaining large and small petals and the 2 leaves.
5. **Painting:** With the right side up, brush half the petal, from the base up, with water. Brush on the Crimson paint, shading and softening the color as you work up and over one-third of the petal (see photo, page 46). Lightly color the edges of the petal with the green felt pen, then brush with water to soften. For the leaves, sketch in the veins, then color the edges with the green pen and soften with water.
6. **Flower Center:** Using 8 per flower, thread one 3" wire through 1 bead, ends even; twist the ends. Repeat for the remaining 7 red, pink and green beads. Then twist the wire ends of the 8 heads together, leaving ½" wire.
7. **Assembly:** Place the 6 small petals, evenly spaced, around the bead center, twisting the wire ends together. Repeat, adding the large petals. From the top down, wrap the wire stem with the floral tape, adding 2 leaves as you wrap. Attach the ornament hangers.

GARLAND TIPS

• *Drape garlands around your mantel, windowsill, banister or from a chandelier.*

• *To attach evergreen roping to a door or window frame, staple the center of a length of thin florist's wire to the frame. Wrap this wire along the roping at several points along its length.*

• *To attach evergreen roping to a staircase or banister, use ribbon or fabric lengths to tie the roping onto your rails.*

• *Try attaching dried flowers, ornaments, ribbon bows, pinecones, small oranges, kumquats, apples or nuts to your garlands.*

• *When preparing popcorn for garlands, keep the lid on your pot while the popcorn cools. This way, the steam will soften the popcorn and make it easier to string the kernels.*

Why limit wreaths to windows and doors? Use them in centerpieces, hang them over mirrors or stand one up on the entry table.

PEPPERMINT CANDY WREATH
(16"-dia.)

EASY: Achievable by anyone.
MATERIALS: Two 16"-dia. flat Styrofoam® wreath forms; cellophane-wrapped peppermint candy; 45' #16 wire; flexible wire; wire cutters; floral tape; 6 small school scissors; glue. *For each bow:* 5 yds. ⅜"-wide polka-dot ribbon; 6 yds. ⅝"-wide and 1 yd. ¼"-wide green ribbon.

DIRECTIONS:
1. Cut the six 5"-long wires for the bows and set aside. Cut the remaining wire into 4" lengths.
2. Wrap the twisted cellophane ends of 2 candies together with the flexible wire. Continue adding candy by wrapping in the ends until there are about 5 candies per cluster, then wrap the cluster to 4" wires. Using floral tape, wrap the whole stem.
3. Glue 2 Styrofoam® wreaths together. When dry, insert the candy clusters into the top and sides of the wreath.
4. Make the bows and streamers from the polka-dot and ⅝" ribbon, following the directions for Basic Bows and Streamers (page 44) and adding 1 extra-long length of narrow ribbon at each bow to tie on the scissors.

Peppermint Candy Wreath

CENTERPIECES

Gold and Silver Balls

💲⚡
GOLD AND SILVER BALLS

DIRECTIONS:
Pile gold and silver Christmas tree balls in a crystal, gold or silver bowl and fill any spaces with metallic roses from gift ties.

💲⚡
GLASS BOWL CENTERPIECE

EASY: Achievable by anyone.
MATERIALS: 12″-dia., 10″-high glass bowl; 3″-dia., 7″-tall red candle; 6 sprigs artificial holly with greenery; 1½ yds. 1″ green and red plaid craft ribbon; floral clay; thin wire; 10 stems of red berries; 6 small pinecone clusters with berries on wire; 8 twigs of varied sizes, but each with several branches.

DIRECTIONS: Place the candle in the center of the bowl and secure with the floral clay. Arrange the holly, then pinecones, around the base of the candle. Wrap the berries singly to the branches. Place low in the bowl. Cut the 1″ ribbon into 3 pieces. Form into bows; space the bows in the bowl. (**Note:** Do *not* burn the candle.)

Twig Creche

FIG. 9

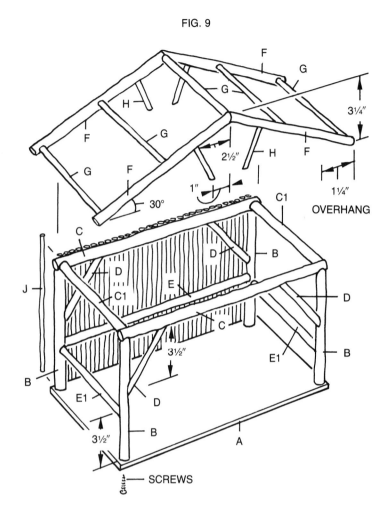

30°

2½"

1"

OVERHANG

SCREWS

3½"

3½"

FIG. 9A

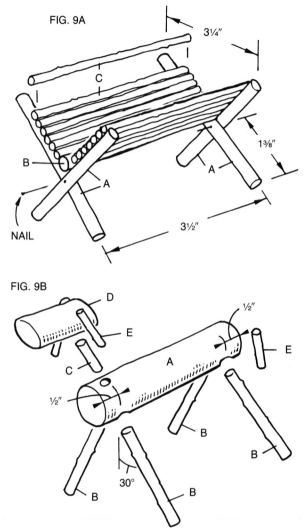

3¼"

1⅜"

3½"

NAIL

3¼"

1¼"

FIG. 9B

30°

½"

½"

TWIG CRECHE
(8"dia. x 16"w. x 13½"h.)

AVERAGE: For those with some experience in woodworking.

MATERIALS: ¼" x 8" x 16" plywood; four ¾" screws; two ¾" brads; collection of various-size twigs; hot glue; brown stain.

TOOLS REQUIRED: Saw; round file; ¼" drill bit and drill; screwdriver; hot glue gun.

CUTTING DIRECTIONS:

CODE	PIECES	SIZE
A(PLY)	1	¼" x 8" x 16" Bottom
B(TW)	4	½"-dia. x 9" Posts
C(TW)	2	⅜"-dia. x 16" Beams
C1(TW)	2	⅜"-dia. x 7" Cross beams
D(TW)	4	⅜"-dia. x 5¼" Braces
E(TW)	1	⅜"-dia. x 15" Brace
E1(TW)	1	⅜"-dia. x 7" Braces
F(TW)	4	½"-dia. x 10" Rafters
G(TW)	5	⅜"-dia. x 7" Roof beams
H(TW)	4	⅜"-dia. x 2¾" Trusses
J(TW)	63	⅛"-dia. x 10" Back wall

DIRECTIONS:
1. Select twigs; cut off branches. Where 1 twig meets another, file a slightly concave shape to give the glue a better surface. Cut the twigs to size (see Cutting Directions).
2. The posts (B) are screwed to the corners of the bottom (A), through A into B (see Fig. 9).
3. Hot-glue the cross beams (C) to the tops of posts (B). Hot-glue the cross beams (C1) between and at the ends of the beams (C). Glue the diagonal braces (D) in place (see Fig. 9).

Glue the braces (E) and (E1) to the posts, 3½" above the bottom (A).

4. Cut the rafters' (F) center angles 30°. Glue the front beams together at the center, then to the top of the posts/beams (B/C). Glue the trusses (H) between F and C (see Fig. 9). Repeat at back. Glue the roof beams (G) between and to the rafters (F).

5. Place the structure face down; run a bead of hot glue along the bottom (A), brace (E) and beam (C). Place the backwall sticks in the glue and butt against each other to form the back wall.

6. Crib:

CODE	PIECES	SIZE
A(TW)	4	¼"-dia. x 3½"
B(TW)	1	¼"-dia. x 4" Ridge
C(TW)	18	⅛"-dia. x 4" Sides

Lay one leg (A) on top of another and cross them 1⅜" from one end. Drive a nail (¾") through the 2 legs (A) to form an "X." Repeat for the other set of legs. Glue the ridge (B) to the top of the legs where they cross (see Fig. 9A). Before the glue sets, adjust the top of the legs to measure 3¼" apart.

7. Lay a bead of glue along the top of the legs and place the side (C) twigs, butted against each other, in place, to form the crib sides. When the glue has dried, place grapevine tendrils (or straw) in the crib as a mat.

8. Lamb:

CODE	PIECES	SIZE
A(TW)	1	¾"-⅞"-dia. x 3¼" Body
B(TW)	4	¼"-dia. x 2" Legs
C(TW)	1	¼"-dia. x ¾" Neck
D(TW)	1	⅝"-dia. x 1" Head
E(TW)	3	⅛"-dia. x ⅝" Ears/Tail

Cut the body twig (A) 3¼" long. Drill ¼"-dia. holes about ¼" deep at 30° angles and ½" from each end of A for legs. Drill a ¼"-dia. hole slanted about 10° forward for the neck (C). Drill a ¼"-dia. hole in the head (D), about ⅜" from one end.

9. Glue the legs in the holes (see Fig. 9B). Glue the head and the neck to the body. Glue the ears to the side of the head and tail to the body.

CLOTHING FOR FIGURES

MATERIALS: 1 yd. muslin; fiberfill; coat hangers; ecru button-twist thread; masking tape; twine for hair.

DIRECTIONS:

1. For Mary and Joseph: Make armature pieces from the coat hangers: Cut one 10" piece (arms), one 9" piece (body). Wrap the sharp ends with tape.

2. Shape the bottom end of the body piece to resemble an egg dipper; for Mary, bend the wire so the figure will be kneeling.

3. Heads: On paper, draw an oval, 2½" wide x 3" high, for the head. Erase the bottom of the oval and extend the lines downward 3" to make the body (draw a straight line across the bottom). Cut out the pattern.

4. Sleeves: Draw a triangle with a 6½" base and 14" sides. Cut off the point, 5½" from the center bottom. Cut out the lower portion for the sleeve pattern. Cut 2 sleeves each for Joseph and Mary.

5. Baby body: Cut the paper pattern 2½" wide x 3¼" long; cut the shape from muslin. Seam (⅜") the side and bottom edges; turn the right side out. Sew gathering stitches at the top edge. Stuff the body firmly; pull up the gathering at the neck. Cut/gather/stuff a 3" circle for the baby's head. Flatten, with the gathering at the back, and stitch to the neck. Sew twine loops to the head for hair.

6. Cut Joseph and Mary head pieces. Seam (½") and trim; turn inside out; stuff firmly. Place the head on the straight end of the body wire and wrap tightly around the wire with the thread under the chin. With the heads in place, Joseph is approximately 10" tall. Mary is approximately 8" tall.

7. For both Joseph and Mary, seam (½") sleeves; turn the right side out. Slip onto wire arms and sew ½" below the chin to the body front and back, raw edges turned under.

8. Tunics: Cut 10" x 14" muslin on the bias. Seam (½") the short sides. Fold under the top edge ½"; gather tightly and tack to the waist. Hem the tunic. Repeat for Mary, using a 9" x 12" piece.

9. Joseph's hair: Glue strands of burlap or yarn across the head from front to back; trim evenly. Repeat for Mary's hair, stitching for a center part.

10. Joseph's beard: Fold 4" threads in half and stitch or glue onto his face; trim.

11. Joseph's coat: Cut muslin 7" x 21" on the bias. Drape the coat over the head and across the shoulders, making tucks in the back to form a hood; tack to the head, shoulders and back. Turn under the bottom edges of the tunic and coat to make Joseph stable.

12. Mary's veil: Cut a 19"-dia. half-circle. Turn under the raw edges and stitch. Turn the front edge under and center on the head. Tack the folded veil edges together at the chin.

13. Swaddling: Cut a 7"-square muslin; fold diagonally and wrap around Jesus, point up behind the head; pin ends in the back.

Gingerbread House

GINGERBREAD HOUSE

Average: For those with some experience in cake decorating.

Makes 1 cookie house.

> *Gingerbread Dough (recipe follows)*
> 2 *pieces 16 x 12-inch foam-core board*
> *(available in art supply stores)*
> *Brown paper*
> *Red and blue hard candy drops*
> *Hammer*
> *Heart-shaped canapé cutter*
> *Sharp paring knife*
> *Shirt cardboard*
> *Natural sliced almonds*
> *Royal Frosting (recipe follows)*
> *Assorted candies (see Directions)*
> *Green and red food colorings*
> *Ice-cream sugar cones*
> *Silver dragées*
> *Gummie bears*
> 1/3 *cup granulated sugar*
> *Swedish fish candy*
> *10X (confectioners' powdered) sugar*

1. **Baking the House Pieces:** Prepare the Gingerbread Dough. Refrigerate for at least 3 hours, or overnight.

2. Enlarge the patterns in Fig. 10 on brown paper, following the directions on page 291. Cut out house pieces from 1 piece of the ⅛-inch-thick foam-core board.

3. Preheat the oven to moderate (350°).

4. Roll out the cookie dough, one-quarter at a time, to ⅛-inch thickness on a well-floured pastry cloth or board.

5. **To make the walls:** Using the prepared pattern pieces, cut out the house front and back and 2 house sides with a sharp knife. Place 1 inch apart on large cookie sheets.

6. Using the prepared pattern pieces, cut out the entrance front and sides; place the cutout dough on a third cookie sheet. Reroll the trimmings for the roof strips; set aside.

7. Bake, 1 cookie sheet at a time, in the preheated moderate oven (350°) for 12 minutes, or until the cookie dough is firm.

8. **To make the stained glass windows:** Crush the red hard candies with a hammer. Arrange the candies in the window openings.

9. Return the cookie sheets to the oven and bake for 3 minutes longer, or until the candies melt. Cool the cookie pieces on the cookie sheets for 3 minutes; loosen the cookie pieces from the cookie sheets with a long knife. Slide the pieces onto wire racks and cool completely.

10. **To make the roof:** Cut the rolled-out Gingerbread Dough into 10 x 1-inch strips. Arrange the strips 1 inch apart on a cookie sheet. Make a shaggy edge by making the ½-inch cuts close together along the long edge of strips.

11. Bake in the preheated moderate oven (350°) for 10 minutes, or until firm. Cool on the cookie sheet on wire racks for 5 minutes. Loosen the cookie strips with a long spatula and slide onto the wire racks to cool completely.

12. **To make the shutter, fence and gingerbread men:** Roll out the remaining Gingerbread Dough and cut out 8 shutter pieces. Place on a cookie sheet, matching 4 pairs. Cut out heart shapes with the canapé cutter or the tip of the paring knife. Make the fence by cutting the dough into 4 x 6-inch rectangles and making decorative tops with the sharp knife or canapé cutters. Make cuts down at ¾-inch intervals for the fencing. Arrange on a cookie sheet. Cut out the gingerbread men with a 1- to 2-inch gingerbread cookie cutter. Cut out N, S, E and W to ¾-inch size with the knife.

13. Bake in the preheated moderate oven (350°) for 8 minutes, or just until firm. Cool.

14. **To assemble the house:** Prepare the Royal Frosting.

15. Spread a thin layer of the Royal Frosting on the back of all cookie pieces and press gently, but firmly, onto the cutout foam core pattern pieces. Allow to dry for at least 1 hour. Join the house front to 1 house side on a second piece of foam-core board with the Royal Frosting. Hold the edges in place for 5 minutes, or until the frosting sets. Join the house back and side wall to the front two, using the Royal Frosting. Allow to firm up for 30 minutes.

16. Assemble the entrance front and sides; join with the Royal Frosting. Allow to dry for at least 1 hour. Attach to the house front with Royal Frosting.

17. Fold a 9 x 14-inch piece of the cardboard in half, crosswise, to make two 9 x 7-inch sections. Spread some of the Royal Frosting along the top edge of the house front and back and side walls. Arrange the roof over the points of the tall walls and allow to firm up for 30 minutes.

18. Fold a 1 x 8-inch piece of the cardboard in half, ☞

crosswise, to make two 1 x 4″ sections. Secure on top of the entrance front with Royal Frosting. Spread the top with the frosting and cover with the natural sliced almonds.

19. Spread the side edges of the shirt cardboard chimney pieces with the Royal Frosting and assemble to make a box shape. Spread outside "box" with the frosting and cover with the candy pebbles. Allow to firm up for 30 minutes; arrange on top of the roof.

20. Decorate the house with the candy pebbles, chocolate mints, tiny pastel mints, Life Savers®, Smartees, pastel candy sticks, silver dragées, Gummie Bears, blue hard candy balls, natural sliced almonds, Swedish fish and candy dots on paper, or use your own selection, using the Royal Frosting as "glue" and following the photograph as a guide.

21. **Making the trees and wreaths:** Prepare another batch of the Royal Frosting and tint part a bright green with the food coloring. Tint a small amount a deep pink with the red food coloring; cover with damp paper toweling. Spread the green frosting over the inverted ice-cream cones and sprinkle with the silver dragées. Top the trees with the Gummie Bears. Fit a pastry bag with a small star tube and fill the bag with the remaining green frosting. Pipe out 1-inch wreaths onto aluminum foil; allow to dry. Pipe pink-tinted frosting bows and "glue" onto the house door with the green frosting in the pastry bag.

22. **Making the weathervane:** Melt the ⅓ cup granulated sugar very slowly in a small heavy skillet. Dip the tip of halved toothpicks in this syrup; attach a cookie letter to 1 end of each and attach the other end to a tall toothpick inserted into the peak of the roof. Stick a Swedish fish candy on top of the weathervane.

23. **Making the icicles:** Break the blue hard candies with the hammer and melt a few at a time in a small heavy skillet. Pour from the tip of a spoon over the edge of the roof to form icicles. Cut 2 pieces of 3 x 6-inch cardboard. Frost the back of the fence pieces with the Royal Frosting; allow to dry. Arrange the fence, trees and gingerbread men as shown in photograph (page 54). Spread additional granulated sugar on the foam-core board and sprinkle the 10X sugar on the roof.

GINGERBREAD DOUGH

1   cup vegetable shortening
2   cups molasses
½   cup warm water
8   cups all-purpose flour
3   teaspoons ground ginger
1   teaspoon salt

1. Melt the shortening in a large saucepan. Stir in the molasses and the water, blending well.
2. Stir in the flour, ginger and salt until the mixture is smooth. Chill for at least 3 hours, or overnight, until firm enough to roll.

ROYAL FROSTING

Makes 1¼ cups.

2   egg whites
½   teaspoon cream of tartar
3   cups sifted 10X (confectioners' powdered) sugar

1. Beat the egg whites with the cream of tartar in a small bowl with an electric mixer at high speed until foamy.
2. Beat in the 10X sugar gradually until the frosting stands in firm peaks and is stiff enough to hold a sharp line when cut through with a knife. Keep the frosting covered with damp paper toweling and plastic wrap.

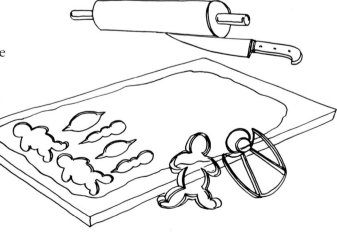

FIG. 10 GINGERBREAD HOUSE

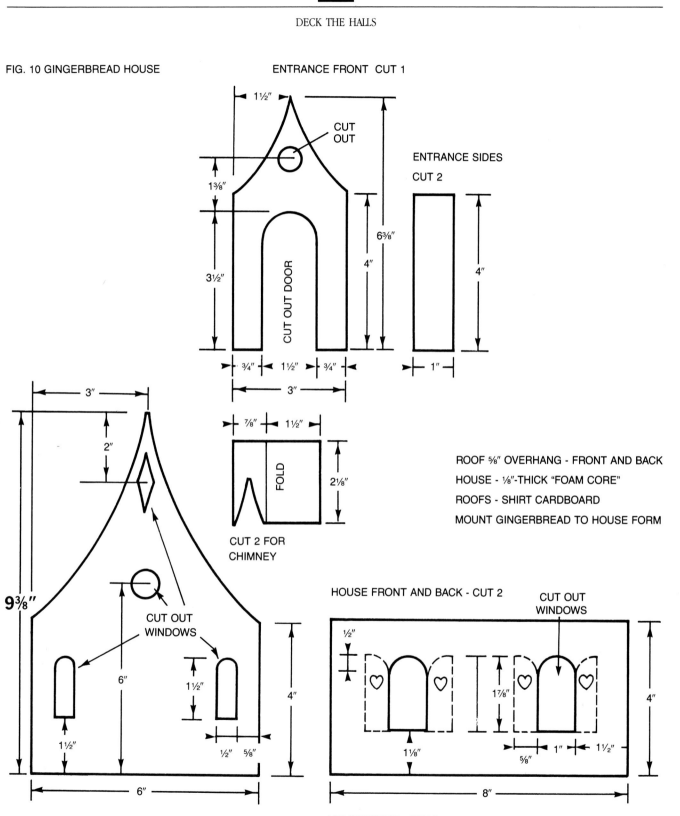

ENTRANCE FRONT CUT 1

CUT OUT

ENTRANCE SIDES

CUT 2

1½"

1⅜"

3½"

6⅜"

4"

CUT OUT DOOR

4"

¾" 1½" ¾"

3"

1"

⅞" 1½"

FOLD

2⅛"

CUT 2 FOR CHIMNEY

ROOF ⅝" OVERHANG - FRONT AND BACK

HOUSE - ⅛"-THICK "FOAM CORE"

ROOFS - SHIRT CARDBOARD

MOUNT GINGERBREAD TO HOUSE FORM

3"

2"

9⅜"

CUT OUT WINDOWS

6"

1½"

4"

1½"

½" ⅝"

6"

HOUSE FRONT AND BACK - CUT 2

CUT OUT WINDOWS

½"

1⅞"

1⅛"

⅝"

1" 1½"

4"

8"

HOUSE SIDES - CUT 2

Tree Angels and Lace Stars will add a golden touch to your tree (pages 69-70).

YULETIDE TREE
TRIMMINGS
FROM THE TOP DOWN

As the focal point of your holiday home, your Christmas tree is also a reflection of personal style. You may prefer a fresh evergreen or an artificial one to light from year to year. You may cover the tree with bright lights and lots of tinsel or pretty it up using dried flowers and bows. You may look for the biggest tree in the nursery or opt for a charming tabletop size. Whatever your preferences, choosing and decorating your tree are integral parts of the season's preparations.

In this chapter, you'll find our favorite finial tree ornaments—decorations to adorn the very top of your tree. Create a natural corn-husk angel (page 65) or a whimsical clown (page 62). Over half a dozen other ornaments run the gamut from a delicate crocheted dove (page 70) to elegant satin-covered balls (page 69).

Garlands are as important to a Christmas tree as ribbon is to a gift-wrapped package. You can create a Victorian-style lace garland (page 79), a garland fashioned from pasta (page 79) or a fun one just for kids that combines candy canes, elves and snowmen (page 75).

To set the stage for your beautifully wrapped gifts (and to catch needles as they fall), try one of our colorful tree skirts made from felt or patchwork fabric. You'll use them season after season!

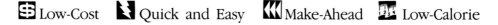

💲 Low-Cost   ⚡ Quick and Easy   ⫸ Make-Ahead   📏 Low-Calorie

BUYING A CHRISTMAS TREE

● Determine where in your home you will display your tree. With this in mind, you will be able to tell what height you will need and whether all four sides must be suitable for display.

● You should select a tree that is the right height for the space you have chosen for it. Cutting large portions off either end will alter the natural taper of the tree.

● Freshness is the key when selecting your tree. The needles should be resilient, but not brittle. Run your finger down a branch—needles should adhere to twigs.

● Shake or bounce the tree on the ground lightly to see that the needles are firmly attached. If only a few drop off, the tree is fresh and with proper care should retain its freshness indoors throughout the holiday season.

● The limbs should be strong enough to hold ornaments and strings of electric lights, and the tree should have a strong fragrance and good green color.

● Be sure it displays the best qualities for that particular species.

A SECOND TREE

Why limit your house to one tree? Place a second, smaller tree in the children's room, dining room or at the top of the stairs.

CHRISTMAS TREE CARE

● If you buy your tree several days before it will be set up and decorated, store it outside. Cut the butt of the tree at a diagonal about one inch above the original cut—this opens the pores and aids in the absorption of water. Place the butt end in a container of water.

● When you bring it into the house, saw the butt again, squaring off the diagonal. This facilitates placing the tree in a stand as well as aiding absorption.

● Keep the butt end of the tree in a container of water the entire time it is in the house. Refill the container daily, as the tree requires a lot of water. Sprinkling water on the branches and needles before you decorate the tree will help retain freshness.

● Be sure that the base of the tree is well supported and the tree is placed away from fireplaces, radiators, electric heaters, televisions or any other source of heat.

● Open flames, such as lighted candles, should never be used on or near the tree. In addition, never leave your home with the Christmas tree lights still on.

QUICK PAPER ORNAMENTS

To make inexpensive ornaments fast, glue designs cut from your favorite Christmas wrapping paper onto index cards or light cardboard and let dry. Trim carefully around the designs. Punch a hole through the top of each, then thread some string or ribbon through for hanging.

CHRISTMAS TREE SAFETY

● Make sure the tree stand you use is large enough to support your tree, or else it may topple over.

● Use only fire-resistant ornaments.

● Never put lit candles on a tree.

● To reduce risk of fire, choose a fresh tree that has no evidence of drying—brown needles or needles that fall off easily.

● More fire prevention: Spray the tree with a fire retardant before you decorate it, and keep it well watered and away from all heat sources.

● Dispose of the tree when it becomes so dry that large amounts of needles fall off.

● Avoid angel hair, since it's made of spun glass, a skin irritant to some people.

STORING ORNAMENTS

● *Wrap strings of tree lights around cardboard paper towel tubes. Taping down the ends prevents unraveling.*

● *Use the divided boxes from wine or soda to store your other ornaments.*

● *Store tiny ornaments in egg cartons to prevent loss or breakage.*

● *When packing your decorations away in boxes, store your heavier ornaments on the bottom and the lighter ones on top, with layers of paper towels or newspapers in between.*

TREE TOPPERS

Satin Angel Ornament

SATIN ANGEL ORNAMENT

EASY: Achievable by anyone.
MATERIALS: ¼ yd. satin fabric (white or pastel); ¼ yd. fusible webbing; two 4″ squares lace or lace fabric; ¼ yd. piece flexible trimming; ¼ yd. ¼″-wide satin ribbon; one 25mm round wooden bead with center hole; one ⅞″-diameter gold-color ring; glue; scissors; pins; ruler; compass; paper for patterns; pencil.

DIRECTIONS:
1. Following the directions that come with fusible webbing, fuse the squares of lace together. Cut two 6″ squares of the satin. Fuse them with their wrong sides together. Cut a 2″ x 6″ piece of satin. Cut a 1″ x 6″ strip of fusible web. Place the webbing strip, centered, on the wrong side of the satin and fold the long edges of the satin over the webbing to the center of the strip. Fuse.
2. Fold the strip, right sides together, and sew the short ends together (¼″ seam). This is the arm piece, and the seam is center front.
3. Draw a 4¾″-diameter circle on the paper. Divide the circle into quarters. Cut out one-quarter for the body pattern. Measuring from the center, mark 1¼″ on each straight edge. Connect these points and cut across this line and discard the triangle. Using the pattern, cut the fused satin. Glue the ribbon down one side of the body piece, starting at the hem and allowing 5½″ free at the top edge.
4. Fold the free end of the ribbon to the inside of the body piece to make a loop. With about ¼″ of ribbon inside the body piece, glue in place.
5. Glue the trimming to the bottom (curved) edge of the body piece. Overlap the straight sides of the body piece, with the ribbon on top, by ¼″. Glue. Pin until set. This is the center back of the body.
6. Glue the center back of the arm piece to the top portion of the center back of the body. Dry.
7. Glue the center front of the arms to the body where the two touch. Thread the ribbon loop through the wooden bead. Glue the bottom of the bead to the top of the body. Dry.
8. Glue the halo (gold-color ring) to the head.
9. Cut a paper rectangle 3½″ x 3¾″. Fold it in half lengthwise and draw an outline of a half heart using the entire size of the paper. Cut. Open the pattern. Use the pattern to cut the lace for the wings.
10. Glue the wings to the back of the body.

HOLIDAY CLOWN

EASY: Achievable by anyone.
MATERIALS: One 25mm white-wood center-hole white bead; one 8mm center-hole white bead; 4″ piece white trimming (for hat); two 5″ squares and two 4″ squares percale-type fabric for body, hat and collar; ¼ yd. fusible webbing; fine-tip marking pens in permanent red and black; heavy thread; needle; glue; scissors; hole punch; compass; pencil; ruler; paper for patterns.

DIRECTIONS:
1. Make patterns: Draw a 2½″-radius circle. Draw the diameter. Measure 1½″ from one end of the diameter line along the circumference of the circle and mark. Draw the radius from the center of the circle to the mark. The body pattern is the half-circle plus the 1½″ piece. Draw another 2½″-radius circle. One-quarter of that circle is the hat pattern. Draw a ¾″ radius circle for the collar pattern.
2. Fuse the fabric squares of the same size together. Cut the body from the 5″ square, the hat and collar from the 4″ square. Overlap the straight sides of the body piece slightly; glue the overlap. Secure with a pin or paper-clip and dry.
3. Repeat the instructions for the hat. Punch a hole in the center of the collar circle. Paint the face on the larger bead with the marking pens. Dry. Glue the smaller bead to the tip of the hat cone. Dry.
4. Centering the punched hole in the collar over the hole in the bottom of the head bead, glue the head to the collar. Glue the head plus the collar to the tip of the body cone. Dry. Glue the hat cone to the head.
5. Glue trimming around the base of the hat. Cut off any excess trimming.
6. Using the needle, attach a hanger loop of thread to the hat.

Holiday Clown

Raffia and Calico Star Finial

RAFFIA AND CALICO STAR FINIAL

AVERAGE: For those with some experience in sewing.
MATERIALS: Twenty 4¼″ x 3¼″ diamond-shape plastic needlepoint canvas forms; 30 gram natural (color #20) artificial matte raffia; ¼ yd. cotton or polyester/cotton fabric with red background and tiny print; red and beige sewing threads; tapestry and large sewing needles; scissors; ruler.

DIRECTIONS:
1. Using a single strand of the natural raffia, overcast all edges of each diamond shape. Insert the needle in the first row of holes. Using the doubled natural raffia, fill the entire surface of the canvas with stitches parallel to the outer edges. Bring the raffia from the underside of the canvas, pass over 2 holes and insert the needle in the third hole. Bring the raffia up to the right side of the canvas again through the fourth hole and repeat. It will be necessary in some cases to pass over only 1 hole in order to stagger the stitches. Cover 10 canvas shapes in the same way.
2. For the remaining 10 shapes, overcast the first plastic line parallel to the outer edge to form a second band of raffia.
3. Cut a piece of fabric the same size as each plastic canvas form (10 pieces). Turn in the raw edges so the fabric fits exactly within the area edges with the raffia bands. Sew the fabric as invisibly as possible to the canvas.
4. Arrange the all-raffia shapes as 2 stars (5 diamonds each). Join the shapes with the overcast-stitch done over the adjacent sides. Stop sewing 1¼″ from the center of the star. Sew the fabric-raffia pieces over all the raffia star with points placed between those of the raffia star. The edges of the upper layer shapes do not quite touch each other.

5. Cut two 3″-diameter fabric circles. Gather each near the edge and pull the thread to form a 2″-diameter puff with the raw edges turned under. Sew 1 to the center of each star.
6. Sew the crossed 2″ pieces of raffia to each circle. Place the completed stars, wrong sides together, with their points even. Overcast-stitch to join the 4 pairs of the all-raffia points. Join *only* the outer points of pairs of the fabric-raffia shapes. The non-stitched all-raffia point allows an opening to slip over the tip.

CORNHUSK TREE-TOP ANGEL

CHALLENGING: Requires more experience in craftwork.
MATERIALS: Cornhusks; 1″ Styrofoam® ball; fabric dye; Manila file folder; white glue/glue gun; 14″ #18 wire; natural-colored heavy thread; cotton balls; miscellaneous miniature dried star flowers, baby's breath; 1 skein embroidery floss in hair color; miscellaneous narrow lace; ecru buttontwist thread; scissors; plastic lid; crochet thread.

DIRECTIONS:
Note: Cornhusks are either fine- or coarse-grained; one side is ribbed, the other smooth and "milky." Use the milky side for the head, hands and sleeves, or where the husks are to be turned or bent. We used both dyed and undyed husks.
1. Color: Decide upon your angel's .dress color and dye 25 husks with a solution of ½ package dye to 1 gallon hot water in an old pail (keep husks as flat as possible). For pastel colors, check after 2 minutes; deeper colors need more dye and time. Rinse well in cold water; squeeze out the water and place in the plastic bag.
2. For the head: Roll and "pinch" the Styrofoam ball into a more oval shape. Using 6″ x 8″ undyed husk, grain running lengthwise, place the head (at bottom third of the husk) with the chin toward the short end. Roll until covered, twist the leftover husks at the top and pull to the bottom at the back of the head. Twist the husk at the neck and wrap with the ecru buttontwist thread, leaving the tag ends of the husk hanging. Cut 4″ of wire and insert from the bottom into the head.
3. Cut 10″ of wire for one-piece shoulders/arms, making tiny loops at each end for the hands. Tear 2 pieces of the undyed husk ¾″ wide. Put the strip through the loop, covering the end of the hand, and wrap up around the hand to the "elbow." Secure by winding thread around the wrist and up the arm wire. Do the second hand.
4. For the sleeve: Use the 6″-wide undyed husk, for the lower sleeve, placing it downward from the wrist, milky side facing the wrist. Gather it around the wrist and tie securely. Do the other sleeve. Carefully pull the husk back to the center of the arm, "puff" the sleeve and tip securely in the middle of the wire arm. Double-layer sleeves are made by placing a second piece of dyed husk starting at the middle of the first sleeve and turning the husk to the center, puffing it and tying it off at the "shoulder."
5. Taking the head, wrap a narrow (½″) strip of husk several turns around the neck area. Center the arm/shoulder piece between the head's 2 husk tag ends and wind thread around the bottom over the shoulders; tie off securely.
6. For the bodice *(use dyed husk):* ☞

Cornhusk Tree-Top Angel

Place 2 cotton balls in the center of a 6"x8" husk, turning each edge inward about 1", turning the top half to bottom. Place this section against the center of the wire arm/shoulder piece (already covered by the head's tag ends). Tear 4 pieces of husk about 1½" wide and 8" long and cover the bodice piece from the waist *diagonally* over the shoulder to the back; next piece goes the other direction over the shoulder diagonally to the back. Repeat with 2 more pieces. Gather and pinch all layers inward at the waistline and bind around 5 times. Tie off tightly.

7. For the skirt: Use the full-length dyed husk pieces. Bend the arms upward, out of the way; lay the first skirt piece at the center of the figure, pointing upward from the body and head. Continue lapping the pieces around the entire waist. Holding all the pieces and the body securely, wrap thread around the waist area many times and tie off. Turn the skirt pieces downward and cut the skirt husks off evenly at the hem. Bend the arms down again. Place crumpled tissue under the skirt and stand the figure in a 5" or 6" plastic bowl from your kitchen. The skirt will conform to the roundness of the bowl. Bend the head, if necessary, and position, the arms now. Dry thoroughly.

8. Wings: On tracing paper, trace the wing pattern *(see Fig. 1)* and cut out. Cut 4 wings from the undyed cornhusk and 2 from the Manila folder. Glue the cornhusk wings on each side of the Manila wings. Place in a heavy book to dry flat.

9. Hair: When the figure is completely dry, add the hair. Cut the entire skein of embroidery floss at the loops at each end. *For front curls:* Cut 4 pieces of floss in half. Dip a ⅛"-round stick or 2" nail into a puddle of glue and then wind the floss piece around and around, smoothing the floss ends with more glue on your finger. Then slide the curl off the stick

and glue to the front of the angel's head. (Have a damp washcloth handy to wipe off fingers.) Continue with about 6 or 8 curls for the front. *For*

FIG. 1

long curls: Use 5 full-length pieces and tie in the middle with the 6th strand of floss. Curl a group of 3 strands on the nail, then curl the next 3 strands. Curl the opposite ends in groups of 3's. Glue to the top of the head. The tie in the center of the strands should be at the center "part" of the head. Continue with all the floss strands, placing and gluing until the whole head is covered, ending with a ⅝" donut-shaped chignon on top. "Style" the long curls by pushing and gluing to the shoulder area and back area. The curls will dry stiff.

10. For halo: Wind 6" of thread over and under the pieces of baby's breath to form a circle. Tie off in the circle to fit the angel's head.

11. Hanging wreath: From the Manila folder, cut a 3"-dia. circle, then cut the 1¾"-dia. circle from the middle. Glue the ½" buttontwist thread loop to the center back. Cover the front with white glue, placing bits and pieces of baby's breath, star flowers and tiny leaf-shaped pieces of the *dyed* cornhusks all over the wreath. Let dry; trim with a lace bow at the top.

12. Attach the wings: Cut a folder piece ½" wide by 3" long. Fold 1" of each end toward the center. Glue the wings to this folded piece at the ends. When dry, glue the center section to the back of the angel.

13. Finishing: Trim the figure with strips of lace on the bodice, a bow at the waist. With a swab, add blush makeup to the angel's cheeks. Glue the baby's breath halo to the head. Cut a Manila cone piece for the stand (half-circle with a 5¾" radius): Bend and overlap, making the cone. Staple. Cut the top hole slightly larger and, with lots of glue on top of the cone, insert under the skirt. Drop more glue in, if necessary. Dry; trim the cone bottom if necessary. Hang the wreath on the angel's hand, and your cornhusk Christmas angel is ready to top the tree or stand alone.

ORNAMENTS

Decorated Satin Balls

DECORATED SATIN BALLS *(3″-dia.)*

EASY: Achievable by anyone.
MATERIALS *(for each ball):* 3″-dia. shocking pink satin-covered ball; 45″ of ⅜″-wide green grosgrain ribbon; 32″ of ⅛″-wide double-faced red satin ribbon; red, shocking pink and green small Christmas glass beads, ¼″ to ⅜″ in dia.; white glue *(see Materials Shopping Guide, page 293, for items listed above)*; fern pins; short straight pins; ornament hangers.

DIRECTIONS:

1. Dip 1 straight pin into the glue and pin one end of the green ribbon at the top of the ball. Wrap the ribbon around the ball to divide the ball into 6 equal parts. Glue a pin at the top and at the center bottom. Repeat with the red ribbon, wrapping between the green ribbon segments. Make a small bow from 12″ of the green ribbon and pin to the center top.
2. Glue the pink, red and green beads along the green ribbon on each side of the bow *(see photo)*. Insert 1 fern pin at the center top of the ball and attach hanger.
Note: For Poinsettias shown in photo, see page 46.

PASTA ORNAMENTS

EASY: Achievable by anyone.
MATERIALS: Pasta wheels; wax paper; white glue; toothpicks.

DIRECTIONS:

1. For small snowflake ornaments: Place 4 pasta wheels on wax paper and glue them together where their sides touch.
2. For large snowflake ornaments: With toothpicks, arrange wheels on wax paper to about a 4″ dia. Glue where the wheels touch *(see photo, page 79)*.

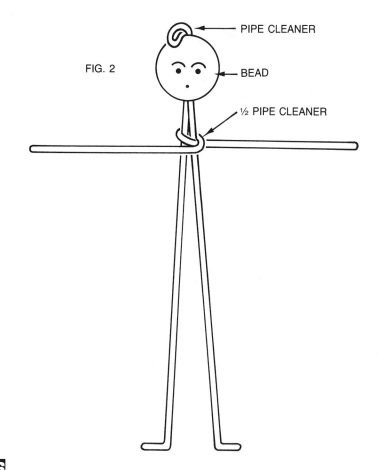

FIG. 2 — PIPE CLEANER — BEAD — ½ PIPE CLEANER

TREE ANGEL

EASY: Achievable by anyone.
MATERIALS: Scraps of lace, as follows—1½″ wide for sleeves, 1″ wide for skirt border, 3″ wide for pantaloons and 2″ wide (both edges finished) for bodice; two white "craft" pipe cleaners; ¾″-dia. Wooden ball "face"; white glue; 7″ x 17″ tulle; craft "pearls"; scrap of white felt and gold paper; gold stars; toothpick; cotton ball; ⅛″ gold braid; purchased gold paper wings; gold Christmas card for sandals.

DIRECTIONS:

1. Body: Fold a pipe cleaner in half; push the folded center through a wooden bead and bend the fold to hold the bead on. At each end, bend for a ½″ foot. Cut the second pipe cleaner in half and wrap it around the body to make arms *(see Fig. 2)*.
2. Sleeves: Fold a 4″ x 1½″ strip of lace over both arms (clipping at the center back); glue the long edges together to make a pair of 2″ x ¾″ sleeves; tack the center of the strip to the back of the body.
3. Pantaloons: Cut a 4″ strip of 3″-wide lace; seam the cut (3″) edges together. With the scalloped edge at the bottom, pull the lace over one "leg" and tie the top around the leg with a piece of thread. Repeat for the other leg.
4. Bodice: Cut a 2½″ strip of 2″-wide lace, finished on both edges. From one (back) end, cut down the center of the strip for 1¼″. Place it on the body, uncut lace in front, cut edges in back; tie around it at the "waist." ☞

5. Skirt: Fold the 7″ x 17″ piece of tulle in half (3½″ x 17″). Lap 1″-wide lace over the double raw edges and topstitch. Seam at the short ends; gather along the fold (waist). Pull the skirt over the pantaloons; draw up the gathering, wrapping thread around the waist, and tie securely.

6. Fasten the string of "pearls" to the front of the bodice. Wrap gold braid around the waist; fasten with thread and trim with a single pearl.

7. Hands: Roll ½″-wide white felt around the end of one "arm," cutting "fingers"; glue. Roll the gold paper around a toothpick; glue one end to the other arm for wand. Add a felt "hand" and gold stars.

8. Glue a cotton ball to the head. Add braid and a pearl. Sew the gold paper wings to the back of the angel. Glue gold braid over the "foot." Glue a gold "sole" under each foot to complete a "sandal."

$

LACE STAR

EASY: Achievable by anyone.
MATERIALS: Fleecy interlining; lace; lace edging; stuffing.

DIRECTIONS (¼″ seams allowed):
1. Trace the star segment in Fig. 3.
2. Follow Step 2 in the directions for Muslin Star (page 91) to complete the star shape.
3. Cut 1 fleece star. Pin it to 2 layers of lace; stitch ¼″ from the edges, leaving an opening at one edge. Turn the lace sides out; stuff; slipstitch closed. Slipstitch lace edging along the seam. Sew a loop to one point, for hanging.

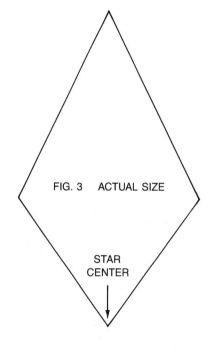

FIG. 3   ACTUAL SIZE

STAR CENTER

CHRISTMAS TREE LIGHT SAFETY

Remember—lights can be fire hazards, too.
● *Look for the "UL Approved" label on all lights and artificial trees.*
● *Avoid overloading wall outlets— one plug per outlet is the safest.*
● *Do not use more than 200 midget lights or 50 larger lights per string.*
● *Never use indoor lights outside.*
● *Never use light strings with frayed wires or damaged sockets.*
● *Before plugging in your lights, make sure there are no empty sockets.*
● *Disconnect lights at bedtime and whenever you leave your home.*
● *If you have a metal tree, the Consumer Product Safety Commission warns: "The only way to illuminate a metal tree safely is to use colored floodlights, where children can't reach them." Don't use ordinary tree lights on a metal tree, as they may cause electric shock.*

$

WHITE DOVE *(4½″ long x 1″ wide)*

AVERAGE: For those with some experience in crocheting.
MATERIALS: J. & P. Coats "Knit-Cro-Sheen": 1 (175-yd.) ball of White; steel crochet hook No. 7; 2 black seed beads; white glue; paintbrush.

DIRECTIONS:
Head: Starting at the center top of the Head with a single strand of thread and No. 7 hook, ch 2. **Rnd 1:** Work 6 sc in 2nd ch from hook. Join to first sc. **Rnd 2:** 2 sc in each sc around—12 sc. Join with sl st to first sc. **Rnd 3:** *Sc in each of next 2 sc, 2 sc in next sc; rep from *3 more times—16 sc. Join with sl st. **Rnds 4-9:** Sc in each sc around. Join. **Rnd 10:** Sc in **back** lp of each sc—ridge formed for neck. **Rnd 11:** *Sc in each of ☞

White Dove

3 sc, 2 sc in next sc; rep from * 3 more times—20 sc. Join. Stuff Head.

Body: Rnd 12: Ch 3 (counts as 1 dc), dc in same place as sl st, dc in each of next 11 sc, *2 dc in next sc, dc in each of next 3 sc; rep from * once—23 dc. Join with sl st to top of beg ch-3. **Rnd 13:** Ch 3 (counts as 1 dc), dc in same place as sl st, dc in each of next 15 dc, 2 dc in next dc, dc in each of next 3 dc, 2 dc in next dc, dc in each of next 2 dc—26 dc. Join with sl st to top of beg ch-3. **Rnds 14 and 15:** Ch 3, dc in each dc around. Join to top of beg ch-3. Stuff Body. **Rnd 16 (dec rnd):** Ch 3 (counts as 1 dc), dc in same place as sl st, dc in each of next 14 dc, sk 1 dc, dc in each of next 2 dc, * sk 1 dc, dc in next 3 dc; rep from * once—24 dc. Join to top of beg ch-3. **Note:** Continue to stuff Body as you work remainder of rnds. **Rnd 17:** Ch 3 (counts as 1 dc), dc in each of next 14 dc, sk 1 dc, dc in next 4 dc, sk 1 dc, dc in each of next 2 dc, sk 1 dc—21 dc. Join. **Rnd 18:** Ch 3 (counts as 1 dc), dc in each of next 20 dc. Join. **Rnd 19:** Ch 3 (counts as 1 dc), dc in each of next 12 dc, sk 1 dc, * dc in each of next 2 dc, sk 1 dc; rep from * once, ending with dc in next dc—18 dc. Join. **Rnd 20:** Ch 3 (counts as 1 dc), dc in each of next 12 dc, sk 1 dc, dc in each of next 2 dc, sk 1 dc, dc in next dc—16 dc. Join. **Rnd 21:** Ch 3 (counts as 1 dc), dc in each of next 7 dc, sk 1 dc, dc in next dc, sk 1 dc, dc in each of next 2 dc, sk 1 dc, dc in next dc, sk 1 dc—12 dc Join. Fasten off.

Note: Tail is worked with two strands of thread held tog throughout. **Tail:** Flatten lower Body in half so there is a front section and a back section. **Row 1:** Working through both thicknesses (to close opening) with No. 3 hook, 1 dc in each dc across—6 dc. Ch 3, turn. **Row 2:** Work 1 dc, ch 1, 2 dc between first 2 dc, ch 1, (dc between next 2 dc, ch 1) 3 times; 2 dc, ch 1, 2 dc between last 2 dc. Ch 1, turn. **Row 3:** Sl st in each st to first

ch-1 sp, sl st in ch-1 sp, in same ch-1 sp work ch 3, 1 dc, ch 1, 2 dc; ch 1, (dc in next ch-1 sp, ch 1) 4 times; 2 dc, ch 1, 2 dc in last ch-1 sp. Ch 1, turn. **Note: To make 1 hdc—**Yo hook, draw up a lp in next sp or st, yo and through 3 lps. **Row 4:** Sl st in each st to first ch-1 sp, sl st in ch-1 sp, in same ch-1 sp work ch 2, 2 hdc, ch 2, sl st in 2nd ch from hook—**picot made;** and 2 hdc, * in next ch-1 sp work 3 hdc, picot st, 2 hdc; rep from * across. Fasten off.

Wings (Make 2): Starting at top of Wing with 2 strands of thread and No. 3 hook, ch 16. **Row 1:** Sc in 2nd ch from hook and in each ch across—15 sc. Ch 3, turn. **Row 2:** * Skip 1 sc, 1 hdc in next sc, ch 1; rep from * 3 more times; sk 1 sc, 1 hdc in each of next 4 sc, 2 sc in next sc, sl st in last sc. Ch 1, turn. **Row 3:** Sl st in first sl st and sc, sc in next sc, 1 hdc in each of next 4 hdc, ch 1, sk 1 hdc, in next ch-1 sp work 2 hdc, ch 1, 2 hdc—**shell made;** ch 1, (sk next ch-1 sp, 1 hdc in next hdc, ch 1) 2 times; 1 hdc in 2nd ch of ch-3 turning ch. Ch 3, turn. **Row 4:** Skip first hdc, (1 hdc in next hdc, ch 1) 2 times; in next ch-1 sp of shell work 1 shell. **Do not** work rem sts. Ch 1, turn. **Row 5:** Sl st in each st of shell and first ch-1 sp, ch 2, in next ch-1 sp work 3 hdc, ending with a sl st in next hdc and in top of ch-3 turning ch. Fasten off.

To Assemble: Sew flat narrow edge of Wing to Rnd 13 of body.

Beak: With a single strand of thread and No. 7 hook, attach thread to Rnd 4 of Head and ch 3. Join with sl st to first ch. Fasten off. Work ends in .

Eyes: Sew on 2 black beads for eyes.

To Shape and Stiffen: Place on wax paper. With slightly diluted glue, paint Body, Wings and Tail, smoothing and shaping (see photo, page 71) as they dry.

CHRISTMAS PUDDING MOUSE

EASY: Achievable by anyone.

MATERIALS: One 9″ x 12″ sheet gray felt; scrap of pink felt; gray thread; scraps of red calico, white cotton fabric, ⅜″ lace trim; eyelet edging; ⅛″ ribbon in red, white and black; 1 acorn; green and white acrylic paints; 3 straight pins with black beads for eyes and mouth; polyester fiberfill; cardboard; tracing paper; 5″ gray pipe cleaner.

DIRECTIONS:

1. On tracing paper, trace the mouse body (see Fig. 4). Cut 2 shapes from the gray felt. Also cut a 1½″-dia. circle from the gray felt and a 1⅜″-dia. circle from the cardboard; cut gray ear and pink ear liners (trace the shapes on page 74). The remaining pieces will be cut as you go along.

2. Mouse: Leaving the bottom open, sew the bodies together with tiny overcasting stitches. Stuff. Insert the cardboard base at the bottom, cover with the felt circle and stitch.

3. Skirt: Cut a 9″ x 2½″ piece from the calico. Hem the long edge ½″. Topstitch the lace trim; sew a ½″ seam for the center back. Sew a gathering row ½″ from the edge and pull up the fullness to fit around the waist at the top of the base, turning the raw edge under.

4. Sleeves: Cut a 1½ x 4″ piece from the calico; seam (¼″) the long edges, right sides together; turn right side out. Insert the pipe cleaner. Add lace at the wrist, bend the arms and glue to the mouse at the back, just above the skirt.

5. Bodice: Arrange a 3″ length of eyelet edging (raw edge turned under) around the neck and tuck the ends under the skirt in front. Glue the center back edge to the top of the "sleeve."

Christmas Pudding Mouse

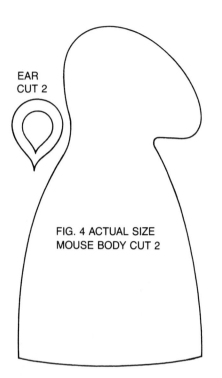

EAR
CUT 2

FIG. 4 ACTUAL SIZE
MOUSE BODY CUT 2

CANDY APPLE

EASY: Achievable by anyone.
MATERIALS: Redwood macrame bead, 1⅝"-dia.; 3 artificial candy canes from craft store; 1 fluted candy paper liner with holly design; fast-drying white glue.

DIRECTIONS:
Glue the bead to the paper liner with the hole at the top. Fill the bead with glue (work fast) and insert the cane immediately. When dry, hang on the tree from the hook of the cane.

Candy Apple

6. Apron: Stitch together two 2" x 1⅜" pieces of white cotton around 3 edges, leaving the top open. Turn; trim the bottom edge with lace and ⅛" ribbon insertion. Gather the top edge slightly and stitch centered under the 10" white ⅛" ribbon apron band. Tie over the skirt with a bow at the back.

7. Dust Cap/Face: With pinking shears, cut a 3¼"-dia. circle from the white cotton fabric. Gather with running stitches ¼" from the edge. Stuff. Glue to the mouse head. Glue a tiny black bow to the front. Glue pink lining to the gray ear, then glue to the side of the head over the cap. Insert the eyes and nose pins. Pull three 1½" pieces of black thread through the nose, ends extending.

8. Christmas Pudding: Paint green and white icing on the acorn; glue on red bead cherries, if desired. Glue the pudding on the hands.

GARLANDS

Snowman, Elf and Candy-Cane Tree Garland

💲

SNOWMAN, ELF AND CANDY-CANE TREE GARLAND

EASY: Achievable by anyone.
MATERIALS (Enough to make approximately a 12½'-long garland, 23 of each figure): 9" x 12" felt squares—14 white, 1 each of red, blue, black, green, yellow; 91 flat toothpicks; white glue; 12½' of

¼"-wide grosgrain ribbon in desired color; fine-point felt-tip pens in red, black; scissors; pinking shears; paper for pattern pieces.

DIRECTIONS:
Note: The cutting instructions on the diagram are enough for 1 of each figure. Be careful to keep all pieces for each figure in separate piles.
1. Enlarge the patterns in Fig. 5, following the directions on page 291.

Cut out 23 elves, snowmen and candy canes; the red collar can be done with pinking shears.
2. Elf: On 1 white body piece, glue the pants, jacket and hat. Glue the collar to the jacket. Following the diagram, draw the eyes on the face in black and the nose and mouth in red. Glue a toothpick vertically to the elf's back.
3. Snowman: Glue the hat, boots, scarf to 1 body piece. Following the ☞

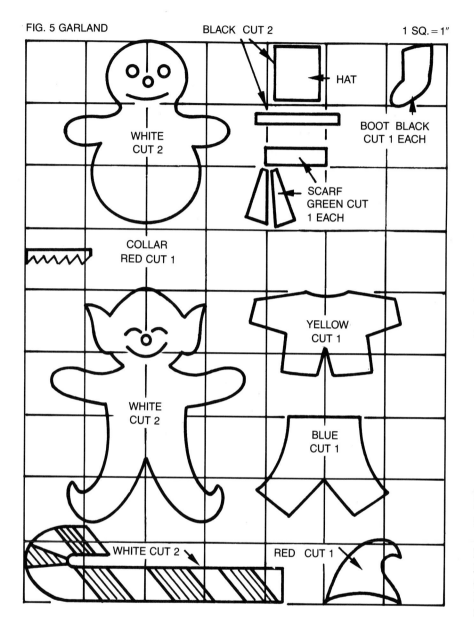

FIG. 5 GARLAND   BLACK CUT 2   1 SQ. = 1"

HAT

WHITE CUT 2

BOOT BLACK CUT 1 EACH

SCARF GREEN CUT 1 EACH

COLLAR RED CUT 1

YELLOW CUT 1

WHITE CUT 2

BLUE CUT 1

WHITE CUT 2   RED CUT 1

diagram, draw the eyes on the face in black and the nose and mouth in red. Glue the toothpick to the back vertically.

4. Candy Cane: Following the diagram, cut small red strips of red felt and glue to the candy canes (make strips extra long and trim later). Glue a toothpick to the back vertically, closer to the top than the bottom.

5. Repeat the instructions for each figure until 23 of each are finished up to this point.

6. Glue all of the pieces to the grosgrain ribbon, repeating the sequence of the 3 figures: The ribbon should follow the arms of the snowmen and elves, and the candy canes should be centered. Let dry.

7. Glue the remaining pieces to the backs of each figure, covering the ribbon.

CHENILLE TREE GARLAND

EASY: Achievable by anyone.
MATERIALS: Red and white Jumbo chenille stems; gold and silver metallic chenille stems; wire-cutting pliers; ruler.

DIRECTIONS:
1. Cut the Jumbo stems into 6" pieces. Cut the metallic chenille stems into 4" pieces. Make a circle of 1 red piece and hook ½" on each end to fasten. Place a silver piece through the red circle and make a circle of the silver piece to create a chain.
2. Repeat with white, then gold, then red, and continue until the chain is the required length.

SIMPLE TREE GARLANDS

- *Cranberries*
- *Unsalted popcorn*
- *Peanuts in shells, sprayed gold or silver*
- *Big sequins*
- *Miniature bows*

Chenille Tree Garland

Lace Tree Garland

LACE TREE GARLAND

EASY: Achievable by anyone.
MATERIALS: White lace *(see Materials Shopping Guide, page 293);* silver chenille stems, 2 for each yard of lace; ruler; wire-cutting pliers.

DIRECTIONS:
1. Cut each silver chenille stem into 3″ pieces. Pleat the lace crosswise between two scallops and wrap with 1 piece of chenille.
2. Repeat 7 scallops beyond the first wrapping. Repeat between every 7 scallops.

PASTA TREE GARLAND

EASY: Achievable by anyone.
MATERIALS: Small tubular and wagon-wheel-type pasta; wax paper; tacky glue; button thread or crochet cotton; blunt needle; toothpicks.

DIRECTIONS:
Start and end with the tubular shape. Using the needle, alternately string round and tubular shapes on 3-yd. lengths of button thread, securing at each end by bringing the thread-ends out of, then back around the last tube. *Note:* For Pasta Ornaments, see page 69.

Pasta Tree Garland

TREE SKIRTS

Fig. 6. Glue to the skirt, overlapping where necessary. Refer to the photo (left) for placement.

5. Also, cut 5 strips of white about 1" wide for the border between the snow hills.

6. For the bird, cut 1 beak and 2 feet from yellow; 1 eye from black. Cut a brown broomstick. Cut 3 white snowballs. Cut a brown branch for holly and 6 red berries. Cut a red mouth for each snowman.

7. Glue all felt pieces to the skirt.

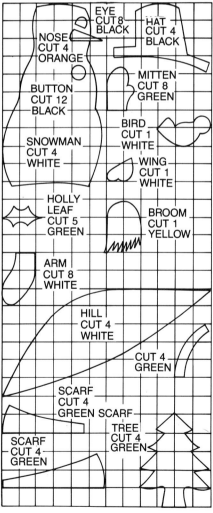

FIG. 6 SNOWMAN TREE SKIRT   1 SQ. = 1"

EYE CUT 8 BLACK
HAT CUT 4 BLACK
NOSE CUT 4 ORANGE
MITTEN CUT 8 GREEN
BUTTON CUT 12 BLACK
BIRD CUT 1 WHITE
SNOWMAN CUT 4 WHITE
WING CUT 1 WHITE
HOLLY LEAF CUT 5 GREEN
BROOM CUT 1 YELLOW
ARM CUT 8 WHITE
HILL CUT 4 WHITE
CUT 4 GREEN
SCARF CUT 4 GREEN SCARF
TREE CUT 4 GREEN
SCARF CUT 4 GREEN

$

SNOWMAN TREE SKIRT

EASY: Achievable by anyone.
MATERIALS: 1¼ yds. white felt; ¼ yd. 36"-wide green felt; 9" x 12" piece of black felt; scraps of orange, yellow and brown felt; white glue; paper for pattern; pencil; scissors; nonstretch cord or string; compass.

DIRECTIONS:
1. Fold the red felt in half lengthwise, then in half crosswise to find the center. Using a 22" length of nonstretch cord or string to serve as a compass, knot one end and pin to the center point of the felt.

2. Tie a pencil to the other end of the string and draw a circle on the felt, 44" in diameter. Cut out with sharp scissors. With the compass, draw a 3" circle in the center of felt and cut out. Cut a slit from the center of the felt to the outer edge.

3. Enlarge the patterns in Fig. 6 on paper, following the directions on page 291.

4. Cut out the appliqués from the assorted colors of felt as specified in

PATCHWORK TREE SKIRT

AVERAGE: For those with some experience in sewing.

MATERIALS: 1¼ yds. 45″-wide unbleached muslin; 2½ yds. polyester fleece; sixty-four 6″ squares in any assortment of red/green/white print or solid cotton or polyester-cotton fabrics; 1½ yds. 45″-wide green (or red) cotton or polyester-cotton fabric; thread to match fabrics; embroidery thread or fine yarn (for tying quilt); scissors; ruler; pins; yardstick. ☞

DIRECTIONS *(½" seams allowed):*

1. Assemble the 6″ squares in a pleasing combination as an 8-square by 8-square patchwork. Mark the center with a pin. Using the yardstick as a guide, mark a 20″-radius circle. Cut the circle out. Using the same center point, cut out a 6″ circle at the center of the large circle. Discard the small circle. Cut once from the outer edge of the skirt to the center in a straight line.

2. Cut 2 pieces of fleece and one of muslin, using the patchwork skirt as the pattern.

3. Cut six 7″-wide strips from solid green (or red) crosswise from the full 45″ width of fabric. Sew the short ends of the pieces together to make one continuous strip. Fold the strip in half, wrong sides together, lengthwise, and press. Hem the short ends. Make a gathering stitch near the cut edge and pull the strip to fit the outer edge of the patchwork circle.

4. Baste a ruffle to the right side of the patchwork with a folded edge of the ruffle facing the center of the circle and cut the edges even with the cut edge of the patchwork. Keep the hemmed ends of the ruffle ⅝″ from the center-to-edge cut edges.

5. Place the muslin piece right side down on patchwork. Place the fleece on the muslin. Baste and sew all layers together ½″ from the cut edges, being careful not to catch the hemmed ends of the ruffle in a seam. Leave a 5″ opening in the seam for turning. Turn the skirt to the right side. Sew the opening closed.

6. Cut six 9″ x 4″ pieces of the same fabric as the ruffle. Fold each lengthwise and sew along one short and the raw long edge. Turn each to the right side and turn in the raw edge at the short end. Sew in pairs to the back opening of the skirt for ties.

7. Tie-quilt with thread or yarn through all layers at the patchwork-square intersections.

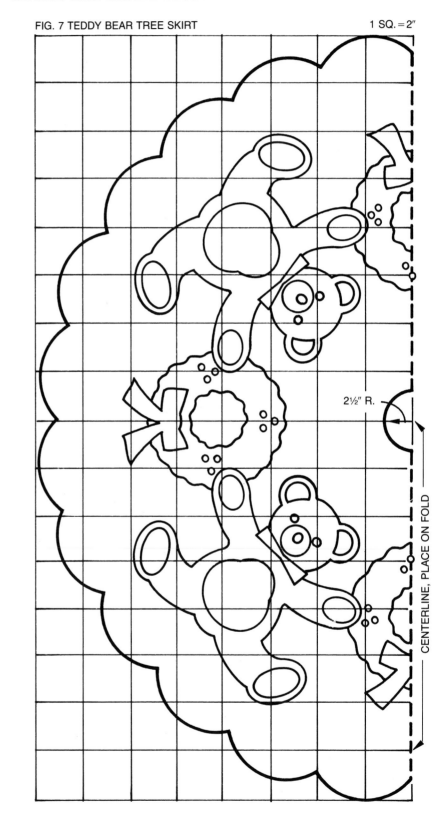

FIG. 7 TEDDY BEAR TREE SKIRT

1 SQ. = 2″

2½″ R.

CENTERLINE, PLACE ON FOLD

TEDDY BEAR TREE SKIRT

EASY: Achievable by anyone.

MATERIALS: 36"-square white felt; 9" x 12" pieces felt—4 tan, 2 green; scraps of felt—light beige (or white), red, black; 4 small bells; Velverette in a Tube glue; red thread; hole paper punch; sewing needle; pencil; ruler; paper for patterns; scissors.

DIRECTIONS:

1. Cut a 36"-diameter circle from the white felt. Using the same center point, cut a 5"-diameter circle and discard the small circle.

2. Enlarge the patterns in Fig. 7 on paper, following the directions on page 291. Cut out the shapes from the appropriate colors of felt.

3. Glue the paw pads, ear linings and muzzle on the bear shapes. Glue the eyes and nose to the face. Dry.

4. Cut scallops on the edge of the tree skirt. Lay out the skirt on a flat surface. Arrange the trimmings as shown with the bear paws under the wreaths. Glue the bears and wreaths to the skirt. Glue bows on the wreaths and at the bear's neck.

5. For the outer edge to the inner hole, mark a straight line through the middle of one wreath. Cut along the line.

6. With the hole punch, make 36 holly berries of red felt. Glue to the wreaths.

7. When the glue is dry, hand-sew the bells to the centers of the bows on the bears.

Christmas, Victorian-Style. Charming Hearts, Bells and Stars (page 90) complement Boy and Girl Doll ornaments (page 89) for a very Victorian feeling.

THEMES
TO SET THE
MOOD

If your family's tastes run along one central theme, use it throughout the house at Christmastime. From the tree and its decorations to wreaths, stockings and table centerpieces, choose similar motifs and materials to give a unified effect.

To inspire you, we offer four themes:

"Christmas, Victorian-Style" (pages 86-91) takes you back to holiday homes during the turn of the century. This is the look for the romantic at heart, with its antique-like dolls and lace-adorned ornaments and centerpieces.

"The Natural Touch" (pages 92-95) relies on the unspoiled look of the outdoors. Decorate a live Christmas tree simply, using baby's breath, little lights and ornaments made from pinecones and dried flowers.

"Country Casual" (pages 96-99), with its rough-hewn objects and calico-fabric decorations, is for those families who like to bring the subtle beauty of the great outdoors into their homes. Patchwork, stenciling and barnyard animal motifs will make your home glow with that special warmth of the country.

"With Kids in Mind" (pages 100-105) fulfills Christmas fantasies for children of all ages. From a Santa Claus-bedecked tree to decorations with a candy motif, this is the theme to use if you want a house that's cheerful and young at heart!

$$ Low-Cost   ◤ Quick and Easy   ◖ Make-Ahead   ▦ Low-Calorie

Button and Bow Wreath

CHRISTMAS
VICTORIAN STYLE

It was Queen Victoria and her taste for the elaborate that influenced Christmas celebrations during the latter half of the 19th century. Trees trimmed with garlands of cranberries or popcorn, colored ribbon bows and gilded nuts became fashionable, as did the rich food we now associate with the classic Christmas dinner.

TO ADD A VICTORIAN FEELING

● Use lots of lace, doilies, satin and velvet all over the house.
● Find old dolls and toys at flea markets and display them on mantels, in windows and in hutches.
● Buy antique Christmas cards (or facsimiles). Use them to make place-cards, elegant ornaments and mantel decorations.
● Wrap gifts in satin or moiré fabric. Decorate with lace ribbon and baby's breath.

Muslin Star; Boy and Girl Dolls; Candlewick Heart and Bells

FIG. 1A DOLL

1 SQ. = 1″

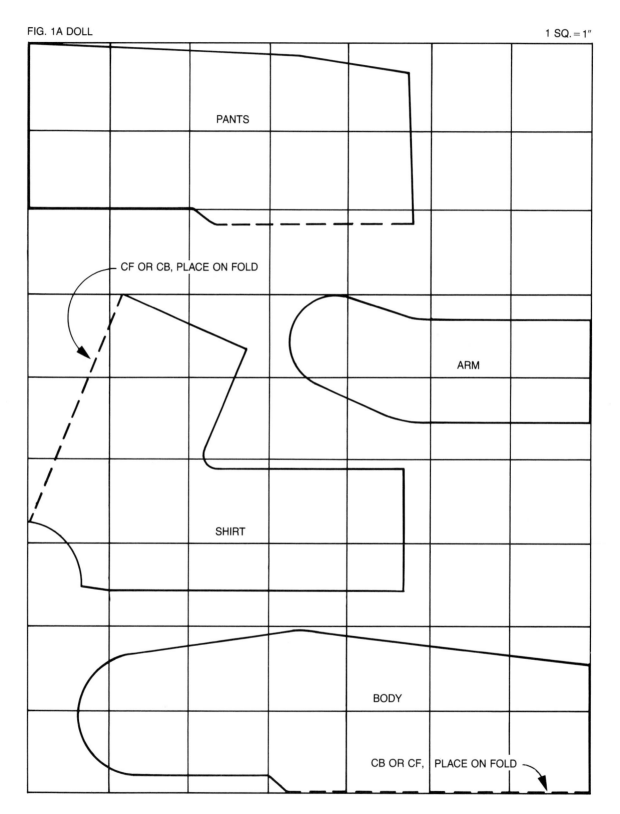

PANTS

CF OR CB, PLACE ON FOLD

ARM

SHIRT

BODY

CB OR CF, PLACE ON FOLD

BOY AND GIRL DOLLS

AVERAGE: For those with some experience in sewing and crafts.
MATERIALS: Modeling compound; mock-wool fiber for hair; satin-finish spray-varnish *(see Materials Shopping Guide, page 293, for items listed above)*; acrylic paint and #0 brush for face; white glue; muslin for body; scraps of fabric for clothes; stuffing; button thread.

DIRECTIONS *(see photo)*:
1. Head: Between your palms, roll a 1½"-dia. ball of the compound until it is smooth. With your thumbnails, pinch up a little nose and 2 brows. Form a chin and cheeks. With a toothpick, make a small mouth opening and draw the lips. To the base of the head, press more compound and shape it into a neck and shoulders, ending in a "lip" *(see Fig. 1)* over which the muslin body can be drawn up. Push a small screw eye "hanger" into the top of the head.
2. Shoe: Mold a ½" ball of the compound into a shoe about 1" long x ¼" high x ½" wide at the heel *(see Fig. 1)*. Depress a circle (for the leg to fit into) and, within it, with a toothpick, make 2 little holes to sew through. Make 2 shoes.
3. Bake and Color: Bake the head and shoes in a preheated moderate oven (350°) until light brown; let them cool. Sand the surface smooth with extra-fine sandpaper. Paint the head flesh color. Add rouge and a touch of eyeshadow. Paint the eyes, brows and lips. Paint the shoes black. After the paint has dried, spray 5 or 6 light coats of satin-finish spray-varnish to get a translucent "waxed" effect.
4. Wig *For girl:* Tear or cut off 8" of wool and sew a "part" at the side or

FIG. 1 DOLL   ACTUAL SIZE

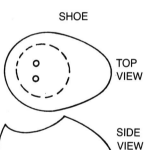

SHOE

TOP VIEW

SIDE VIEW

center (add braids, buns, curls or pigtails, following the package directions). *For boy:* Use 4" of wool; "part" or tie at the center, then distribute hair over the head, gluing with tacky glue and using pins or string to hold in place while drying; trim the boy's hair. Keep the screw eye accessible and add hats and bows as you wish.
5. Body: Enlarge the patterns in Fig. 1A, following the directions on page 291. From the muslin, cut 2 bodies and 2 pairs of arms. Seam a pair of bodies and each pair of arms except at the straight top edge. At the raw edge of the body, stitch a ¼" hem and draw a piece of button thread through it. Stuff the body and insert the baked neck; pull the thread up snugly over the base of the neck and tie the thread ends; also glue. Turn and stuff the arms; turn in the raw ends and slipstitch; then sew them (at the top edges) to the body.
6. Clothes *For skirt:* Seam the short ends of a 4½" x 12" piece of fabric; hem both long edges; run a thread through one hem and pull it up to fit the waist. *For pants:* Cut 2 pants *(see Fig. 1A)* and seam them together, except at the top and bottom edges. Turn under ½" at the waist and stitch a 4" length of narrow elastic to the wrong side, stretching it as you sew. Hem the bottom edges. *For shirt:* Cut 2 shirts *(see Fig. 1A)* and seam them together at the sleeve and side edges. Cut the center opening at the back or front, turn the raw edges under and stitch. Clip and turn the neck edge under and stitch (over lace or other trim if you like). Hem the sleeves and lower edges.
7. Assembly: Dress the body. Stitch and glue the shoes to the legs. Fasten 8" of wire to the screw eye for hanging.

FIG. 2

1 SQ. = 1"

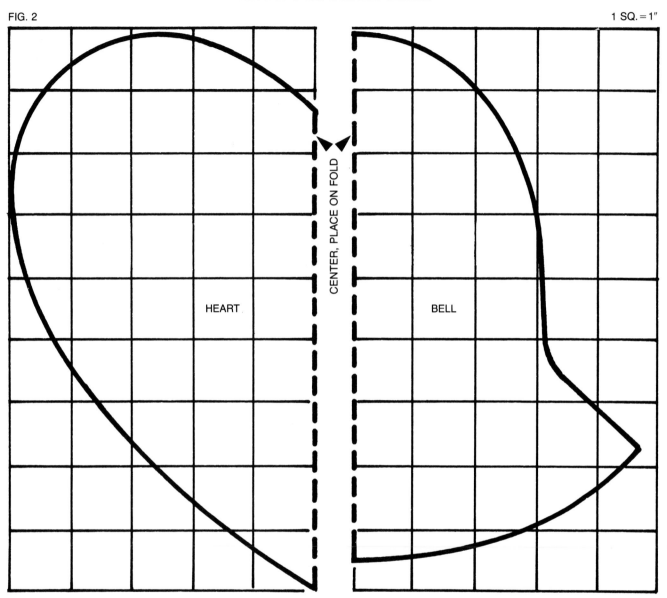

HEART

CENTER, PLACE ON FOLD

BELL

CANDLEWICK HEART AND BELLS

AVERAGE: For those with some experience in embroidery and sewing.
MATERIALS: Scraps of muslin and ruffled edging; candlewicking thread and needle; embroidery hoop; stuffing. *(See Materials Shopping Guide, page 293.)*

DIRECTIONS *(¼" seams allowed):*
1. Embroidery: Enlarge the patterns in Fig. 2, following the directions on page 291. Trace them twice (for front and back) to the muslin *without cutting* and place the muslin in a hoop. Lightly mark on the fabric (or improvise) a design *(see photo, page 86),* leaving the seam allowance empty. Work French knots with the candlewicking thread *(see Stitch Guide, page 290).* Wash and press on the wrong side.
2. Assembly: Cut out the embroidered muslin pieces. On one (front), stitch the edging, right sides together and raw edges matching. Stitch the muslin back on top, right sides together, leaving a 1" opening. Turn the right side out, stuff and slipstitch closed. Sew a thread loop at the center top for hanging.

⊞ MUSLIN STAR *(about 12" wide)*

AVERAGE: For those with some experience in embroidery and sewing.
MATERIALS: See Candlewick Hearts and Bells.

DIRECTIONS:

1. Trace Lace Star illustration, Fig. 2, on page 70, in order to copy the central "angel." Enlarge the pattern by extending both inside edges to 3¼", then draw the central length of 6½" *(see Fig. 3, below)*. Connect the 3 points to draw the outside edges.
2. Draw the complete star by tracing the new pattern 5 times around the center, with the inside edges matching. Embroider and assemble, without edging *(see Candlewick Hearts and Bells, page 90)*.
3. Hand-sew a double ruffle along the seam.

BUTTON AND BOW WREATH *(18"-dia.)*

EASY: Achievable by anyone.
MATERIALS: 16"-dia. flat Styrofoam® wreath form; fiberfill; 16 yds. pink and 5 yds. white 2"-wide craft ribbon; 5 yds. 1¼"-wide pink craft ribbon; 12 yds. 1"-wide lace ribbon; assorted buttons; pink thread; heavy-duty thread; flexible wire; glue stick; silicone glue.

DIRECTIONS:

1. Pad the wreath form on all sides with about 1" of fiberfill. Secure by wrapping the wreath with heavy-duty thread.
2. Wrap the wreath with 2"-wide craft ribbon, overlapping slightly. Secure the end with the glue stick.
3. Cut 24 lengths of lace ribbon, equal to the girth of the wreath. Wrap around the wreath in groups of threes *(see photo, page 86)*. Glue the ends.
4. Sew thread through the button holes to simulate stitching. Glue the "stitched" buttons to the wreath in groups *(see photo)* with the silicone glue.
5. Make 3 sets of bows and streamers using the 1¼" ribbon, leftover 2" ribbon and lace, following the directions for Basic Bows and Streamers *(see page 44)*. Sew a large button in the center of the bow to cover the wire. Trim the ribbon ends as shown in the photo.

SMALL WREATHS—Use 6" and 3" flat wreath forms. Make in the same manner as the large wreath, omitting fiberfill from the 3" wreath and scaling the bows down to the size of the wreath.

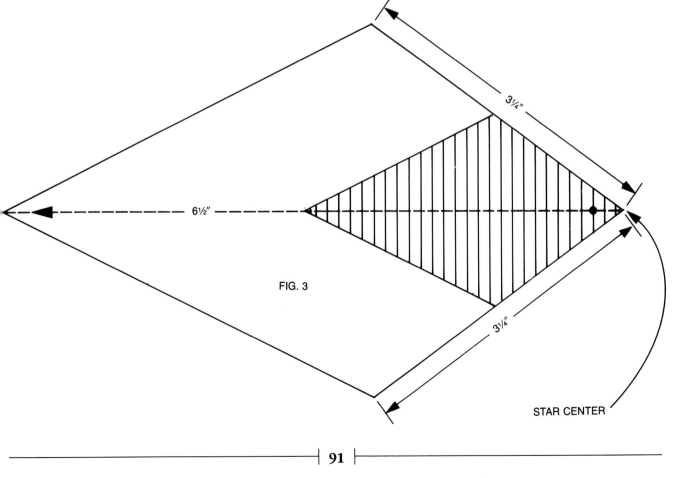

FIG. 3

Natural Christmas Tree. Decorate the Christmas tree with red velvet ribbons, clumps of baby's breath and tiny white lights for a festive, yet simple effect. After the holidays, you can plant the tree in your garden.

THE
NATURAL
TOUCH

Do you prefer wood, dried flowers and the muted colors of heather, rust and olive? Then let your home reflect this feeling! Bring the outdoors inside by using evergreens, pinecones and other items salvaged from your garden. If you don't have access to these things at home, look for them at your nearest florist shop or craft store.

Cornhusk Wreath

QUICK WAYS TO BRING THE OUTDOORS INSIDE

● *Hollow out oranges and fill them with white votives. Tuck these into a flat basket lined with greenery.*
● *Arrange holly and boxwood with loops of aspidistra leaves and bright accents of cranberries.*
● *Add fruit and whole cinnamon sticks to a white basket filled with pine, variegated holly and dusty miller.*
● *Line a window ledge or dining room nook with rows of baskets of all shapes and sizes, each filled with an abundance of dried flowers and ribbon streamers.*
● *Arrange fresh sprays of pine and cedar with green plants from your garden. Tuck in some dried seed pods such as okra and roadside weeds that you've spray-painted red.*

CORNHUSK WREATH

EASY: Achievable by anyone.
MATERIALS: 24″ Styrofoam® or cardboard wreath; 4″-square piece of Styrofoam®; craft glue; spool wire; cornhusks; 7 large dried yarrow heads; 6 wired pinecones; bunch of dark brown dried grasses or wheat; cinnamon sticks.

DIRECTIONS:

1. On the Styrofoam or heavy cardboard ring, wire cornhusk loops, 3 across, leaving a 2″ overlap and using the spool wire for continuous wiring of the ends. Use the darker shades of cornhusks to create the design, as pictured, blending light to dark.
2. Secure the piece of Styrofoam at the base of the wreath, using craft glue, wire or glue gun.

3. In the open design, place the yarrow heads into the Styrofoam base. Fill in with the pinecones, the bunches of the dark brown grasses or wheat and the cinnamon sticks.

FRAGRANT KEEPSAKE WREATHS

EASY: Achievable by anyone.
When decorated with ribbons, miniwreaths make the prettiest room fresheners. Hang them in a sunny window or above a fireplace, where they'll release their fragrance when they're warmed.

You can use homemade or store-bought potpourri, recycled wedding flowers, chopped thyme and oregano leaves accented with berries (for the men on your gift list), chopped or shredded flowers in color-coordinated combinations. Unleash your imagination and experiment!

THREE WAYS TO DRY BUDS, FLOWERS, LEAVES AND BERRIES.
For all methods: Pull apart flower clusters, shred large petals and remove woody stems to speed drying.
1. Air drying: Flowers, buds, leaves and berries. Hang bundles of 3 to 4 stems, secured with a rubber band, upside down in a warm sunless spot, such as a cellar, attic or garage. Or spread the plant material 1 layer deep on a screen or cheesecloth; stir daily. *Drying time:* 10 days to 2 weeks. (Berries may require up to 1 month.)
2. Oven drying: Flowers, buds and leaves (not berries). Set oven at the lowest temperature. Spread plant material 1 layer deep on a screen or wire rack placed on a cookie sheet. Leave the oven door ajar to allow moisture to escape. Stir once or twice. *Drying time:* 10 to 30 minutes.

3. Microwave-oven drying: Flowers and leaves (not buds or berries). If available, follow the manufacturer's instructions for drying herbs. Generally, place a few sprigs of flowers or leaves (stripped from their stems) between 2 paper towels and set the microwave oven at *high* for 2 to 3 minutes. If necessary, replace the towels and dry the sprigs again at *high* for 1 minute, or until crumbly.

PREPARING INGREDIENTS
● Flowers and leaves should be crumbly dry. Berries are dry when wrinkled and hard; flower buds will feel papery.
● Shred dried flowers and leaves by briskly rubbing them between your hands. Or, chop them in a blender.
● Use dried berries as wreath accents; all-berry wreaths may mold.
● Fragrance is easily added to potpourri mixtures with a few drops of scented oil.

HOW TO MAKE MINI-WREATHS
You'll need:
1 gelatin mold (⅓-cup capacity)
   Shortening
1 tablespoon white glue
3 tablespoons water
¾ cup potpourri
1. Lightly grease the interior of the gelatin mold with shortening; set aside.
2. Blend the glue and water together in a small bowl. Add the potpourri; stir to coat evenly and set aside for 5 minutes.
3. Spoon the potpourri into the mold, including all the liquid. Pack the potpourri firmly; set aside for 30 minutes.
4. Carefully pour off the excess liquid by holding the mold nearly vertical. Place the mold, face down, on a screen in a warm, dry room. Leave undisturbed overnight, or for 12 hours.
5. Sharply rap the rim of the mold, face down, against a table edge to dis-

lodge the wreath. Place the wreath, face up, on a screen and dry in a warm (70°) room for 2 days, or until the wreath is quite firm.

PLANTS FOR MINI-WREATHS

Flowers:	**Leaves:**
Aster	Camomile
Broom Camomile	Lavender
Carnation	Lemon Balm
Chrysanthemum	Lemon Verbena
Clarkia	Marjoram
Coral bells	Mint
Dahlia	Oregano
Delphinium	Rosemary
Dusty Miller	Scented
Forget-Me-Not	Geranium
Freesia	Thyme
Geranium	**Berries:**
Heather	Barberry
Heliotrope	Bayberry
Lavender	Bittersweet
Lilac	Cotoneaster
Marigold	Firethorn
Nasturtium	Juniper
Peony	
Petunia	
Poppy	
Rose	
Salvia	
Stock	
Violet	
Yarrow	
Zinnia	

PINECONE WREATH

EASY: Achievable by anyone.

MATERIALS: 12″ square of plywood; 12″ square of felt for backing; 6″-square tile for top; quick-drying glue; acrylic spray coating; wood stain; an assortment of pinecones (1½″ to 3″ or 4″ high); an assortment of nuts in their shells, including acorns, hazelnuts, walnuts, almonds and chestnuts.

DIRECTIONS:

1. Stain the plywood; allow to dry.

2. Glue the 12″ felt square to the bottom. Glue the 6″-square tile to the center of the top.

3. Select the largest pinecones and form a square around the outside edge of the plywood square, using glue sparingly. Next, glue a second square of pinecones inside the first, leaving a 3″ circle for your candle. Pinecones should not be perfectly aligned. Now glue a third square of pinecones on top of the first two. Let this set overnight.

4. To build up: In between your pinecone squares, start to fill in with smaller cones, gluing them down as you go along. As you look down, fill in the space with the various nuts and small cones. Let them set.

5. If you wish, you can fill in the sides with nuts and acorns as you go around the wreath. When you are satisfied with the appearance of having filled in all voids, let the wreath set overnight.

6. Next, spray the wreath with 3 coats of acrylic spray coating, allowing each coat to dry thoroughly before applying the next coat.

Tree in a Basket

COUNTRY CASUAL

*The ever-growing popularity of country-casual decorating
has had its effects on Christmas decorating, too. Wreaths made
from straw and calico are almost as common as the classic
evergreen varieties. If you are a collector of Americana, be sure
to bring it all out for the holidays! A few carefully placed ribbons
can add a holiday look to all your treasured pieces.*

COUNTRY FLAVOR

● *Hang hand-crafted cookie cutters
from bright red ribbons of different
lengths. Attach ornament hooks and
hang in your window.*
● *Try sewing calico or gingham fabric to wrap presents. Either fold it as
you would gift wrap, or place the gift
on a square of fabric, then gather up
diagonally the opposite ends and tie
with a ribbon or yarn.*
● *Place cheery baskets all over the
house. Weave some calico-patterned
ribbon through the top of each.*
● *Use an old quilt as a Christmas tree
skirt. Cut out pieces of the quilt, then
stuff and hang as ornaments.*

TREE IN A BASKET

Trim your tree with painted wooden
barnyard animals and miniature
baskets lined with red-checked
gingham. Place the tree in a wooden
bushel basket. Surround the base
with gifts wrapped in paper made
from brown paper bags embellished
with stencil designs or rubber-stamp
imprints.

Heart Christmas Card Holder

💲 HEART CHRISTMAS CARD HOLDER

EASY: Achievable by anyone.
MATERIALS: ¼ yd. 45″-wide solid red cotton fabric; ¼ yd. 45″-wide red print cotton fabric; ¼ yd. iron-on interfacing; ½ yd. 1″- or 1½″-wide red grosgrain ribbon; red thread.

DIRECTIONS:
1. Enlarge the pattern in Fig. 4, following the directions on page 291. Cut the pattern out twice along the outer edges in the interfacing.
2. Place the interfacing pattern pieces on the wrong side of the cotton fabrics: one piece on the solid red and one piece on the red prints.
3. Iron the pieces on, following the instructions for the type of interfacing used. Cut the 2 pieces out.

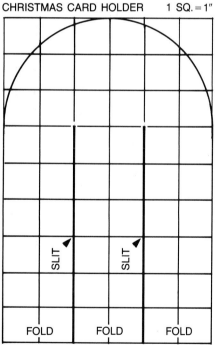

FIG. 4
CHRISTMAS CARD HOLDER   1 SQ. = 1″

Rustic Wreath

4. Cut the pattern once in the solid red and once in the red print. Place the solid red pieces together, right sides out, and the red print pieces together, right sides out. Stitch close to the outer edges. Stitch 1 row around the slit lines. Cut along the slit lines. Stitch with zigzag along all the cut edges.
5. "Weave" the 2 halves of the card holder together as shown in the photo. Sew the grosgrain ribbon on for hanging as shown, forming loops on the front.

💲 RUSTIC WREATH

EASY: Achievable by anyone
MATERIALS: Wooden cutting board; stencils and stencil paints; excelsior or straw wreath; assorted ribbons and a bow in country motifs.

DIRECTIONS:
1. Stencil the designs on the cutting board; let dry.
2. Place the stenciled board in the middle of the wreath.
3. Trim with the ribbons and the bow.

STRIP QUILTING FOR RUNNER AND NAPKINS

AVERAGE: For those with some experience in sewing.

MATERIALS: Quantities are not specified because both runners and place mats of any desired size can be made using these instructions. Coloring can be non-seasonal as well as in the red-green mixture shown. Select at least 6 different but compatible prints in all-cotton percale-type fabric. Allow sufficient extra fabric in one of the prints to make the backing and bias for edging (or for napkins). For batting, use either a lightweight quilt batting or 1 or 2 layers of polyester fleece. *(See Materials Shopping Guide, page 293, for material suggestions.)* Ruler; scissors; pins; thread to match fabrics.

DIRECTIONS:

1. Wash and press all fabrics to be used. Cut the backing piece slightly longer and wider than the dimensions chosen for the finished item. Cut the batting the same size as the backing piece.

2. Baste the batting to the wrong side of the backing piece with contrasting thread. Place the basted piece, batting side up, on a flat surface.

3. Cut 2"-wide strips of fabrics for quilting. Arrange the pattern in a pleasing repeat. Place one strip, of the same fabric as the backing, centered crosswise on the batting. This strip is right side up. Place the next strip, wrong side up, on top of the first strip. Using thread to match the backing fabric, sew along one long edge of the doubled strips with a ¼" seam. Open the strips and flatten strip 2 against the batting. Pin in place. Repeat on the opposite long edge of strip 1, using another strip. Reverse the sewing direction to keep the runner straight.

4. Repeat with additional strips, working to right and left of the center

Strip Quilting for Runner and Napkins

strip. If possible, end with the same color strip as the backing.

5. Cut the long edges of the finished piece even and, if desired, cut the short ends as a curve or to a point. Baste all edges.

6. Make 1½-wide bias strips. Sew the bias to the striped side of the runner for the first seam. Turn to the back and sew by hand to finish binding. Remove any basting thread visible. If desired, a ruffle may be used to finish the piece instead of a bias.

Felt Santas

WITH
KIDS
IN MIND

*Christmas wouldn't be Christmas without children—
of all ages! For a houseful of decorations with the kids in
mind, use Santa, toy and candy motifs with abandon.
Also try to have decorations that invite kids to play with
them—pull-toy wall decorations, Advent calendars
and cuddly stuffed pillows in Yuletide colors.*

Kiddy Tree

KIDDY TREE

Spray-paint some branches white (or use birch) and insert them into a piece of Styrofoam® you've placed in a basket. Trim with gift tags, glitter-sprayed stars and blue bows. Make "presents" from colorful cartons filled with tiny stocking-stuffers.

POISONOUS HOLIDAY PLANTS

The following holiday plants are considered poisonous if ingested. Contact your local Poison Control Center if a child or pet nibbles on any of the following:

- *Amaryllis*
- *Azalea*
- *Boxwood*
- *Castor bean*
- *Christmas cactus*
- *Christmas rose*
- *Crown of thorns*
- *English and American ivy*
- *Holly berries*
- *Jerusalem or Christmas cherry*
- *Jimson weed*
- *Mistletoe*
- *Mountain laurel*
- *Pokeweed*
- *Privet*
- *Rhododendron*
- *Yew berries*

ADDITIONAL HAZARDS

Call your local Poison Control Center (have the product container with ingredient list handy) if your child ingests any of the following:

- *Fluid inside of bubbly lights.*
- *Spray snow in an aerosol can—the snow is nontoxic, but the propellants may be toxic.*
- *Alcohol (present not only in holiday drinks but also in aftershaves, perfumes and colognes), which is poisonous to a small child.*
- *Fireplace color crystals, which are powdered substances that may contain salts of heavy metals.*

FIG. 5   1 SQ. = 1″

FELT SANTA

EASY: Achievable by anyone.
MATERIALS: Red, white, pink and black felt*; scrap of gold soutache braid; white glue; fusible web; buckram; iron-on interfacing; red cord for hanging; paper punch (¼″ and ³⁄₁₆″); fine-tip ballpoint pen; oak tag.
*Note: 1 yd. 72″-wide red felt makes about 28 Santas.

DIRECTIONS:

1. Enlarge the patterns (*in Fig. 5 for large Santa, Fig. 6 for small Santa, following the directions on page 291*). Fuse the iron-on interfacing to the felt; with the ballpoint pen, trace the patterns to the interfacing side. From red, cut 1 Santa, following the broken lines in Figs. 5 and 6. From the white, cut a pair of cuffs and 1 each of a beard, pompons, suit and hat trim. From the black, cut a pair of boots and a belt. From the pink, cut a 1½″ x 1″ face to underlap the white felt hat/beard. From the green, cut 1 tree. From the buckram and from the fusible interfacing, cut a Santa (like the red felt one) and a tree.

2. For hanging ornaments, fuse the buckram to the back of Santa and tree (omit the buckram for appliqués). Glue the pink hatband/beard behind the white. Glue the white cuffs, trim and pompon over Santa. With the paper punch, cut two black eyes and a red mouth; glue to the face. Glue the gold braid to the belt for the buckle. Glue the tree behind one hand.

3. For a hanging ornament, make a small hole at the X. Cut a 6″ cord and tie the ends together; push the loop through the hole and tie a slipknot.

FIG. 6 SMALL SANTA AND STOCKING   1 SQ. = 1"

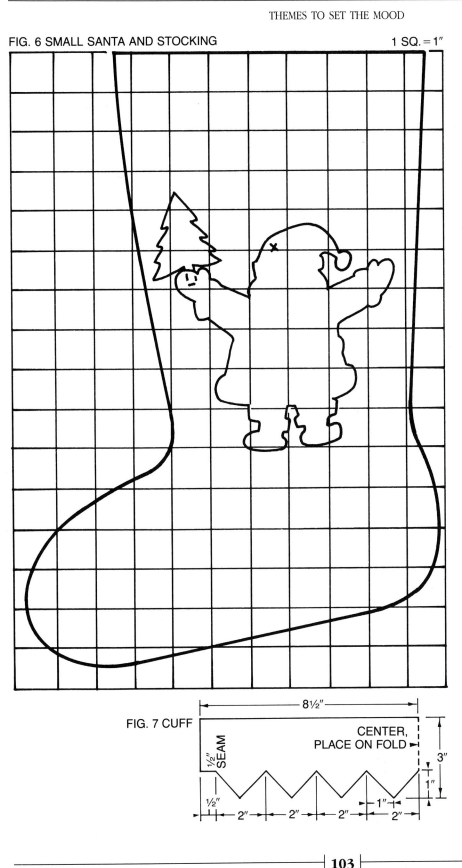

FIG. 7 CUFF

8½"

½" SEAM

CENTER,
PLACE ON FOLD ►

3"

1"

½"

2"   2"   2"   2"

1"

TO KEEP KIDS BUSY

● *Little ones can trim their own tree if you cut a tree outline from paper or felt and tape it to a wall. Let them create ornaments from paper, yarn, etc., and tape or glue to the tree.*
● *Make up a "guest box" for little visitors with art supplies, games and books. Present on arrival.*
● *Staple plain paper together in book form for kids to write their own Christmas story.*
● *Have a decoration contest with small Styrofoam® shapes such as balls, plus sequins, felt and gold stars. Give a prize for the best snowman, face and tree trim.*

GINGHAM STOCKING

AVERAGE: For those with some experience in sewing.
MATERIALS: ½ yd. each of 44"-wide gingham and muslin (makes 2); stick-on gold craft trim; iron-on interfacing; white glue; small Santa and tree *(see Fig. 6)*.

DIRECTIONS:
1. Enlarge the stocking patterns *(in Fig. 6, following the directions on page 291, reversing the pattern if desired.)* Cut one pair each of gingham and muslin stockings. Cut a 3" x 17" cuff and fuse it to the iron-on interfacing.
2. With the edges even, stack the stockings as follows: muslin, gingham and gingham (right sides together) and muslin; pin and seam all except the top edges. Clip the curves and turn the gingham side out.
3. Draw a serrated edge on the cuff *(see Fig. 7)* and cut away where shaded. Seam the cuff at the ends to make a loop. Stitch the top edge to the stocking edge. Cover the raw edges with the gold trim.
4. Glue on the small Santa and small tree *(see Felt Santa, page 102)*.

GINGHAM TREE SKIRT

AVERAGE: For those with some experience in sewing.

MATERIALS: 1 yd. each of 45″-wide gingham and muslin; package of adhesive gold craft rickrack; 1 yd. adhesive ¼″ gold soutache braid; 7 large Santas and trees *(see Felt Santa, page 102).*

DIRECTIONS:

1. Draw the pattern *(see Fig. 8)* for the skirt segment and cut 8 from gingham, 7 from muslin. Also cut a 1½″-wide bias strip for binding, ½ yd. long.

2. Seam the gingham segments together, side by side, to make a circle. Seam the muslin pieces the same way. Press the seams open.

3. With the right sides together, stitch the muslin to the gingham skirt at each end. Fold the extra gingham segment in half vertically (this will be an underlap). Pin the lower edges together with the seams matching; stitch.

4. Bind the inside edges with the binding strip, turning the raw ends under.

5. Stick rickrack to the outside edges. Glue 7 large Santas and large trees to the skirt.

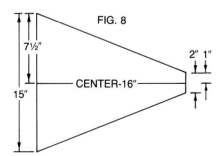

FIG. 8

7½″

15″

CENTER-16″

2″ 1″

Lollipop Advent Calendar

LOLLIPOP ADVENT CALENDAR

(approximately 2' x 3')

AVERAGE: For those with some experience in sewing.

MATERIALS: ⅞ yd. 45"-wide green and white tiny-check gingham; 1½ yds. 36"-wide (or wider) bright green cotton-blend fabric; scraps of green, orange, red and yellow print fabrics for bias binding and star; two pieces polyester batting, one 26" x 36", the other 29" x 24"; threads to match star and trees; 24 red, green, orange and yellow lollipops; scraps of worsted yarn to match lollipops; straight pins.

DIRECTIONS:

1. Enlarge and cut out the patterns in Fig. 9, following the directions on page 291.

2. Fold the gingham in half and draw the tree shape on the back. Pin 2 layers of gingham, right sides together, with a small piece of batting under. Sew around the outline; cut out, clip and slit the top layer of gingham.

3. Turn through the hole made, so that the gingham is right side out with the batting in between. Press very lightly with a warm iron, if necessary.

4. Cut 2 pieces of bright green fabric to cover the larger piece of batting. Sandwich the batting between the fabric, right side out.

5. Pin the tree, slit-side down, to the sandwiched materials, going through all layers and allowing room for the star above.

6. Stuff and sew the star the same way as the tree; pin slightly over the tip of the tree.

7. Sew the tree and star onto the background, using appliqué stitches. Quilt aroung the tree and star, ¼" from the edge, using straight stitches and green thread and going thtrough all layers. Trim the edges of the background evenly.

8. Cut bias binding from the prints; sew the strips together to form a continuous piece of binding; pin to the edge of the quilt front, right sides together. Sew by machine; turn to the back; turn the edge under and sew down by hand.

9. Cut twenty-four 9" lengths of yarn to match the lollipops; affix to the tree by running yarn through all layers in a side-to-side single stitch and spacing the rows evenly in the following order: 1 piece; 4 pieces; 5 pieces; 6 pieces; 7 pieces; 1 piece. Tie in bows over the lollipop sticks.

10. Slip one lollipop out each day of December, until the last one is removed on Christmas Eve.

PLAYFUL TOUCHES

- *Hang candy canes in different colors on the tree, along wall moldings and from the banister.*
- *Trim the tree with paper-wrapped candies. Wrap them a second time, if you wish, with colorful tissue paper.*
- *Arrange stuffed animals in groups on the landing, on window ledges or on top of the piano.*
- *Let the kids draw on brown paper and use it to wrap gifts.*

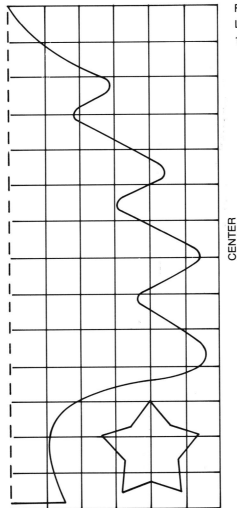

FIG. 9
LOLLIPOP ADVENT CALENDAR
1 SQ. = 2"

CENTER

Two quilts sure to become heirlooms: *left*, Trip Around the World and, *right*, Kentucky Mountain Chain (both page 110).

FILLING THE
GIFT LIST

Gifts you make yourself have a special charm all their own. Whether you're looking for some inexpensive stocking-stuffers or a few special items for those important people on your list, our collection of homemade gifts has something for everyone.

"For Grandma and Grandpa," choose from picture frames made with fabric (page 109), a wine rack (page 114) and lightweight breakfast trays (page 115).

Make some warm clothing for that special man in your life. How about a cozy sweater knitted from two strands of yarn (page 117) or a whimsical scarf with musical flourishes (page 118)? For your No. 1 lady, decorate a keepsake box with decals (page 121). Social events of the season make fashion demands on us all, so you'll find extra-quick ideas for adding sparkle with sequins (page 122). Useful gifts that will please any avid chef are featured on pages 123–125.

Christmas is especially for kids, so we've included projects to make clothing and toys for all the children on your list—"From Tots to Teens." Kids can help you fill the gift list, too, with a group of easy-to-make projects that use simple materials in new ways (page 145–147).

"The Gift Bazaar" (page 148) is full of thrifty projects that are equally suitable as small gifts or as profitable bazaar items. And if you're short on time or money, you can still feel generous with our list of "Last-Minute Gifts" (page 154–157) and "Gifts From the Heart" (they're marked with hearts!) interspersed throughout the chapter.

Finally, "Wrapping It Up" (page 158) provides useful information on packaging and sending all the presents you've lovingly created.

💲 Low-Cost   **⚡ Quick and Easy**   **🎚 Make-Ahead**   **🍴 Low-Calorie**

Gathered and Padded Frames

GATHERED FRAME

AVERAGE: For those with some experience in sewing.
MATERIALS: 12″ x 20″ cardboard; ¼ yd. each of 44″-wide fabric for frame front and frame back; white glue.

DIRECTIONS:
1. Enlarge the quarter pattern in Fig. 1 on 8″ x 10″ tracing paper folded in half both ways (4″ x 5″), following the directions on page 291; trace on each layer and unfold for the full pattern. Cut one cardboard oval for the back. Cut another for the front, with its center cutaway at the broken line.
2. Cut 2 fabric strips, each 4″ x 42″, and seam together at one end. Fold the strip in half, right sides together, and stitch ¼″ from the raw edge. Turn the right side out.
3. Slash through the frame front at the lower center. Slide the fabric tube over the frame, with the seam in back. Tape the cut ends of the cardboard together again. Turn under one fabric end and slipstitch it over the other raw end.
4. Frame Back: Trace that cardboard oval to the fabric and cut out. Trace again and cut out 1″ outside the traced line. Center the cardboard on the wrong side of the larger fabric oval; turn the fabric edges over the cardboard and glue. Glue the smaller fabric oval on top.
5. Glue the frame front over the frame back, right side out, leaving open one end to insert the photo.
6. Easel: Cut a 2½ x 6½″ piece of cardboard; trim the long (side) edges to 1″ wide at the top. Score across the easel 1″ from the top. Cover it with fabric and glue the top inch to the frame back so it sets well.

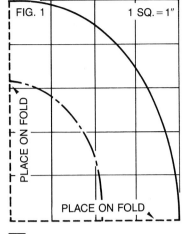

FIG. 1 — 1 SQ. = 1″
PLACE ON FOLD
PLACE ON FOLD

PADDED FRAME *(8″ square)*

EASY: Achievable by anyone.
MATERIALS: 8″ wooden canvas stretcher (4 pieces); 12″ x 14″ fabric; 12″ square of batting; 8″ x 11″ firm cardboard; ¼ yd. fabric for frame back.

DIRECTIONS:
1. Frame: Assemble the stretchers. Stretch the batting on top; fold and tape the edge to the back of the frame. From the center, cut the batting diagonally toward each inside corner; turn each triangle of batting to the frame back; trim and tape.
2. Frame Front: Cut an 11″ square from the 12″ x 14″ fabric. Cut the 2″ strips remaining into four 3″-long pieces. Fold one 3″ piece over each inside corner of the frame, clipping from the ends toward the center in order to smooth the fabric against the inside edge. Tape to the batting. Pin the 12″-square fabric (centered) on top and tape the edges to the frame back, as you did in Step 1. Fold cord or ribbon over the corners and tape the ends over the back.
3. Frame Back: Fold a 9″ x 20″ piece of fabric over an 8″-square cardboard; turn in the edges and glue.
4. Easel: See Steps 5 and 6 for Gathered Frame.

TIED "TRAY"

AVERAGE: For those with some experience in sewing.
MATERIALS: Two 10″ squares of fabrics and scraps for ties; corrugated cardboard.

DIRECTIONS:
1. Ties: Cut 8 strips, each 1½″ x 7″. Press them in half lengthwise, right side out; press the raw edges to meet the centerfold; stitch along the open edge to make ties. Pin the ties to one of the fabric squares, 2″ from each corner, right sides together and raw edges even; stitch across the end of each tie; knot the opposite end.
2. Seam (½″) the 2 squares (enclosing ties) around 3 edges. Turn the right side out and press. Lightly draw a line 1¾″ from each edge.
3. Cardboard: From the cardboard, cut one 5¼″ square and four 1¾″ x 5¼″ strips. Stitch the fabric across a pair of opposite drawn lines (one at each side of the open edge). In between them, drop a cardboard strip; push its long edge against the opposite seam; with a zipper foot, stitch across the lower line parallel to that seam. Drop a strip into each border and drop the square between them. Stitch across the top drawn line; drop in the last strip; turn in the open edges and slipstitch.

♥ *Tape-record a conversation with your children. Then send the tape to a faraway grandparent or other relative to enjoy for Christmas.*

♥ *Photographed with love: Are you a good photographer? Try this last-minute gift idea. Wrap up an inexpensive 8" x 10" frame and attach a note promising to take—and enlarge—an adorable photo of a friend's son or daughter.*

KENTUCKY MOUNTAIN CHAIN QUILT (page 106)
(about 70" x 78")

AVERAGE: For those with some experience in quilting.

MATERIALS: 45"-wide fabric—3 yds. green, 2¼ yds. red and 1⅝ yds. yellow; 72" x 80" batting; bed sheet (at least 72" x 80") for quilt-back; 9 yds. yellow single-fold bias tape for binding.

DIRECTIONS:

1. Cut the following 2¼" squares: 756 green, 576 red and 144 yellow. Also cut 36 yellow 5¾" squares.

2. A-Blocks: Seam alternating red and green squares together to make 5 rows of 5 patches, starting 3 rows with green and 2 rows with red. Sew the 5 rows together, checkerboard fashion, to make an A-Block. Make 35 more A-Blocks.

3. B-Blocks: Seam 2 rows of 5 patches, alternating 3 red and 2 green. Seam 2 rows of 3 patches alternating 2 green with 1 yellow. Seam a short row to the opposite sides of a large yellow square. Seam a long row to the remaining edges to make a B-Block. Make 35 more. Lightly draw 9 overlapping circles (3 rows of 3) on the large yellow square (we traced around a thread spool).

4. Quilt-Top: Seam 5 rows of 8 blocks each, alternating A and B, starting with B. Seam 4 rows the same way, starting with A. Seam the 9 rows together, checkerboard fashion, starting with a B-Block.

5. Follow Step 5 of "Trip Around The World" quilt (right), using the sheet for the quilt-back. Also quilt over the drawn circles in the B-Blocks.

6. Trim off the quilt-back and batting flush with the quilt-top. Stitch bias tape to the quilt-top, right sides together and raw edges even, mitering at the corners. Fold the tape to the quilt-back and slipstitch to bind.

TRIP AROUND THE WORLD QUILT (page 106) *(about 75" x 80")*

CHALLENGING: For those with more experience in quilting.

MATERIALS: 45"-wide fabric as follows—4½ yds. for quilt-back/binding; ⅛ yd. fabric C; ¼ yd. each of fabrics A, G, I, J and K; ⅜ yd. each of fabrics E, L, N, O, P and Q; ½ yd. R; ⅝ yd. H; ¾ yd. M; 1 yd. F; 1⅜ yds. B; and 1½ yds. D; 81" x 89" batting.

DIRECTIONS:

1. Cutting: Cut the required 2¼"-square patches *(see page 111, Fig. 2)*.

2. Seam the ABC patches into rows, then seam the rows together to make the central oblong within the arrows *(see Fig. 2)*.

3. Seam 27 patches to make the repeat row *(see bracketed D-D in Fig. 2)*. Seam 17 more rows the same. Stitch 9 of them to the right of the central oblong. Stitch the others to the left, turning them upside down so the final DBD's are at the outside.

4. Seam the patches to make the remaining row of partial repeats, starting with the letters in the vertical, central row. Stitch them right of center. Repeat at left (omitting the central letters) with the rows turned upside down to complete the pattern of concentric borders.

5. Quilt-Back: Cut the quilt-back fabric in half crosswise and sew the two 2¼-yd. lengths together at a long edge; press the seam to one side. Spread it out, wrong side up, on a clean surface and tape down the corners. Over this, spread the batting (edges even), then the quilt-top (right side up and centered). Baste the 3 layers together from the center outward diagonally to each corner and straight to each edge. Add more basting rows about 10" apart. To quilt, sew running stitches around each patch ¼" from the seams.

6. Bound Edges: Mark the outside edge diagonally through the D squares and baste along the mark, through all layers. Cut off (⅜" outside the basting) *the quilt-top and batting only.* Trim off the quilt-back so it extends ¾" *outside the quilt-top;* then fold it over the quilt-top, turn the raw edges under and slipstitch along the basting to bind.

FIG. 2 QUILT

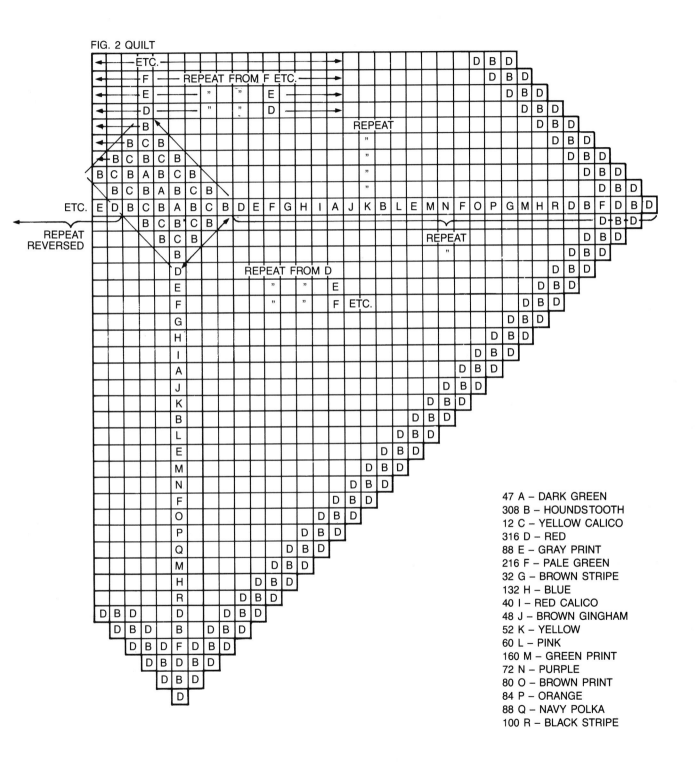

47 A – DARK GREEN
308 B – HOUNDSTOOTH
12 C – YELLOW CALICO
316 D – RED
88 E – GRAY PRINT
216 F – PALE GREEN
32 G – BROWN STRIPE
132 H – BLUE
40 I – RED CALICO
48 J – BROWN GINGHAM
52 K – YELLOW
60 L – PINK
160 M – GREEN PRINT
72 N – PURPLE
80 O – BROWN PRINT
84 P – ORANGE
88 Q – NAVY POLKA
100 R – BLACK STRIPE

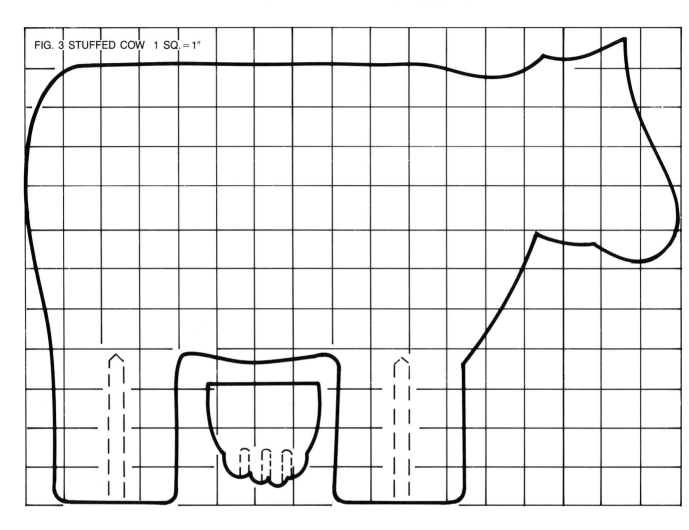

FIG. 3 STUFFED COW 1 SQ. = 1"

♥ *Have your child make a drawing and send it (mounted on cardboard) to a doting grandma or grandpa. If you have an extra picture frame, that's even better.*

💲
STUFFED COW

EASY: Achievable by anyone.
MATERIALS: Two 12" x 18" pieces of fabric*; ¾ yd. ribbon; synthetic stuffing; small bell *(optional)*.

DIRECTIONS:
Note: To make "your own" patchwork fabric, seam strips (1" to 2" wide) of fabric side by side.
1. Enlarge the pattern in Fig. 3, following the directions on page 291
2. Over the 2 fabric pieces (right sides together), pin the pattern and cut on the solid lines. Stitch ¼" inside the cut lines (and along the broken lines at legs), leaving open between the circles. Clip at the inside curves and corners. Slash halfway between the broken lines. Turn the right side out and stuff.
3. Udder: Stitch the same way as the cow, leaving the top edges open. Turn and stuff. Sew gathering stitches ¼" from the top edges and pull up the thread slightly.
4. Turn in the open edges of the cow, insert the udder against the back legs *(see photo, page 113)* and slipstitch closed.
5. Tie the ribbon (pulled through a bell, if you wish) around the neck.

Stuffed Cows

Wine Rack and Tray

WINE RACK

AVERAGE: For those with some experience in woodworking.

MATERIALS AND DIRECTIONS:
1. To make the lattice grid (C), draw a 19¾″ square on a piece of scrap wood. Mark 2½″ and 10″ from each corner on all 4 sides *(see Fig. 4)*.
2. Place the lattice on this plan and cut each piece to size; lightly tack in place. Complete the lattice in one direction, then cut and size for the opposite directions. Staple the lattice pieces together where they cross.
3. Remove from the plan and make one more lattice grid.
4. Rip the frame parts from a 1 x 8 (A/A/B/B). Glue/nail (1½″) B to the edges of A *(see Fig. 4)*.
5. Glue/nail (1″) the lattice grids (C) to the frame (A/B) with the lattice staples facing in.
6. Miter, cut and glue/nail (1″) the corner-guard trim (D) on 8 edges. Paint.

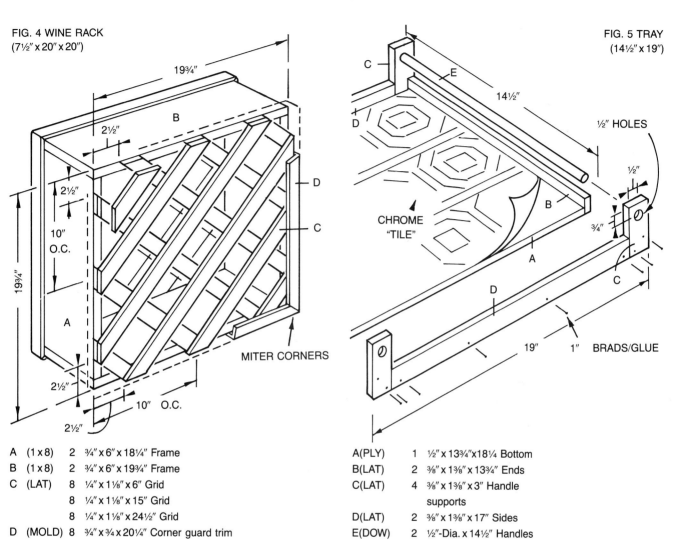

FIG. 4 WINE RACK
(7½" x 20" x 20")

19¾"

B

2½"

2½"

10"
O.C.

19¾"

A

2½"

10" O.C.

2½"

D

C

MITER CORNERS

FIG. 5 TRAY
(14½" x 19")

C

E

D

14½"

½" HOLES

B

½"

CHROME
"TILE"

A

¾"

D

C

19"   1"   BRADS/GLUE

A	(1 x 8)	2	¾" x 6" x 18¼" Frame
B	(1 x 8)	2	¾" x 6" x 19¾" Frame
C	(LAT)	8	¼" x 1⅛" x 6" Grid
		8	¼" x 1⅛" x 15" Grid
		8	¼" x 1⅛" x 24½" Grid
D	(MOLD)	8	¾" x ¾ x 20¼" Corner guard trim

A(PLY)	1	½" x 13¾"x18¼ Bottom
B(LAT)	2	⅜" x 1⅜" x 13¾" Ends
C(LAT)	4	⅜" x 1⅜" x 3" Handle supports
D(LAT)	2	⅜" x 1⅜" x 17" Sides
E(DOW)	2	½"-Dia. x 14½" Handles

TRAY

AVERAGE: For those with some experience in woodworking.

MATERIALS AND DIRECTIONS: See Fig. 5.

♥ **Personal-service gift certificates:** *Give an "I.O.U." for babysitting to a mother who never seems to get a break from the kids, breakfast in bed to a close relative or some other thoughtful gift of your time. Make it special by writing it like a gift certificate and including a personal note or private joke.*

SPAGHETTI GAUGE

AVERAGE: For those with some experience in woodworking.
MATERIALS: ½" x 6" x 7" scrap wood; 1", 1¼", 1½" and 1¾" drill bits; saber saw; fine sandpaper; wax.

DIRECTIONS:
1. Drill 1", 1¼", 1½" and 1¾" holes in the scrap wood.
2. Draw a pig shape freehand; cut out with the saber saw.
3. Sand and wax.

FOR HIM, FOR HER

Twisted-Rib Pullover

TWISTED-RIB PULLOVER

AVERAGE: For those with some experience in knitting.

Directions are given for Size Small (36-38). Changes for Sizes Medium (40-42) and Large (44) are in parentheses.

MATERIALS: Caron "Wintuk" (3½-oz. skein): 8 (8, 10) skeins of No. 3003 bone *(see Materials Shopping Guide, page 293);* knitting needles, one pair No. 13 and No. 17 (14″ length), or any size needles to obtain gauge below; stitch holder.

GAUGE: With two strands of yarn and larger needles in reverse stockinette stitch (p on right side, k on wrong side)—9 sts = 4″; 3 rows = 1″. Be sure to check your gauge.

Sizes:	Small (36-38)	Medium (40-42)	Large (44)
Body:			
Chest	38″	42″	44″
Finished Measurements:			
Chest:	39″	42½″	46″
Width Across Back or Front at Underarms:			
	19½″	21¼″	23″
Width Across Sleeve at Upper Arm:			
	18½″	19″	20″

BACK: With smaller needles and two strands of yarn held together, cast on 37 (41, 45) sts. *Row 1 (wrong side):* P 1, *k 1, p 1; rep from * across. *Row 2:* K 1, *p 1; k 1; rep from * across. Rep these 2 rows for ribbing for 2″, ending with Row 2. K 1 row, inc 9 sts evenly across—46 (50,54) sts. Change to larger needles and pat. *Row 1 (right side):* P 3, (5,7), *k next st going through back loop*—**k lb made;** (p 1, k lb) 3 times, * p 4, k 1b, (p 1, k 1b) 3 times*; rep between *'s twice more, p 3 (5,7). *Row 2:* K 3 (5, 7), p 1 (k 1, p 1) 3 times, * k 4, p 1, (k 1, p 1) 3 times; rep from * twice more, k 3 (5, 7). Rep these 2 rows for pat. Work until 14″ from beg. **Mark beg and end of next row for start of armholes.** Work even until arm-

holes measure 10 (10½, 11)″, ending with a wrong-side row.

Shoulder Shaping: Keeping to pat, bind off 6 (7, 7) sts at beg of next 2 rows, then bing odd 6 (7, 8) sts at beg of next 2 rows—22 (22, 24) sts. Bind off rem sts for back neck.

FRONT: Work same as Back until armholes measure 4½ (5, 5½)″, ending with a right-side row—46 (50, 54) sts.

Neck Shaping: Keeping to pat, work 18 (20, 21) sts, sl these sts to a st holder, bind off center 10 (10, 12) sts loosely and complete row. Working on one side **only,** dec at neck edge one st every right-side row 6 times—12 (14, 15) sts. Work even in pat until armhole measures same as Back to shoulder, ending at armhole edge.

Shoulder Shaping: Keeping to pat, bind off 6 (7, 7) sts once. Work 1 row, bind off rem 6 (7, 8) sts. Sl sts from st holder to larger needle. Work to correspond to other side, reversing shaping.

Neckband: Sew left shoulder seam. With right side facing, using smaller needles and two strands of yarn held tog, beg at right back neck, pick up and k 53 (53 ,57) sts around neck. K 1 row on wrong side. Work in k 1, p 1 rib for 4 rows. Bind off loosely in rib. Sew right shoulder and neckband seams.

SLEEVES: With right side facing, using smaller needles and two strands of yarn held tog, beg at one armhole marker, pick up and k 43 (45, 47) sts to other armhole marker. K 1 row. Change to larger needles and pat. *Row 1 (right side):* P 18 (19, 20), k lb, (p 1, k 1b) 3 times; p 18 (19, 20). *Row 2:* K 18 (19, 20), p 1, (k 1, p 1) 3 times; k 18 (19,20). Rep these 2 rows for pat. Work even for 6″ from beg. Keeping to pat, dec one st each end of next row, then every 1½″, 6 times more—29 (31, 33) sts. Work to 18″ from beg, or 3″ less than desired length, ending with a right-side row. Change to smaller needles and k 1

row, dec 3 sts across each k section (**do not** dec across panel)—**6 sts dec**—23 (25, 17) sts. Work in k 1, p 1 rib for 3″. Bind off in ribbing. Sew side and sleeve seams. **Do not** block.

TIE/BELT RACK

AVERAGE: For those with some experience in woodworking.

MATERIALS AND DIRECTIONS: See Fig. 6.

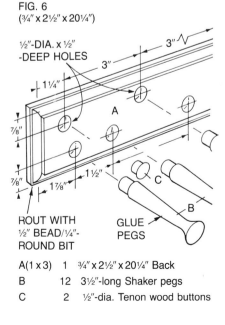

Tie/Belt Rack

FIG. 6
(¾″ x 2½″ x 20¼″)

½″-DIA. x ½″ -DEEP HOLES

3″

3″

1¼″

7/8″

A

7/8″

1½″

1 7/8″

ROUT WITH ½″ BEAD/¼″- ROUND BIT

GLUE PEGS

B

C

A(1 x 3)	1	¾″ x 2½″ x 20¼″ Back
B	12	3½″-long Shaker pegs
C	2	½″-dia. Tenon wood buttons

PIANO KEY SCARF

AVERAGE: For those with some experience in knitting.

Directions are given for a Scarf measuring 8″ wide x 52″ long.

MATERIALS: Lion Brand Sayelle 4-Ply Worsted Weight Yarn (3.5-oz. skein): 1 skein each of white (A) and black (B) *(see Materials Shopping Guide, page 293)*; knitting needles, one pair No. 8, or any size needles to obtain gauge below.

GAUGE: In stockinette stitch (st st)—5 sts = 1″; 7 rows = 1″. Be sure to check your gauge.

Note 1: When changing color, pick up the new color from under the dropped color to prevent holes. Carry the color not in use loosely across the wrong side of the work.

Note 2: The horizontal duplicate-stitch rows are worked after the Scarf is completed to divide the keys.

FIG. 7 PIANO KEY CHART

⊡ = Duplicate stitch with B
☐ = A
▲ = B

HORIZONTAL DUPLICATE STITCH
Bring up the needle threaded with contrasting color yarn; insert the needle under the stitch above *(see diagram);* insert the needle in the same place where the yarn was brought up, thus covering the stitch completely.

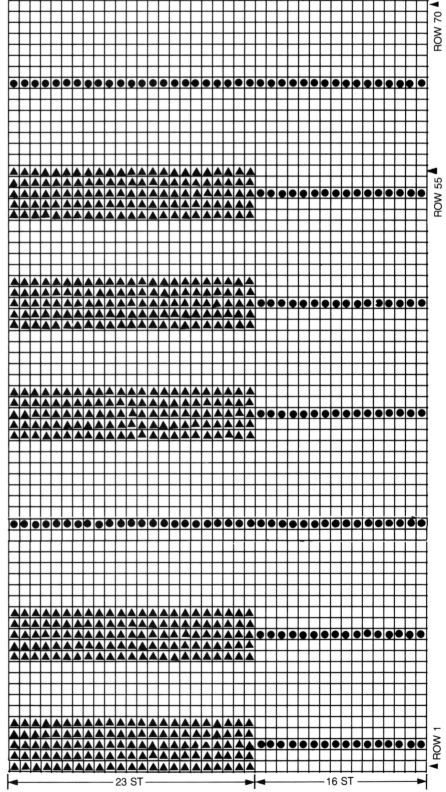

ROW 70

ROW 55

ROW 1

23 ST   16 ST

Piano Key Scarf

SCARF: Starting at narrow end with A, cast on 39 sts. Work in garter st (k every row) for 2 rows. Change to stockinette stitch (k 1 row, p 1 row) and work 5 rows with A, ending with a p row. **Now start** piano key chart *(see Fig. 7)*, starting with row 1 until completion of Row 70, then rep Rows 1 to 55 once. Cut B. Continuing in st st, work with A **only** for 14″ more, ending with a p row. **Now repeat** chart *(see Fig. 7)*, working in reverse order from Rows 55 to 1 once, then rep Rows 70-1 once. Cut B. With A **only,** work 5 rows of st st, then 2 rows of garter st. Bind off.

Horizontal Duplicate Stitch: Work in duplicate stitch *(see Fig. 7)* with B across the rows indicated on chart *(see Fig. 7)*.

♥ *Romantic dinner for two:* *Whip up a batch of homemade spaghetti sauce and put it in a plastic container. Combine with a box of pasta, small bottle of red wine and a loaf of bread. Present it in a colored shopping bag tied with ribbon. (Be sure your friends open it right away!)*

Scarf, Tam, Earmuffs

Keepsake Box

SCARF, TAM, EARMUFFS

AVERAGE: For those with some experience in sewing.
MATERIALS: 1¼ yds. of 60″-wide wool.* *For Tam:* fold-over braid. *For Earmuffs:* purchased earmuffs.
Note: With careful cutting, you can make two scarves, one tam and one pair of earmuffs from the 1¼ yds. of fabric.

DIRECTIONS:
1. For Scarves: Cut two 12″ strips from the full width of the fabric. Zigzag both long sides, then the short ends, 2″ from the edges.

2. Pull away the end threads to make a fringe.
3. For Tam: Cut a 16″-diameter circle. Cut out a pie-shaped wedge, measuring 8″ at the arc edge. Seam-cut the edges.
4. Sew a gathering row, ½″ from the edge, and pull up the fullness to measure 22″.
5. Bind the edges with the fold-over braid.
6. For Earmuffs: From the remaining fabric, you should be able to make several sets of earmuffs. Cut 8″ circles; sew a gathering row around the edge; place over the earmuff and pull up the fullness to cover.
7. Tie the thread-ends securely.

KEEPSAKE BOX

EASY: Achievable by anyone.
MATERIALS: Fabric for outside and contrast for lining; synthetic batting; wooden box or old silver chest; illustration board; ⅜″-wide ribbon; paper memorabilia; white glue.

DIRECTIONS:
1. Lid top: If the box has hinges, remove them. Spread the batting over the lid top. Spread the fabric over the batting and glue its edges to the lid sides. Arrange 4 ribbons diagonally— 2 between the corners and 2 between the edge centers. ☞

2. Lid sides: For the fabric length, measure around the 4 sides and add 1″; for the width, measure down the sides and add 2″; cut the fabric. Turn under ½″ at the top edge. Start at the center back to glue the strip to the lid sides, with the fold at the top edge. Turn under ½″ at the final end and glue it over the initial raw end. Glue the extra width, mitering the corners, up inside the lid. Glue a ribbon just below the top fold.

3. Box sides: Measure as in Step 2 and cut the fabric. Place the fabric, centered, over the box sides; glue the center back seam (like the lid). Turn 1″ to the box bottom and 1″ to the inside, mitering the corners, and glue.

4. Lining: From the illustration board, cut a rectangle and four strips to line the box; cover them with fabric, glued in place. Repeat for the box lid.

5. Glue fabric to the outside bottom. Glue the memorabilia to the box top. Replace the hinges.

FANTASY FASHION TRIMS

EASY: Achievable by anyone.
MATERIALS: *See Materials Shopping Guide, page 293,* for the trims used to make these fashions.

DIRECTIONS:
Note: Always work from right side.
1. Applying Sequins to Scarf/Gloves: Using single strand of thread to match garment, bring needle from back, through sequin, through matching bead, then through sequin; tie off in back.

Fantasy Fashion Trims

Canisters; Apple Pot-holder Set

CANISTERS

AVERAGE: For those with some experience in woodworking.
Note: All the canisters and lids are the same size except for the height.

DIRECTIONS:

1. *See Fig. 8* for construction details.
2. Sand and fill with white spackle thinned with water. Rub a thin coat over all surfaces. Fine-sand.
3. The finishes are polyurethane color thinned to 2 parts paint to 1 part mineral spirits. Apply with a brush. Let set for 3 to 5 minutes, then rub with a cloth slightly dampened with thinner. When dry, lightly sand with 220-grit paper. Apply 2 coats of clear finish. *Do not finish the inside of the canisters.*

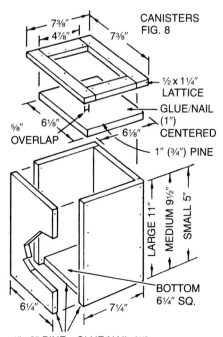

CANISTERS
FIG. 8

7⅜″
4⅞″
7⅜″
½ x 1¼″
LATTICE
GLUE/NAIL
(1″)
CENTERED
5/8″
6⅛″
6⅛″
OVERLAP
1″ (¾″) PINE
LARGE 11″
MEDIUM 9½″
SMALL 5″
BOTTOM
6¼″ SQ.
6¼″
7¼″
½″ x 8″ PINE—GLUE/NAIL (1″)
Sizes are the same (except height) for all canisters.

APPLE POT HOLDER

EASY: Achievable by anyone.
MATERIALS *(for 5 pieces shown):* ½ yd. 45″-wide plaid fabric; scraps red and green fabric; scraps bias tape; ½ yd. 45″-wide fleece interlining.

DIRECTIONS *(¼″ seams allowed):* Enlarge the patterns in Fig. 9, following the directions on page 291.

POT HOLDER

1. Cut 2 large apples from the plaid and fleece; 2 small apples from the red and 2 leaves from the green.
2. Cut a 5″ length of brown bias tape; edgestitch and fold in half, raw ends even. Sew to the right side of one large apple at the center top, raw edges even, as "stem." ☞

3. Pin the fleece to the wrong side of each plaid apple.

4. With the right sides together, seam the apples, leaving an opening to turn. Clip and turn; slipstitch the opening.

5. Repeat Step 4 for the small apple and leaf; slip stitch to the Pot Holder.

HOT PAD

1. Cut two 9"-dia. circles from the plaid fabric and fleece; cut 2 small apples from the red fabric.

2. Follow Steps 3 and 4 for Pot Holder.

3. Stitch around the pad, ½" from edge. Repeat Step 4 for Pot Holder; slipstitch the small apple to the center.

MITT

1. Cut 2 Mitts each from the plaid, lining fabric and fleece; cut 2 apples from the red.

2. Pin the fleece between the lining and plaid fabric, right sides out. Bind the wrist edge with bias tape.

3. To form tab, cut a 5" piece of bias tape. Edgestitch and fold in half, raw edges even. Pin to the wrist edge *(see photo, page 123)* of one piece.

4. With the right sides together, seam the 2 mitts together, leaving the wrist edge open. Clip and turn.

5. For the apple, see Steps 4 and 5, Pot Holder.

POT HANDLE COVER

1. Cut two 2½" x 7" rectangles from the plaid, lining and fleece, rounded at one end.

2. Follow Steps 2 and 3, Mitt.

3. Pin the 2 sections together, right sides out, and bind the raw edges with bias tape.

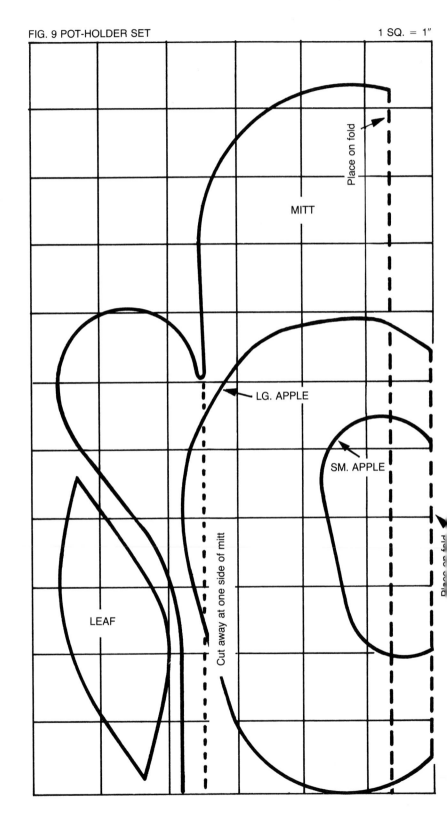

FIG. 9 POT-HOLDER SET   1 SQ. = 1"

Knife Box; Recipe Stand

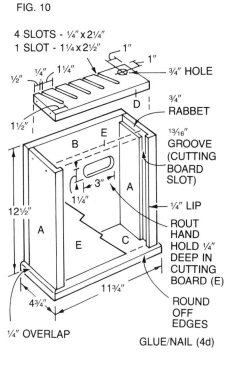

FIG. 10

4 SLOTS - ¼" x 2¼"
1 SLOT - 1¼ x 2½"

¾" HOLE
¾" RABBET
¹³⁄₁₆" GROOVE (CUTTING BOARD SLOT)
¼" LIP
ROUT HAND HOLD ¼" DEEP IN CUTTING BOARD (E)
ROUND OFF EDGES
GLUE/NAIL (4d)

12½"
4¾"
11¾"
¼" OVERLAP
1½"
½"
¼"
1¼"
1¼"
3"
1"
1"

CUT FROM 1 x 12 x 4" COMMON PINE

A 2 ¾" x 3¾" x 11¾" Sides
B 1 ¾" x 11¼" x 11¾" Back
C 1 ¾" x 4¾" x 11¾" Bottom
D 1 ¾" x 2¾" x 10¼" Top
E 1 ¾" x 10⅛" x 11¾" Cutting board

Use nontoxic walnut oil on cutting board, early American satin on the box.

♥ *Write out your favorite recipes on index cards and put together a package for that special person. For instance, a working mom would love some quick-dinner ideas, and a friend with high blood pressure would really appreciate some good-tasting low-salt recipes.*

KNIFE BOX

(4¾"D x 11¾"W x 12¾"H)

AVERAGE: For those with some experience in woodworking.

MATERIALS AND DIRECTIONS: See Fig. 10. *Note:*The back of the Knife Box becomes a cutting board.

RECIPE STAND

EASY: Achievable by anyone.
MATERIALS: Ring binder; ribbons; stapler and staples.

DIRECTIONS:
1. Staple ribbons inside the front edges of the binder.

2. Open the binder and tie the ribbons.

FIG. 11 1 SQ. = 1″

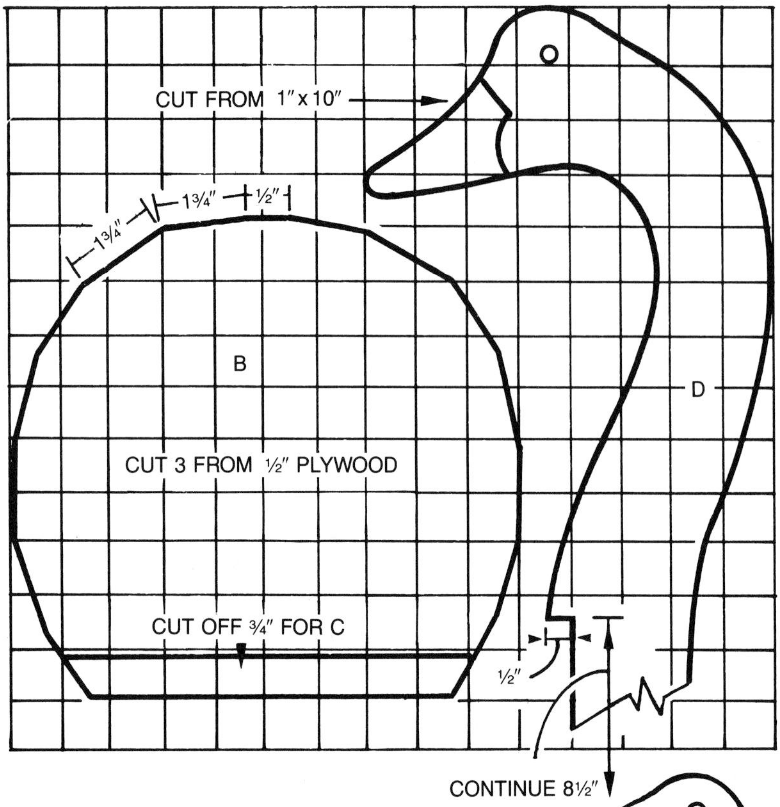
CUT FROM 1″x 10″
1¾″
1¾″
½″
B
D
CUT 3 FROM ½″ PLYWOOD
CUT OFF ¾″ FOR C
½″
CONTINUE 8½″

FIG. 11A

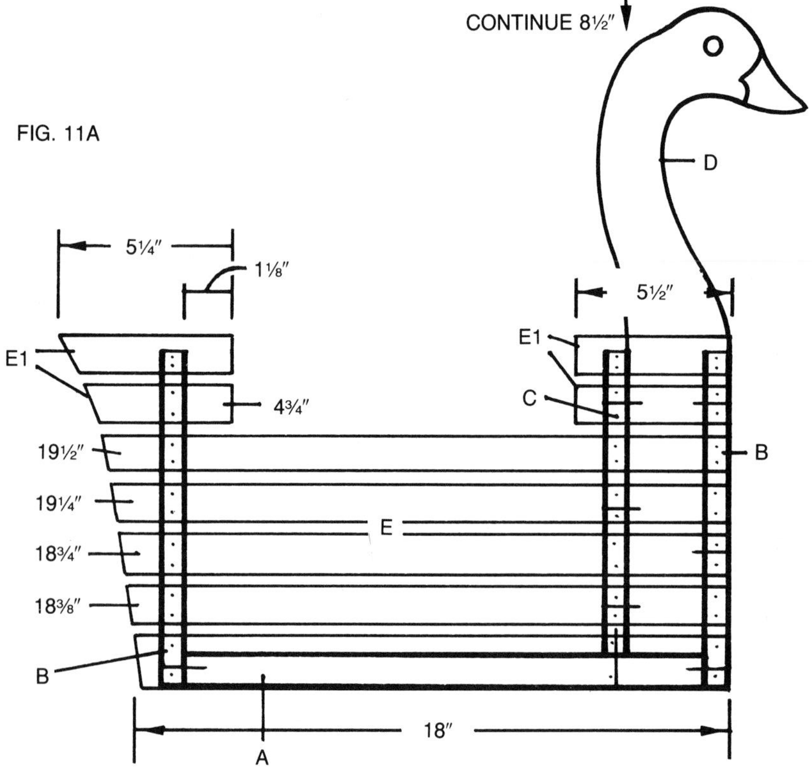
D
5¼″
1⅛″
5½″
E1
E1
C
4¾″
19½″
19¼″
18¾″
18⅜″
B
B
E
18″
A

GOOSE PLANTER

(10½″W x 21″H x 20½″L)

AVERAGE: For those with some experience in woodworking.

MATERIALS: ½″ x 10″ x 30″ plywood; 1 x 10 x 4′ pine board; ¼″ x 1⅝″ x 20′ lattice; 4d finishing nails; ¾″ wire brads; glue; paint.

CUTTING DIRECTIONS:

Code	Pieces	Size
A(1 x 10)	1	¾″ x 7¾″ x 16″ Bottom
B(PLY)	2	½″ x 10″ x 9″ Body
C(PLY)	1	½″ x 10″ x 8¼″ Body
D(1 x 10)	1	¾″x7¾″x19¾″Neck/Head
E(LAT)	10	¼″ x 1⅝″ x 19″ Sides
E1(LAT)	8	¼″ x 1⅝″ x 5½″ Top

DIRECTIONS:

1. Enlarge the patterns in Fig. 11, following the directions on page 291. Transfer to the plywood and 1 x 10.

2. Cut the bottom (A) 16″ long from the 1 x 10; angle the side edges *(see Fig. 11)*.

3. Glue/nail (4d) the body (B) pieces to each end of the bottom (A). Glue/nail (4d) the neck/head (D) to the front (B), through B into D. *See Fig. 11A.*

4. Glue/nail (4d) the body (C) to the bottom (A) and the neck/head (D). *See Fig. 11A.*

5. Cut the lattice to length *(see Cutting Directions)*. Lay the pieces, butted edge to edge, in position on a flat surface. Mark off the sizes shown in Fig. 11A. Draw a line across the lattice at the marks for the tail curve. Cut the lattice and nail (¾″) to B/B/C, leaving equal spaces (about 3⁄16″) between the slats.

6. Sand; paint white, then paint the bill orange.

Goose Planter; Three Nesting Trays

FIG. 12
1 SQ. = 1″

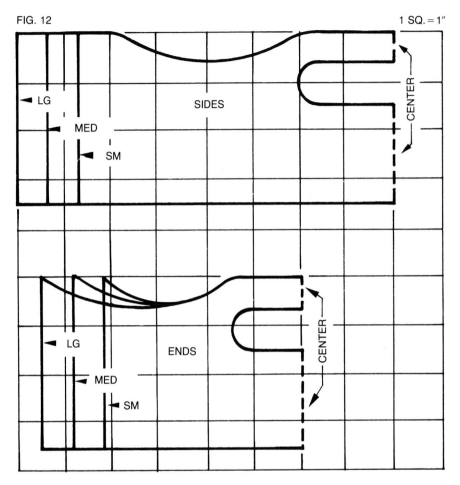

LG
SIDES
MED
SM
CENTER

LG
ENDS
MED
SM
CENTER

THREE NESTING TRAYS

(Small 3½″H x 9½″W x 13½″L)
(Medium 3½″ x 10¾″W x 14¾″L)
(Large 3½″H x 12″W x 16″L)

AVERAGE: For those with some experience in woodworking.
MATERIALS: ½″ x 16″ x 30″ birch plywood; ½″ x 4″ x 14′ pine; 3d finishing nails; glue; filler; paint.
CUTTING DIRECTIONS:

Code	Pieces	Size
Small		
A(PLY)	1	½″ x 8½″ x 12½″ Bottom
B(½ x 4)	2	½″ x 3½ x 8½″ Ends
C(½ x 4)	2	½″ x 3½ x 13½″ Sides
Medium		
A(PLY)	1	½″ x 9¾″ x 13¾″ Bottom
B(½ x 4)	2	½″ x 9½″ x 13¾″ Ends
C(½ x 4)	2	½″ x 3½ x 14¾″ Sides
Large Tray		
A(PLY)	1	½″ x 11″ x 15″ Bottom
B(½ x 4)	2	½″ x 3½″ x 11″ Ends
C(½ x 4)	2	½″ x 3½″ x 16″ Sides

DIRECTIONS:
1. Enlarge the half patterns in Fig. 12, following the directions on page 291.
2. Transfer the patterns to the ½″ pine and cut out with a saber or jigsaw. For the hand holes, drill a ⅞″-dia. hole at each end, then cut out the remaining wood with a saber or coping saw. File; sand.
3. Cut the bottoms to size from the ½″ plywood.
4. Glue/nail (3d) the ends (B) to the short edges of the bottoms (A). Glue/nail (3d) the sides (C) to the ends (B) and bottoms (A).
5. Round off all the top edges, corners and hand holes. Set and fill the nail holes. Sand and paint.

♥ ***Coupon-clipper's delight:*** *Help a friend save time and money by giving her a well-stocked grocery coupon organizer. Buy a coupon wallet and fill it with a batch of cents-off coupons that you probably already have stashed in a kitchen drawer.*

FROM TOTS TO TEENS

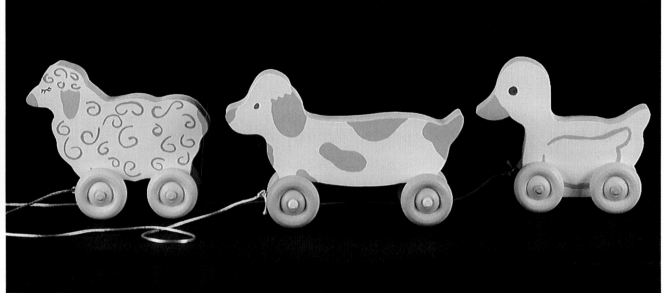

Pull-Toys

♥ *A "coupon" book for your kids works well, too, and reminds them that gifts of the heart are often more special than material things. You might include a one-time, no-penalty coupon for a day when they just don't feel like cleaning their rooms, and a coupon good for playing the game of their choice with one or both parents.*

FIG. 13 PULL-TOYS   1 SQ. = 1"

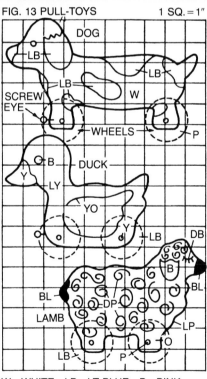

W = WHITE   LB = LT BLUE   P = PINK
B = BLUE   LY = LT YELLOW   LP = LT PINK
YO = YELLOW OUTLINE   DP = DK PINK
DB = DK BLUE   Y = YELLOW   BL = BLACK

$
PULL-TOYS
(about 6" x 10")

AVERAGE: For some experience in woodworking.
MATERIALS *(for one):* ¾" x 10" pine; ¼"-dia. x 6" dowel; four 2"-dia. purchased wood wheels; thumbtacks or wood beads for hub caps; screw eyes; pull-string; paint.

DIRECTIONS:
1. Enlarge the patterns in Fig. 13, following the directions on page 291. Transfer the patterns to the ¾" pine and cut out with a saber saw.
2. Drill ¼"-dia. holes for the wheel axles and insert the dowel. Use thumbtacks as hubcaps to secure the purchased wood wheels. Paint as shown. Knot a piece of string around a screw eye and use it as a pull.

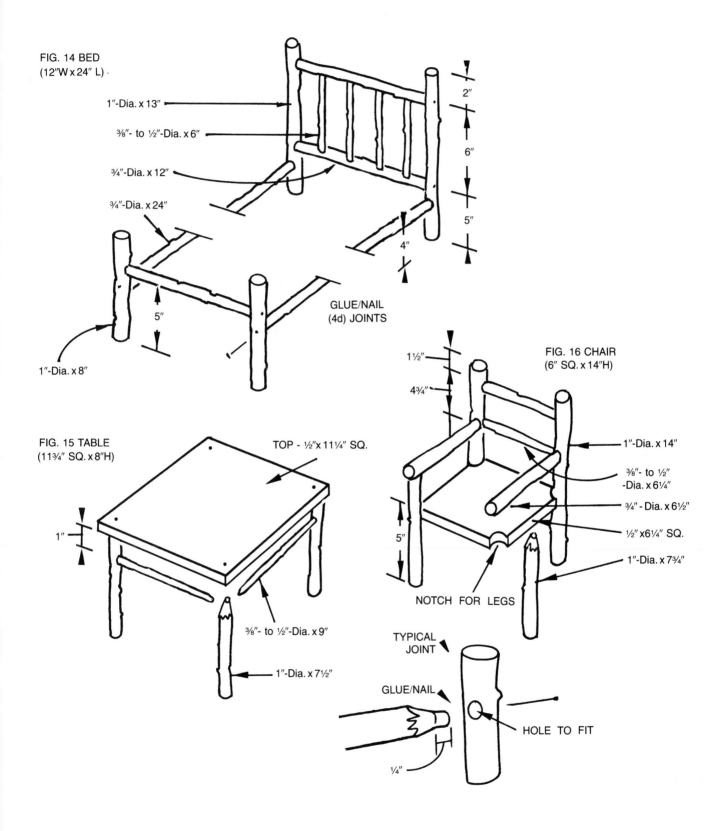

FIG. 14 BED
(12″W x 24″ L)

1″-Dia. x 13″

⅜″- to ½″-Dia. x 6″

¾″-Dia. x 12″

¾″-Dia. x 24″

2″

6″

5″

4″

GLUE/NAIL
(4d) JOINTS

5″

1″-Dia. x 8″

FIG. 15 TABLE
(11¾″ SQ. x 8″H)

TOP - ½″x 11¼″ SQ.

1″

⅜″- to ½″-Dia. x 9″

1″-Dia. x 7½″

FIG. 16 CHAIR
(6″ SQ. x 14″H)

1½″

4¾″

5″

1″-Dia. x 14″

⅜″- to ½″
-Dia. x 6¼″

¾″ - Dia. x 6½″

½″ x 6¼″ SQ.

1″-Dia. x 7¾″

NOTCH FOR LEGS

TYPICAL
JOINT

GLUE/NAIL

HOLE TO FIT

¼″

Twig Doll Furniture

💲 TWIG DOLL FURNITURE
(photo, page 131)

AVERAGE: For those with some experience in woodworking.
MATERIALS: Twigs—1″-dia., ¾″-dia., ⅜″- to ½″-dia.; ½″ x 12″ x 18″ common pine, rough on one side; 3d finishing nails; glue; stain.
TOOLS: Drill; ¼″, ⅜″, ½″ drill bits; hammer.

DIRECTIONS:
1. Since various sizes of twigs are used, 3 drill-bit sizes are needed—¼″, ⅜″, ½″.
2. Drill ¼″, ⅜″ and ½″ holes in a scrap block of wood. This is your test block. With a razor blade or knife, trim ¼″ of bark from the end of the twig and fit it into the appropriate hole in the block (snug). If it is too large, trim it with a rasp or rough file. Use that size drill for the support hole.
3. Put glue on the end of the twig and in the hole. Fit it in tight. Drive a nail through the joint from the opposite side to secure.
4. Note that the seat has quarter-circle notches for the legs; see Fig. 16.

♥ *Give a gift certificate promising to do a chore the person dreads or a service he or she needs. Some suggestions: You could donate a few hours of babysitting for a young mother who'd like a little free time; or promise a month of lawn mowing for an elderly neighbor.*

BEDDING AND CUSHION FOR TWIG FURNITURE

DIRECTIONS:
1. Mattress: Cut 2 pieces of fabric and one of batting, all 14″ x 22″. With the fabric sides facing, seam them around 3 sides and 4 corners. Turn the right sides out; turn in the open edges and slipstitch. Tack or tie the layers together in 6 to 8 places.
2. Quilt: In a different fabric, make the quilt like the mattress, but with 20″ x 24″ pieces—2 of fabric and 2 of batting.
3. Pillow: Seam two 11″ x 14″ pieces around 3 sides and 4 corners; turn the right side out and press. Topstitch about 1¼″ from the 3 closed sides. Fill with synthetic stuffing. Turn in the open ends and slipstitch; then topstitch this edge.
4. Chair Cushion: Cut two 8″ squares and one strip 2¼″ x 16″. Fold the strip in half and press; fold the raw edges to meet the centerfold and edgestitch the open side. Cut the strip in half and knot the four ends (2 ties). Fold each tie in half and pin 1 fold to each of two adjacent corners of one of the squares, with the knotted ends pointed toward the center. Pin the other square on top, right sides together (over ties), and stitch around 3 sides and 4 corners. Turn the right side out and stuff; turn in the open ends and slipstitch.

TOYS FOR TOTS
- *Remember to suit toys to the child's age and stage of development. Many toy-related accidents occur when a young child is playing with a toy meant for an older child.*
- *Avoid projectile toys that shoot objects that can cause eye injury or choking.*
- *For children under 3 years of age, avoid toys with small parts.*
- *Don't allow cap guns to be shot indoors or within one foot of a child's ear—hearing can be damaged.*

Look for:
- *The words "nontoxic," "flame retardant/flame resistant" on fabric toys and "washable hygienic materials" on dolls and stuffed toys.*
- *The "UL Approved" label on any electric toy.*
- *Wheels that are attached with screws, not staples.*
- *Ropes or strings on toys that are threaded through holes, not attached with tacks or staples.*
- *Electric toys with heating elements—they are only appropriate for children older than 8, and then only with adult supervision.*
- *Sharp points, flimsy construction, pinch spots and unprotected edges.*
- *Toy arrows or darts with blunt tips or suction cups; check that tips are firmly attached to shafts.*

Orange Tweed Cardigan and Hat

ORANGE TWEED CARDIGAN AND HAT *(photo, page 133)*

AVERAGE: For those with some experience in knitting.

SIZE: Children's Size 6.

MATERIALS: Plymouth Persian yarn (4-oz. skein): 2 skeins each of Orange #406 and Yellow #416 *(see Materials Shopping Guide, page 293)*; knitting needles, sizes 8 and 10, or any size needles to obtain gauge below; cable stitch holder; stitch holders; 5 toggle buttons.

GAUGE: 5 sts and 6 rows = 1″ ribbing size 8 needles. Be sure to check your gauge.

PATTERN STITCHES:

T Cable (TC): Worked over 7 sts. **Row 1:** (Right side) Sl 2 sts onto holder and hold in back, k1, k2 from holder, k1, sl 1 st onto holder and hold in front, k2, k1 from holder. **Rows 2, 4, 6:** Purl. **Rows 3 and 5:** Knit. Rep Rows 1 to 6 for **TC**.

Black Berry (BB): Worked over 16 sts. **Row 1:** (Right side) Purl. **Row 2:** k2, [p3 tog, (k1, p1, k1) in next st] 3 times, k2. **Row 3:** Purl. **Row 4:** K4 [(k1, p1, k1) in next st, p3 tog] twice, k4. Rep Rows 1 to 4 for **BB**.

Double Moss (DM): Row 1: *K1, p1; rep from * across row. **Row 2:** Knit all k sts, purl all p sts. **Row 3:** Purl on k sts, knit on p sts. Rep Rows 2 and 3 for **DM**.

Chain Cable (CC): Worked over 6 sts. **Row 1:** Sl 2 sts onto st holder and hold in front, k2, p2, k2 from holder. **Row 2:** P2, k2, p2. **Row 3:** K2, p2, k2. Rep Rows 2 and 3 fourteen times, then Row 2 once. Rep Rows 1-18 for **CC**.

DIRECTIONS—Note: Work with double yarn—1 orange, 1 yellow—throughout. **Back:** Using smaller needles cast on 62 sts. Work in k1, p1 ribbin for 7 rows, knitting into back of k sts. Change to larger needles. **Next Row:** (Wrong side) Purl across. **Row 2:** DM-9 sts, TC, k1, CC, BB, CC, k1, TC, DM-9 sts. Work in established

pat until piece measures 10½″ from beg. **Shape Raglan Armholes:** Bind off 3 sts at beg of next 2 rows. **Row 3:** K1, s1, k1, psso, work in at until 3 sts rem K2 tog, K1 Dec one st each side of every other row 17 times more, 20 sts rem. Place sts on holder. **Left Front:** On smaller needles, cast on 35 sts and work 3 rows in k1, p1, ribbing, knitting into back of all k sts. **Buttonhole:** Work 2 sts in rib, bind off 2 sts, finish row in rib. **Next Row:** Work in rib, cast on 2 sts above 2 bound-off sts. Work 2 more rows of rib. Change to larger needles. **Next Row:** Rib for 6 sts, purl inc 3 sts evenly spaced (38 sts). **Row 1:** DM on 7 sts, TC, p1, CC, p11, rib for 6 sts. **Row 2:** Rib, BB-k2 [p3 tog (k1, p1, k1) in next st] twice, k1; CC, k1, TC, DM-7. **Row 3:** Rep Row 1: **Row 4:** Rib; BB-k2 [(k1, p1, k1) in next st, p3 tog] twice, k1, CC, k1. TC, DM-7. Continue working even in established pat, making buttonholes on every 15th row, until piece measures 10½″, ending on wrong side. **Shape Raglan Armhole—Next Row:** (Right side) Bind off 3 sts at beg of row; finish row in pat. **Row 2:** Work in pat k last st. Continue working in pat and on every right-side row; k1, sl1, k1, psso, finish row in pat. Work until 25 sts rem, ending on right side. **Shape Neck:** (Wrong side) Place 6 sts of rib on st holder. Continue working in pat but dec 1 st at beg of every row for Raglan Armhole and Neck Shaping until 2 sts rem. K2 tog. Fasten off. **Right Front:** Work in the same manner as left front, but reverse armhole and neck shaping and omit buttonholes. **Sleeves:** On smaller needles, cast on 29 sts and work in k1, p1, ribbing for 9 rows. Change to larger needles. **Next Row:** Purl, inc 5 sts evenly across row (34 sts). **Row 1:** (Right side) DM-2, TC, BB, TC, DM-2. Continue working pat, inc 1 sts on each end of every 7th row until there are 42 sts. Work even until piece measures 11½″, ending on wrong side. **Shape Shoulder Cap:** Bind off 2 sts at beg

of next 2 rows. **Row 3:** (Right side) K1, sl1, k1, psso, work in pat until 3 sts rem, k2 tog, k1. **Row 4:** Work in pat to last st, k1. Rep Rows 3 and 4 until 16 sts rem. Place on holder with back. Rep exactly for 2nd sleeve.

Finishing: Sew sleeves to back along raglan armhole. Sew fronts to sleeves along raglan armholes. Sew sleeve and side seams. **Collar:** Using smaller needles and working in k1, p1, ribbing starting from right side, pick up 6 sts from holder from rib, pick up 10 sts on right front, 4 sts from right shoulder, 20 sts from back on holder, 4 sts from left shoulder, 10 sts from left front and 6 from left ribs. Work 15 rows in rib. Bind off loosely. Sew on buttons.

HAT DIRECTIONS: Using smaller needle, cast on 69 sts and work 7 rows of k1, p1 ribbing, working through back of all k sts. Change to large needle. **Row 1:** K1, TC, p1, CC, pl TC, p12, TC, p1, CC, p1, TC, p11, k1. **Row 2:** K1; BB—k1; [p3 tog, (k1, p1, k1) in next st] twice, k2; TC, k1, CC, k1, TC; BB—k2, [p3 tog, (k1, p1, k1) in next st] twice, k2; TC; k1, CC, k1 TC, k1. **Row 3:** Rep Row 1. **Row 4:** K1; BB—k1, [(k1, p1, k1) in next st, p3 tog] twice, k2; TC, k1, CC, k1, TC; BB—k1, [(k1, p1, k1) in next st, p3 tog] twice, k2; TC, k1, CC, k1, TC, k1. Continue in established pat until piece measures 6½″ from beg, ending on wrong side. Work in k1, p1 ribbing for next 2 rows. **Next Row:** (Right Sides) *K5, k2 tog; rep from * 8 times, k4, k2 tog. **Row 2:** K1, purl until last st, k1. **Row 3:** *K4, k2 tog; rep from * 8 times, k3, k2 tog. **Row 4:** Rep Row 2. **Row 5:** *K3, k2 tog; rep from * 8 times, k2, k2 tog. **Row 6:** Rep Row 2. **Row 7:** *K2, k2 tog; rep from * 8 times K1, K2 tog. **Row 8:** Rep Row 2. **Row 9:** *K1, k2, k1, tog; rep from * 8 times, k2 tog. **Row 10:** P2 tog 9 times, k1. Break yarn and thread through rem 10 sts. Sew seam. Make a pompon and sew on top.

BABY BOOTIES

AVERAGE: For those with some experience in crocheting.

Directions are given for Sizes Infant to about 6 Months.

MATERIALS: 1.5 oz. any bulky-weight leftover yarn in 8 colors or 2 strands thinner-weight yarn held together to obtain the same gauge; crochet hook, Size G, or any size hook to obtain gauge below; tapestry needle.

GAUGE: 3 sc = 1″; 3 rows = 1″. Be sure to check your gauge.

BOOTIES *(Make 2):* Starting at sole of Bootie with A, ch 31. *Row 1 (row side):* Sc in each ch across—30 sc. Ch 1, turn. **Mark center st for center front of Bootie. Rows 2-5:** Sc in each sc across—30 sc. Ch1, turn. *Row 6 (dec row):* Sc in each sc across, decreasing 3 sts on each side of center st—24 sc. At end of this row, change to B as follows: Work last sc of row until there are 2 lps on hook; with new color, yo and draw through 2 lps on hook. Fasten off old color. **Hereafter change colors in this way.** *Row 7:* With B, ch 2, turn, skip first sc, * 2 hdc in next sc, skip next sc; rep from * across, ending with 2 hdc in last sc—24 hdc. Ch1, turn. **Row 8:** Sc in front lp **only** of each hdc across—24 sc. Change to C. *Row 9 (dec row):* With C, ch 1, turn, sc in each sc across, decreasing 2 sts on each side of center st—20 sc. Change to D, **but do not** fasten off C. *Row 10:* With D, ch 1, turn, work * 1 sc with D, 1 sc with C; rep from * across row—20 sc. Fasten off D **only.** *Row 11:* With C, ch 1, turn, skip first sc, * 2 sc in next sc, skip next sc; rep from * across, ending with 2 sc in last sc—20 sc. Change to E. *Row 12:* With E, ch 1, turn, sc in front lp **only** of each sc across to within last sc, *2 sc in last sc*—**inc made**—21 sc. Change to F. *Row 13:* With F, ch 1, turn, sc in each sc across—21 c. change to E. *Row 14:* With E, ch 1, turn, sc in **both** lps of each sc across to within last sc, inc 1 sc—22 sc. Change to G. *Row 15:* With G, rep Row 7—22 hdc. Change to H. *Row 16:* With H, ch 1, turn, * sc bet next 2 hdc groups, ch 1; rep from * across, ending with sc bet next 2 hdc groups—22 sts. Ch 1, turn. *Row 17:* Sc in each st across—22 sc. Change to I or C if you desire. *Row 18:* With I, ch 1, turn, sc in each sc across. Fasten off.

Finishing: Sew ends of rows together for center back of Bootie. Sew foundation chain row together for bottom of sole.

Drawstring: With I, work an 18″-long chain. Weave drawstring through sps of Row 9 and tie into a bow at center front. With B and tapestry needle, work a running st through sps of Row 17.

♥ *Merry outing for a youngster:* *Treat your favorite kid to tickets to the local zoo or amusement park. Wrap them with a written promise to take the child on a Saturday afternoon of his or her choosing.*

Rose Vest

ROSE VEST

AVERAGE: For those with some experience in knitting.

Directions are given for Size Petite (8). Changes for Sizes Small (10-12), Medium (14) and Large (16) are in parentheses. **Note:** Rose and Bud motifs are worked in duplicate stitch after Vest is completed.

MATERIALS: Brunswick "Germantown" Knitting Worsted Yarn (3.5-oz. skein): 3 (3, 4, 4) skeins of No. 482 Burgundy Heather (A); DMC tapestry wool (8.8-yd. skein): 2 each of No. 7370 Soft Green (B), No. 7204 Medium Rose (C) and No. 7202 Light Rose (D) *(see Materials Shopping Guide, page 293);* knitting needles, No. 8, or any size needles to obtain gauge below; crochet hook, Size G; five ¾"-dia. buttons.

GAUGE: In Stockinette Stitch (k1 row, p1 row)—5 sts = 1"; 6 rows = 1". Be sure to check your gauge.

Sizes Petite Small Medium Large
    (8)   (10-12) (14)   (16)
Body
Bust: 31½"   34"   36"   38"
Finished Measurements:
Bust: 34"   36"   38"   40"
Width Across Back or Front at Underarms:
    17"   18"   19"   20"
Width Across Sleeves at Upper Arms (without crocheted bands):
    8½"   9"   9½"   10"

Back: Starting at lower edge with A, cast on 85 (89, 95, 99) sts. Work in seed st as follows: **Row 1:** * K1, p1; rep from * across, ending with k1. **Row 2:** Rep Row 1. Rep Rows 1 and 2 for a total of 5 rows. Change to stockinette stitch (k 1 row, p 1 row) and work until total length is 2½" from beg, ending with a p row.
Waistline Shaping—Next Row: K across row, decreasing 20 sts evenly spaced, and place a marker after each decrease—65 (69, 75, 79) sts. Work
(Continued on next page.)

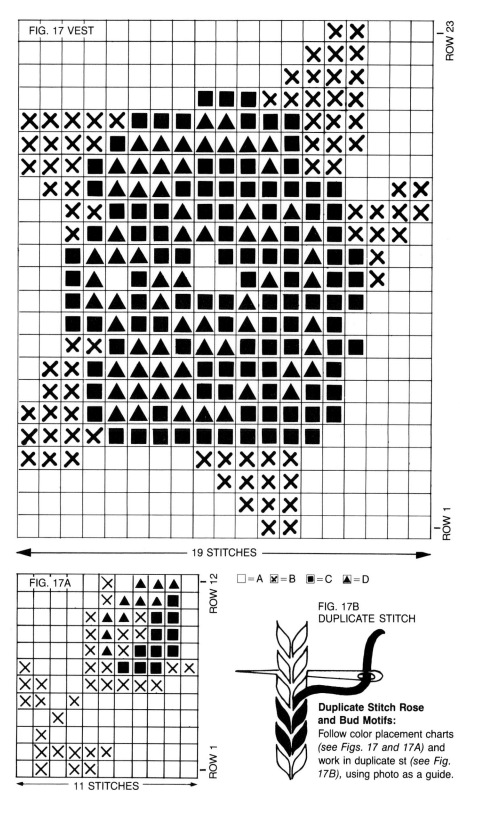

FIG. 17 VEST

ROW 23

ROW 1

19 STITCHES

FIG. 17A

ROW 12

ROW 1

11 STITCHES

□=A ☒=B ■=C ▲=D

FIG. 17B
DUPLICATE STITCH

Duplicate Stitch Rose and Bud Motifs:
Follow color placement charts *(see Figs. 17 and 17A)* and work in duplicate st *(see Fig. 17B),* using photo as a guide.

even in stockinette stitch (st st) for 3 rows, slipping markers every row. **Next Row:** K across row, increasing one st before each marker, then remove markers—85 (89, 95, 99) sts. Work even in st st until total length is 12½ (12½, 13, 13½)" from beg or desired length to underarm, ending with a p row.

Armhole Shaping: Bind off 5 sts at beg of next 2 rows. Dec one st each end every other row 4 (4, 5, 6) times. Work even on 67 (71, 75, 77) sts until armhole measures 8 (8, 8¼, 8½)" from first row of armhole shaping. Bind off all sts.

Left Front: Starting at lower edge with A, cast on 43 (45, 47, 49) sts. Work in seed st as for back until 5 rows have been completed. Change to st st and work until total length is 2½" from beg, ending with a p row.

Waistline Shaping—Next Row: K across row, decreasing 10 sts evenly spaced, and place a marker after each decrease—33 (35, 37, 39) sts. Work even in st st for 3 rows, slipping markers every row. **Next Row:** K across row, increasing one st before each marker, then remove markers—43 (45, 47, 49) sts. Work even in st st until same length as back to underarm, ending with a p row.

Neck and Armhole Shaping— Next Row: Bind off 5 sts at beg of row, k rem sts. **Next Row:** P across. Dec one st at armhole edge every other row 4 (4, 5 6) times. And at the same time dec one st at neck edge **every** row 10 times, then every **other** row 10 times—14 (16, 17, 18) sts. Work even until length of armhole is the same as on back. Bind off.

Right Front: Work right front to correspond with left front, reversing shaping.

Finishing: Sew shoulder and side seams.

Armhole Edging—Rnd 1: With right side facing you and crochet hook, work 1 rnd of sc around armholes, decreasing as necessary. Join to first sc. **Rnd 2:** Work in reverse sc as follows: Working from left to right, draw up a lp in next st to the right, yo and draw through 2 lps on hook. Fasten off.

Front Bands—Row 1: With right side facing you, join yarn at lower right front edge and work 1 row of sc up right front side edge, around neck edge, and down left front side edge, making 3 sc at upper corners of fronts. Ch 1, turn. Mark right front side edge for buttonhole, having one marker ½" from upper and lower corners and 3 more evenly spaced in between. **Row 2 (buttonhole row):** Work 1 row of sc to first marker as for Row 1, making buttonholes at each marker as follows: Ch 2, skip 2 sc, sc in next sc. Ch 1, turn. **Row 3:** Work 1 row of sc, along fronts and neck edge, making 2 sc in each ch-2 sp. Ch 1; **do not** turn. **Row 4:** Work 1 row of reverse sc along fronts and neck edges. Fasten off. Sew button onto left front bank opposite buttonholes.

The heart teen box.

♥ ***Especially for teens:*** *Getting a car on the weekend is often a problem for young drivers. Lend your responsible teenage son or daughter or niece or nephew your car for a Friday or Saturday night out. It'll be a gift he or she won't forget.*

TWIN STUFFED DOLLS

AVERAGE: For those with some experience in sewing.

MATERIALS: ½ yd. (36"- or 45"-wide) peach percale; scrap of nonwoven bondable interfacing; 1 skein (2 oz.) four-ply wool or synthetic yarn; one bag polyester stuffing; thread to match fabric and yarn; 4 flat 2-hole buttons, ½"-dia.; rug thread and extra-large darning needle; scissors; pencil; paper for pattern; pins; embroidery thread scraps and needle; sewing needle; white percale or muslin for lining *(optional)*.

Note: If fabric of proper color is not available, white cotton can be easily dyed peach or flesh color.

DIRECTIONS:
1. Bodies: Enlarge and cut out all the pattern pieces in Fig. 18, following the directions on page 291. Pin the pieces to the fabric and cut out the fabric. *(Note: If you want a smoother result, cut all the pieces again out of thin white cotton and baste to the wrong side of each major part of the doll. Treat the results as you would the fabric alone.)* Sew all darts as indicated.

2. Sew the center back seam, leaving an opening as indicated. Sew the back to the front of the body. Slash the seam allowance as indicated. Turn to the right side. Stuff very firmly. This is most important. Pack the stuffing until the "skin" is almost as firm as that of a composition doll. Sew the back opening closed.

(Continued on page 141.)

Twin Stuffed Dolls

FIG. 18   TWIN DOLLS   1 SQ. = 1″

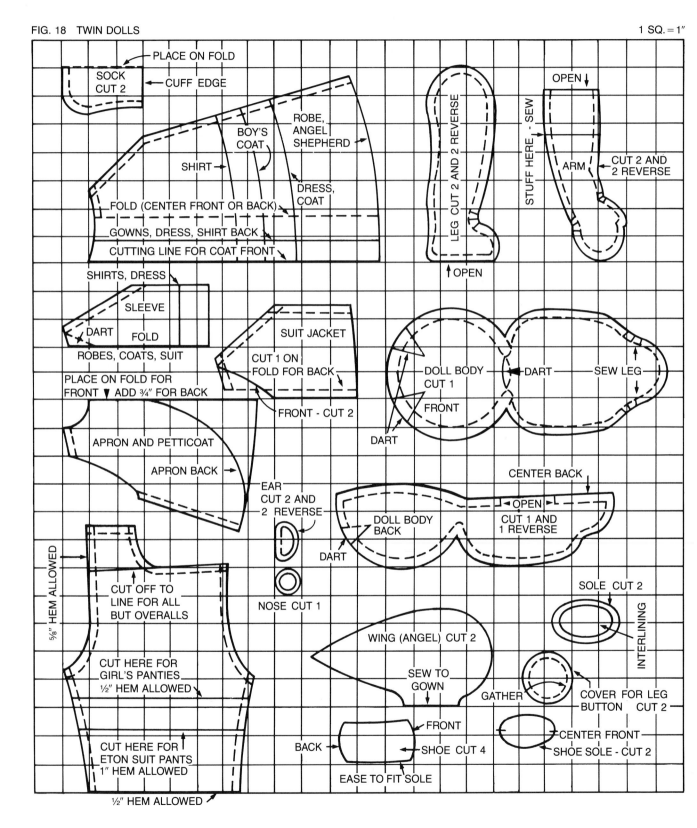

3. Sew the legs in pairs, leaving the bottom of the foot open. Slash the seams as indicated. Turn to the right side. Stuff as firmly as the body. Iron the sole interfacing and tack. Gather the open end of the leg lightly so that it curves under and position the sole, facing side inside, over it. Sew the sole in place to cover the seam (gathering) at the opening.

4. Attach the legs to the body with the rug thread on the darning needle. The thread is knotted on the outside of a button and pulled as tightly as possible. Gather the edge of the cover for the button and pull to make the edge turn under. Sew over the button to cover it.

5. Sew the arm pieces in pairs. Slash the seams as indicated. Turn to the right side. Stuff firmly to line and sew across by hand. Turn in the top seam allowance and stitch closed. Pin the top edge to the body at a right angle to the side seam at the shoulder. Sew to the body.

6. Cut the nose, gather the edge, stuff and sew to face. Sew the ear pieces in pairs (boy only), leaving opening. Turn to the right side, sew the opening closed and sew to head. Lightly mark the eyes and mouth with a pencil and embroider with satin and outline stitches.

7. To sew hair to dolls: Using yarn, make hair. For the boy, fringe around the edge of the head first, then work down the center part. (Sew strands centered on the seam.) For the girl, work with two needles, one working down the center part and the other at the hairline. (Some loops do not return quite to the ear; work to cover the scalp.) Add braids when the head is covered.

CLOTHING

MATERIALS: Two pairs of infant-size white stretch socks; one square yellow felt (for angel wings); one pair, size 9 to 11, white stretch socks; size 3/0 snaps; fabric remnants (if fabric is to be purchased, ¼ yd. is sufficient in almost all garments; floor-length garments require ⅓ yd.); thread to match all fabrics and trim; paper for patterns; pins; needle; scissors; pencil; for trim, see individual item.

DIRECTIONS:

1. Enlarge and cut out the desired patterns in Fig. 18, following the directions on page 291.

2. Socks: Cut according to the pattern, using the finished edge of the infant's sock as the top of the doll sock. Sew. Turn to the right side.

3. Girl's Panties: Cut the pattern out of white cotton. Leave back opening. Make a narrow hem on the legs and back opening. Turn in ½" at the top and make a hem. Sew a snap to back. Adjust the waist with tiny tucks, if necessary.

4. Petticoat: Cut the pattern out of white cotton; sew as indicated. Make a rolled hem at the neck and arm openings (⅜") and a ½" hem at the bottom. Overlap the back when the edges have been finished (see diagram note). Tack for about ½" up from the bottom edge. Sew lace to the bottom over the hem stitch line. Sew snaps to the back.

5. Plaid Dress: Cut fabric according to the pattern. Sew the diagonal seam of the sleeve to the diagonal seam of the dress front. Repeat to join the back. Sew the underarm seams. Make a dart at the shoulder. Turn up ½" on

---

♥ *Scrapbook starter set: Great for kids who love collecting memorabilia—wrap up a plain scrapbook, a bottle of glue, some fun stickers and photo-mounting corners.*

---

the sleeve and make a hem. Turn in ½" on the back opening and make the hem. The bottom edge has a ¾" hem. Cut a bias of the same fabric and bind the neck opening. Sew lace to trim the sleeves. Finish the back the same way as the Petticoat.

6. Apron: Cut fabric according to the pattern. Make a ⅜" hem on all the unseamed edges. Sew lace trim as shown. Sew a snap to the back at the neckline.

7. Flowered Dress: Follow the directions for Plaid Dress, except make 1" sleeve hems. Sew lace trim to the front before binding the neck edge.

8. Girl's Coat: Cut material as for Plaid Dress, but use a wider pattern for the front. Make ½" hems on the sleeves and bottom, and turn in the front edge 1". Sew darts on the sleeve. Cut the lining in the same way and sew into coat, but do not sew a dart in the sleeve top. The neck edge of the coat and lining are sewn together but are raw edges. Bind the neck with a matching bias. Sew snaps to the front. Sew tiny buttons to the outside of the front.

9. Hood of Coat: Cut a 3½" x 11" piece from the same fabric. Fold in half crosswise and seam to form the hood. Cut a 2½" x 11" piece of fur cloth. Seam, right sides together, to the front edge. Allow ⅝" for the "fur" to show on the outside and turn the rest to the inside of the hood. Turn up ½" on the neck edge. Cut the lining and sew to form the hood. Line the hood. Sew a large white pompon to a point of the hood on the outside. Sew the front points (neck edge) of the hood to the collar at the front sleeve seam. ☞

Gather the back to match the neck of coat. Tack at the center back.

10. Girl's Robe: Cut fabric according to the pattern. Sew in the same way as the Plaid Dress. Sew the hem as follows: sleeves ¾", front edges ¾", bottom ½". Add lace trim on the front before binding the neck. Sew a snap at the neck. Add a ribbon bow.

11. Nightgown: Cut a piece according to the pattern without sleeves. Sew the side seams. Bind the arm openings. Turn in ½" on the back edges and hem. Tack the arm openings together at neck and bind the neck edge. Make a ¾" bottom hem. Sew lace trim. Finish the back as for Plaid Dress.

12. Angel Petticoat: Follow the directions for Nightgown, but make a narrow hem instead of binding the neck and arm openings (tack at shoulders). Use no lace.

13. Gown: For the sleeve, place the pattern ½" from the fold line. Assemble as for the Plaid Dress, but use a very narrow hem on the sleeve and bottom edges. Make no dart at the shoulder and gather the fullness in tightly. Turn in the back edge and finish as for Dress. Bind the neck. Sew narrow gold rickrack as shown. Cut the wings of yellow felt. Sew the trim. Sew the wings to the back of the Gown by stitching tabs to the Gown (top of the tab begins just below the neck binding). The halos are two 12" gold pipecleaners twisted together and shaped. Or use wire, wrapped with gold tinsel. Shape. Pin to the back of the head.

14. Shepherd: Cut and make undergown, following the directions for Angel Petticoat. Cut the outer robe according to the pattern, but allow ¼" beyond the fold line for the front opening. Turn in and hem the front and sleeve edges ½". Make a 1" hem at the bottom. Bind the neck. The crook is a pipecleaner.

15. Head Cloth: Cut an 8½" x 9½" piece of thin fabric. Make a narrow hem on all edges. The band is ½"-wide black elastic, cut 9½" long and seamed at the cut edges.

16. Boy's Coat: Cut fabric to the length shown on the pattern. Assemble in the same way as for Girl's Coat, but omit the hood.

17. Scarf: Cut one yard of 1"-wide ribbon in half and sew together to make a piece 2" wide x 18" long. Fringe the ends.

18. Cap: Cut off the ribbed portion of a man's acrylic sock. Gather the cut end tightly on the wrong side. Turn to the right side. Sew a large pompon to the outside of the gathered end. Turn up the cuff.

19. Mittens: Make like Socks, but fit to the hands.

20. Shirt: Cut fabric to the length indicated on the pattern. Assemble as for Plaid Dress, except make the sleeve hem ⅝" and turn it up on the right side to make the cuff. The plaid shirt has a "tie" of a 3" square of fabric fringed on all edges and gathered diagonally. Sew to the neck edge. The white shirt has tiny buttons sewn down the center front. Add a ribbon bow tie.

21. Overalls: Cut fabric according to the pattern. For the top edge, sew the bias binding, but turn it entirely to the inside. Make a narrow hem at the back opening. Cut 2¼"-square pockets and turn in all the edges. Sew to

Overalls. Cut 6" x 2" straps. Fold in half, lengthwise; turn in the raw edges and sew closed. Attach to the bib. Cross in back and snap to the top of back.

22. Long Pants: Cut fabric according to the pattern. Make like Overalls but without bib and pockets. Turn in the top edge ⅝" and hem. Sew a snap to the back. Adjust the waist with tucks, if necessary.

23. Pajamas: Make the bottoms like Long Pants. Sew the top like Shirt, but make it ½" longer and make an opening at the front.

24. Robe: Cut as for Plaid Dress. Turn in ½" on the front edges and hem. Turn up sleeves to make a narrow bottom hem. Bind the neck with pajama fabric. Sew snaps to the front. Add cord tie.

25. Shoes (and Slippers): Cut the pieces out of felt according to the pattern. Sew the front and back seams of tops with tiny overcast stitches. Sew the sole to the bottom edge (ease if necessary) in the same way. Add trim—pompon for slippers, felt bow for girl's dress shoes, cross stitches of embroidery thread for "ties."

26. Suit—Jacket: Cut fabric according to the pattern, using the same sleeve as for the other garments but adjusting the sleeve length afterward (bind the edge, no hem). Assemble the Jacket. Bind all edges. Sew a Soutache just above the binding. Sew snaps to the front and buttons to the outside.

27. Suit—Pants: Cut fabric according to the pattern. Turn up 1" and hem the bottom edges. Finish otherwise like the Girl's Panties.

♥ *If you're artistic, neatly copy one of your favorite poems on a piece of parchment-like paper and share this sensitive part of yourself as a special Christmas present.*

Stenciled Sweatshirts

STENCILED SWEATSHIRTS

EASY: Achievable by anyone.
MATERIALS: Sweatshirt (poly/cotton or 100% cotton); heavy (#10) sheet of acetate, or stencil-acetate with one adhesive side; acrylic or fabric paint; stencil brush; masking tape; cutting board; X-acto knife or single-edge razor blade.

DIRECTIONS:
1. Pattern: You will cut 2 stencils for each of the 2 patterns. Cut a piece of acrylic at least 6″ square for each stencil.
2. Stencil No. 1: Trace the figures using tracing paper, then thumbtack them to a cutting board. Tape down the corners of an acrylic square, centered over one of the patterns. With the X-acto knife, cut along the *darker edges only* (3 cutouts for the dog, 2 cutouts for the cow). Ignore the eyes and the dotted lines. This will be Stencil No. 1 for the principal color. Remove the tape; leave the page on the board.
3. Stencil No. 2: Now tape down an acrylic square for Stencil No. 2 and cut out *the lighter areas only* (ribbon for the dog, 4 spots, 4 hooves and an eye for the cow). This will be Stencil No. 2 for the second color.
4. Placement: For allover stenciling, baste a vertical line to mark the center front of the sweatshirt. Measure the design to find the space needed for each row. Baste horizontal guidelines across the sweatshirt to mark the bottom of each one. Now you can stencil a centered animal on alternate rows, then stencil an animal at each side of it. On the intervening rows, it will be easy to stagger an animal in between those above it.
5. Painting: With cardboard inside (between front and back), spread out the sweatshirt. It will be easier to work if you keep the fabric taut with pushpins. Tape Stencil 1 to the sweatshirt and paint the principal color. Use the paints just as they come, straight from the jars or tubes. *Don't mix* them with water. Pick up a little paint off the end of a dry stenciling brush. Gently pounce the top up and down on paper towels. This removes excess paint and distributes paint evenly throughout the bristles. Gently dab the brush, in an up-and-down, stippling motion, through the stencil openings, working from the outside inward to apply a thick, even covering of color. (White paint may require another coat after the first one has dried.) Lift the stencil straight up and let the paint dry before you apply the second color. Tape Stencil No. 2 over the first color, so the spaces match and the design registers; paint, with the second color, as before. Cut a second stencil for reversed animals or wash the first one *(see Step 6)* and turn it over.
6. Clean the brushes with water before the paint gets hard; dry them with a paper towel. Stencils can be cleaned in hot water for 5 minutes; wipe off loosened paint.
7. Acrylic paint is water-soluble when it is wet. When it dries, it becomes permanent and washable if you follow the manufacturer's directions. Turn the garment inside out before laundering. Wash and rinse with cold water (using permanent press "colored" cycle). Do not dry-clean.

■ STENCIL NO. 1   ▨ STENCIL NO. 2

FOR KIDS TO MAKE

Wallpaper Note Paper

WALLPAPER NOTE PAPER

EASY: Achievable by anyone.
MATERIALS: Note paper with matching envelopes; wallpaper remnants or samples*; scissors; ruler; pencil; rubber cement.

DIRECTIONS:
1. Note Paper: Cut wallpaper in one of three ways: If the wallpaper is a small print, cover the entire face of the front flap of the note paper with a rectangle of the wallpaper. Coat the back of the wallpaper with rubber cement and smooth in place. Line the envelope to match.
2. If the wallpaper is a bold stripe, cut a length of the stripe to fit the width of the front flap of the note paper. Glue, centered, to the face of the note paper. Line the envelope to match. Or, if the wallpaper has two distinct types of striping, use a different one to line the envelope.
3. If the wallpaper has medallions or bold motifs, cut these and glue, centered, to the front flap of the note paper. Line the envelope to match, using random portions of the same paper.
4. Envelopes: Cut the envelope linings of the wallpaper to fit inside the front and triangular closing flap (except glued edges). Insert into the envelope, fold the flap down to crease the lining. Glue down the flap area *only*.
Note: If wallpaper samples are used, watch for printing on the reverse side; it will show through the note paper and envelope. Do not use these areas on the note paper. For the envelopes, keep the print off the flap portion. If used inside the envelope, insert a rectangle of white paper between the back of the lining and envelope before gluing the flap in place.

Stick-on Graphics

♥ *Make a certificate saying that since the recipient understands and appreciates the true meaning of Christmas, you are going to work a certain number of hours for a charity, in her honor.*

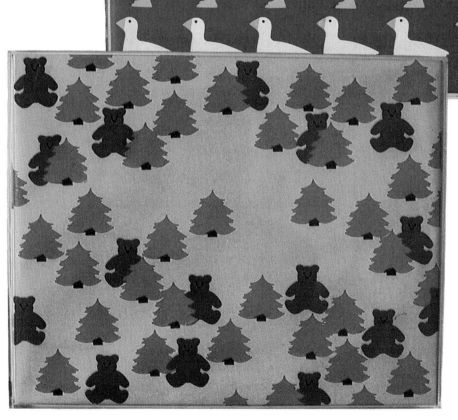

STICK-ON GRAPHICS

EASY: Achievable by anyone.
MATERIALS: Plastic box frame (available at dime stores); colored gift wrap; self-adhering gift-wrap stickers.

DIRECTIONS:
1. Cover the inset of the frame with the gift wrap.
2. Using this as a canvas, arrange stickers in a design.
3. Replace the inset in the frame.

THE GIFT BAZAAR

Gifts to sell at a holiday bazaar or to use as stocking-stuffers.

FOR A SUCCESSFUL BAZAAR

- **Know your customers.** Determine whom you are selling to, how much they will spend and what items will be the most popular. Grandmothers look for gifts for their grandchildren, while young marrieds want gifts and decorative crafts for their own home.
- **Take the time for a "market survey."** Go to the best shops in town. What's the latest in fashion and decorating news? Don't forget to look at children's stores, too!
- **Choose items that are inexpensive to make** but are usually overpriced in stores, such as sachets, pillows and pot holders.
- **Also think of seasonal items** like colorful ornaments, stocking-stuffers and Christmas cards.
- **Choose at least one "star"** that can be used to draw in the crowd and then be raffled off at the end of the day. This is a surefire way to bring in the highest profit.
- **Don't overprice items.** Check prices at your local boutiques and specialty stores, then price your items at least 30% to 50% lower than their retail costs. If an item isn't selling, reduce its price even more.
- **Accept all donations.** Take every bit of yarn, fabric and trim that's donated and design a craft item that can utilize these items.

PADDED HANGERS

EASY: Achievable by anyone.

MATERIALS—_Note:_ Materials given are for one hanger. Substitute desired fabrics for other hangers. One 20-oz.-size "LOVE MY CARPET"™ "Soft Scent" rug and room deodorizer _(see Materials Shopping Guide, page 293);_ 1 package quilt batting; ¼ yd. fabric; ½ yd. ¼"-wide ribbon; ¾ yd. ½"-wide ribbon; 1 wooden hanger; masking tape; thread to coordinate with fabric; muslin or scrap sheeting.

DIRECTIONS:

1. Wrap a layer or two of batting around the wooden part of the hanger and tape to fasten. Stitch the ends closed.

2. Make a 1" x 17"-wide muslin pocket for the "LOVE MY CARPET" powder. Attach the muslin pouch to the underside of the hanger. Wrap another layer of batting over it and secure.

3. Stitch the raw ends of batting together, making sure the batting is secure on the hanger and will not shift when inserted into the fabric covering.

4. Cut 2 pieces of 11" x 5" fabric and two 22" x 5" pieces. Stitch one basting line along each 22" side. Gather the sides to measure 11". With the right sides together, stitch one gathered piece of material to one ungathered piece of material, leaving one 5" side unstitched. Clip the corners. Repeat for the 2 remaining pieces of fabric. Turn both pieces right side out.

5. Slip one fabric tube on each side of the hanger. Turn the raw edges under so that the edges of the tubes just meet. Tack the fabric together at the top and bottom of the hanger.

6. Using the ¼"-wide ribbon, tape one end to the tip of the wire hook and wrap, covering the metal completely. Slipstitch the end of the ribbon to the fabric on the hanger. Fold the ½"-wide ribbon in half and place the fold around the base of the wire hook. Wrap the ribbon around the hanger in 2 parallel bands, returning to the starting point. Wrap the 2 ends around the wire hook, crisscrossing them behind the hook and returning them to the front of the hook.

7. Tie a bow and stitch to fasten.

♥ *A pamper-yourself potpourri:* *Give a busy girlfriend a collection of bubble bath, scented soap and a romantic novel or magazine. Throw in a bottle of bright red nail polish as well.*

💲 RICE-PAPER JARS

EASY: Achievable by anyone
MATERIALS: Glass jar with cork top; textured rice paper (24″ x 36″); Mod Podge® matt *(see Materials Shopping Guide, page 293)*; sponge paintbrush; wax paper; floral paper cutouts.

DIRECTIONS:
1. Cut the rice paper 1″ taller than the jar height and ½″ wider than the jar girth. Place the rice paper on wax paper and paint it with 1 part Mod Podge mixed with about 2 parts water.
2. Place the wet paper around the jar; overlap the edges and turn ½″ to the bottom, ½″ to the inside. Mold the paper around the jar neck. Let it dry.
3. With full-strength Mod Podge, glue the paper flowers to the jar; press the edges with a spoon to avoid curling. Let it dry. With a dampened sponge brush, paint 4 or 5 coats of Mod Podge over the jar, drying between coats.
4. Turn the jar upside down and cover bottom with rice paper in the same way.

💲 LINGERIE CASE

AVERAGE: For those with some experience in sewing.
MATERIALS: 15″x36″ rectangles—1 of bag fabric, 1 of lining fabric and 1 of batting; snap or Velcro closure *(optional).*

DIRECTIONS:
1. Cut one 15″ x 27″ rectangle for the bag and another for the lining. Cut two 3½″ x 8½″ strips for the side boxing; curve the corners at one (bottom) end of each strip.
2. Baste the batting to the wrong side of the bag and boxing pieces. Quilt around the flowers if you like. Seam the boxings to the bag, starting at one end of a 27″ edge; this will form the pouch. Sew the boxing to the lining the same way.
3. With the right sides together, pin the flap end of the bag to the flap end of the lining. Stitch around the 3 flap edges. Turn the flap right side out and poke the lining pouch into the bag pouch. Turn in the raw edges and slipstitch around the top edges. Press.
4. Topstitch ½″ from the flap edge and continue, through all layers, around the boxing edges. Sew on the snap or Velcro closure, if desired.

♥ *Create your own "I love you" book for the man in your life. Offer him a coupon good for a candle-lit dinner for two, a car wash, a back rub or anything else you know he'll find special. Make sure he turns in his coupon for each service requested. That's half the fun!*

💲 POCKET TISSUE CASE

AVERAGE: For those with some experience in sewing.
MATERIALS: 6″ x 8″ rectangles—2 of fabric and 1 of batting; bias tape or 1″-wide fabric for binding; pocket pack of tissues.

DIRECTIONS:
1. Place the batting between the fabric pieces (right side out) and baste along the edges. Bind the two 6″ edges.
2. With the right sides together, fold the bound edges inward to meet at the center. Stitch ¼″ from each end. Turn the right side out. At each end, slipstitch the bound edges for ½″. Fill the case with the tissue packet

💲 EYEGLASS CASE

AVERAGE: For thoses with some experience in sewing.
MATERIALS: A 7″-long x 8″-wide piece each floral fabric, lining fabric and batting.

DIRECTIONS:
1. Pin the batting to the wrong side of the floral fabric and quilt along the flower outlines. Fold the piece in half (to 7″ x 4″), right sides together, and seam (¼″) the side and bottom edges. Seam the lining the same way.
2. Turn the quilted piece right side out; slip the lining inside; turn in ¼″ at the top edges and slipstitch.

Rice-Paper Jars, Lingerie Case, Pocket Tissue Case and Eyeglass Case

QUICK & EASY FABRIC GIFTS

1. BOTTLE BAG

AVERAGE: For those with some experience in sewing.
MATERIALS:
¾ yd. 45″-wide fabric (makes six).

DIRECTIONS:
1. Cut a 13″ square of fabric; pin one (top) edge. Seam 2 opposite edges to form a tube. At the bottom edge, turn under ¼″ and sew gathering stitches along the fold. Pull up the thread (to a round opening about ¾″ wide) and fasten the thread-ends securely.
2. Pull the bag over the bottle and tie a fancy cord or ribbon around the neck.

2. LACE-PANEL PILLOW

AVERAGE: For those with some experience in sewing.
MATERIALS: Lace panel, about 12″ square *(see Materials Shopping Guide, page 293);* ⅓ yd. red fabric; stuffing.

DIRECTIONS:
Pin the lace panel over the red fabric and edgestitch, for the pillow front; cut out close to the edges of the lace. Cut the red pillow back in two 8″ x 12″ pieces. Hem (1″) one 12″ edge of each piece. With the right sides together, pin the back pieces to the pillow front, all around (the hemmed edges will overlap at the center back). Stitch; turn; insert the pillow.

Quick & Easy Fabric Gifts

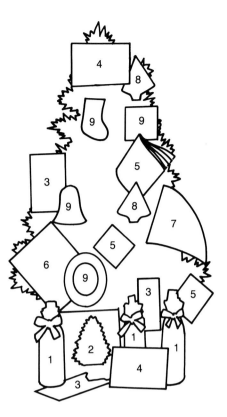

3. HAND TOWELS

AVERAGE: For those with some experience in sewing.
MATERIALS: ½ yd. and ⅛ yd. (for border of 44"-wide fabric and 1½ yds. woven braid (makes three).

DIRECTIONS:
1. Cut a 14" x 18" towel, 14" x 4" border and 14" length of braid.
2. With the right sides together, seam a long edge of the border to the short edge of the towel; press. At the other long edge of the border, turn under ¼" and press. With the right sides together, fold the border in half (with the turned-under edge matching the seam) and stitch across the short ends. Turn the border right side out.
3. Stitch a ¼" hem at the top and side edges. Topstitch the braid along the border, turning under the raw ends.

4. NOEL PANEL

EASY: Achievable by anyone.
MATERIALS: "NOEL" lace panel, 4½ x 7½" *(see Materials Shopping Guide, page 293);* 5½" x 8½" red felt; frame *(optional).*

DIRECTIONS: Glue the panel to the red felt. Frame, if desired.

5. COCKTAIL NAPKINS

EASY: Achievable by anyone.
MATERIALS: Scraps of fabric from other projects.

DIRECTIONS:
With pinking shears, cut 6" squares of fabric. Or, cut 6" x 8" pieces; fray ¼" at each edge; fold in half (6" x 4") and press.

6, 7. APPLIQUED AND QUILTED POT HOLDERS

AVERAGE: For those with some experience in sewing.
MATERIALS: ½ yd. each 45"-wide fabric and fleecy interfacing (makes 5); 1 panel (12 motifs) of fabric appliqués *(see Materials Shopping Guide, page 293);* bias tape.

DIRECTIONS:
6. Appliquéd Pot Holder: Cut two 9" squares of fabric and 3 of fleecy interfacing. Cut out the appliqué; turn under ¼" at the edges and press; center it on a fabric square and edgestitch. Bind the edges with bias tape.
7. Prequilted Pot Holder: Cut a 9" square prequilted fabric; topstitch ¼" from the edges. Bind edges with bias tape; fold over the tape at one corner and stitch to make the loop.

8. CHRISTMAS TREE COASTERS

AVERAGE: For those with some experience in sewing.
MATERIALS: Printed tree appliqués *(see Materials Shopping Guide, page 293);* coordinating fabric.

DIRECTIONS: Seam the tree appliqués to fabric, right sides together and leaving an opening. Trim the seam allowance once to ¼" and clip at the corners. Turn the right sides out and slipstitch closed. Press. Sew a thread loop at top for hanging.

9. FABRIC-COVERED FRAMES

EASY: Achievable by anyone.
MATERIALS: Purchased cardboard frames; fabric; white glue.

DIRECTIONS:
1. Glue the frame face down to the wrong side of fabric, leaving at least ½" fabric, extending all around, for a fold-over. Trim the fold-over to ½" outside the frame and inside the opening. Turn the fabric to the wrong side of the frame, clipping at the curves; glue in place.
2. Tape the photo to the wrong side. Tape the ends of yarn or ribbon to the wrong side at the center top to make a loop for hanging.

♥ ***At-home manicure kit:*** *Give a "nail-conscious" friend a pampering collection that includes a bottle of her favorite nail polish, emery boards, nail polish remover and a fragrant hand lotion.*

LAST-MINUTE GIFTS

These gifts can be made in a single evening!

Set-to-Cook Apron

♥ **A busy cook's casserole:** *An ideal present for the woman who has no time to cook: Give a casserole dish with three of your no-fail quick recipes. Or, promise to fill it with two dinners in the next two months.*

SET-TO-COOK APRON

A practical item for a cooking enthusiast. Buy 2 lettered linen towels. Cut the red printed stripes from one and sew together to make a waistband and ties. Gather one edge of the second and stitch to the waistband (as shown). Substitute a solid-color ribbon or fabric to make the waistband, if you like. Sew on terry-cloth pot holders as pockets and give 2 matching pot holders or mitts to complete the set.

SPLIT-SECOND ORNAMENTS

Create any of the designs here for a fraction of what they'd cost to buy! Dress up dime-store headbands, barrettes or elasticized ponytail holders. Bows, ribbon streamers, bits of eyelet, appliqués, buttons, charms and miniature fake flowers work well for the materials. Use an all-purpose glue to affix everything. Simply attach the decorations as shown. Even buttons threaded on ribbon should be reinforced with a drop of glue. (Tip: Use a metal hair clip to hold trims in place, while glue is drying.) Very little sewing is required; you need only a few stitches to gather circles of eyelet, secure the bows or sew on buttons.

Split-Second Hair Ornaments

DIRECTIONS:
Wash the empty containers thoroughly. Dry. The baby food jar requires 2 candles, the tuna can 3. Melt or heat wax (candles) in the container which is placed in a larger water container to prevent any possible contact of wax with the flame. Check to see if the candle fits in the jar. If too wide, shave off wax as necessary. Soften the bottom of the candle by heating over water and set in the jar (or can). Melt another candle. Pour this wax *around* the first candle in the jar (or can). Do not cover the top of the candle. Add wax from the second melted candle if necessary. Allow the wax to harden. Decorate the container by gluing fabric or ribbon to the outside and adding trimmings as desired.

"EMERGENCY" GIFTS

Caught off guard by a gift-bearing friend? You won't be found empty-handed with help from these snappy, last-second gift ideas.
- *Write up a menu for a gourmet meal—and specify the date you'll cook it.*
- *Tie a ribbon around a magazine and attach a gift tag saying "subscription to come."*
- *For a woman friend: A coupon, redeemable to you, for a visit to a beauty salon.*
- *Take a matchbook from a favorite restaurant and attach a dinner invitation to it.*
- *Clip off a stem cutting from a pretty plant; trim with a bright-colored bow and add a card with care instructions.*
- *Make a last-minute gourmet basket. Line a basket or decorative tin with tissue, then fill with prewrapped treats, nuts, cookies, etc.*
- *Snip an item from a catalog, glue onto a greeting card and write: "Real McCoy is on the way." Or, cut out a store logo and offer a "gift certificate to come in the mail."*
- *Hire a friend a maid for the day.*

♥ **Winter-storm survival kit:** *For those nasty stay-at-home days, put together a set of checkers, a deck of fun cards, like "Old Maid" or "Crazy Eights," and candles for atmosphere (or just in case).*

💲⚡
SCENTED CANDLES

MATERIALS: Baby food jars, tuna cans; scented votive light candles; scraps of fabrics (nontransparent), trimmings, felt, ribbon; Quik glue; container which is placed in larger heatproof container for water; scissors.

DESK SET
EASY: Achievable by anyone.

PENCIL HOLDER
Cover a soup can with batting. Cut a strip of fabric 2″ wider than the height of the can and 1″ longer than its circumference. Wrap it around the can, turning 1″ to the outside bottom and 1″ to the inside top. Turn under the final raw edge and slipstitch the vertical seam. Glue a paper circle to the outside bottom over the raw edges. Glue the paper to the inside of the can, edges flush.

THREE-RING NOTEBOOK
Trace an open notebook on the wrong side of the cloth. Cut it 1″ outside the traced lines. Spread batting over the outside of the book cover. Spread fabric on top; turn the edges to the inside cover, clipping at the spine, and glue. Glue paper to each inside cover.

DESK BLOTTER
From illustration board, cut one 17″ x 22″ and two 17″ x 3½″ pieces. Center the larger board over the wrong side of 20″ x 25″ fabric; fold the raw edges over the board and glue. Place batting over one side of the 2 small boards and cover with fabric that is cut 2″ larger (all around) than the board. At one long (inside) edge of each board, turn 1″ of fabric to the wrong side and glue. Turn the other 3 sides to the wrong side of the blotter and glue. Glue paper over the wrong side of the blotter.

WRAPPING IT UP

Now that you've finished making your gifts, wrap them in style and mail them off well protected.

- Begin to buy wrapping paper, ribbons, transparent tape, parcel wrapping paper and labels in November. (Or better yet, buy these just after Christmas, the year before.)
- Clear a space on a table or counter that is large enough to accommodate the largest package.
- Assemble all the packages to be wrapped, dividing them by sizes.

WRAPPING BASICS

- To wrap square and rectangular boxes, center the wrapping paper beneath the box. The paper should extend over both ends a little more than half the box's depth. Fasten the ends by folding the top flap down, sides in and the bottom flap up. Secure with tape.
- For round or tubular packages, you have three options. The first is to wrap the package, leaving extra wrap at both ends, and then gather the ends and tie with ribbon or yarn (this leaves a crinkle of gift wrap at each end). Or you can cut a large circle of gift wrap and gather the wrap at the top for a perfect ruffle of paper. Finally, for larger items, such as a basketball, lay out two rectangles of paper on an "X." Gather the ends and tie.
- Label each box, as soon as it has been wrapped.
- Save the small pieces of wrapping paper for the smaller packages.

Ribbons and Bows

- Try placing ribbons slightly off center. Split the ribbon to varying widths for a decreasing stripe effect. Two colors or shades of ribbon can easily be woven into a nostalgic basket-weave pattern.
- Use paper for wrapping and trimming. Make a bow by stapling strips of paper together like the spokes of a wheel. Draw the paper over a dull edge to create curls.
- Ordinary items such as small toys, candy and old greeting cards make eye-catching trims and may be used to hint at the contents of the package.
- If you run low on a favored gift-wrapping paper, wrap the gift in a matching solid and use the scraps as trim.
- Dress up the obvious. If the gift is a tie or a giveaway shape, use trims and bows to give the package a little extra pizzazz. You may even be able to hide the shape.
- Coordinate the wrapping of different gifts for a dazzling foot-of-the-tree array.

IDEAS FOR CLEVER PACKAGING

There are many other ways you can wrap up your presents besides the ordinary ribbon-and-paper routine.

Decorate with unusual trims:
- Deck out a hostess gift with tinsel and an ornament she can hang on her tree!
- Tie up a home-sewer's present with pretty eyelet trim she'll use later on.
- Use leftover yarn as "ribbon" on a knitter's gift; a pair of knitting needles makes an interesting "bow."
- Please a little girl with a streamer of hair ribbons to wear all year long.
- Tuck a silk flower into a bow—it will look lovely in a bud vase for the rest of the year.
- Guarantee a thank-you: Put a sprig of artificial mistletoe atop his tie box!
- Delight a gardener with a bright bunch of seed packets strung together.

REVIVING OLD GIFT WRAP AND BOWS
- *To take the wrinkles out of gift wrap, spray the underside with starch; iron.*
- *To perk up a ribbon bow, run a curling iron in and out of each loop.*

Wrap up with your local newspaper:
- Make kids laugh with the comics; top with lollipops.
- Give a crossword buff a clue with the puzzle page; trim with pencil and eraser.

- Put a new homeowner's gift inside the real estate ads.
- Impress a businessperson with the stock market pages (or *The Wall Street Journal*). Top with a bag of chocolate gold coins.

Try other clever paper substitutes:
- Wrap a magazine subscription card in the cover of an old issue.
- Point your favorite jogger in the right direction with a map of the city; tie with a pair of shoelaces.
- Fancy up plain brown paper with gold cord and a First Prize blue ribbon.
- Strike the right note with sheet music for a record or concert tickets.
- Ask your child to draw a picture—this wrapping gets raves from Grandma!
- Decorate colored tissue paper with stickers for a youngster's gift.
- Turn on the holiday glow with wine bottles wrapped in aluminum foil. Put confetti inside the foil and tie with paper streamers.
- Use a travel poster for someone on the go.

- Appeal to a lawyer with a blank legal form and close with gold notary seals. (Try graph paper for an architect or engineer.)

STORING GIFT WRAP
- *Store rolls of gift wrap in long cardboard floral boxes used for long-stemmed roses. Or, reroll it tightly, then insert it inside the wrapping's cardboard tube.*

Use containers instead of paper:
- Cover an empty candy box with plush red velvet; make a bow with lace.
- Fill an apothecary jar with a batch of your best cookies. Top with a cookie cutter.
- Glue fabric to the cover of a gift box, then to the bottom—it will be a handy storage box after the holidays.
- Put cash or gift certificates in old-style tins or piggy banks.
- Give a casserole dish with some of your favorite recipes and a few of the herbs and spices needed—just tie with a big bow!

Note: *See page 277 for tips on packaging food gifts.*

♥ *Yuletide wine wish: Select an out-of-the-ordinary wine and top it off with a written toast for a happy holiday.*

TO SEND A GIFT BY MAIL

Time it right

The Postal Service offers a wide range of delivery options for mailing packages, depending on the amount of money you want to spend and the time you've allowed for delivery. A good general rule to follow is to mail early in the day and early in the month. As for first-class letters and cards, those sent coast-to-coast should arrive within 3 to 4 days; those greetings sent within the state should arrive within 2 to 3 days; and those mailed to an address within a city should reach their destination in 2 days. However, as we all know, the Christmas season is the busiest time of the year for mail carriers, so it's best to allow at least two weeks for domestic delivery of holiday cards and gifts just to be on the safe side.

Select the proper container

Fiberboard containers (commonly found in supermarkets or hardware stores) are generally strong enough for mailing things of average weight and size—up to 10 lbs. Paperboard cartons (similar to suit boxes) can also be used for items of up to 10 lbs. Some boxes have what is known as a "test board" rating, which indicates how strong they are. For example, a corrugated fiberboard box (125-lb. test board) is good for mailing weights up to 20 lbs. High-density items, such as tools, require a stronger container (strength is indicated by a round imprint on a bottom corner of the box).

Insure your packages

Any gift sent by mail should be insured. You can insure your package in varying amounts for up to $400. The cost is minimal, and you have the added security of knowing that in case anything does happen to the package, you will be reimbursed. If you are mailing something that is worth more than $400 or if you are sending cash or an irreplaceable item through the mail, send it by registered mail.

Use ZIP codes

The easiest way to delay delivery of mail is to forget the ZIP Code, or to use the wrong one. So, when addressing your package, be sure to include the ZIP code in both the recipient's and your return address.

How to package your gifts

Soft goods, like clothing, pillows and blankets, should be placed in a self-supporting box or tear-resistant bag—the box closed with reinforced tape, the bag sealed properly.

Perishables, such as cheese, fruit, vegetables, meat or anything with an odor, must be placed in an impermeable container, filled with absorbent cushioning and sealed with filament tape.

Fragile items, such as glasses, dishes or photography equipment, are safest packaged in fiberboard containers (minimum 175-lb. test board) and cushioned with foamed plastic or padding. Seal the package and reinforce with filament tape.

Shifting contents, including books, tools or nails, should be packaged in fiberboard containers (minimum 175-lb. test board). Make sure that you use interior fiberboard separators or tape to prevent the contents of the parcel from shifting in transit. Seal the package and reinforce it with filament tape.

Awkward loads, such as gloves, pipes or odd-shaped tools or instruments, require special packaging. Use fiberboard tubes or boxes with length not more than 10 times their girth. Cushioning must be of preformed fiberboard or foamed plastic shapes, and the closure should be as strong as the tube itself.

Use adequate cushioning

If you are mailing several gift items in one package, wrap them individually and protect each one from the other with padding or foamed plastic. To prevent one item from damaging another, make sure you fill the box completely with cushioning material, leaving no empty space. Polystyrene, shredded, rolled or crumpled newspaper, "bubble" plastic and fiberboard are all good cushioning materials. Commercially available foam shells or airpocket padding can also be used, as well as padded mailing bags (good for small items).

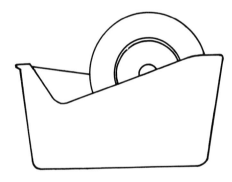

Seal your carton properly

Use one of three recommended types of tape to secure your parcel: pressure-sensitive filament tape, nylon-reinforced Kraft paper tape or plain Kraft paper tape. All three types are available in stationery stores or dime stores. There's no need to wrap your container with brown paper or tie it with twine. Paper sometimes rips in handling, and twine often gets entangled in mail-processing equipment.

Request special markings

Certain phrases printed on the outside of your parcel will alert Postal Service employees to the nature of its contents. Mark breakable objects FRAGILE in three places; above the address, below the postage and on the reverse side. Packages of food or other items which can decay should be marked PERISHABLE in the same locations. The words DO NOT BEND on your package will signal a fragile item, but the sender must have first protected these and similar articles with stiffening material. When you take your packages to the post office for mailing, ask the clerk to stamp them appropriately.

Traditional Christmas Dinner

THE HOLIDAY SPREAD

Whether you're just having a few couples over or planning a large party for family and friends, here's a quintet of menus planned from beginning to end. Each includes a handy meal preparation countdown, with make-ahead tips where possible.

A "Traditional Christmas Dinner" for 8 (pages 164-173) focuses around a maple-glazed ham with all the trimmings. For dessert, choose between two special recipes using holiday ingredients—cranberries and pumpkins.

A "Danish Open House Buffet" for 24 (pages 174-183) is built around a Danish theme. Assorted open-faced sandwiches—Smørrebrød—are accompanied by delicious meat, fish and vegetable side dishes, all to be enjoyed with Gløgg, a Danish mulled wine. A regal Kransekage teams up with assorted rich butter cookies for an irresistible dessert.

A "Christmas Morning Brunch" for 10 (pages 184-191) is heartier than breakfast—and more exciting! Worthy of robust Victorian diners, this meal features breakfast meats, eggs and mouth-watering pastries.

An "International Feast" for 12 (pages 192-203) combines salad and quick breads with the distinctive flavors of Italy and Holland. For dessert, classic Bûche de Noël is paired with an apple custard pie.

Because many of us have to loosen our belts a few notches as the holiday season progresses, "Dinner on the Light Side" (pages 204-213), a meal for 10, pares away some of the calories lurking in holiday fare. But your guests won't miss them, because the meal is colorful and full of flavor. Its crowning glory, Velvety Creme Chocolate, weighs in at a mere 104 calories per serving!

⑤ Low-Cost　　**⚡** Quick and Easy　　**《《《** Make-Ahead　　**▓▓▓** Low-Calorie

TRADITIONAL CHRISTMAS DINNER

(for 8)

Mulled Cider*
Butternut Squash Bisque*
Maple-Glazed Ham* with
Pineapple Doughnuts* and Raisin Sauce*
Yankee Succotash*
Fluffy Mashed Potatoes*
Buttered Brussels Sprouts*
Creamed Beans and Onions*
Assorted Relishes
Lemon-Caraway Muffins*
Colonial Cranberry Pie*
Pumpkin Steamed Pudding*
Rich Butterscotch Sauce*
Hot Coffee
Cordials

*recipe follows

A Note About Flour

Unless sifted flour is specified in a recipe, gently spoon the flour straight from your canister into a dry measuring cup. Level the top with a knife.

From the glazed ham to the cranberry pie, this spread includes delectably rich fare for an unforgettable holiday feast.

Up to 1 month ahead:
● Prepare Pumpkin Steamed Pudding and Lemon-Caraway Muffins, then put them in the freezer after labeling and dating them.
The day before:
● Bake Colonial Cranberry Pie and store it at room temperature.
● Parboil the beans and onions for Creamed Beans and Onions.
● Trim and wash Brussels sprouts for Buttered Brussels Sprouts.
● Dice the bacon and onion for Yankee Succotash.
● Make and freeze Pineapple Doughnuts.
● Prepare Butternut Squash Bisque through Step 2, then cover and refrigerate.
At party time:
● Roast Maple-Glazed Ham.
● Make Rich Butterscotch Sauce.
● Prepare Yankee Succotash, Fluffy Mashed Potatoes, Buttered Brussels Sprouts and Creamed Beans and Onions.
● Reheat and glaze Lemon-Caraway Muffins.
● Bake Pineapple Doughnuts.
● Make Raisin Sauce.
● Heat and complete Butternut Squash Bisque.
During dinner:
● Reheat Pumpkin Steamed Pudding, then Colonial Cranberry Pie and Rich Butterscotch Sauce.
● Prepare the coffee.

For most families, Christmas dinner is a time to enjoy traditional holiday foods—turkey or ham roasted to a turn, a harvest's worth of fruits and vegetables, freshly baked breads and warm-from-the oven pies and puddings.

This Traditional Dinner begins with a spiked hot cider punch, then a creamy soup made from butternut squash. A whole ham, glazed with cranberry jelly and maple syrup, is served with a variety of taste-tempting vegetable side dishes. Offer a tangy cranberry pie and pumpkin pudding served with a buttery brown sugar sauce for dessert.

MULLED CIDER

For a nonalcoholic version of this punch, substitute one additional cup of cider for the applejack.

Makes 8 servings.

 4 **cups apple cider**
 ¼ **cup sugar**
 3 **cinnamon sticks**
 4 **whole cloves**
 1 **cup applejack**
    Orange slices

1. Combine the cider, sugar, cinnamon sticks and cloves in a large saucepan.
2. Bring to boiling over low heat, stirring several times.
3. Remove the saucepan from the heat. Stir in the applejack; add the orange slices. Return to the heat and simmer for 2 minutes.
4. Transfer the mixture to a heatproof punch bowl. Serve in demitasse cups.

Make-ahead Note: A few hours ahead, simmer 1 cup of the cider with the sugar and the cinnamon sticks. Heat until the sugar dissolves; reserve. At serving time, add the remaining cider and complete the recipe from Step 2.

CAPTURING CHRISTMAS IN PHOTOS

Capture the intimate, hilarious, surprising and gratifying moments of the season. Experts at Kodak share some picture-taking tips:
● *Begin photographing early. Look for shoppers returning from a spree, a wreath on the front door, newly baked Christmas cookies still on the sheet.*
● *Shoot photos from different angles. Kneel on the floor, for example, to shoot the tree from below.*
● *Be sure that a shot has a central point of interest because too much clutter makes for an unconvincing photo.*
● *Move in close on little gifts, step back for big ones. Be sure to catch the new owner beside his treasure.*
● *Watch out for sparkling or shiny objects—glassware, mirrors, polished metal, silver, chrome—that may cause reflection. Choose an angle that reduces glare.*

BUTTERNUT SQUASH BISQUE

A delicious way to use the season's produce.

Makes 8 servings.

> 2 **pounds butternut squash, pared, halved,**
>   **seeded and cubed**
> 4 **tart apples, pared, cored, cubed**
> 1 **large onion, chopped**
> 4 **slices white bread, trimmed and cubed**
> 2 **quarts chicken broth**
> ½ **teaspoon pepper**
> ½ **teaspoon ground rosemary**
> ½ **teaspoon ground marjoram**
> 4 **egg yolks, slightly beaten**
> ½ **cup heavy cream**
>   **Salt, if necessary**
>   **Apple slices and fresh rosemary sprig for**
>   **garnish (optional)**

1. Combine the squash, apples, onion, bread, chicken broth, pepper, rosemary and marjoram in a saucepan. Bring to boiling. Lower the heat; simmer, uncovered, for 35 minutes, or until the squash and apples are tender. Remove from the heat. Cool to lukewarm.
2. Working in batches, spoon the soup into the container of an electric blender or food processor. Cover; whirl until puréed. Return the soup to the saucepan. Reheat the soup gently over very low heat.
3. Mix together the egg yolks and the cream in a small bowl. Beat in a little of the hot soup; return the yolk mixture to the saucepan, stirring. Heat gently to serve. Do not boil, or the eggs will curdle. Taste and add salt, if necessary. Transfer to a soup tureen. Garnish with thin unpeeled apple slices and a fresh rosemary sprig, if you wish.

Make-ahead Note: Prepare the soup through Step 2, but do not reheat. Cover and refrigerate. At serving time, slowly reheat the soup and continue with Step 3.

WINTER SQUASH

● *Choose squash that are firm, unblemished and have a hard skin (butternut squash has a waxy exterior).*
● *Acorn squash that weigh about one pound each make edible containers for entrée and vegetable fillings.*
● *Bake squash whole or halve, scoop out the seeds and string, then pare and cut up. Steam or boil until tender. Serve as is with butter, cinnamon and honey, or mash and season with butter, milk and sweet sherry.*

MAPLE-GLAZED HAM

Maple syrup combined with cranberry jelly gives ham a delicious flavor and an attractive color.

Roast at 350° for 3 hours, 30 minutes.
Makes 8 servings, plus leftovers.

> 1 **whole, fully cooked, bone-in ham**
>   **(about 14 pounds)**
> ½ **teaspoon ground cloves**
> 1 **can (12 ounces) ginger ale**
> 1 **can (1 pound) cranberry jelly**
> ½ **cup maple OR: pancake syrup**
> 1 **can (1 pound) fruits for salad, drained**
>   **Green grapes**
>   **Pineapple Doughnuts (recipe follows)**
>   **Salt and pepper**
> 1 **cup raisins**
> 2 **tablespoons white Port wine**

1. Preheat the oven to moderate (350°).
2. Trim the excess fat from the ham and score the remaining fat in a diamond pattern. Rub the ham with the ground cloves. Place, fat-side up, in a shallow roasting pan; pour the ginger ale over.
3. Roast in the preheated moderate oven (350°) for 3 hours, basting often with the ginger ale.
4. Heat the cranberry jelly in a small saucepan; stir in the maple or pancake syrup and heat to bubbling. Brush the glaze on the ham.
5. Roast 20 minutes, basting the ham several times. Arrange the fruits for salad and the green grapes in a decorative pattern on the ham, then brush with the remaining glaze. Roast for 10 minutes longer, or until richly glazed.
6. Place the ham on a heated platter and garnish the platter with the Pineapple Doughnuts (recipe follows).
7. Pour the fat from the roasting pan. Stir 1 cup of water into the pan. Bring to boiling. Lower the heat; simmer, stirring up all baked-on juices, until thickened. Taste and season with salt and pepper. Add the raisins and the wine. Pour the sauce into a heated sauceboat.

Cook's Tip: After baking the Maple-Glazed Ham, reheat the Lemon-Caraway Muffins, then raise the oven temperature to hot (425°) and bake the doughnuts.

HAM

- *Do not freeze ham. Instead, keep it refrigerated, whether cooked or uncooked. Be sure to use it within a week.*
- *"Fully cooked" ham is completely cooked and ready to eat without further cooking. If desired, it may be reheated.*
- *"Ready to eat" ham improves in texture and flavor if you cook it before serving.*
- *"Cook before eating" ham must be cooked before serving.*
- *Canned ham is ready to use, cold or reheated. Slice it before heating to reduce the cooking time.*
- *Do not glaze a ham until 30 minutes before the end of the baking time. Otherwise, the glaze may burn.*

PINEAPPLE DOUGHNUTS

Bake at 425° for 30 minutes.
Makes 8 servings.

1 can (20 ounces) sliced pineapple in heavy syrup, drained
1 package (17 ounces) frozen puff pastry
Granulated sugar
Pumpkin pie spice
1 egg, lightly beaten

1. Three to 4 hours before serving time, place 8 of the pineapple slices on paper towels and let drain for 30 minutes. (Reserve the remaining 2 slices for another use.)
2. Thaw the puff pastry, following the package directions. Cut each sheet into 4 squares; roll out each square 1 inch longer and 1 inch wider on a lightly floured pastry cloth or board.
3. Sprinkle the pineapple with the sugar and pumpkin pie spice; place each slice on a pastry square. Wrap the pastry around the pineapple, pinching the ends to seal and trimming the excess dough from the bottom. Turn right-side up and shape the pastry around the pineapple to form a circle. Carefully cut an "X" in the middle with a sharp paring knife; enlarge to neaten the hole with your finger.
4. Place the doughnuts on a medium-size ungreased cookie sheet. Freeze until 30 minutes before serving.
5. Preheat the oven to very hot (425°).
6. Brush the doughnuts with the beaten egg.
7. Bake in the preheated very hot oven (425°) for 30 minutes, or until puffed and golden brown. Serve warm as a garnish around the ham.

YANKEE SUCCOTASH

Bacon and chunks of tomatoes turn everyday succotash into a holiday vegetable dish.

Makes 8 servings.

4 slices bacon, diced
1 large onion, chopped (1 cup)
1 bag (1 pound) frozen whole-kernel corn
1 bag (1 pound) frozen lima beans
1 can (1 pound) whole tomatoes, undrained
1 teaspoon salt
1 teaspoon leaf thyme, crumbled
¼ teaspoon pepper

1. Fry the bacon until crisp. Remove with a slotted spoon and drain on paper towels.
2. Sauté the onion until soft in the bacon drippings. Stir in the frozen corn and lima beans. Drain the tomato liquid into the saucepan. Add the salt, thyme and pepper; cover the saucepan.
3. Bring to boiling. Lower the heat and simmer for 5 minutes. Cut the tomatoes into chunks and add along with the bacon to the saucepan. Simmer for 5 minutes longer. Spoon into a heated serving dish, just before serving. Garnish with parsley, if desired.

Make-ahead Note: Dice the bacon and onion. Wrap and refrigerate.

SHINING EXAMPLES—Party fare demands glowing crystal, flatware and china.
Crystal Clear
- *Place a towel in the bottom of sink to act as a cushion; remove rings. Fill the sink with warm soapy water. Wash the crystal, one piece at a time. Rinse in clear warm water, then dry with a lint-free cloth.*
- *For decanters and vases, gently pour in sand or raw rice. Add warm soapy water and swirl.*
Spotless Flatware
- *Wash the pieces as soon after use as possible.*
- *Hand-wash in hot soapy water. Rinse, then dry at once.*
- *Never use steel-wool pads, coarse powders or abrasives.*
- *Remove flatware from dishwasher after last rinse and hand-dry, or use detergent with a watershedding additive.*
- *Use silverplate or sterling silver frequently so you won't have to polish it very often.*
- *Store less-used silver in tarnish-proof bags.*
China Care
- *When washing in a dishwasher, use a mild detergent.*
- *Never use harsh detergents or abrasives.*

FLUFFY MASHED POTATOES

An electric hand mixer makes quick work of mashed potatoes.

Makes 8 servings.

8 large boiling potatoes (about 3 pounds)
¼ cup (½ stick) butter or margarine
½ cup milk
1 teaspoon salt
¼ teaspoon freshly ground pepper
** Butter or margarine**
** Paprika**

1. Pare and quarter the potatoes. Cover with salted water in a large kettle; bring to boiling.
2. Lower the heat; simmer for 20 minutes, or until the potatoes are tender when pierced with a two-tined fork. Drain.
3. Return the potatoes to the kettle and toss over low heat until potatoes fluff up. Add the ¼ cup of butter or margarine and the milk. Heat slowly until the butter melts.
4. Mash the potatoes, first with a potato masher, then with an electric hand mixer, until light and fluffy. Season with the salt and pepper and spoon into a heated serving bowl. Top with a few slices of butter and sprinkle with the paprika. Keep warm in the oven until serving time.

Cook's Tip: The cooking water from potatoes and other vegetables is vitamin-rich and flavorful, so don't throw it out. Strain it into a large bowl; when cool, pour it into glass or plastic jars and refrigerate. Use in soups, sauces and stews.

BUTTERED BRUSSELS SPROUTS

Chestnuts add seasonal flair to a favorite winter vegetable.

Makes 8 servings.

1 container (1 pint) Brussels sprouts
** OR: 2 packages (9 ounces each) frozen**
** Brussels sprouts**
1 cup chicken broth
** Salt, if desired**
¼ teaspoon freshly ground pepper
¼ teaspoon ground mace
1 can (15 ounces) whole chestnuts, drained
¼ cup (½ stick) butter or margarine

1. Remove only the bruised leaves from the fresh Brussels sprouts; cut an "X" in the stem-end of each sprout. Wash in salted warm water.
2. Bring the chicken broth to boiling in a large saucepan; add the fresh or frozen sprouts, salt, pepper and mace. Bring to boiling. Lower the heat to simmering and break apart the frozen sprouts with 2 forks. Stir in the drained chestnuts and cover the pan.
3. Cook the frozen sprouts for 5 minutes, the fresh sprouts for 15 minutes, or until crisp-tender. Remove with a slotted spoon to a heated vegetable bowl, reserving the cooking liquid for soup making. Add butter or margarine to the bowl; toss.

Watch Cooking Time: To avoid unpleasant odors, be careful not to overcook the sprouts.

CANDLE CARE AND USAGE

- *Store candles flat in a dark, dry place, to prevent warping.*
- *Revive less-than-new candles by rubbing them clean with an old nylon stocking or soft cloth moistened with salad oil.*
- *Freeze candles for one hour to make them burn longer, drip less.*
- *Char wicks before the party, so they'll light in an instant.*
- *Choose dripless candles; otherwise, set them on a plate or tray to catch drips and save furniture and tablecloths.*
- *Never leave a candle-lit room unattended.*
- *If a candle is too small for its holder, wrap the bottom in aluminum foil. If it's too big, gently whittle the bottom down to size with a sharp knife.*
- *To lessen candle wax stains on a tablecloth, lift off as much solid wax as possible, then place the stained area between clean paper towels. Press lightly with a warm iron.*
- *Place wax-coated candle holders in the freezer for one hour. The wax will peel off.*
- *To remove wax from wooden finishes, soften the wax with a hair dryer and remove with paper towels. Wipe off residue with a mixture of vinegar and water.*
- *To remove wax stains from a carpet or rug, scrape off the excess. Cover with several layers of paper towels, then carefully press with a warm iron.*

CREAMED BEANS AND ONIONS

A traditional holiday side dish.

Makes 8 servings.

1 pound small white onions
¼ cup (½ stick) butter or margarine
¼ cup all-purpose flour
2 cups light cream
1 teaspoon salt
¼ teaspoon pepper
¼ teaspoon ground nutmeg
1 bag (1 pound) frozen cut green beans,
   cooked and drained

1. Pour boiling water over the onions in a small bowl; allow to stand for 2 minutes; drain the water and peel the onions. Cut an "X" in the root-end of each onion.

2. Cook in salted boiling water in a large saucepan for 15 minutes, or until the onions are tender when pierced with a two-tined fork; drain. (This can be done the day before. Place in a bowl and cover with plastic wrap and refrigerate.)

3. Melt the butter or margarine in a large saucepan. Stir in the flour and cook until the mixture bubbles. Stir in the cream, salt, pepper and nutmeg. Cook, stirring constantly, until the sauce thickens and bubbles for 2 minutes.

4. Add the boiled onions and cooked green beans, and heat for 5 minutes, or until bubbly hot. Spoon onto a heated serving dish.

LIGHT FANTASTIC

Depending on the mood you want to create, indoor lighting can be bright and cheery or soft and subtle.
● *A brightly lit entrance makes guests feel welcome.*
● *Bring a museum technique to your home: Use spotlights to show off plants, prized art or personal collections.*
● *Keep serving areas at buffet parties well lit, so guests can see the food.*
● *Electrical light dimmers save money and let you adjust overhead light to the perfect level.*
● *Candles cast a soft romantic glow on the dining table and your guests. (See below for usage tips and decorative ideas.)*
● *Bright lights are an easy way to signal the end of a party to guests who've overstayed their welcome.*

CANDLELIGHT

Cast the soft, gentle glow of flickering candles whenever you give a party.
● *Burn classic tapers at formal affairs, rounds or votives for more casual parties.*
● *Place long candles on the buffet table; candles on the dining table should be short enough for guests to see each other.*
● *Color-coordinate candles with the rest of the table decor.*
● *Break the rules. Mix colors and heights instead of using traditional matched sets. Set candles at each place setting, instead of using one large centerpiece.*
● *Candle holders can be as formal as crystal, as casual as small flowerpots—use whatever is appropriate to the occasion.*
● *Use scented candles to create special effects: Try vanilla and cinnamon at a dessert buffet, bayberry at a traditional meal.*
● *Set floating candles in a punch bowl or shallow container filled with water.*

💲 🔊
LEMON-CARAWAY MUFFINS

The old-fashioned taste of caraway complements these lemon-glazed muffins.

Bake at 400° for 20 minutes.
Makes 1 dozen muffins.

2 cups all-purpose flour
¼ cup sugar
1 tablespoon baking powder
½ teaspoon salt
 Grated rind of 1 lemon
¼ cup (½ stick) butter or margarine
1 teaspoon caraway seeds
1 cup milk
1 egg, beaten
 Lemon Glaze (recipe follows)

1. Preheat the oven to hot (400°).
2. Sift the flour, sugar, baking powder and salt into a medium-size bowl. Stir in the grated lemon rind.
3. Melt the butter or margarine with the caraway seeds in a small saucepan over low heat; cool slightly, then add the milk and beaten egg.
4. Add the liquid all at once to the flour mixture, stirring only until just moistened—the batter will be lumpy.
5. Spoon the batter into 12 greased muffin-pan cups, filling ⅔ full.
6. Bake in the preheated hot oven (400°) for 20 minutes, or until golden. Cool for 5 minutes in the pan on a wire rack; invert onto the rack. Brush with the Lemon Glaze and serve warm.

Make-ahead Note: To freeze the muffins, let cool completely and do not glaze. Label, date and freeze, following the directions on page 191. Heat in a preheated moderate oven (350°) for 15 minutes, or until heated through. Glaze and serve.

LEMON GLAZE: Makes enough to top 1 dozen muffins. Mix 1 teaspoon of lemon juice with 2 tablespoons of 10X (confectioners' powdered) sugar in a 1-cup measure until blended; brush onto the warm muffins.

THE PERFECT MUFFIN

● *Always sift the dry ingredients together.*
● *Cool the melted shortening slightly before you use it, to prevent cooking the egg when you mix the batter together.*
● *Stir liquid into the dry ingredients just until mixed. (Batter should be lumpy.) Overmixing causes tough, coarse-textured results.*
● *Fill greased muffin-pan cups only two-thirds full.*

COLONIAL CRANBERRY PIE

Applejack adds extra zest to a rich cranberry-raisin crisscross pie.

Bake at 400° for 35 minutes.
Makes one 10-inch pie.

2 cans (1 pound each) whole cranberry sauce
1 cup raisins
¼ cup applejack
½ cup all-purpose flour
¼ cup sugar
½ teaspoon ground mace
1 cup chopped pecans
Rich Pastry (recipe follows)

1. Preheat the oven to hot (400°).
2. Combine the cranberry sauce, raisins and applejack in a large saucepan; bring to boiling; simmer for 5 minutes. Combine the flour, sugar and mace in a small bowl and stir into the cranberry mixture. Cook, stirring constantly, for 3 minutes. Remove from the heat and cool completely; stir in the nuts.
3. Prepare the Rich Pastry and roll out half to a 13-inch round on a lightly floured pastry cloth or board. Fit into a 10-inch pie plate.
4. Pour the cooled cranberry mixture over the pastry.
5. Roll out the remaining pastry into a 12x6-inch rectangle; cut the pastry into twelve ½-inch-wide strips.
6. To weave the lattice top: Lay half the pastry strips evenly on top of the cranberry filling. Fold alternate strips halfway back; lay the first cross strip near the center of the pie. Bring the folded strips back over it; continue, alternating folded-back strips each time a cross strip is added.
7. Trim the edges to ½ inch; turn under and flute.
8. Bake in the preheated hot oven (400°) for 35 minutes, or until the filling bubbles up and the pastry turns golden brown. Cool in the pan on a wire rack.

Make-ahead Note: Bake the pie a day ahead and store at room temperature. Reheat in a slow oven (325°) for 15 minutes.

ANOTHER WAY TO WEAVE A PASTRY LATTICE

Weave pastry strips on a sheet of wax paper. Carefully invert the whole lattice over the filling, then peel off the wax paper. Trim and crimp edges.

RICH PASTRY

Makes one 10-inch double crust.

3 cups all-purpose flour
1 teaspoon salt
1 cup vegetable shortening
⅓ cup very cold water

Combine the flour and salt in a medium-size bowl. Cut in the shortening with a pastry blender until the mixture is crumbly. Sprinkle the water over, one tablespoon at a time, tossing with a fork until pastry holds together. Wrap in wax paper.

PERFECT PIECRUSTS

- *Avoid overhandling the dough.*
- *Only use as much flour as is needed to prevent sticking.*
- *Never pull or stretch the dough. Ease it into the pan.*
- *To minimize shrinking, chill the pastry shell before baking.*
- *To prevent soggy bottom crusts, pour your filling into the crust just before baking. Or, partially bake the empty crust and line it with aluminum foil. Fill it with raw beans or rice to weigh down the dough. Bake until partially set but not colored, then carefully remove the foil and beans. Fill and finish baking.*
- *If crust browns too fast, lightly cover it with aluminum foil, shiny-side up. Continue baking until the filling is set.*

💲 𝕂𝕂
PUMPKIN STEAMED PUDDING

A different way to enjoy one's holiday pumpkin.

Steam for 2 hours.
Makes 8 servings.

- **1½ cups all-purpose flour**
- **1 cup instant mashed potato powder**
- **1 teaspoon baking soda**
- **½ teaspoon salt**
- **1½ teaspoons pumpkin pie spice**
- **¼ cup (½ stick) butter or margarine**
- **¾ cup firmly packed brown sugar**
- **2 eggs**
- **1 teaspoon vanilla**
- **1 teaspoon grated orange rind**
- **¼ cup orange juice**
- **1 cup pumpkin (from an about-1-pound can)**
- **½ cup chopped walnuts**
  Packaged unseasoned bread crumbs
  Rich Butterscotch Sauce (recipe follows)
  Flaked coconut and chopped walnuts for garnish (optional)

1. Combine the flour, instant mashed potato powder, baking soda, salt and pumpkin pie spice in a medium-size bowl.
2. Beat the butter or margarine with the brown sugar in a large bowl with an electric mixer at high speed; beat in the eggs, vanilla and orange rind.
3. Add the dry ingredients, alternately with the orange juice, beating well after each addition. Fold in the pumpkin and the walnuts with a rubber scraper.
4. Grease an 8-cup tube mold. Sprinkle with the bread crumbs; tap out the excess. Pour the batter into the prepared mold. Cover with a double thickness of heavy-duty aluminum foil and fasten with string to hold tightly.
5. Place on a rack or trivet in a kettle or steamer. Pour in boiling water to half the depth of the pudding in the mold; cover the kettle tightly.
6. Steam for 2 hours, or until a long, thin skewer inserted near the center comes out clean. (Keep the water boiling gently during the entire time, adding more boiling water, if needed.)
7. Cool the mold for 5 minutes. Loosen the pudding around the edge with a knife; unmold onto a serving plate; cool slightly. Spoon about ¼ cup hot Rich Butterscotch Sauce over the pudding. Top with

flaked coconut and chopped walnuts, if you wish. Cut in wedges and serve with the remaining sauce.

Make-ahead Note: After unmolding the pudding, cool completely. Wrap in heavy-duty aluminum foil; label, date and freeze. To reheat, bake the thawed pudding in a preheated slow oven (300°) for 20 to 30 minutes.

Baker's Tip: Steamed puddings make wonderful gifts to give to special friends. The above recipe can be made in two 4-cup molds and steamed for 1½ hours.

RICH BUTTERSCOTCH SAUCE: Makes 1½ cups. Combine 1¼ cups of firmly packed light brown sugar, ¼ cup of heavy cream, 2 tablespoons of light corn syrup and ¼ cup (½ stick) of butter or margarine in a small saucepan. Heat to boiling, then cook for 1 minute. Remove from the heat; stir in 1 teaspoon of vanilla. Serve hot.

Pumpkin Steamed Pudding

DANISH OPEN HOUSE BUFFET

(for 24)

Gløgg*
Smørrebrød Buffet*
Herring Salad*
Leverpostej (Liver Pâté)*, Crackers
Frikadeller (Meatballs)*, Pickled Beets
Mushrooms and Tomatoes*
Mustards, Pickles
Sprutter (Pressed Cookies)*
Jødekager (Jewish Cakes)*
Kransekage (Wreath Cake)*
Hot Coffee
Aquavit

*recipe follows

Danish Open House Buffet

*For a tasty departure from your usual holiday meals,
try this sumptuous Scandinavian buffet.*

Up to 1 month ahead:
● Bake and freeze Sprutter and Jødekager (or bake and store for up to 1 week).

Up to several days ahead:
● Bake and refrigerate Leverpostej.
● Bake rings for Kransekage.

The day before:
● Prepare and refrigerate the following Smørrebrød ingredients: butter-mustard, hard-cooked eggs and chopped parsley for Savory Ham, and dill mayonnaise and cooked shrimp for Rejer.
● Assemble Kransekage.
● Make and refrigerate Herring Salad.
● Make and refrigerate meat mixture for Frikadeller.
● Make and refrigerate Mushrooms and Tomatoes.

Several hours before:
● Make Smørrebrød, cover it with plastic wrap, then refrigerate.
● Unmold Leverpostej onto platters and refrigerate.
● Place Herring Salad and Mushrooms and Tomatoes in bowls. Cover and refrigerate.
● Make the spiced base for Gløgg.
● Arrange the cookies on platters.

At party time:
● Arrange Smørrebrød on platters and add garnish.
● Fry Frikadeller. Keep them warm or place the dish on a hot plate.
● Finish Gløgg.
● Make coffee.

In Denmark, this buffet would be served around midnight on New Year's Eve. But you can serve 24 people also on Christmas Eve or Christmas Day with this generous spread.

Gløgg—Danish mulled wine—blends spiced red wine with caraway-flavored aquavit, raisins and almonds.

Like many Danish meals, this feast centers around Smørrebrød, a lavish assortment of open-faced sandwiches. Frikadeller, light and fluffy meatballs, Leverpostej, a cream-enriched liver pâté, and Herring Salad are rich accompaniments to the sandwiches. For dessert, serve hot coffee and more aquavit with rich butter cookies and Kransekage, the crowning glory of cakes.

PARTY ICE CUBES

Fill containers of an ice cube tray with small strawberry halves, mint sprigs or pieces of orange. Add water or juice and freeze.

GLØGG

A Danish-style mulled wine, made with caraway-flavored aquavit.

Makes 24 servings.

  4 bottles (1 liter each) Burgundy wine
  2 cups sugar
20 whole cardamom seeds, peeled
20 whole cloves
  8 two-inch pieces stick cinnamon
¼ cup finely grated orange rind
  1 bottle (750 ml.) Danish aquavit
  2 cups raisins
  1 cup sliced blanched almonds

1. Pour the wine into a very large kettle. Add the sugar, cardamom, cloves, cinnamon and orange rind. Simmer slowly, without boiling, until the sugar dissolves completely.

2. Add the aquavit. Heat, then light with a long match and let burn down.

3. Strain part of the mixture into a fondue pot over a candle warmer and add part of the raisins. Keep hot and serve in mugs or in heatproof cups with handles. Add the almonds just before serving. Replenish wine and raisins as needed.

Make-ahead Note: Several hours ahead, simmer 2 cups of the wine with the sugar, cardamom seeds, cloves, cinnamon and orange rind, until the sugar dissolves completely. Set aside. At serving time, heat the spiced mixture with the remaining wine. Continue with Step 2.

HOLIDAY PARTY BAR

Always be prepared for unexpected guests, as well as what's planned, with a well-stocked bar. To keep costs under control:
● Comparison-shop when you're buying liquid refreshments for any gathering.
● When purchasing sizable quantities of beer, soda, wine or liquor, ask if you can buy at case price.
● Save money by purchasing store brands and private-label liquors.
● Let the use of wine or liquor determine the price you pay for it. If you're mixing drinks where the liquor will be heavily masked by spices or fruit juices, buy an inexpensive brand. The same goes for wines. Buy nonvintage jug wines for punch bases and sangria. You should, however, buy reputable brands of spirits such as scotch or bourbon.

How to Convert to Metric Measures

Metric measure replaces:	U.S. measure
500 milliliter or ½ liter (16.9 oz.)	the pint
750 milliliter (25.4 oz.)	the fifth
one liter (33.8 oz.)	the quart
two liters (67.6 oz.)	the ½ gallon
four liters (135.2 oz.)	the gallon

How Much to Buy

Below is a chart indicating how many drinks you should get from bottles of liquor or wine. If serving wine with dinner, however, figure on fewer glasses to a bottle: 5 to 6 to a liter (quart); 3 to 4 to 750 milliliter (fifth).

	Number of drinks per bottle	
	liter	750 milliliters
Whiskey, gin, vodka (mixed drinks, highballs— 1½-oz. servings)	22	17
Table wines (red, white, rosé— 4- to 5-oz. servings)	6 to 8	5 to 6
Sherry (3-oz. servings)	11	8
Cordials (1-oz. servings)	33	25
Champagne, sparkling wine (4- to 5-oz. servings)	6 to 8	5 to 6

SMØRREBRØD BUFFET

Open-faced sandwiches, called Smørrebrød or buttered bread, are probably the best-known feature of Danish cuisine. They are the perfect choice for holiday entertaining since they can be made ahead and refrigerated—and they add a festive touch to any holiday table. Plan on a minimum of three sandwiches for each guest, plus a few extra for the tray.

For 24 servings, make one batch of each of the 5 recipes below.

SALMON AND SCRAMBLED EGG: Makes 16 sandwiches. Top 16 slices of well-buttered square white bread with 2 cans (1 pound each) of salmon, drained, boned and flaked, OR: 1 pound of sliced smoked salmon and 8 eggs scrambled with cream, salt and pepper. Garnish with sprigs of fresh dill.

SAVORY HAM: Makes 16 sandwiches. Spread a mixture of ¼ cup of butter or margarine and 2 tablespoons of sharp mustard on 16 slices of square pumpernickel bread. Place 1 pound of sliced boiled ham over and top with hard-cooked egg slices and sliced radishes. Garnish the edges with chopped parsley or a piping of yellow mustard.

SMOKED TURKEY: Makes 16 sandwiches. Spread 16 slices of square whole-wheat bread with butter or margarine. Place 1 pound of sliced smoked turkey over the bread and top with a strip of crisply cooked bacon. Garnish with sliced mushrooms.

CHEESE AND HAM: Makes 16 sandwiches. Spread 16 slices of square rye bread with butter or margarine. Arrange 1 pound of sliced Havarti cheese and ½ pound of sliced boiled ham on the bread. Garnish with radish slices.

REJER (Tiny Shrimp): Makes 16 sandwiches. Spread 16 slices of square rye bread with a mixture of 6 tablespoons of mayonnaise or salad dressing, 2 tablespoons of lemon juice and 2 teaspooons of dillweed. Pile with 2 packages (1 pound each) of frozen shelled deveined shrimp, cooked, drained, chopped (if large) and chilled. Drizzle with lemon juice and garnish with lemon peel twists.

GENERAL DIRECTIONS: Place the sandwiches on large cookie sheets. Cover with plastic wrap and refrigerate until serving time. Arrange an assortment of the sandwiches on each of 3 or 4 serving platters. Garnish the platters with rolls of cold meats, watercress and cherry tomatoes. For a distinctive Danish touch, buy some Danish flags at a party supply shop and decorate the platters with them.

HERRING SALAD

The salty tang of herring and the earthy flavor of potatoes and beets blend into a savory fish salad.

Makes 24 servings.

> 4 **jars (12 ounces each) pickled herring**
> 4 **cups finely diced, peeled, cold boiled**
> **potatoes**
> 4 **cups finely diced pickled beets**
> 2 **cups finely diced peeled apples**
> 1⅓ **cups finely chopped onions**
> 4 **teaspoons mustard**
> 2 **teaspoons sugar**
> 2⅔ **cups heavy cream, whipped**
> **Salt**
> **Pepper**
> **Hard-cooked egg slices for garnish**

1. Soak the herring overnight in cold water in the refrigerator. Drain and finely dice.
2. Combine the herring with the potatoes, beets, apples, onions, mustard and sugar in a medium-size bowl.
3. Fold in the whipped cream and season with salt and pepper to taste. Chill until serving time. Spoon onto a chilled serving platter and garnish the top with the hard-cooked egg slices.

PERFECT HARD-COOKED EGGS

Put room-temperature eggs in a saucepan and cover them with cold water. Place the pan over medium heat and bring the water to boiling. Then lower the heat and simmer for 12 minutes. Immediately plunge the eggs into cold water. Crack the shells all over, then roll the eggs between your hands. Carefully peel them under running water. Use an egg slicer for uniform slices or a sharp knife dipped into water before cutting.

LEVERPOSTEJ (Liver Pâté)

A flavorful pâté that's quick to prepare.

Bake at 325° for 1 hour, 30 minutes.
Makes 24 servings.

> 4 **pounds pork or calf's liver**
> 1 **large onion, quartered**
> 2 **pounds pork fat**
> ½ **cup (1 stick) butter or margarine**
> ½ **cup all-purpose flour**
> 4 **cups light cream**
> 4 **eggs, well beaten**
> 4 **teaspoons anchovy paste (or to taste)**
> 4 **teaspoons salt**
> 2 **teaspoons pepper**
> 1 **teaspoon ground ginger**
> **Spinach leaves for garnish**

1. Preheat the oven to slow (325°).
2. Process the pork or calf's liver and the onion, half at at time, in a food processor for 30 seconds, or grind twice in a food grinder, using the finest blade. Grind the pork fat in the processor or grinder.
3. Melt the butter or margarine in a large saucepan. Add the flour and cook, stirring constantly, until bubbly. Stir in the cream and cook, stirring constantly, until the sauce thickens and bubbles for 2 minutes. Add the ground pork fat and cook until the fat melts; remove from the heat.
4. Add the ground liver and onion mixture, the eggs, anchovy paste, salt, pepper and ginger; stir until well blended. Pour into two 8-cup pâté molds or 8-cup springform pans. Place in a baking pan and place on the center rack of the oven. Fill the baking pan to a depth of 2 inches with boiling water.
5. Bake in the preheated slow oven (325°) for 1 hour, 30 minutes, or until the pâté is firm, covering the top with aluminum foil if it darkens too quickly. Remove from the water and cool in the molds on a wire rack. Chill until serving time. Unmold and arrange on a chilled serving plate. Garnish with the spinach leaves and serve with crisp crackers.

S$

FRIKADELLER (Danish Meatballs)

These savory meatballs are extra light because of the addition of club soda.

Makes 4 dozen.

1 **pound ground veal or beef**
1 **pound ground pork**
1 **onion, very finely chopped (1 cup)**
6 **tablespoons all-purpose flour**
3 **cups club soda OR: milk**
2 **eggs, well beaten**
2 **teaspoons salt**
½ **teaspoon pepper**
⅔ **cup butter or margarine**

1. Combine the ground veal or beef and pork in a large bowl and add the onion.
2. Stir in the flour and beat thoroughly. Beat in the club soda or milk, 2 tablespoons at a time, beating constantly to aerate the mixture. Beat in the eggs, salt and pepper. Beat the mixture until fluffy.
3. Shape the mixture into oblongs with 2 teaspoons dipped in water. (If the mixture is hard to shape, refrigerate for 30 minutes, or until thoroughly chilled.)
4. Fry the meatballs in a large skillet in the hot butter or margarine until brown on all sides. Serve with pickled beets, if you wish.

·**Make-ahead Note:** The meat mixture may be prepared a day ahead. Cover well and refrigerate.

SAFETY FIRST

Make your party a safe one:
● *Never wax floors super-slick just before a party.*
● *Store small rugs away from pedestrian traffic.*
● *Tuck all stray electrical cords out of the way.*
● *Don't spray air freshener near food preparation or serving areas (read labels carefully).*
● *Place candles on flameproof trays or holders, away from all flammable materials.*
● *Keep candles and lanterns away from crowded areas.*
● *If glass breaks, insist on taking care of it yourself. Bring a pot holder or towel to pick up the pieces, and a paper bag to carry them away.*

↘ ⦉⦉ ▦

MUSHROOMS AND TOMATOES

Save the marinade and use as a dressing for tossed salad.

Makes 24 servings.

1½ **pounds fresh mushrooms**
2 **pints cherry tomatoes**
2 **lemons, cut up**
1½ **cups vegetable oil**
⅔ **cup lemon juice**
½ **cup snipped fresh dill**
2 **cloves garlic, minced**
  Salt and pepper to taste

1. Halve the mushrooms, if large. Place them in a large glass or ceramic bowl with the cherry tomatoes and lemon pieces.
2. Combine the oil, lemon juice, dill, garlic, salt and pepper in a jar with a screw-top lid. Cover and shake well. Pour over the mushroom mixture; toss to mix. (Coating will be thin.)
3. Cover the bowl with plastic wrap. Marinate for 12 hours, or for up to 24 hours.

LOW-CAL SWITCH CHART

Try serving this	Instead of this
Wine spritzers; light beer; mineral water or club soda with lime; alcohol mixed with water or club soda	Sweet wines; liqueurs; punch; eggnog; alcohol with sugary mixes
Lean, sliced poultry or roast beef; shrimp	High-fat cold cuts; pâté; sausage; Swedish meatballs
Lower-calorie cheeses like Gouda, Camembert, provolone, Neufchâtel	High-calorie cheeses like creamed cottage cheese, Brie, Roquefort
Flatbreads; pretzels; popcorn; breadsticks; whole-grain crackers	Potato, corn or taco chips; salted nuts
Plain crudités	Crudités with dips
Oil and vinegar or plain lemon juice	Blue cheese, Roquefort and Russian dressings
Raisins; dried fruits; fresh apples and pears; hard candy	Fruitcake; gingerbread; Christmas cookies; pie; fudge

SPRUTTER (Pressed Cookies)

Almond extract flavors a butter-rich cookie that gets an even better flavor if allowed to mellow in a tin.

Bake at 400° for 8 minutes.
Makes 5 dozen.

   1 cup (2 sticks) butter or margarine
   ⅔ cup sugar
   3 egg yolks
2½ cups all-purpose flour
   1 teaspoon salt
   ¼ teaspoon almond extract

1. Preheat the oven to hot (400°).
2. Beat the butter or margarine and sugar until fluffy in a large bowl with an electric mixer at high speed. Beat in the egg yolks, one at a time, until creamy-smooth. Blend in the flour, salt and almond extract to make a soft dough.
3. Fit a cookie press with a decorative plate or disk. Fill with part of the dough and press out onto ungreased cookie sheets.
4. Bake in the preheated hot oven (400°) for 8 minutes, or until lightly browned around the edges. Remove with a spatula and cool completely on wire racks. Store in a metal tin with a tight-fitting lid. If desired, freeze, following the directions on page 258.

Baker's Tip: Use the leftover egg whites to brush on the Jødekager (recipe on page 182).

Mulled Cider for a Crowd

If you want to serve mulled cider in a large bowl, use a fondue pot or flameproof bowl. For an added touch of elegance, brush unpeeled apple slices with lemon juice and float them in the hot cider.

HOW TO KEEP YOUR PARTY MOVING

- *The traffic flow of a party must be carefully pre-arranged. Guests should be able to circulate without bumping into furniture—or each other.*
- *Don't invite more guests than your party area can hold.*

Arranging Furniture

- *For large, stand-up affairs, remove unneeded chairs and tables to the side of the room, or out of the room entirely.*
- *Minimize slipping and tripping by rolling up small rugs and tucking electrical cords out of the way.*
- *For small gatherings, be sure that one or two seats aren't isolated. Groupings of three or four are perfect settings for conversation.*
- *Once the party's started, examine the traffic flow to make sure you haven't overlooked an in-the-way object.*

Serving Food

- *Leave an uncluttered route between the kitchen and serving table, so you can bring out food without detours.*
- *Large buffet parties require special furniture arrangements: Make a triangle out of the entrance door, bar and food table, with several snack areas in between. Alternatively, place a long, narrow island in the center of the room, so guests can circulate on all sides. A third option is a table in the corner.*
- *Set up food, cutlery, plates and napkins so guests can move quickly in one direction. For very large groups, two smaller, identical settings are better than one big one.*
- *Don't overcrowd the table. Use side tables for cutlery, drinks, dessert and coffee.*

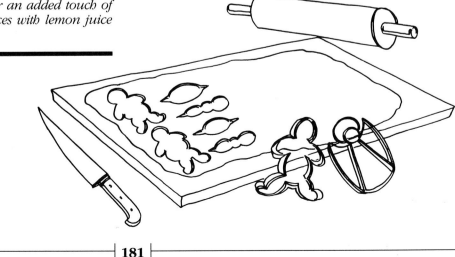

JØDEKAGER

Denmark's traditional Christmas cookie is usually made with carbonated ammonia (hartshorn salt) which is hard to find here. This recipe was developed using double-acting baking powder.

Bake at 350° for 12 minutes.
Makes 8 dozen.

1½ cups (3 sticks) butter or margarine
1 cup sugar
2 eggs
1 teaspoon vanilla
5 cups all-purpose flour
2 teaspoons baking powder
1 teaspoon salt
3 egg whites, beaten
¼ cup sugar
½ cup sliced natural almonds

1. Preheat the oven to moderate (350°).
2. Beat the butter or margarine and the 1 cup of sugar until fluffy in a large bowl with an electric mixer at high speed. Beat in the whole eggs, one at a time, until creamy, then beat in the vanilla.
3. Sift in the flour, baking powder and salt. Stir to make a stiff dough.
4. Roll out the dough, a part at a time, to a ¼-inch thickness on a lightly floured pastry cloth or board. Cut with a 3-inch scalloped cookie cutter. Arrange on ungreased cookie sheets.
5. Bake in the preheated moderate oven (350°) for 10 minutes, or until golden around the edges.
6. Brush the hot cookies with the egg whites; sprinkle with the ¼ cup of sugar and top with the sliced almonds. Bake for 2 minutes longer, or until the top is set. Remove with a spatula to wire racks; cool completely. Layer between wax paper in a metal tin with a tight-fitting lid. If desired, freeze, following the directions on page 258.

KRANSEKAGE

"Wreath cake" is the traditional Scandinavian party cake that's made with almond cookie rings.

Bake at 350° for 15 minutes.
Makes 11 rings.

3¼ cups all-purpose flour
1¼ cups (2½ sticks) butter or margarine
1 egg

1½ teaspoons almond extract
2 cans (8 ounces each) almond paste
Ornamental Frosting (recipe follows)

1. Preheat the oven to moderate (350°).
2. Place the flour in a large bowl. Cut in the butter or margarine with a pastry blender until the mixture forms small balls when pressed between the fingers. Beat in the egg and almond extract with a wooden spoon.
3. Turn the dough out onto a pastry board. Top with the almond paste, then press together and knead for about 5 minutes, or until the dough is smooth and well blended.
4. Make the rings: Pack a small amount of the dough at a time into a pastry bag fitted with a ¾-inch metal tip (#9 B is a good size). Press out 11 graduated-length strips onto ungreased cookie sheets, using a ruler to measure each accurately. The first strip, for the smallest ring, should be 4 inches long; make each succeeding strip 1 inch longer, until the eleventh measures 14 inches. For the longest strips, press the shorter strips together. (Press gently, if the strips break.)
5. Shape each strip into a ring; press the ends with the fingers to join. Shape and bake each large ring on a separate cookie sheet; shape 2 or 3 smaller rings on one sheet, allowing at least 3 inches between them.
6. Press out large "S" shapes with the remaining dough. Place on the cookie sheets.
7. Bake in the preheated moderate oven (350°) for 15 minutes, or until lightly browned. Cool for 10 minutes on the cookie sheets on wire racks, loosen and slide onto the wire racks to cool.
8. Assemble and decorate the cake: Slide the largest ring onto a serving plate. Decorate with loops of Ornamental Frosting, using a #7 writing tip. Place the next largest ring on top before the frosting has set; continue until the smallest ring has been decorated.
9. Decorate the "S" shapes with Ornamental Frosting. Arrange around the assembled Kransekage, using the photo as a guide.

ORNAMENTAL FROSTING: Makes about 1 cup. Combine 1 cup of 10X (confectioners' powdered) sugar, 1 tablespoon of light cream or water and ½ teaspoon of vanilla in a small bowl with a wire whip. Add 1 to 1½ teaspoons more liquid, if necessary, to make a spreadable frosting.

Kransekage

CHRISTMAS MORNING BRUNCH

(for 10)

Blend of Tangerine Juice and Cranberry Juice Cocktail
Continental Fruit Compote*
Broiled Breakfast Steaks*
Baked Sausage and Bacon*
Creamy Scrambled Eggs*
Marbled Waffles*, Syrup
Butter-Broiled Vegetables*
Pumpkin Muffins*, Butter
Aprikosenflek*
Kugelhopf Coffee Cake*
Cocoa with Crème de Menthe*
Café au Lait*
Milk

*recipe follows

Christmas Morning Brunch

Hearty brunch fare includes sausage, steak and eggs, marbled waffles, pumpkin muffins, fruit compote and apricot cake.

Up to 3 months ahead:
● Bake and freeze Aprikosenflek, Pumpkin Muffins and Kugelhopf Coffee Cake.

Up to 1 month ahead:
● Make and freeze parsley butter balls (or refrigerate for 1 or 2 days) to go with Broiled Breakfast Steaks.

The day before:
● Prepare and refrigerate the oranges for Continental Fruit Compote.
● Blend and refrigerate juices.

Early in the day:
● Make the batter for Marbled Waffles.
● Combine the eggs, seasonings and cream for Creamy Scrambled Eggs.

At party time:
● Make coffee for Café au Lait.
● Place the oranges for Continental Fruit Compote in a dish and top with plums.
● Bake the Sausage and Bacon, then reheat Aprikosenflek, Pumpkin Muffins and Kugelhopf. Keep warm.
● Make Marbled Waffles. Keep warm.
● Make Butter-Broiled Vegetables, then Broiled Breakfast Steaks.
● Meanwhile, make Creamy Scrambled Eggs and heat the water and milk for drinks.

Big breakfasts are, for the most part, meals of the past. Yet, come Christmas morning, after the last package has been opened and before the first toy needs repair, everyone has an appetite for more than a quick piece of toast and coffee. Our menu is large and varied, so you can choose those dishes you know your family and friends would most enjoy on a cold winter's morning.

CONTINENTAL FRUIT COMPOTE

Luscious oranges have been an important part of Christmas since Victorian days.

Makes 10 servings.

> 8 medium-size California oranges
> 1 cup water
> ¼ cup sugar
> 3 tablespoons Liquore Galliano (optional)
> 1 can (1 pound, 13 ounces) purple plums, chilled

1. Pare the rind from 1 orange, removing white pith. Cut into tiny strips. Pare the remaining oranges and cut all into thin slices, crosswise. Place in a large glass bowl.
2. Cover the rind strips with water in a small saucepan and bring to boiling; drain.
3. Combine the 1 cup of water, the orange rind strips and sugar in the same saucepan. Bring to boiling. Lower the heat; simmer for 5 minutes.
4. Stir in the Galliano, if desired, and pour over the orange slices. Cover the bowl with plastic wrap and chill until serving time.
5. Arrange the orange slices with syrup in a serving bowl; then drain the plums, reserving the juice for fruit punch. Place the plums in the center of the orange slices.

BROILED BREAKFAST STEAKS

Steak, often part of a hearty breakfast in the "good old days," makes any brunch menu extra special.

Broil for 6 to 14 minutes.
Makes 10 servings.

**10 breakfast chicken or individual steaks
        (about 6 ounces each)
        Instant meat tenderizer**
½ cup (1 stick) butter or margarine, softened
2 tablespoons finely chopped parsley
1 teaspoon Worcestershire sauce

1. Preheat the broiler to high.
2. Remove the steaks from the refrigerator 1 hour before serving. Sprinkle with the meat tenderizer, following the label directions.
3. Combine the butter or margarine, chopped parsley and Worcestershire sauce in a small bowl until well blended. Shape into 10 balls and chill until serving time.
4. Broil the steaks, 4 inches from the heat, for 3 minutes on each side for rare, 5 minutes for medium and 7 minutes for well done. Transfer to a heated platter and serve with the parsley butter balls.

Make-ahead Note: The parsley balls may be prepared in advance and frozen for up to 1 month or refrigerated for 1 or 2 days.

BEATING EGGS

To quickly blend a lot of eggs, place the eggs with cream or milk and seasonings in the container of your electric blender or food processor. Cover and process until blended.

BAKED SAUSAGE AND BACON

Oven-baking your breakfast meats is far less time-consuming than frying them.

Bake at 400° for 30 minutes.
Makes 10 servings.

1 package (1 pound) breakfast sausage links
1 package (1 pound) sliced bacon

1. Preheat the oven to hot (400°).
2. Arrange the sausage on a broiler pan, or on a wire rack on a jelly-roll pan.
3. Place the sliced bacon on a second broiler pan, or line a large cookie sheet with heavy-duty aluminum foil and turn up the edges to contain the fat.
4. Bake in the preheated hot oven (400°) for 15 minutes. Turn the sausage with tongs. Separate the bacon slices into a single layer. Bake for 15 minutes longer, or until the sausage is golden and the bacon is crisp. Drain on paper toweling and keep warm until ready to serve.

CREAMY SCRAMBLED EGGS

Cooking eggs over simmering water produces a very creamy texture.

Makes 10 servings.

15 eggs
1 teaspoon salt
½ teaspoon white pepper
⅔ cup light cream or milk
¼ cup (½ stick) butter or margarine

1. Beat the eggs with the salt and pepper in a large bowl with a wire whip until foamy. Beat in the cream or milk until smooth.
2. Melt the butter or margarine in the top of a double boiler over simmering water. (Or place a large saucepan in a large skillet and add simmering water to the skillet to a depth of 1 inch.)
3. Add the egg mixture and cook, stirring often, for 15 minutes, or until the eggs are creamy and set. Serve immediately.

Make-ahead Note: The eggs, seasonings and cream may be blended several hours ahead; refrigerate.

💲

MARBLED WAFFLES

Have the batter ready and make to order as guests arrive.

Makes 10 servings.

6 eggs
3 cups buttermilk
½ cup vegetable oil
3½ cups all-purpose flour
¼ cup sugar
4 teaspoons baking powder
2 teaspoons baking soda
1 teaspoon salt
⅓ cup cocoa powder (not a mix)

1. Beat the eggs until light and fluffy with a wire whip. Beat in the buttermilk and oil until smooth.
2. Sift the flour, sugar, baking powder, baking soda and salt over the egg mixture; stir in with the wire whip, just until smooth. Pour half the batter into a pitcher. Stir the cocoa powder into the remaining batter until smooth. Pour into a second pitcher.
3. Heat the waffle iron, following the manufacturer's directions. Pour about ½ cup of the batter from each pitcher in a random pattern onto the hot waffle iron; cover.
4. Bake for 5 minutes, or until the waffles stop steaming. Serve hot with butter or margarine and pancake syrup, or keep warm in a low oven.

EXTRA-LIGHT WAFFLES

• *After conditioning the waffle iron, following the manufacturer's directions, never grease or wash the grid—just brush out the crumbs.*
• *Blend batter until the flour mixture is barely blended. It should be lumpy, like muffin batter.*
• *Beat the egg whites separately, then fold them into the batter.*
• *Wait until the waffle iron indicates it is hot enough.*
• *Pour the batter from your pitcher to cover ⅔ of the grid surface.*
• *Cook the waffles until they stop giving off steam.*

EASY POUR

To pour maple syrup more easily, rinse the cup with cold water before measuring.

BUTTER-BROILED VEGETABLES

Mushroom caps and tomato halves add the British touch to a brunch.

Broil for 6 minutes.
Makes 10 servings.

1 pound mushrooms
8 medium-size tomatoes
⅓ cup butter or margarine
3 tablespoons lemon juice
2 tablespoons chopped chives
1 teaspoon salt
¼ teaspoon seasoned pepper
Chopped parsley

1. Wipe the mushrooms with a damp paper towel. Remove the stems and reserve for another dish (such as a creamed mushroom soup or a mushroom omelet). Core the tomatoes and halve, crosswise.
2. Arrange the mushroom caps, rounded-side up, and the tomatoes, cut-side up, in a 15x10x1-inch jelly-roll pan. Cover with plastic wrap and chill until ready to broil.
3. Preheat the broiler to high.
4. Combine the butter or margarine, lemon juice, chopped chives, salt and seasoned pepper in a small saucepan. Heat until bubbly. Brush the mixture over the mushrooms and tomatoes.
5. Broil, 4 inches from the heat, for 6 minutes, or until bubbly hot. Keep warm until ready to serve. Sprinkle with the chopped parsley.

CORING TOMATOES

Use a grapefruit spoon to core tomato halves.

APRIKOSENFLEK

You can also use cherries, peaches or Italian plums in this recipe.

Bake at 350° for 1 hour.
Makes one 9-inch-round or one 13 x 9 x 2-inch cake.

> 4 eggs, separated
> 1¼ cups sugar
> 1¼ cups (2½ sticks) butter or margarine
>   Rind of 1 lemon, grated
> 2 cups all-purpose flour
> ½ teaspoon salt
> 1 can (1 pound) pitted apricots, drained and halved

1. Preheat the oven to moderate (350°).
2. Beat the egg whites until foamy and doubled in volume in a small bowl with an electric mixer at high speed. Gradually beat in ¼ cup of the sugar to make a soft meringue.
3. Beat the butter or margarine and the remaining 1 cup of sugar until light and fluffy in a large bowl with an electric mixer at high speed. Beat in the egg yolks, one at a time, until well blended, then stir in the lemon rind.
4. Fold in the egg whites with a wire whip until well blended. Gradually stir in the flour and salt, just until smooth.
5. Spread the batter into a buttered 9-inch quiche/flan pan or a 13 x 9 x 2-inch baking pan. Arrange the apricots, rounded sides up, on top of the batter. Sprinkle with additional sugar.
6. Bake in the preheated moderate oven (350°) for 1 hour, or until a wooden pick inserted into the center comes out clean. Cool in the pan on a wire rack for 10 minutes. Loosen the cake around the edge and remove from the pan.

Make-ahead Note: Cool completely, then wrap and freeze, following the directions on page 191. To serve: Loosen foil around the cake and heat in a preheated moderate oven (350°) for 20 minutes. Garnish with a ring of red maraschino cherries.

PUMPKIN MUFFINS

A breakfast treat for pumpkin pie lovers.

Bake at 400° for 20 minutes.
Makes 2 dozen.

> 3 cups all-purpose flour
> 1 cup sugar
> 4 teaspoons baking powder
> 1 teaspoon salt
> 1 teaspoon pumpkin pie spice
> 1 cup milk
> 1 cup canned pumpkin
> ½ cup (1 stick) butter or margarine, melted
> 2 eggs, beaten

1. Preheat the oven to hot (400°).
2. Sift the flour, sugar, baking powder, salt and pumpkin pie spice into a large bowl.
3. Add the milk, pumpkin, melted butter or margarine and eggs. Mix with a wooden spoon just until the flour is moist. (The batter will be lumpy.)
4. Fill 24 well-greased muffin tin cups ⅔ full with the batter.
5. Bake in the preheated hot oven (400°) for 20 minutes, or until the muffins are golden. Cool in the muffin cups for 10 minutes on a wire rack. Loosen the muffins around the edge with a sharp knife, then invert onto wire racks. Pile into serving baskets and serve warm.

Make-ahead Note: Muffins can be frozen, following the directions on page 191. To reheat, place the frozen muffins on a cookie sheet in a moderate preheated oven (350°) for 15 minutes.

THE SCOOP ON MUFFINS

Use an ice-cream scoop for easy, even division of muffin batter.

KUGELHOPF COFFEE CAKE

German in origin, this rich coffee cake takes its name from the pan it's baked in; however, you can bake it in any 12-cup tube pan.

Bake at 350° for 50 minutes.
Makes one large cake.

½ **cup milk**
½ **cup (1 stick) butter or margarine**
¾ **cup sugar**
2 **teaspoons grated lemon rind**
1 **envelope fast-rising active dry yeast***
1 **teaspoon sugar**
½ **cup very warm water**
4 **cups all-purpose flour**
½ **teaspoon ground mace**
4 **eggs**
1 **teaspoon salt**
½ **cup sliced almonds**
½ **cup golden raisins**

1. Heat the milk, butter or margarine, sugar and lemon rind in a small saucepan, just until the butter or margarine melts. Cool to lukewarm.
2. Dissolve the yeast and 1 teaspoon of sugar in very warm water in a large bowl with an electric mixer using a dough hook. ("Very warm" water should feel comfortably warm when dropped on the wrist.) Stir until well blended and allow to stand for 5 minutes, or until the mixture begins to bubble.
3. Add the cooled milk mixture, 2 cups of the flour and mace to the bowl. Beat at high speed for 2 minutes, then add the eggs, one at a time, beating well after each addition. Add the remaining 2 cups of the flour and the salt. Lower the speed to medium; beat for 5 minutes longer. Cover the bowl with plastic wrap.
4. Let rise in a warm place, away from drafts, for 45 minutes, or until doubled in volume; beat the dough down with a spoon. Stir in the almonds and raisins.
5. Spoon into a well-greased 12-cup kugelhopf or fluted tube pan. Cover with plastic wrap and let rise in a warm place for 25 minutes, or until doubled in volume.
6. Preheat the oven to moderate (350°).
7. Bake in the preheated moderate oven (350°) for 50 minutes, or until the cake gives a hollow sound when tapped. (Cover the top with aluminum foil during the last few minutes of baking, if it browns too quickly.) Cool in the pan on a wire rack for 5 minutes. Loosen around the edge and tube of the pan; turn out onto the wire rack and cool completely.

Make-ahead Note: Wrap and freeze, following the directions on page 191. To serve: Loosen the foil from the bread. Heat in a preheated moderate oven (350°) for 30 minutes, or until heated.

Note: If using active dry yeast, increase rising time to 10 minutes in Step 2; let rise for 1 hour, 30 minutes in Step 4; let rise 45 minutes in Step 5.

RISE AND SHINE

If you have a gas oven with a pilot light, place yeast dough in the unlit oven to rise. Or, preheat oven at 300° for 5 minutes; turn off heat. This way, it will be warm and free from drafts. Never place your dough in a hot oven or directly on a radiator to rise because the heat will kill the yeast.

TO GRATE ORANGE RIND IN A FLASH

Combine pieces of orange zest (with no white pith attached) with part of the sugar called for in your recipe. Place in the container of an electric food processor fitted with a metal blade. Cover and pulse-process until very finely chopped.

COCOA WITH CRÈME DE MENTHE

The "grown-up" version of hot cocoa.

Makes 10 servings.

- **8 envelopes (1 ounce each) hot cocoa mix**
- **6 cups boiling water**
- **½ cup white crème de menthe**

1. Pour the hot cocoa mix into a large heatproof pitcher.
2. Add the boiling water and crème de menthe; whisk until well mixed and foamy with a wire whisk. Pour into mugs.

CAFÉ AU LAIT

Breakfast coffee, French-style.

Makes 10 servings.

- **4 cups hot strong coffee**
- **4 cups hot milk or liquid cream**
  Sugar

Pour equal parts of the coffee and the hot milk or cream into heated coffee cups. Sweeten, to taste, with sugar. Serve immediately.

FREEZING MUFFINS, BREADS AND CAKES

● *Wrap unfrosted items in heavy-duty aluminum foil, plastic wrap or plastic bags. Label, date and freeze for up to 4 months. Thaw at room temperature for 1 hour. Reheat your muffins and breads for a just-baked flavor.*

● *Freeze frosted cakes on a piece of heavy cardboard or a cookie sheet. When firm, wrap in heavy-duty aluminum foil, plastic wrap or plastic bag. Label, date and freeze for up to 3 months.*

● *Remove the wrapping while your cake is still frozen, so the frosting doesn't smear. Thaw at room temperature for 2 hours.*

● *Glaze breads and muffins only after they have thawed.*

INTERNATIONAL FEAST

(for 12)

Sangria* (Spain)
California Artichoke Platter* (U.S.A.)
Chicken and Peanut Kabobs* (Africa)
Striped Oriental Salad* (The Orient)
Cuban-Style Pork Platter* (Cuba)
Rice Pilaf*, Peas à la Française* (France)
Navy Bean Picadillo* (Mexico)
Gouda Muffins* (Holland), Butter
Pizza Breads* (Italy),
Bûche de Noël* (France)
Marlborough Pie* (England),
Brandy-Flavored Whipped Cream
Spiced Cappuccino* (Italy), Tea

*recipe follows

International Feast

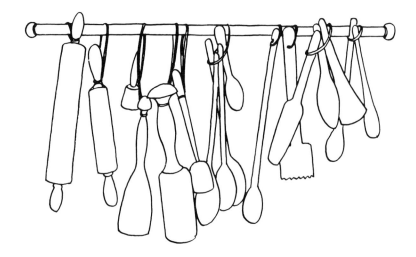

An around-the-world buffet offers unique and delicious regional specialties.

Up to 3 months ahead:
● Bake and freeze Gouda Muffins and Pizza Breads.
Up to 1 week ahead:
● Prepare the Chocolate Butter Frosting, Coffee Cream Filling and Mushroom Meringues for Bûche de Noël, then refrigerate the filling and frosting.
Up to 3 days ahead:
● Prepare and refrigerate Navy Bean Picadillo.
The day before:
● Prepare and chill the Sangria base.
● Cook the artichokes and make the dips for California Artichoke Platter; refrigerate.
● Prepare the Chicken and Peanut Kabobs, then cover them and chill.
● Wash the lettuce, cook the bacon curls, blanch the broccoli flowerets and fresh snow pea pods (or drain the frozen pea pods) for Striped Oriental Salad. Wrap them in separate plastic bags and refrigerate. Make and chill Oriental Dressing.
● Marinate pork for Cuban-Style Pork. Refrigerate, turning it several times.
● Chop the onion and garlic for Rice Pilaf.
● Prepare and refrigerate Bûche de Noël.
Early in the day:
● Bake Marlborough Pie.
● Make the spice base for Cappuccino.
Several hours ahead:
● Start roasting Cuban-Syle Pork.
● Decorate Bûche de Noël with Mushroom Meringues.

At party time:
● Make Rice Pilaf and Peas à la Française.
● Fill the artichokes with dip and arrange with the vegetables on your platter.
● Arrange the lettuce and vegetables for the salad in a bowl. Cover and refrigerate.
● Heat Pizza Breads and Gouda Muffins.
● Heat Navy Bean Picadillo.
● Finish Sangria.
● Broil Chicken and Peanut Kabobs.
During meal:
● Whip, then chill the cream for the pie.
● Finish Spiced Cappuccino.
● Decorate Marlborough Pie with apple slices.

A few twists on ingredients can lend a foreign air to any dish. This hearty buffet for 12 takes its inspiration from the classic fare of different countries. Served together, the dishes will take your guests abroad for the holidays!

Begin with Sangria, the traditional wine punch of Spain, served with an American artichoke hors d'oeuvre and Chicken Kabobs encrusted with an African staple—peanuts. Striped Oriental Salad blends Oriental-style vegetables with a soy vinaigrette. Cuban-style marinated loin of pork is served with rice and peas prepared in the French manner. Navy Bean Picadillo, the piquant Mexican bean dish made with olives and raisins, is made with navy beans from Michigan. Gouda Muffins and Pizza Breads are quick breads with the taste of Holland and Italy, respectively. Team up English-style Marlborough Pie with the traditional Christmas cake of France—Bûche de Noël— for a delicious dessert.

SANGRIA

A lighter version of the Spanish wine punch.

Makes 12 four-ounce servings.

> 1 **bottle (1 liter) dry red wine**
> 2 **cups orange juice**
> ¼ **cup superfine sugar**
> ¼ **cup brandy**
> 2 **cups club soda, chilled**
>   **Lime slices for garnish** (optional)

1. Combine the red wine, orange juice, sugar and brandy in a tall pitcher; stir until the sugar dissolves. Chill for at least 2 hours to blend the flavors.
2. At serving time, add the club soda and fill the pitcher with ice cubes. Pour into stemmed glasses and float a lime slice in each glass, if you wish.

CALIFORNIA ARTICHOKE PLATTER

Use artichokes as edible dip containers.

Makes 12 servings.

> 3 **large artichokes**
>   **Pimiento-Sour Cream Dip (recipe follows)**
>   **Tangy Tomato Dip (recipe follows)**
> 2 **small yellow squash**
> 1 **bunch baby carrots**
> 2 **small zucchini**
> 1 **box (1 pint) cherry tomatoes**
> 1 **small cauliflower**
> 1 **pound asparagus**

1. Cook the artichokes in salted boiling water in a large kettle for 40 minutes, or until the leaves are easily pulled off; drain. When cool enough to handle, remove artichokes with a teaspoon. Wrap in a plastic bag and chill.
2. Prepare the Pimiento-Sour Cream Dip and Tangy Tomato Dip, and chill.
3. Trim the yellow squash and cut into sticks. Pare the carrots, then trim the zucchini and cut into sticks. Wash and hull the tomatoes. Separate the cauliflower into flowerets and trim the asparagus. Wrap the vegetables in plastic bags; chill.

4. To serve: Separate the leaves of one artichoke and chop the heart into chunks. Insert a small glass container into the remaining 2 artichokes and spoon the Pimiento-Sour Cream Dip into one and the Tangy Tomato Dip into the second.
5. Arrange the whole artichokes in a large serving dish and pile the artichoke leaves, heart pieces and raw vegetables around them.

ARTICHOKES

Look for artichokes that are compact and bright green, with few discolored leaves. Wash by immersing them, stem-end up, in a deep bowl of lukewarm water. Shake them vigorously to dislodge any dirt.

PIMIENTO-SOUR CREAM DIP

Makes 1½ cups.

> 1 **container (8 ounces) dairy sour cream**
> ¼ **cup finely chopped, pared and seeded**
>   **cucumber**
> 2 **tablespoons chopped parsley**
> 2 **tablespoons chopped pimiento**
> 1 **teaspoon dry mustard**
> ½ **teaspoon salt**
> ¼ **teaspoon freshly ground pepper**

Combine the sour cream, cucumber, parsley, pimiento, dry mustard, salt and pepper in a small bowl. Cover with plastic wrap and chill for at least 2 hours.

PERFECT CHOPPED PARSLEY

Remove the stems. Wash the leaves to remove all traces of grit, then dry them thoroughly (a salad spinner is ideal for this). Place the leaves in the dry container of a food processor fitted with a metal blade. Pulse-process until very finely chopped (the larger the amount of parsley, the more finely chopped the parsley can become). Transfer the chopped parsley to an airtight container or plastic bag. Refrigerate it for up to one week.

TANGY TOMATO DIP

Makes 1½ cups.

1 bottle (10 ounces) chili sauce
1 tablespoon finely chopped chives
1 tablespoon lemon juice
1 teaspoon Worcestershire sauce

Combine the chili sauce, chives, lemon juice and Worcestershire sauce in a small bowl. Cover with plastic wrap and chill for 2 hours.

CHICKEN AND PEANUT KABOBS

Skewers of peanut-encrusted chicken.

Makes 12 appetizer servings.

2 pounds boned chicken breasts
¼ cup (½ stick) butter or margarine
¼ cup prepared mustard
1 clove garlic, minced
1 teaspoon salt
1 cup chopped unsalted peanuts

1. Cut the chicken into 48 cubes. Thread 4 chicken cubes on each of 12 skewers. Lay the skewers on wax paper.
2. Melt the butter or margarine in a small saucepan; remove from the heat. Add the mustard and stir until smooth with a wire whip; stir in the garlic and salt (if the sauce is very thick, add 1 teaspoon of water). Brush the sauce on both sides of the chicken, then roll the chicken in the chopped peanuts, coating evenly.
3. Cover the skewers with plastic wrap; refrigerate until serving time.
4. Preheat the broiler to moderate.
5. Broil the skewers, 4 inches from the heat, for 10 to 15 minutes, turning occasionally or until the chicken is golden.

STRIPED ORIENTAL SALAD

A salad of Oriental vegetables and crisp bacon curls, served with a soy vinaigrette.

Makes 12 servings.

2 heads Boston lettuce
1 pound sliced bacon
2 heads broccoli
¾ pound fresh snow pea pods, trimmed, OR: 2 packages (6 ounces each) frozen snow pea pods, thawed
1 pound fresh bean sprouts OR: 1 can (16 ounces) bean sprouts, rinsed and drained
1 can (5 ounces) water chestnuts, drained and sliced
Oriental Dressing (recipe follows)

1. Wash the lettuce heads and dry thoroughly. Break one lettuce head into bite-size pieces. Keep the remaining leaves whole. Wrap in separate plastic bags and refrigerate.
2. Halve the bacon slices, crosswise. Brown, a part at a time, in a large skillet, just until they begin to crisp; roll up with 2 forks and continue frying, turning the rolls with a fork until cooked. Drain on paper toweling. Cover with plastic wrap; chill.
3. Trim the broccoli and cut into small flowerets (save the stems for another use, such as soup). Drop the flowerets into boiling salted water; cook for 3 to 5 minutes, or until barely tender. Refresh in a colander under cold running water. Drain well; place in a plastic bag and refrigerate.
4. Drop the fresh snow pea pods into the boiling water; cook for 1 minute, or until barely tender. Refresh in the colander under cold running water, drain, wrap and refrigerate. Or, drain the frozen pea pods on paper toweling; place in a plastic bag and refrigerate.
5. At serving time, line a large salad bowl with the whole lettuce leaves; spread the bite-size lettuce pieces on the bottom. Top with rows of the bean sprouts, broccoli, bacon and snow pea pods mixed with sliced water chestnuts. Serve with the Oriental Dressing.

ORIENTAL DRESSING: Makes about 1 cup. Place ½ cup of vegetable oil, ¼ cup of wine vinegar, 3 tablespoons of soy sauce, ¼ teaspoon of garlic powder, a dash of dry Sherry, a few drips of liquid red-pepper seasoning and a few drops of sesame oil (*optional*) in a screw-top jar. Cover tightly and shake until very well blended.

CUBAN-STYLE PORK

Marinate a pork loin in garlic vinaigrette for extra flavor.

Roast at 325° for 3 hours.
Makes 12 servings.

- **1 center-cut pork loin (about 7 pounds)**
- **2 teaspoons salt**
- **1 teaspoon pepper**
- **1 teaspoon leaf oregano, crumbled**
- **6 cloves garlic, chopped**
- **2 tablespoons olive or vegetable oil**
- **2 tablespoons lemon juice**
- **1 tablespoon white vinegar**
  Rice Pilaf (recipe follows)
  Peas à la Française (recipe on page 198)

1. Have your butcher cut the pork loin from the bones in one piece. (Save the bones to barbecue or make into a soup.)
2. Prick the pork loin with a 2-tined fork.
3. Combine the salt, pepper, oregano, garlic, oil, lemon juice and vinegar in a large plastic bag; add the pork loin. Close the bag securely and turn the meat to coat with the marinade. Place in a shallow pan and refrigerate at least 8 hours, or overnight, turning several times.
4. Preheat the oven to moderate (325°). Place the pork loin in a shallow roasting pan; pour part of the marinade over. Insert a meat thermometer, if using, near the center of the roast.
5. Roast in the preheated moderate oven (325°) for 3 hours, or until the thermometer registers 170°.
6. Place the roast on a wooden carving board and cover with aluminum foil to keep warm. Allow to "rest" for 20 minutes; cut into thin slices.
7. Line a large serving platter with Rice Pilaf, then arrange the pork slices to overlap on the top and ring with the Peas à la Française.

RICE PILAF

Bake at 325° for 1 hour, 30 minutes.
Makes 12 servings.

- **3 cups raw long-grain rice**
- **¼ cup vegetable oil**
- **1 large onion, chopped (1 cup)**
- **2 cloves garlic, minced**
- **8 cups boiling water**
- **8 envelopes or teaspoons instant chicken broth**
- **1 cup sliced natural almonds**
- **1 cup golden raisins.**

1. Preheat the oven to moderate (325°).
2. Toast the rice in the oil in a large kettle until golden; push to one side. Sauté the onion and garlic until soft in the same kettle.
3. Stir in the boiling water and instant chicken broth; bring to boiling. Pour the mixture into a 16-cup casserole and cover.
4. Bake in the preheated moderate oven (325°) for 1 hour, 30 minutes, or until the liquid is absorbed and the rice is tender. Stir the almonds and raisins into the rice with a fork.

PEAS À LA FRANÇAISE

The French add lettuce to their peas before cooking them.

Makes 12 servings.

2 **bags (1 pound each) frozen peas**
3 **tablespoons butter or margarine**
2 **teaspoons sugar**
1 **teaspoon salt**
¼ **teaspoon pepper**
2 **outer iceberg lettuce leaves**
2 **whole pimientos, diced**

1. Combine the peas, butter or margarine, sugar, salt and pepper in a large saucepan. Top with the lettuce leaves and cover the pan.
2. Bring to boiling over low heat, then shake the pan, but do not uncover. Simmer for 5 minutes. Remove the lettuce leaves and discard. Toss in the diced pimientos.

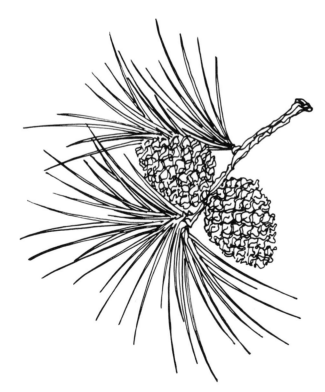

NAVY BEAN PICADILLO

Inspired by the Mexican beef stew, this dish is enlivened with raisins and olives.

Makes 12 servings.

1 **pound dry navy beans**
6 **cups water**
1 **pound kielbasi, or Polish sausage (about 1 pound)**
½ **cup olive or vegetable oil**
1 **large onion, chopped (1 cup)**
2 **cloves garlic, minced**
½ **pound beef chuck, cut into strips**
1 **cup chopped celery**
1 **can (28 ounces) peeled whole tomatoes**
1½ **cups dry white wine**
½ **cup raisins**
½ **cup sliced stuffed green olives**
   Dash cayenne pepper
2 **teaspoons salt, or to taste**

1. Place the beans in a large saucepan with the water. Bring to boiling; boil for 2 minutes, then remove from the heat. Cover the pan and allow to stand for 1 hour.
2. Score the kielbasi and brown in the oil in a large kettle; remove and reserve. Brown the onion and garlic in the pan drippings until soft. Add the beef and stir until the beef loses its pink color; add the celery and sauté for 2 minutes.
3. Add the tomatoes, wine, raisins, olives and cayenne pepper. Bring to boiling. Add the beans along with the cooking water and the kielbasi to the kettle, pushing the sausage ring under the cooking liquid; cover the kettle.
4. Simmer for 2 hours, or until the beans are tender. Taste and add salt, if needed. Ladle into a heated tureen. Cut the kielbasi into pieces, as portions are served.

Make-ahead Note: For an even more flavorful dish, make a day ahead. Cool, then refrigerate. Heat, just before serving.

Cook's Tip: This dish is really so satisfying and hearty you can also serve it by itself on one of the busy evenings before Christmas. Just add a crisp salad and crusty bread.

💲⚡《《
GOUDA MUFFINS

If you can't find Dutch Gouda or Edam, substitute Gruyère or Jarlsberg cheese.

Bake at 425° for 20 to 25 minutes.
Makes 1 dozen.

- **3** *tablespoons vegetable shortening*
- **2** *cups sifted all-purpose flour*
- **1** *tablespoon baking powder*
- **1** *tablespoon sugar*
- **½** *teaspoon dry mustard powder*
- **½** *teaspoon salt*
- **¼** *teaspoon cayenne pepper*
- **½** *cup grated Gouda or Edam cheese (2 ounces)*
- **1** *cup milk*
- **1** *egg, beaten*

1. Preheat the oven to very hot (425°). Grease twelve 2-inch muffin-pan cups.
2. Melt the shortening in a small saucepan; cool slightly.
3. Sift together the flour, baking powder, sugar, mustard powder, salt and cayenne pepper into a medium-size bowl; stir in the cheese.
4. Combine the milk, egg and melted shortening, then add all at once to the flour mixture, stirring only until just moistened. Do not overmix.
5. Drop the batter into the prepared muffin-pan cups, filling ⅔ full.
6. Bake in the preheated very hot oven (425°) for 20 to 25 minutes, or until golden brown.
7. Cool in the muffin-pan cups on a wire rack for 15 minutes. Unmold. Serve warm, or cool completely and freeze, following the directions on page 191.

Make-ahead Note: Reheat the muffins in a preheated moderate oven (325°) for 15 minutes.

💲⚡《《
PIZZA BREADS

The tangy taste of pizza, in compact loaves.

Bake at 400° for 35 minutes.
Makes 8 small loaves.

- **4** *cups all-purpose flour*
- **2** *tablespoons baking powder*
- **1** *teaspoon salt*
- **1** *large onion, chopped (1 cup)*
- **1** *teaspoon leaf oregano, crumbled*
- **¼** *teaspoon garlic powder*
- **½** *cup (1 stick) butter or margarine*
- **2** *cups milk*
- **2** *eggs, beaten*
- **1** *package (4 ounces) sliced pepperoni, chopped*
- **1** *package (4 ounces) shredded mozzarella (1 cup)*

1. Preheat the oven to hot (400°). Grease eight 3 x 5 x 1½-inch loaf pans.
2. Sift the flour, baking powder and salt into a large bowl; make a well in the center.
3. Sauté the onion with the oregano and garlic powder in the butter or margarine in a medium-size saucepan for 5 minutes, or until the onion is soft; cool slightly. Add the milk, then the eggs.
4. Add the liquid all at once to the dry ingredients. Toss in the pepperoni and cheese. Stir lightly, just until the liquid is absorbed—the batter will be lumpy.
5. Spoon the batter into the loaf pans, dividing evenly and smoothing the tops.
6. Bake in the preheated hot oven (400°) for 35 minutes, or until a wooden skewer inserted in the center comes out clean. Let cool in the pans on a wire rack for 15 minutes, then loosen around the edges with a long, sharp knife. Invert onto the wire rack and serve warm.

Make-ahead Note: To freeze, cool completely on the rack, then label, date and freeze, following the directions on page 191. Reheat in a preheated moderate (325°) oven for 15 minutes, or until heated through.

BÛCHE DE NOËL

The Yule log of Christmas past is recreated with a chocolate jelly roll coated with a rich frosting to resemble the tree's bark. Mushroom Meringues are the classic garnish.

Bake at 375° for 12 minutes.
Makes 12 servings.

1 cup unsifted cake flour
¼ cup cocoa powder (not a mix)
1 teaspoon baking powder
¼ teaspoon salt
3 eggs
1 cup granulated sugar
⅓ cup water
1 teaspoon vanilla
10X (confectioners' powdered) sugar
Coffee Cream Filling (recipe follows)
Chocolate Butter Frosting (recipe follows)
Chopped pistachio nuts
Mushroom Meringues (recipe on page 202)

1. Preheat the oven to moderate (375°).
2. Grease a 15 x 10 x 1-inch jelly-roll pan, then line with wax paper and grease again.
3. Sift the flour, cocoa, baking powder and salt onto wax paper.
4. Beat the eggs until thick and creamy in a small bowl with an electric mixer at high speed. Beat in the granulated sugar, 1 tablespoon at a time, beating all the time until the mixture is very thick. Stir in the water and vanilla; fold in the flour mixture. Spread the batter evenly in the pan.

5. Bake in the preheated moderate oven (375°) for 12 minutes, or until the center springs back when lightly pressed with the fingertip.
6. Loosen around the edges of the pan with a sharp knife, then invert the pan onto a clean towel dusted with 10X sugar; peel off the wax paper. Starting at a long side, roll up the cake, jelly-roll fashion; wrap in the towel and cool completely.
7. Unroll the cake carefully. Spread with the Coffee Cream Filling; reroll.
8. Cut a ½-inch-thick slice from one end of the cake roll. Remove the inner coil and reshape tightly to form a "knot" on a log; frost with a bit of the Chocolate Butter Frosting. Frost the cake roll with the remaining frosting, then draw the tines of a fork, lengthwise, through the frosting to resemble "bark"; press the "knot" onto the side. Sprinkle the ends of the roll with chopped pistachio nuts as photographed. Chill until serving time. Decorate the plate with the Mushroom Meringues. Cut crosswise into slices.

COFFEE CREAM FILLING: Makes 2 cups. Combine 1 cup of heavy cream, 1 tablespoon of instant coffee powder and ½ cup of 10X (confectioners' powdered) sugar in a medium-size bowl. Beat until stiff with an electric mixer at medium speed.

CHOCOLATE BUTTER FROSTING: Makes enough to frost a jelly roll. Melt ¼ cup (½ stick) of butter or margarine and 2 squares of unsweetened chocolate in a small saucepan; cool slightly. Add 2 cups of 10X (confectioners' powdered) sugar, ¼ cup of milk and ½ teaspoon of vanilla. Beat with a wire whip until the frosting is smooth.

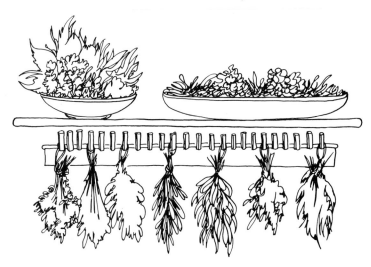

Bûche de Noël

MUSHROOM MERINGUES

Bake at 250° for 30 minutes.
Makes 2 dozen.

2 egg whites
⅛ teaspoon cream of tartar
½ teaspoon almond extract
⅔ cup sugar
¼ cup semisweet chocolate pieces
Cocoa powder for garnish (optional)

1. Grease 2 large cookie sheets; flour lightly, tapping out any excess. Preheat the oven to slow (250°).
2. Beat the egg whites, cream of tartar and almond extract until foamy-white and doubled in volume in a small bowl with an electric mixer at high speed.
3. Sprinkle in the sugar, 1 tablespoon at a time, beating until the sugar dissolves completely and the meringue stands in firm peaks when the beaters are lifted.
4. Fit a pastry bag with a #10 plain tip; spoon the meringue into the bag.
5. To make mushroom caps, press out the meringue in 1½-inch rounds; smooth the top of each, if needed, with a knife, but do not flatten.
6. To make stems, hold the pastry bag upright, then press out the meringue, pulling straight up on the bag for 1½ inches.
7. Bake in the preheated slow oven (250°) for 30 minutes, or until firm but not brown. Let stand for several minutes on the cookie sheets. Loosen carefully with a small knife; remove to wire racks with a spatula and cool completely.
8. Melt the chocolate in a cup placed in a small skillet of hot water.
9. Working carefully, make a small hollow in the underside of each cap. Add a dab of the melted chocolate and press a stem into the hollow. Let stand until the chocolate is firm.
10. Sprinkle the tops of the mushrooms with the cocoa powder, if you wish. Store in a tightly covered container in a dry place.

PERFECT MERINGUES

● *Separate eggs while they're cold, but allow the egg whites to come to room temperature before beating.*
● *Drop egg whites into a clean, grease-free bowl, making sure no particles of egg yolk fall in. (If they do, remove all traces with a piece of eggshell.)*
● *Beat egg whites until foamy before adding sugar, a little at a time, so the sugar granules can dissolve instantly.*
● *After all the sugar has been added, beat the meringue only until it forms stiff peaks.*
● *After baking meringues, let them stand in the turned-off oven, with the door slightly ajar, for 5 minutes. Remove from the oven. Cool on cookie sheets, away from drafts, then remove from the sheets.*

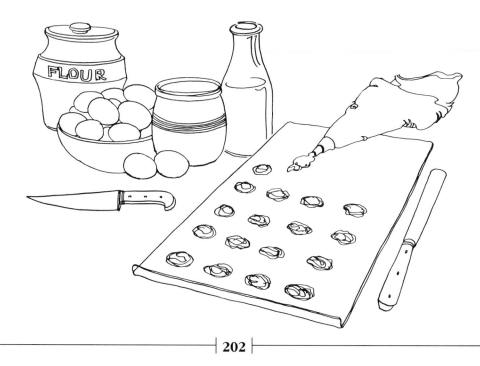

MARLBOROUGH PIE

An English-style apple-custard pie.

Bake at 400° for 10 minutes, then at 325° for 40 minutes.
Makes one 10-inch pie.

1 **package piecrust mix**
1 **jar (1 pound) applesauce**
¾ **cup firmly packed brown sugar**
   Grated rind and juice of 1 lemon
½ **teaspoon grated nutmeg**
4 **eggs, beaten**
1 **cup light cream**
   Red apple slices for garnish

1. Preheat the oven to hot (400°).
2. Prepare the piecrust mix, following the label directions. Roll out to a 13-inch round on a lightly floured pastry cloth or board. Fit into a 10-inch pie plate and trim the edge to ½ inch; turn the pastry under and flute to make a stand-up edge. Refrigerate while making the apple-custard filling.
3. Combine the applesauce, brown sugar, rind and juice of the lemon and the nutmeg in a large bowl. Stir in the eggs and cream until well blended. Pour into the prepared pastry shell.
4. Bake in the preheated hot oven (400°) for 10 minutes; reduce the oven temperature to slow (325°); bake for 40 minutes longer, or until the top is golden and the filling starts to firm up. Cool in the pan on a wire rack. Serve at room temperature, garnished with the slices of apple. Serve with a dollop of brandy-flavored whipped cream and a sprinkling of ground nutmeg, if you wish.

SPICED CAPPUCCINO

This shortcut recipe is made with instant espresso powder.

Makes 12 servings.

3 **three-inch pieces stick cinnamon**
12 **whole cloves**
½ **cup instant espresso coffee**
6 **cups boiling water**
½ **cup sugar**
3 **cups half and half (½ cream, ½ milk), warmed**
2 **cups (1 pint) heavy cream**
   Ground nutmeg

1. Tie the cinnamon sticks and cloves in cheesecloth; drop into a large saucepan. Add the instant espresso coffee and boiling water; cover and steep for 5 minutes.
2. Remove the spice bag. Stir in the sugar and half and half; continue stirring until the sugar dissolves.
3. Beat the cream in a medium bowl with an electric mixer at high speed until soft peaks form.
4. Serve the cappuccino in warmed mugs or stemmed glasses. Top each serving with a spoonful of whipped cream; sprinkle with ground nutmeg.

Make-ahead Note: Prepare the spiced espresso mixture with 1 cup of the water; remove the spice bag and stir in the sugar until it dissolves; set aside. At serving time, add the remaining water and the half and half, then top with the whipped cream and nutmeg.

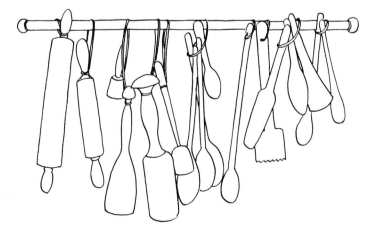

DINNER ON THE LIGHT SIDE
(for 10)

Rosé Spritzers*
Golden Punch*
Curried Chicken Liver Pâté*
Tzatziki*, Raw Vegetables
Oriental Spinach Rolls*
Party Meatballs*
Stuffed Turkey Breast*
with Boiled New Potatoes and Onions*
Zucchini Boats with Red Pepper-Bulgur Pilaf*
Winter Salad of Julienne Vegetables*
Tossed Salad, Buttermilk Dressing*
Velvety Creme Chocolate*
Espresso Coffee with Lemon Rind
Spiced Tea

*recipe follows

Stuffed Turkey Breast

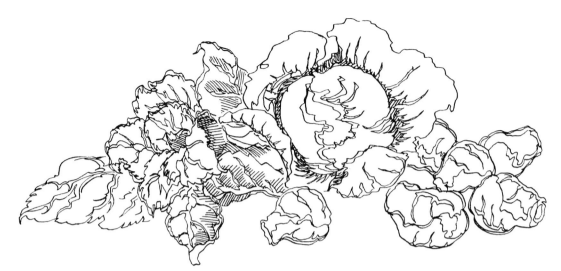

A stuffed turkey breast, served with a medley of julienne-cut winter vegetables, makes a light holiday entrée.

Up to 1 month ahead:
● Bake and freeze the cake layer for Velvety Creme Chocolate.

The day before:
● Make and refrigerate Curried Chicken Liver Pâté.
● Make Tzatziki. Cut the vegetables for dipping, then refrigerate.
● Make and refrigerate Golden Punch.
● Make and chill Oriental Spinach Rolls.
● Shape Party Meatballs, then cover and refrigerate.
● Parboil the zucchini for Zucchini Boats.
● Chop the vegetables and shred the cheese for Stuffed Turkey Breast.
● Parboil vegetables, make the dressing for Winter Salad and refrigerate separately.
● Wash the lettuce and make Buttermilk Dressing for your Tossed Salad, then refrigerate separately.
● Make and chill Velvety Creme Chocolate.
● Stuff the Turkey Breast and chill until ½ hour before roasting time.
● Make the spiced wine mixture for Rosé Spritzers.

Several hours ahead:
● Start roasting Stuffed Turkey Breast.
● Prepare the bulgur and stuff the zucchini.
● Unmold and refrigerate Velvety Creme Chocolate.

At party time:
● Unmold Curried Chicken Liver Pâté.
● Decorate and chill Velvety Creme Chocolate.
● Finish Rosé Spritzers and Golden Punch.
● Cook Party Meatballs.
● Cook New Potatoes and Onions.
● Heat Zucchini Boats.
● Toss together the dressing and vegetables for Winter Salad of Julienne Vegetables.

During the meal:
● Brew the espresso and make the tea.

Holiday time usually signals winter's battle of the bulge. How can one avoid overeating when extra-rich food lurks in every corner?

This light menu, although satisfying and varied, cuts calories that won't be missed. Serve Rosé Wine Spritzers and a nonalcoholic fruit punch while guests nibble on scrumptious hors d'oeuvres like liver pâté, spinach rolls, meatballs stuffed with olives and a cucumber-yogurt dip for vegetables.

Lean turkey breast is stuffed with leeks, parsley and cheese before being roasted. Serve it with simply boiled new potatoes and onions, a salad of matchstick-sized carrots, snow peas and fennel, zucchini boats with bulgur-pilaf stuffing and a tossed salad with a low-calorie buttermilk dressing.

For dessert, Velvety Creme Chocolate, at 104 calories per serving, only looks calorie-laden. Even the "whipped cream" is pared down.

ROSÉ SPRITZERS

Two kinds of wine and club soda make a bright-colored punch.

Makes 10 servings at 58 calories each.

 1 **cup dry white wine**
 1 **3-inch piece stick cinnamon**
 6 **whole cloves**
    Ice cubes
 2 **cups rosé wine, chilled**
 2 **bottles (32 ounces each) club soda, chilled**
    Red food coloring (optional)
 1 **orange, halved and sliced, 1 lime, sliced, and 1 lemon, sliced, for garnish**

1. Combine the white wine, cinnamon and whole cloves in a small saucepan. Heat slowly to boiling, then lower the heat and simmer for 5 minutes. Cool in the pan with the spices; remove the spices.
2. Fill a tall pitcher with the ice cubes. Add the spiced wine, rosé wine, club soda and red food coloring, if using; stir until well blended. Garnish with the orange, lime and lemon slices.

Make-ahead Note: Prepare the spiced wine mixture; cool. Remove the spices and set aside. Just before serving, proceed with Step 2.

GOLDEN PUNCH

A slightly sweet fruit punch.

Makes 10 servings at 125 calories each.

 2 **quarts orange juice**
 4 **cans (6 ounces each) pineapple juice**
 2 **cans (6 ounces each) apricot nectar**
 ¼ **cup honey (optional)**
 6 **sprigs fresh mint, crushed**

1. A day ahead, combine the orange juice, pineapple juice and apricot nectar in a 2-quart container. Pour some of this mixture into an ice cube tray and freeze. Add the honey, if you wish, and the crushed mint to the remaining juice mixture. Stir to dissolve the honey. Refrigerate overnight.
2. To serve, remove the mint and pour the juice into a large pitcher. Add the frozen punch cubes; stir.

CURRIED CHICKEN LIVER PÂTÉ

Nutritious and tasty, yet low in calories.

Makes 2 cups at 16 calories per tablespoon.

 ½ **pound chicken livers**
 1 **small onion, quartered**
 2 **tablespoons brandy or Cognac**
 1 **envelope unflavored gelatin**
 ½ **cup cold water**
 1 **envelope chicken broth**
 ½ **teaspoon paprika**
 ½ **teaspoon curry powder**
 ½ **teaspoon salt (optional)**
 ⅛ **teaspoon white pepper**
 ½ **cup diet margarine (from a 4-ounce tub)**
 ½ **cup Neufchâtel cheese (from an 8-ounce package), softened**

1. Clean the chicken livers; cut in half and remove connective tissue. Put into a medium-size saucepan with the onion and brandy or Cognac.
2. Soften the gelatin in the cold water in a cup and stir into the saucepan along with the chicken broth. Bring to boiling and cook for 5 minutes.
3. Empty the mixture (including the liquid) into the container of an electric food processor or blender. Add the paprika, curry powder, salt, if using, and white pepper. Cover and process at high speed until smooth. With the blades still spinning, remove the inner cap or cover and slice in the diet margarine and Neufchâtel cheese, stopping the machine to stir down the mixture with a thin rubber spatula, if necessary.
4. Pour into a two-cup glass or mold and refrigerate for at least 2 hours, or until serving time.
5. At serving time, unmold the pâté onto a plate. Serve with sliced cucumber and yellow squash if you wish.

HEALTHY SNACKING

Offer melba toast and unsalted crackers instead of rich, salty crackers and chips.

TZATZIKI

Cucumber purée blends with seasoned yogurt for a low-cal Middle Eastern dip that goes well with raw vegetables.

Makes 1¾ cups at 6 calories per tablespoon.

- **1 large cucumber**
- **¼ cup water**
- **1 small onion, quartered**
- **1 container (8 ounces) plain yogurt**
- **Salt (optional)**
- **1 teaspoon dill weed**
- **¼ teaspoon freshly ground pepper**
- **Snow pea pods, trimmed**
- **Yellow squash, sliced**
- **Cherry tomatoes**
- **Red pepper, halved, seeded and cut into strips**
- **Broccoli, separated into flowerets**
- **Cauliflower, separated into flowerets**

1. Pare the cucumber and cut into chunks. Pour the water into the container of an electric blender. Add 4 of the cucumber chunks; cover and process on high until smooth.

2. Remove the center from the blender cap and add the remaining cucumber chunks, a part at a time, then the onion quarters until smooth.

3. Pour the mixture into a fine strainer and allow the pureé to drain for 15 minutes.

4. Stir the drained pureé into the yogurt in a medium-size glass bowl. Stir in the salt, if using, the dill weed and pepper until well blended. Cover the bowl with plastic wrap; refrigerate until serving time.

5. Spoon the dip into a serving bowl and pile the raw vegetables in a decorative pattern on the serving platter.

DIPS FOR DIETERS

- *Any dip recipe can be calorie-reduced by the simple substitution of plain yogurt for sour cream.*
- *For a festive dip container, hollow out a cabbage, making sure to cut the base flat so the cabbage won't roll. Affix sprigs of parsley around the opening with wooden toothpicks.*

ORIENTAL SPINACH ROLLS

Elegant vegetable rolls flavored with soy sauce and sesame oil.

Makes 18 rolls at 5 calories each.

- **½ pound large fresh spinach leaves**
- **½ cup shredded carrot**
- **1 tablespoon rice vinegar**
- **2 teaspoons soy sauce**
- **1 teaspoon sesame oil (optional)**

1. Trim the stems and tough ribs from the spinach. Place the leaves in a large bowl of warm water; swish gently to dislodge any sand, then gently lift the leaves from the water. Repeat several times with fresh water until the spinach is clean.

2. Place half of the leaves in a metal colander, vegetable steamer or steamer top of a double boiler. Bring salted water to boiling; cover the pan and steam for 3 minutes, or just until wilted.

3. Invert the spinach onto a double layer of paper toweling; press out as much water as possible, using the hands or a plate, to make a flat cake. Repeat with the remaining spinach.

4. When the spinach is as dry as possible, place a mound of the carrot on one end of each leaf. Roll up tightly, jelly-roll style, to form a cigar shape. Cut carefully into ½-inch slices, using a sharp serrated knife. Place the slices, cut-side up, close together on a plate.

5. Mix the vinegar, soy sauce and oil in a small cup; drizzle over the spinach rolls. Cover with plastic wrap and refrigerate for 4 hours or overnight.

Cook's Tip: Sesame oil and rice vinegar are sold in specialty stores and in gourmet sections of supermarkets.

PARTY MEATBALLS

Tiny green olives are hidden in each meatball.

Makes 18 meatballs at 32 calories each.

½ **pound lean ground beef**
1 **small clove garlic, minced**
1 **tablespoon minced onion**
½ **teaspoon seasoned salt**
¼ **teaspoon seasoned pepper**
¼ **teaspoon mixed Italian herbs, crumbled**
1 **egg**
1 **thin slice whole-wheat bread, soaked in
      water and squeezed**
18 **very small pimiento-stuffed green olives**
½ **cup tomato juice**
3 **tablespoons chili sauce
      Dash bottled red-pepper seasoning**

1. Mix the meat, garlic, onion, salt, pepper, Italian herbs, egg and bread in a medium-size bowl just until blended.
2. Shape the meat mixture into 18 balls, placing an olive in the center of each.
3. Brown the meatballs in a large, heavy nonstick skillet, turning often.
4. Remove the meatballs to a medium-size saucepan. Deglaze the skillet with ¼ cup of hot water and pour over the meatballs. Add the tomato juice, chili sauce and red-pepper seasoning; cover.
5. Simmer for 10 minutes, or until bubbly hot. Serve hot.

GROUND BEEF

Ground beef is available with different amounts of fat mixed in:
- *Hamburger or Ground Beef: 20% to 30% fat.*
- *Ground Chuck (may be labeled Lean Ground Beef): 15% to 20% fat.*
- *Ground Round (may be labeled Extra Lean Ground Beef): 10% to 15% fat.*
- *Ground Sirloin or Chopped Sirloin: 15% fat.*

STUFFED TURKEY BREAST

The turkey breast is wrapped around a parsley and Fontina cheese stuffing.

Roast at 325° for 2 hours and 15 minutes.
Makes 10 servings at 573 calories each.

1 **fresh or frozen bone-in turkey breast
    (6 to 6½ pounds), thawed if frozen**
2 **cups fresh bread crumbs**
1½ **cups chopped parsley**
1 **egg, slightly beaten**
2 **leeks, washed and sliced (1½ cups)**
2 **teaspoons finely chopped garlic**
5 **ounces (1¼ sticks) butter or margarine**
1½ **cups (6 ounces) shredded Fontina cheese**
1 **can (13¾ ounces) chicken broth
    OR: 2 cups water**
4 **teaspoons cornstarch**
2 **tablespoons cold water
    Salt and pepper to taste**

1. To bone the turkey, place, skin-side down, on a cutting board. Using a thin-bladed knife, cut between the bone and flesh, keeping the point of the knife close to the bone so as not to pierce the meat; pull the bone away as you loosen it. When you get to the base of the breastbone, be careful not to cut through the skin. (Save the bone for soup.)
2. Place the boned turkey breast, skin-side down, on the work surface. Trim off all excess fat. Cut away the pointed oval fillet from each side of the breast; set aside. Make horizontal slits in the thickest part of the breast, without cutting all the way through. Open the slits toward the top of the breast; pound slightly with the base of the hand or a mallet to make the meat an even thickness. Set aside.
3. Combine the bread crumbs, parsley and egg in a large bowl.
4. Sauté the leeks and garlic in ¼ cup of the butter in a small skillet until soft, for 5 minutes. Add to the bread-crumb mixture.
5. Sprinkle the turkey with the Fontina. Distribute the bread-crumb stuffing over the cheese. Lay the reserved breast fillets, end to end, lengthwise down the center. Roll the breast up from one long side and fasten with skewers to hold its shape. Bring the skin up and over the turkey from both ends; fasten with skewers. Wrap the turkey in a double thickness of cheesecloth. Tie in 4 or 5 places with string. Place, seam-side down, in a small roasting pan. Melt the remaining 6 tablespoons of butter in a saucepan.

Pour over the turkey to soak the cheesecloth. (The turkey can be prepared to this point, 3 hours in advance, and refrigerated.)
6. Preheat the oven to moderate (325°).
7. Roast in the preheated moderate oven (325°), basting often with pan drippings, for 2 hours and 15 minutes, or until a meat thermometer inserted into the thickest part registers 185°. Remove the turkey to a cutting board. Let stand for 20 minutes before unwrapping and slicing. Reserve the pan drippings for gravy. Serve the turkey hot or warm with the pan gravy.
8. Meanwhile, prepare the gravy: Tilt the roasting pan carefully and pour off the fat. Add the chicken broth to the pan. Stir over low heat, scraping up browned bits from the bottom of the pan. Strain into a small saucepan. Skim off and discard any fat. Bring to boiling. Mix the cornstarch with the cold water in a small cup until smooth. Stir into the saucepan. Return to boiling. Cook, stirring, for 1 minute until thickened and smooth. Add salt and pepper to taste.

BOILED NEW POTATOES AND ONIONS: Cook 16 red new potatoes, with skins on, in boiling salted water for 20 minutes, or until tender. Drain. Keep warm. Cook 8 medium-size yellow onions in boiling salted water for 30 minutes, or just until tender. Drain and cut in half. Keep warm. (If red new potatoes are not available, use red potatoes, halved or quartered.)

WINTER SALAD OF JULIENNE VEGETABLES

Fennel is an anise-flavored vegetable. If unavailable, substitute with celery.

Makes 10 servings at 106 calories each.

4 **to 6 carrots, cut into julienne
    (1½ x ¼-inch) pieces (about 2 cups)**
½ **pound snow peas, strings removed, cut
    lengthwise into ¼-inch strips**
1 **large fennel bulb, washed**
1 **teaspoon grated fresh gingerroot**
½ **teaspoon finely chopped garlic**
⅛ **teaspoon cayenne pepper**
3 **tablespoons lemon juice**
3 **tablespoons peanut oil**
2 **tablespoons soy sauce**
1 **tablespoon honey**
1 **head radicchio,* separated into leaves**
1 **head romaine, separated into leaves**

1. Place the carrots in a metal strainer. Immerse in a large pot of boiling salted water. Cook until crisp-tender for 1 to 2 minutes. Lift out the strainer and drain; plunge the carrots into ice water in a bowl. In the same boiling water, immerse the snow peas in a strainer until just bright green, for 5 seconds. Drain; add to the carrots in the ice water. Drain the vegetables well. Place in a large bowl.
2. Trim the stalks from the fennel. Cut the bulb in half, lengthwise. Remove the core from each half. Cut the fennel lengthwise into very thin slices. Add to the other vegetables. Refrigerate.
3. Mix the gingerroot, garlic, cayenne, lemon juice, oil, soy sauce and honey. Let stand for 30 minutes.
4. To serve, toss the vegetables with the dressing. Arrange the radicchio and romaine around the edge of a serving plate. Spoon the salad in the center.

*__Note:__ Radicchio is a pepper-tasting, red-leafed Italian lettuce.

BUTTERMILK DRESSING

Makes 1 cup at 8 calories per tablespoon.

3/4 __cup buttermilk__
2 __tablespoons lemon juice__
1 __teaspoon leaf basil, crumbled__
1/2 __teaspoon crushed red pepper flakes,__
  __or to taste__
1 __clove garlic, finely chopped__

Combine all ingredients in the container of an electric blender. Cover and whirl until smooth, scraping down the sides as necessary. Refrigerate for at least 2 hours before serving.

___CRISP SALADS___

● *Wash your greens well, shaking off the excess water. Wrap in paper toweling in a plastic bag and refrigerate.*
● *To minimize wilting, toss greens with dressing just before serving.*

ZUCCHINI BOATS WITH BULGUR PILAF

___Bulgur is a form of cracked wheat.___

Makes 8 to 10 servings at 123 calories each.

1/4 __cup chopped shallots OR: green onions__
2 __tablespoons butter or margarine__
1 __sweet red pepper, cored, seeded and__
  __finely chopped__
1 __cup bulgur__
2 __cups water OR: chicken broth__
1/2 __cup tomato juice__
3/4 __teaspoon salt__
1/4 __teaspoon ground pepper__
1/8 __teaspoon ground allspice__
8 __to 10 medium-size zucchini (5 or 6 inches__
  __long), halved lengthwise__

1. Sauté the shallots or green onions in the butter or margarine in a medium-size heavy saucepan for 5 minutes. Add the red pepper; sauté, stirring, for 4 to 5 minutes. Stir in the bulgur, water or chicken broth, tomato juice, salt, pepper and allspice. Bring to boiling. Lower the heat, then simmer, covered, for 15 minutes. Remove from the heat. Let stand, tightly covered, for 15 to 20 minutes.
2. Cook the zucchini in boiling salted water to cover in a large skillet for 8 minutes, or until tender. Drain. Run under cold water. Scoop out the insides, leaving a 1/4- to 1/2-inch shell. Spoon the bulgur pilaf into the zucchini shells. Serve hot or at room temperature. To serve hot, preheat the oven to moderate (350°), then bake the zucchini in a shallow baking dish, loosely covered with foil, in the preheated moderate oven (350°) for 20 minutes, or until heated through.

VELVETY CREME CHOCOLATE

Dieters will think they're cheating!

Bake cake layers at 350° for 20 minutes.
Makes 10 servings at 104 calories each.

Cake Layers:
½ **cup** sifted **all-purpose flour**
¼ **cup unsweetened cocoa powder**
¼ **teaspoon ground cinnamon**
¼ **teaspoon salt**
3 **eggs**
⅔ **cup sugar**
Chocolate Creme:
1 **envelope unflavored gelatin**
3 **tablespoons unsweetened cocoa powder**
1 **tablespoon instant coffee**
Dash ground cinnamon
¼ **cup water**
1 **cup cold skim milk**
2 **egg whites**
3 **tablespoons sugar**
Yogurt Topping:
1 **envelope unflavored gelatin**
¼ **cup water**
1 **egg white**
1 **tablespoon sugar**
½ **teaspoon vanilla**
¾ **cup plain yogurt**
4 **to 6 large strawberries, quartered**
Fresh mint leaves for garnish (optional)

1. Preheat the oven to moderate (350°).
2. Prepare the Cake Layers: Grease two 8-inch-round cake pans; line the bottoms with wax paper, then grease the paper.
3. Sift together the flour, cocoa, cinnamon and salt onto a piece of wax paper.
4. Beat the eggs in a small bowl until foamy. Gradually beat in the sugar until thick and fluffy. Fold in the flour mixture. Spoon into the prepared pans, dividing evenly.
5. Bake in the preheated moderate oven (350°) for 20 minutes, or until the tops spring back when lightly pressed with a fingertip. Cool in the pans on wire racks for 10 minutes. Loosen the edges and invert the cakes onto the racks; cool completely. Place one layer on a serving platter. Cover and set aside. Wrap and freeze the second layer for another use.
6. Prepare the Chocolate Creme: Combine the gelatin, cocoa powder, instant coffee, cinnamon and water

in a cup. Stir until the gelatin is softened. Place the cup in hot water; stir to dissolve the gelatin.
7. Combine the cold milk and gelatin-cocoa mixture in a small bowl. Chill until the mixture is the consistency of unbeaten egg whites.
8. Beat the 2 egg whites in a bowl until foamy. Gradually beat in the sugar until soft peaks form. Fold the chilled cocoa mixture into the beaten whites until no white streaks remain. Pour into a 1-quart metal mold or bowl, 6 to 7½ inches in diameter. Shake gently to remove large bubbles. Refrigerate for several hours, or overnight, until firm.
9. To unmold, loosen the edges of the gelatin; quickly dip in warm water. Invert over the Cake Layer; shake to loosen and carefully remove the mold. Refrigerate until the surface of the mold has set again.
10. Prepare the Yogurt Topping: Sprinkle the gelatin over the water in a small cup; let stand for 5 minutes to soften. Set the cup in hot water; stir to dissolve the gelatin. Cool slightly.
11. Beat the egg white in the small bowl until foamy. Gradually beat in the sugar until the meringue forms soft peaks. Fold the gelatin mixture and the vanilla into the yogurt in a medium-size bowl. Fold in the beaten egg white. Spoon the Yogurt Topping into a pastry bag fitted with a large star tip. Pipe up and down over the side of the mold, but leave the top sides of the mold uncovered. Pipe the topping on top of the mold in a small swirl. Garnish the side and top with strawberries. Garnish each strawberry with fresh mint leaves, if you wish.

Make-ahead Note: Freeze both Cake Layers, thawing one the day before party time.

Velvety Creme Chocolate

HOLIDAY
ENTERTAINING GUIDE

Giving a holiday party for the first time? Or do you already consider yourself a pro? This mini-hostess guide will allow you to enjoy the party just as much as your guests will. Also, check out our "Holiday Countdown to a Party" on page 9 for planning strategies.

NAPKIN KNOW-HOW

Napkins add the final touch to a festive table, whatever the occasion.

If you're going beyond the paper napkin route, you'll find a variety of sizes, colors and materials to choose from. Let the occasion, menu and number of guests be your guide.

● Choose luncheon or cocktail napkins for informal meals and light refreshments, larger dinner napkins for more substantial fare.

● Imported linen napkins certainly add a gracious feeling to formal dining. But the newer linen/polyester blends are less expensive and come in a wide variety of contemporary and traditional designs.

● Embroidered or trimmed designs add a more formal look to the table.

● To traditionalists, white is still considered "the" color for posh meals, although many hostesses are breaking out of this formality.

● Coordinate napkin colors with tablecloths and china patterns. More than one color, or two patterns in the same color scheme, adds visual interest.

QUICK TRICKS

● Place napkins to the left of silver for formal occasions. Otherwise, be adventurous: Tuck the napkin in a glass, under the top plate or on top of the plate. For buffet service, line up the napkins next to the cutlery or roll them up and set them in some baskets on each table.

● Gingham napkins are great for country-style meals.

● Colorful tea towels-turned-napkins add a rustic note to your informal suppers.

● Tie striped or checked ribbons around the napkins, as well as around wine bottles.

● Tie thick twine around raw cotton squares, then tuck in a daisy or two just before your guests sit down.

● For a Victorian accent, scent the napkins with your most delicate cologne.

● Glue tiny shells, acorns or trinkets on the ends of thin ribbons and use; these to tie the rolled napkins.

NAPKIN FOLDING—REVIVAL OF AN OLD-FASHIONED ART

The centuries-old custom of napkin folding is easier than it looks and gives any table an elegant aura.

● Use crisply starched and smoothly ironed squares.

● Practice complicated folds on pieces of paper first.

● Sharpen the folds with an iron.

● Here, the shapes illustrated on the next page and how to make them:

1. "The Bishop": Fold the napkin not quite in half, along (A); fold two (BB) portions to the center (C); fold across at the dotted line (E), turning up the portion marked (D); turn down portion (F) onto (G); curl at the base of the triangle; insert the point of 1 side (H) into the pleat of the other (I); pull down the pointed leaves, curl and tuck them into the pleats; place tiny biscuits or muffins in the center.

2. "The Palm": Fold the napkin into quarters, then diagonally across; pleat, beginning on one end of the fold; gently open up; tuck it into a napkin ring.

3. "The Lily": Fold the napkin into quarters, then diagonally; turn 2 loose leaves onto either side. Pleat and pull down the two leaves from either side of the center; insert in a glass.

4. "The Cactus": Fold the napkin into quarters, then diagonally across, as for "The Palm"; pull down the four leaves.

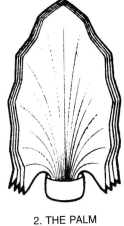

2. THE PALM

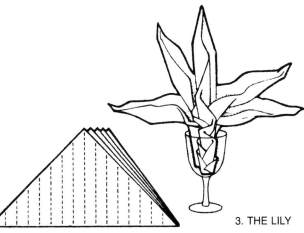

3. THE LILY

1. THE BISHOP

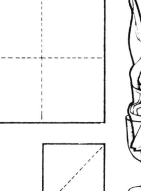

4. THE CACTUS

NIP AND TUCK—four elegant ways to grace a special-occasion table: 1. The Bishop, smart holder for tiny biscuits; 2. The Palm, placed in a napkin ring; 3. The Lily & 4. The Cactus, in goblets.

OFF THE SHELVES

Bring out those seldom-used serving pieces and appliances and give them new functions.

Instead of buying a whole cupboard of new serving pieces, recycle what you already have:

Oversized Wine Goblets—Great for chilled soups, seafood cocktails (the clear glass makes layers of shredded lettuce, seafood and cocktail sauce a real showstopper), dessert mousses or jumbo ice-cream sundaes.

Punch Bowl—Fill with tossed salad, mousse or icy fruit salad for a crowd; pile crushed ice to fill the bowl and nestle bowls of crudités and dips in the ice; use it to serve mixed drinks—Whiskey Sour, Bloody Mary, Screwdriver or Sangria—to a crowd; use as a beer or wine cooler.

Scallop Shells—These make lovely serving plates for butter pats at a seafood luncheon; line with frilly lettuce leaves and top with scoops of seafood salad; use as "tins" for pastry: Place on a cookie sheet, bake and use as an edible container for seafood newburg, bouillabaisse or scrambled eggs and fish.

Individual Soup Tureens (ovenproof)—Use for individual chicken pot pies, soufflés or deep-dish fruit pies; reheat casseroles with cooked noodles or rice in the bottom.

Mugs—Fill with stew or thick soup and serve with long spoons for casual eating in front of the fire or television; fill the bottom with cracked ice and add celery, carrot and zucchini sticks; fill with breadsticks and place between every two seats at the table.

Oval Fish Platters—Ideal for any kind of buffet service, especially asparagus, cold cuts, deviled eggs and fried chicken for a crowd.

Ovenproof Lasagna Dishes—Bake giant lattice pies, gratinéed vegetable casseroles, fruit crumbles and sheet cakes.

Ring Molds—Useful for meatloaf mixtures, cheese rings, baba au rhum (fill the center with softly whipped cream), rice or noodle rings, ice molds and gelatin salads.

Pizza Pans—Pat a meatloaf mixture to cover the bottom, bake it and top with a tomato sauce, grated cheese and spices, for a "pizza"; use this for a crowd-size fruit tart.

Muffin Tins—Bake patty shells, shirred eggs (grease well and line the edge with bacon strip halves) and individual meatloaves.

Ramekins or Custard Cups—Fill with dip, place in the center of a cabbage or hollowed artichoke and surrounded with crisp raw vegetables; use as a container for drawn butter at seafood meals; fill with softened herb or orange butter, level the top, score with a fork and place in a basket of warm muffins and rolls; fill with individual fruit mousse or soufflé mixtures.

Egg Cups—If you're really desperate, use these as Sherry or liqueur cups.

Jam Jars—Fill with mustard for ham, horseradish sauce for roast beef or hollandaise for steamed vegetables.

Large Wood Salad Bowls—Line with pretty dish towels and fill with hot rolls and muffins; fill with chunks of sausage and cheese and provide skewers for spearing; fill with popcorn, pretzels or potato chips for munching by the fireplace.

THE HEAT'S ON

If you've ever had more pots than places to cook them, bring out your smaller electric appliances. They're like extra help in the kitchen.

Electric Frypan—Heat rolls; use as a buffet server for chili, casseroles and hearty stews at informal parties; reheat soups and sauces; cook chops, chicken and fried eggplant.

Electric Wok—Reheat rice or pasta (add a bit of water); stir-fry side dishes (they don't have to be Oriental!); steam rolls and turnovers; heat stews.

Electric Hot Hors d'Oeuvre/Meal Maker—The hot tray lets you make hors d'oeuvre, vegetable or main-dish kabobs while you reheat cooked rice, noodles or rolls on top.

Electric Slow-Cooker—Steam pudding, heat sauces, soup and mulled wine.

Electric Fondue Pot—Keep entrée or dessert sauces warm; use for hot hors d'oeuvre dips.

4 QUICK APPLIANCE RECIPES

FONDUE POT BAGNA CAUDA
Makes 4 servings. Combine ½ cup (1 stick) of butter or margarine, ½ cup of olive or vegetable oil, 8 anchovy fillets (mashed), 2 garlic cloves (minced), and ½ teaspoon of leaf oregano (crumbled) in an electric fondue pot. Simmer, stirring once or twice, for 5 minutes. Stir in ¼ cup of thinly sliced pitted ripe olives. Serve with crisp raw vegetables. Use fondue forks for easy dipping.

ELECTRIC FRYPAN RICE BALLS
Makes 8 servings. Combine 6 cups of cooked rice, 4 egg yolks and ½ of cup shredded provolone cheese in a medium-size bowl, then shape into 24 balls. Roll in 4 slightly beaten egg whites, then in 1 cup of dry bread crumbs. Chill for at least 1 hour. Pour vegetable oil to a depth of 3 inches in a skillet and heat to 375°. Fry the rice balls, 2 or 3 at a time, for 4 minutes, or until golden. Drain on paper towels and serve warm with tomato sauce.

WOK MULLED CIDER
Makes 5 quarts. Mix 4 quarts of apple cider, 1 quart of ginger ale, ¼ cup of golden raisins, ¼ cup of toasted slivered almonds, three 2-inch pieces of stick cinnamon and 4 whole cloves in a 6-quart electric wok. Heat on a low setting (200°) for 10 minutes, or until hot. Do *not* allow to boil. Add 1 thinly sliced navel orange and 1 cup of Calvados or apple brandy. Serve hot in glass punch cups.

TOASTER OVEN CHEDDAR LOAVES
Makes 8 servings. Cut 2 small loaves of French bread into ¾-inch-thick slices almost to the bottom. Spread the cut surfaces with a mixture of 2 cups of shredded Cheddar cheese, ¼ cup (½ stick) of softened butter or margarine, ¼ cup of sliced green onion and ¼ cup of wheat germ. Place the loaves on the baking sheet of a toaster oven. Bake in a moderate oven (350°) for 12 minutes, or until the cheese melts.

STANDING ROOM ONLY

If you're limited on space and furniture, you can still hold a bash for a crowd—buffet-style.
● Invent new functions for old pieces. Covered with a runner, a desk becomes an extra table for dining or serving. An étagére, cleared of most of its bric-a-brac, is transformed into a tiered serving space. Even the old trunk in the attic has its place on the entertaining scene. Besides being the ideal place to hide last-minute junk, it makes a whimsical cocktail table.
● Folding tables and chairs fit well in small quarters. Store them under a bed or in a closet.

FIRST AID FOR FOOD

Don't let last-minute mishaps in the kitchen spoil your party.
Yes, even that collapsed soufflé is salvageable!

A culinary mishap is often the start of a delectable new dish. Remember, only *you* know what was originally on the menu!

- If your soufflé falls, bring out individual portions from the kitchen and serve as baked pudding. Top savory soufflés with a cheese, vegetable or tomato sauce, sweet ones with clouds of whipped cream.
- If your gelatin mold collapses, chop it into cubes and serve on individual lettuce-lined plates.
- If your cheese is overripe, grate or mash it and mix with softened butter or cream cheese. Serve with crisp crackers.
- If your cake sinks, cover the top with a center of fruit salad, surrounded by rosettes of whipped cream.
- If your meatballs fall apart, crush them with a fork and add them to the sauce.
- If your rice forms a crust on the bottom of your saucepan, serve it in wedges.
- If your whipped cream is overbeaten, continue beating until soft butter forms. Beat in 10X (confectioners' powdered) sugar and liqueur, then serve it as a hard sauce topping.

- If your poached eggs are misshapen, place them in a toast-lined casserole, then top with a sauce and bake.
- If your pasta or rice gets mushy, bind it with a thick white sauce. Form it into patties, then dip in beaten egg and bread crumbs. Sauté.
- If your roast chicken falls apart, slice it in the kitchen.
- If your omelet falls apart, cut it into cubes. Mound it on a plate and garnish with colorful vegetables.

PREVENTIVE MEASURES

- *Use a wire whip to stir sauces to silky smoothness.*
- *Heat delicate sauces and stews in a double boiler.*
- *Keep flames low to prevent overcooking.*
- *Stir pasta and rice with a fork to prevent mashing.*
- *Lightly salt long-simmering food before cooking. Taste after cooking and adjust the seasoning.*

COLD STORAGE

A freezer of ready-to-serve food is a welcome head start at party time.
Here's how to stock up.

Here are the solid facts on freezing cooked food for best results:

● Use air- or moisture-proof freezer paper or heavy-duty aluminum foil to keep food in top condition.

● Glass jars are ideal for soups and sauces. Leave 1-inch headroom.

● Squeeze out as much air as possible when wrapping food in paper. Don't let sharp bones cut through the wrapping or air will leak in, causing flavor loss.

● Label and date each item. Keep a list of all the food in your freezer so you know just what you have.

● Only freeze food in serving-size portions, since thawed food should never be refrozen.

● For easy-to-reheat casseroles that keep cooking dishes in circulation: Line a cooking dish with heavy-duty aluminum foil, leaving an overhang on all sides. Fill with prepared food, then seal tightly and freeze until solid. Remove the foil package from the dish and return it to the freezer. At serving time, return the

package to the dish and bake as directed. (Bonus: Cleanup will be easier, too!)

● Unfreezables: Don't freeze fresh raw vegetables (except onions, peppers, cabbage and celery), hard-cooked eggs, boiled potatoes, gelatin dishes, sour cream or mayonnaise, custard and cream pies, stuffed poultry or boiled frostings.

● Wrap unfrosted cakes before freezing. They'll thaw at room temperature in 1 hour. Frosted cakes should be frozen firm, then wrapped, so frosting stays fluffy. Unwrap and thaw at room temperature for 2 hours.

● Freeze baked rolls and breads unglazed. Remove them from wrapping to thaw at room temperature, then glaze.

● Heat straight-from-the-freezer rolls in a slow oven (300°) for 15 minutes, or until heated through.

● Freeze canapes on cookie sheets, then pack them in freezer bags. Place frozen canapes directly on a serving tray. Cover with a cloth; defrost them at room temperature.

GOOD SCENTS—ODOR CONTROL

Since scent has such a powerful influence on a guest's perception of your home, make sure first impressions are sweet, not disturbing:

● Clean and air your house thoroughly before your guests arrive. Use a deodorant rug cleaner to eliminate lingering odors underfoot.

● Keep solid air fresheners in close areas, such as bathrooms, closets and vestibules.

● Place an in-bowl freshener/deodorizer in the toilet.

● Use an aerosol air freshener for immediate control of strong odors such as onions and cigar smoke. Avoid

overpowering single scents, such as evergreen or rose in favor of more subtle combinations.

● For long-lasting effects, sprinkle a cotton ball with a few drops of wintergreen oil and place out of sight.

● Burn special scentless candles that absorb odors.

● For post-party odors, place a bucket of water mixed with a few tablespoons of baking soda in the middle of the room and let stand overnight. Or, place a piece of charcoal in a little water and leave overnight. The air will be sweeter in the morning.

WINNING WAYS TO ENTERTAIN WITHOUT GOING BROKE

Just because you're counting pennies during the holidays doesn't mean you have to scrimp at party time. Here are some tips for painless cost-cutting.

● Serve omelets for brunch or a casual supper. Let guests choose from an assortment of sweet and savory fillings—like chicken in Sherry-cream sauce with toasted almonds and peas; strawberry jam and sour cream; shredded Cheddar with sliced cooked sausage and sautéed apples. Serve with hot homemade biscuits, softly whipped butter and one or two vegetable or fruit salads.

● Buy meat for stews and casseroles in large, uncut pieces, rather than buying cubed stew meat. Whole chickens cost less than parts.

● Give a sausage- and mustard-tasting party. Choose from sweet and hot Italian sausage, Polish kielbasa, German bockwurst or knackwurst and all-American frankfurters. Serve complementary mustards, a hearty baked bean casserole and lots of beer.

● Divide the cost—and labor—of entertaining by hosting a co-op party where everyone brings his or her own dish.

● Invite guests for a dessert smorgasbord. Balance one or two elaborate cakes with tiny butter cookies and a bowl of chilled fresh fruit sprinkled with wine and 10X (confectioners' powdered) sugar.

● Try ethnic cuisines that don't emphasize costly meat and seafood. Our International Feast (pages 192-203) fills this bill.

● Choose from the calendar's bounty, when produce is most plentiful and least expensive.

● Don't eliminate luxury items—just make the most of them. A quarter pound of smoked salmon serves 4 if you add it to a dill-flavored cream sauce for pasta. One pound of crisp asparagus adds elegance to a crudité selection.

● Use up what you've got. Waste is a wicked budget eater. If you've bought 5 chickens, make pâté from the livers. A sauce prepared with egg yolks leaves you egg whites for making meringues.

● Serve bowls of chili with all the trimmings—chopped onions, chopped tomatoes and green peppers, crushed taco chips and cubed Monterey Jack cheese. Mexican beer, orange and avocado salad, and flan with cinnamon butter cookies complete the meal.

● Give a beer-tasting party. Include 6 to 10 domestic and imported varieties. Freeze wet glasses or mugs to keep the beer chilled. Pass hearty nibbles such as cheese-sausage kabobs, onion-quiche squares and miniature caraway-buttermilk biscuits sandwiched with paper-thin slices of corned beef.

● Serve poultry. Many elegant recipes use chicken, turkey, duck or Cornish hens. Not only is poultry the traditional pièce de résistance, your guests will enjoy that roast turkey as much, if not more than Beef Wellington.

● Give a breakfast party—even if it's noon. Traditional early morning fare, such as pancakes, eggs and muffins taste good anytime.

● Soufflés and quiches are always impressive, yet they are neither difficult nor expensive to prepare.

● Replace veal with chicken or turkey in classic recipes.

- Borrow additional chairs, serving pieces and appliances for big parties, instead of buying or renting them.
- Choose local flowers instead of exotic varieties—they're just as festive. Arrange them yourself and save even more.
- Buy good, inexpensive wines for cooking and drinking at party time. Cooking wines cost more per ounce.
- Prepare your own cold-cut and cheese platters. Buy a total of ¼ pound per person. Bulk purchases are great if you've got a slicing machine. Otherwise, buy the items presliced. Arrange the meats and cheeses on the platters, tuck in garnishes, cover with plastic wrap and chill.
- If you're serving turkey, baste it yourself instead of buying more costly self-basting birds.
- Plan a pasta buffet. Serve 2 to 3 kinds of pasta, a meat sauce, a cream sauce and a vegetable sauce. Pass grated cheese, chopped green onions and toasted bread crumbs for toppings.
- Tenderize chuck steak and use this instead of sirloin. Tenderized shoulder lamb chops can replace loin chops.
- Give a grown-up ice-cream buffet. Scoop the ice cream onto jelly-roll pans (3 quarts serve 8 amply). Cover with plastic wrap and freeze for at least 2 hours, or until very firm. Place in a large metal bowl and return to the freezer. Stir creme de cacao into your favorite hot fudge sauce, toasted chopped pecans into butterscotch sauce and a generous splash of Grand Marnier into strawberry sauce. Chopped salted peanuts, toasted coconut and lightly whipped cream top off the gala affair.
- Shop at discount beer and soda distributors for big savings.
- When buying large amounts of beer, soda, wine or liquor, ask the store manager if there are special case prices.
- Before buying alcoholic beverages, find out the return policy of the store, since sometimes it's possible to return unopened bottles for credit.
- Buy store brands and private label liquors. It's a good idea to sample each one before you buy in quantity.

LITTLE EXTRAS THAT DON'T COST MUCH

- *Serve fancy desserts on small doilies.*
- *Form butter or margarine into curls or balls, or use a butter mold.*
- *Use candles.*
- *Fold your napkins in unusual shapes (see page 214 for ideas) or tie them with pretty ribbons.*
- *Add color to punch bowls and tall drinks with decorative ice molds and cubes. For cubes, add lemon, lime or orange rind, mint leaves or halved strawberries.*
- *Garnish food to give it a festive, finished look.*
- *If you can't afford flowers, use a healthy houseplant or bowl of perfect fruit for a centerpiece.*
- *Chill your beer glasses and salad plates, and warm the plates for hot foods.*
- *Serve rolls, breads and muffins warm for a just-baked flavor.*
- *Add sliced lemon to ice water and serve it in your best goblets.*
- *Use place cards for a touch of elegance.*
- *Decant less expensive wines into pitchers or decanters.*

EMERGENCY SHELF

*Unexpected company? No time to cook? Check your well-stocked pantry,
refrigerator and freezer for the makings for a fast and fancy buffet.
Here are some delectable ways to use the staples in your kitchen.*

CHEESE PRODUCTS: One of the most popular varieties is pasteurized process cheese food. It's soft, smooth and richly seasoned, making it an ideal cracker spread. Take it one step further and make it the key flavoring ingredient in recipes.

COLD CUTS: This diverse line includes turkey parts and processed turkey products, including franks, sausage and ham. These turkey versions are prepared to fit breakfast, lunch and dinner—all year round! They offer further convenience because they're sold fully cooked, in packages just the right size and amount for today's smaller households.

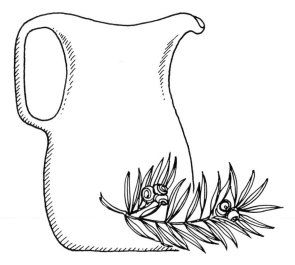

CANNED FRUIT: One of the best-selling canned fruits is pineapple. It's available in slices, chunks and crushed. Like many other canned fruits, it offers a myriad of uses. It's a popular salad ingredient, regal roast accompaniment or convenient dessert by itself or with ice cream.

CANNED MEAT AND SEAFOOD: These are real cook-savers for the hostess. Corned beef hash, ham and tuna are some popular choices. Already cooked and seasoned, they're ready to serve as soon as you open the can. Or, make canned meat and seafood the beginning of a tasty sandwich, casserole or appetizer.

CEREAL: Dry cereal and the addition of a few ingredients are the perfect party-snack combo—No-Cook Party Mix: Combine 1 cup each of bite-size crispy bran, wheat, rice and corn squares with 2 cups of cheese-flavored corn puff balls and 1 cup of peanut-butter flavored chips in a large bowl. Store in a tightly covered container until serving time.

CULTURED BUTTERMILK POWDER: This new product works like liquid buttermilk that give baked goods a lighter, fluffier texture. And it offers the convenience and economy of purchasing buttermilk in shelf-stable form. Use cultured buttermilk powder whenever a recipe calls for liquid buttermilk: Mix ¼ cup of dry buttermilk powder for every cup of liquid buttermilk in your recipe with the other dry ingredients. Then add 1 cup of water when the recipe calls for the addition of liquid buttermilk.

FLAVORED WAFERS: Easy-melting wafers are for candy-making, baking and molding. Available in chocolate and vanilla flavors, they can be the basis of a new repertoire of tempting sweets.

FROZEN SNACK FOODS: What you see is just the beginning of what you get! A frozen French bread pizza, for example, is the starting point of an appetizer extraordinaire: Bake the pizzas, following the package directions. Along one side of the hot pizzas, arrange rolled salami slices stuffed with sliced green onions. Alternate pitted ripe olives and rolled anchovies with capers on the other side, then cut into slices on the diagonal. Serve hot or at room temperature.

INSTANT COFFEE BEVERAGES: Coffee with European flair is whipped up easily, thanks to convenient mixes. Roman style with Amaretto flavoring and Irish mocha mint, to cite two examples, contain the basic flavorings for an exotic hot drink. To finish it off in holiday fashion, stir in a spoonful of the appropriate liqueur and top with a dollop of whipped cream.

MOLASSES: Combine 1 cup of light molasses and ½ cup of prepared mustard in a small bowl. Brush on ham, baked following the directions on its label, during the last hour of cooking time.

NOODLES & SAUCE PRODUCTS: Golden egg noodles in a rich, creamy sauce mixed in a pouch blend the flavor of vegetables and spices. They can be prepared quickly and easily in one saucepan. In just minutes, noodles and sauce products become great-tasting side dishes. When combined with a source of protein and garnished with red and green peppers, for example, they can help create main dishes that look festive and taste fabulous!

NONALCOHOLIC MIXERS: These are designed primarily for making cocktails by mixing with a liquor, but the bottled mixers perk up recipes when you use them in place of all or part of the liquid called for. Some popular flavors are piña colada, peach colada and whiskey sour.

PASTRY FILLING: Here's a product that offers real convenience. Ready-made fruit fillings and nut fillings save you the time and trouble of measuring and mixing your own. In addition, they blend with other ingredients to make delicious baked goods.

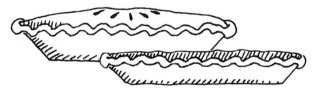

PREPARED PIE SHELLS: These not only save you the time and trouble of mixing your own, they also guarantee perfect crusts. The proof is in the never-fail pies that start with one of the popular convenience products: frozen pastry shell, all-ready piecrust and graham cracker crust. Look for them in the freezer case, in the refrigerator section and on the grocery shelf.

YEAST: No doubt you'll be baking several fragrant yeast breads during the holiday season, so you'll want to keep plenty of active dry yeast on hand. Everyone agrees that yeast bread's lengthy rising time is well worth the end results. But when you use envelopes of the new quick-rise active dry yeast, you can reduce rising time by up to 50%!

WINE GUIDE

Here's all you need to know about wine to serve it with grace. The chart lists the most popular wines, their relative cost (L = low cost, M = medium, H = high) and the foods which provide the best companionship to each wine.

WINE	COST	BEST IF SERVED WITH
WHITE		
Dry, Light-Bodied		
French Chablis	H	Fish, white meat, seafood; as aperitif
California Chablis, Sauternes, French Colombard	L	All foods; as aperitif
California Sauvignon Blanc	M	Fish in sauce, veal, pork, cold meats; hard cheeses; as aperitif
Dry, Medium to Full-Bodied		
Most French White Burgundies	H	Pâté, cold meats, fowl and fish in sauce
California Pinot Blanc	M	Same as for white Burgundies
Italian Soave	L	Seafood, fowl, veal, cold dishes
Semi-Dry to Sweet, Medium to Full-Bodied		
California Chenin Blanc	M	White meat, pork, boiled red meat, picnic food; as aperitif
German Liebfraumilch	M	All foods; as aperitif
French Sauternes	H	Desserts
ROSÉ		
Dry & Sweet		
California, New York, French, etc., Vin Rosé or rosé varietals	L	All foods
RED		
Dry, Light-Bodied		
French Bordeaux	H	Lamb, beef, pork, game; hard cheeses.
California Cabernet Sauvignon	H	Same as for French Bordeaux
California Claret	L	Game, beef; hard cheeses
French Beaujolais	M	All foods
Italian Valpolicella	L	Veal, fowl, cold meats
Spanish Rioja	L	Beef, pork, lamb, ham
Dry, Medium to Full-Bodied		
Italian, California Chianti	M	Italian food; strong cheeses
French Burgundy	H	Beef, pork, game; soft, strong cheeses; spicy dishes
California Burgundy, Hearty Reds	L	Same as for French Burgundy

HOW TO CHOOSE WINE

The first question that causes panic in the wine novice is what kind of wine to serve. Should it be red, white or rosé? Most people learn to enjoy white wine before red wine. If you find that your guests are adverse to reds, it is no crime to serve whites with any food. It is even less of a crime to serve rosé, the most versatile of wine types. If, however, you and your guests enjoy both red and white wines, see our chart (page 224) for wine and food suggestions.

There are, of course, decisions to be made beyond color. European wines, in general, are placed in categories according to the region in which they are produced. The French Burgundies, for example, come from a specific region of France. Not so with California wines. There are two types of California wines: generic and varietal. Generic wines are produced from a blend of grapes and are the inexpensive everyday jug wines. California Burgundy, Chablis and Sauternes have only borrowed their names from the French wines and have little or no resemblance to them.

Varietal wines, on the other hand, bear names like Chenin Blanc and Cabernet Sauvignon. These are the names of special, high-quality grapes used as a principal ingredient in the wine. The grapes are the same ones of which the older, more famous European wines are made. Varietal wines are more expensive and often more subtle and complex in flavor than generic wines. In searching for a wine, don't overlook the tasty, reasonably priced domestic wines from New York State.

Although it is perfectly acceptable to serve a good "jug" wine with most meals, the jug may be too bulky for your table. Pour the wine into an attractive decanter for easy handling and pouring. If, however, you have put special effort into a subtly flavored dish, you may wish to consider serving a more sophisticated wine. A fine imported or California varietal wine would be more suitable. Your wine merchant can point you toward a wine that will best enhance the delights of your culinary efforts.

In developing a taste for wine, you will first learn to distinguish various degrees of dryness and of body. Our wine chart is organized according to these characteristics. Take time to taste a wine. Swirl it in the glass, smell it, take a small sip and roll it around your tongue. Learning to enjoy wine requires a little patience!

HOW TO BUY IT

Cost does not always equal quality in the wine department. Many wines with hefty price tags may be inferior to less expensive wines. Also, a wine producer's product may not be consistent. One California wine producer may make a tremendous Zinfandel, but may put out a bitter Claret. Time and the guidance of a good wine merchant will steer you right.

Wine is available in a variety of bottle sizes. The standard size is 750 milliliters or 25 ounces. Also available: 375 milliliters or 12 ounces; 1 liter or 34 ounces; 1.5 liters or 50 ounces; 3 liters or 100 ounces; and 4 liters or 135 ounces. You should have enough wine on hand to provide at least two 6-ounce glasses for each guest. If you serve wine as a cocktail as well as with the meal, you should have an extra 12 ounces per person. For a buffet that includes a variety of dishes, you should provide both white and red wines, with twice as much white as red.

BUBBLY HOSPITALITY—CHAMPAGNE

Authentic Champagne comes from the Champagne district of northeastern France. Champagne is a sparkling white wine, although slightly sweeter, fuller-bodied pink champagnes are also available. The champagne label will indicate the nature of the drink: "Brut" is very dry; "extra dry" is slightly less dry; "demi-sec" or "semi-dry" is somewhat sweet; and "sec" or "dry" is sweet.

A dryer champagne is best as an aperitif and as an accompaniment to a meal. A sweeter champagne is best with dessert. Champagne should be served chilled, but not ice cold.

Although American champagnes are not duplicates of the French originals, they provide their own special delights. American champagnes, both from California and from New York State, are also considerably less expensive. A superb California champagne costs considerably less but may rival a much higher-priced French Champagne in quality.

Dramatic uncorking of a champagne bottle is for the movies, not for your living room. It is wasteful and harmful to the wine, not to mention your guests! Do not shake up the champagne bottle before opening. In one hand, tilt the bottle at a 45° angle away from the crowd, and in the other hand, grab the cork firmly. Twist the bottle—not the cork—gently, until the cork is removed without a sigh or a fizzle.

CHEESE GUIDE

The following cheeses come from all over the world, but are widely available in the United States and Canada.

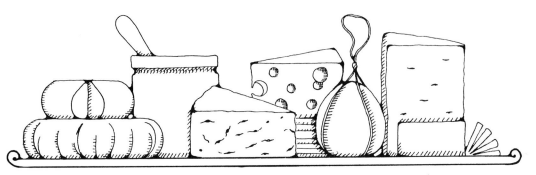

CHEESE	DESCRIPTION	BUYING TIPS	RESEMBLES
SOFT			
Boursin	Strong, rich flavor; white; creamy	Packaged with herbs, spices, garlic or pepper	Boursin is one of many herbed or spiced cream cheeses
Brie	Mild to pungent flavor; creamy yellow interior, edible white crust; creamy	Should bulge and run a little; center should not be collapsed	Camembert
Cheese Spreads	Mild to mellow flavor; various colors; spreads easily	Available in jars and loaves in smoked, blue cheese and other flavors	Coldpack cheese, a spreadable blend of natural cheese
Liederkranz	Strong flavor; white interior; waxy	Should be soft, glossy, fully ripened; package often dated	Limburger, a stronger cheese
SEMISOFT			
American	Mild flavor; pale yellow, orange or white; smooth	Available in loaves, wrapped or unwrapped slices; Swiss, pimiento, other flavors	Brick; Monterey Jack
Bel Paese	Mild, sweet flavor; creamy yellow interior; waxy	Consistently good quality	Port du Salut, a stronger cheese; Bonbel
Blue (Bleu)	Strong flavor; marbled with blue-green mold; crumbly	Should look moist; veins should stand out against background	Gorgonzola, less moist; Stilton, more crumbly; Roquefort
Brick	Mild flavor when young, strong when old; light yellow to orange; small holes	Consistently good quality	Port du Salut; Tilsit
Muenster	Mild to mellow flavor; creamy white interior; smooth, waxy	European Muenster is sharper and darker than American Muenster	Monterey Jack
Port du Salut	Mellow to robust flavor; creamy yellow interior; smooth, buttery	Consistently good quality	Bel Paese; Bonbel

CHEESE	DESCRIPTION	BUYING TIPS	RESEMBLES
FIRM			
Cheddar	Mild to very sharp flavor; white to deep orange; smooth	Should have neither cracks in surface nor spots of mold	Colby, softer than Cheddar, mild flavor
Edam	Mild, nutlike, buttery flavor; golden interior; small holes; mealy	Comes with red wax covering	Gouda, of slightly softer consistency, but similar flavor; wrapped in yellow wax covering
Gjetost	Sweet, caramel flavor; golden brown; buttery	Consistently good quality	Other sweet Norwegian cheeses; Primost; Mysost
Monterey Jack	Mild to mellow flavor; creamy white; semisoft to firm, open	Consistently good quality	Muenster; Colby; Cheddar
Provolone	Smoky, mellow flavor; yellowish-white interior, golden surface; compact	Comes in pear-, sausage- and salami-shaped rolls and is bound with rope	Cacciocavallo
Swiss (Emmenthaler)	Mild, sweet, nutlike flavor; light yellow; smooth with large holes	Switzerland Swiss is the best; domestic can have slightly bitter flavor	Gruyère, sharper flavor; Jarlsberg, blander flavor

SHARPEN YOUR CHEESE SENSE

Serving cheese is perhaps the simplest and most reliable entertaining technique. The cheese board contains within itself a little world of flavors, enough to satisfy every whim of the fickle or fussy palate.

In choosing the cheese you will serve, consider first the nature of the party. For a dinner party with an hors d'oeuvre hour, strong and tangy cheeses, like Blue, Boursin or Port du Salut are preferable. Since strong cheeses are consumed in small amounts, they won't kill the appetite. Bland cheeses, on the other hand, are eaten in big and frequent chunks that prohibit full enjoyment of the meal which follows.

For a cocktail party, your cheese board should feature variety. Serve 3 or 4 cheeses: one mild, firm cheese like Gouda or Edam; one Cheddar or Cheddar-like cheese; one blue-veined cheese; and one soft cheese or spread. Cheese connoisseurs discourage the use of Limburger or Liederkranz for a party because of their strong odors.

Always serve some cheese you know your guests will like, but also include some unusual ones that they have probably never tasted before. If your guests are beer drinkers, put emphasis on Cheddars, Muenster, Gloucester and other British and American cheeses. Generally, the continental cheeses go best with a dry red wine. The stronger the cheese, the fuller the body of the wine should be. A dry, light white wine, however, never did any harm to cheese either.

Cheese can be served between the main course and dessert, as it is in Europe, or as a healthful dessert in itself, combined with fresh fruit. The most compatible fruits are apples, pears, grapes and plums. Cheese is out of order after an Oriental or Indian meal, or after a very rich meal. To serve cheese with style, follow these guidelines:

● For a cocktail party that features cheese, figure on ¼ to ½ pound of cheese per person. For before-dinner drinks, figure ⅙ of a pound per person. Buy plentiful, attractive wedges or bricks of cheese.

● All cheeses, except soft, unripened types like cream and cottage, should be served at room temperature. Soft cheeses take ⅓ as much time to warm up as do hard cheeses, so take the hard ones out of the refrigerator earlier in the evening. It will take between ½ to 3 hours for cheese to warm up, so plan ahead. Leave the cheese in its wrapper as it warms to prevent drying.

● Serve cheese on wooden boards. On china, crystal or silver platters, cheese—that wholesome, earthy food—looks out of place

● In placing cheese on a board, leave plenty of room for cutting. Do not put strong cheeses next to mild ones.

FEEDING FIFTY

Cooking for a crowd? Here's a handy chart to help you buy just the right amount. To save money, buy foods in largest available sizes.

ITEM	WEIGHT OR MEASURE	SERVING PORTION	AMOUNT TO BUY
Meats and Fish			
Bacon, sliced	pound	2 slices	5 pounds
Chicken, roast	2-pound bird	½ chicken	25 2-pound birds
Frankfurters	pound	2 frankfurters	12 pounds
Ham, baked	5-pound ham	4½ ounces	3 5-pound hams
Meatloaf,			
Hamburger	pound	4½ ounces	15 pounds
Turkey, roast	18-pound bird	4½ ounces	3 18-pound birds
Fish Fillets, fresh			
or frozen	pound	4 ounces, cooked	16 pounds
Vegetables			
Canned	1-pound can	½ cup	12 1-pound cans
Frozen	2-pound bag	½ cup	6 2-pound bags
Fresh			
Beans, Carrots	pound	½ cup	10 pounds
Cabbage	pound	½ cup	12 pounds
Lettuce (salad)	large head	⅛ head	7 large heads
Potatoes			
baked, boiled	pound	1 medium-size	25 pounds
French-fried	pound	4 ounces	15 pounds
mashed	pound	½ cup	15 pounds
Tomatoes	pound	3 slices	10 pounds

ITEM	WEIGHT OR MEASURE	SERVING PORTION	AMOUNT TO BUY
Pasta and Rice			
Macaroni	pound	1 cup	3 pounds
Noodles, Spaghetti	pound	1 cup	6 pounds
Rice, long-grain	3-pound bag	⅔ cup	1 3-pound bag
Bread, Crackers			
Bread	2-pound loaf	2 slices	4 2-pound loaves
Crackers	8-ounce package	4 crackers	4 8-ounce packages
Rolls	dozen	2 rolls	8½ dozen
Desserts			
Fruit Cocktail	29-ounce can	½ cup	8 29-ounce cans
Fruit Cup, fresh	quart	½ cup	6½ quarts
Ice Cream	gallon	½ cup	2 gallons
Pie	9-inch pie	⅙ of pie	9 pies
Beverages			
Coffee			
ground	pound	1½ cups	2 pounds
instant	10-ounce jar	1½ cups	1 10-ounce jar
Juices	46-ounce can	½ cup	5 46-ounce quarts
Milk	gallon	1 glass	4 gallons
Tea, bags	dozen	1½ cups	8 dozen
Extras			
Butter	pound	2 pats	2½ pounds
Cream (for coffee)	pint	2 tablespoons	4 pints
Lemons (for tea)	dozen	1 slice	½ dozen
Salad Dressing	16-ounce bottle	2 tablespoons	3 16-ounce bottles

Delicious gifts to give include, *clockwise from top right:* Pickled Peppers (page 234), Green Peppercorn Cheese (page 271), Spiced Fruit Compote (page 234), Dilled Green Beans (page 233), Chunky Tomato Sauce (page 233) and Herbed Vinegar (page 237).

GIFTS FROM THE
KITCHEN

Y*ou can package these holiday delicacies to give away, or set some aside for friends who stop by, your family and, of course, yourself.*

Preserves and condiments can be made well in advance and are excellent to have on hand for last-minute gifts. Our pantry of recipes gives detailed instructions for canning and heating jars in a water bath (page 232). Once you've mastered a few simple steps, you can turn out Chunky Tomato Sauce (page 233), Hawaiian Pear Marmalade (page 234) and other treats using tasty (and nutritious!) fruits and vegetables.

Christmas baking is a category unto itself. From aromatic yeast breads, like Rum-Raisin Ring (page 240) and Pecan Twists (page 242), to quick breads and fruitcakes (pages 238-251), you'll want to bake and freeze an abundance of breads and cakes in different sizes.

Be they rolled by hand, cut into bars or made without any baking at all, Christmas cookies are always in demand. Because you can bake most cookies ahead of time and store them in tins or in the freezer, they, too, can be made before the real holiday crunch begins.

Savory delights such as Wine and Cheese Spread (page 271), Bacon & Cheese Loaves (page 270) and Brandy Pâté (page 272) can make thoughtful gifts or be kept on hand for holiday entertaining.

Finally, if you're short on time but still want to prepare a gift from scratch, look on page 274 for delicious Super-Quick Goodies.

Whether your gifts are going to a faraway friend or just down the street, packing food attractively and safely is important. See page 277 for wrapping ideas and mailing tips.

💲 Low-Cost ⚡ Quick and Easy ⫷ Make-Ahead 🏔 Low-Calorie

PRESERVES AND CONDIMENTS

HOW TO CAN

1. Wash your jars in hot, sudsy water and rinse them well. Leave the jars in hot water until you're ready to use them.
2. Place new domed lids in a bowl and cover them with boiling water. Keep them in the water until ready to use.
3. Follow the individual recipe directions to make the preserves.
4. Remove the jars from the water, one at a time. Place them on paper towels or a clean cloth. Pack and/or ladle food into the jars, leaving the headroom called for in the individual recipe.
5. Wipe the top and outside rim of the jar with a clean cloth. Place a domed lid on top and screw the metal rings on tightly, but do not force them.

HOW TO MAKE A HOT WATER BATH

1. Place your hot-water-bath canner onto a burner, then add enough water to half-fill the canner (a tea kettle does this job easily). Cover the canner and bring the water to boiling.
2. Place your filled and covered jars in the canner rack and lower into the rapidly boiling water, adding more boiling water to the kettle if the level of the water is not two inches above the jars. Cover the kettle and allow the water to return to a full boil.
3. Process, following the times given in the individual recipes and calculated from the time the water comes to the second boil.
4. Remove the jars from the canner and place them, at least three inches apart, on wire racks on a cloth-lined surface. Allow them to stand for 12 hours, or until cool.
5. Test all your jars to be sure they are sealed, by tapping the top with a spoon. (A clear ringing sound means a good seal. A hollow sound means the jar is *not* sealed properly. Improperly sealed jars should be stored in your refrigerator and used within a month. You may also freeze unsealed jars for up to one year.)
6. If you wish, remove the metal rings. Then wipe the jars with a clean, damp cloth. Label, date and store the jars in a cool, dark, dry place for up to one year.

Note: For altitudes above sea level, add one minute for each 1,000 feet when the recipe processes under 20 minutes. When you're processing jars for more than 20 minutes, add two minutes for each additional 1,000 feet above sea level.

⑤ ⟪⟪
CHUNKY TOMATO SAUCE

Accompany this lusty tomato sauce with a basket of pasta and a jar of freshly grated Parmesan cheese.

Makes five 1-quart jars.

- **2 large onions, chopped (2 cups)**
- **2 green peppers, halved, seeded and chopped**
- **2 stalks celery, chopped**
- **4 cloves garlic, minced**
- **½ cup olive or vegetable oil**
- **1 cup red wine**
- **4 cans (2 pounds, 3 ounces each) Italian tomatoes**
- **4 cans (6 ounces each) tomato paste**
- **¼ cup sugar (or to taste)**
- **2 tablespoons leaf oregano, crumbled**
- **2 tablespoons leaf basil, crumbled**
- **2 tablespoons salt (or to taste)**
- **1 teaspoon pepper**
- **½ cup grated Parmesan cheese (optional)**

1. Sauté the onions, peppers, celery and garlic in the oil until soft in a very large saucepan over moderate heat.
2. Pour in the wine; simmer until it is almost evaporated.
3. Add the tomatoes and their liquid, tomato paste, sugar, leaf oregano, basil, salt and pepper. Bring to boiling; lower the heat. Simmer, uncovered, stirring frequently to avoid burning, for 1 hour, or until the sauce thickens. Stir in the cheese, if using; cool.
4. Ladle the sauce into 5 hot, sterilized 1-quart jars. Seal and refrigerate, or freeze in plastic containers. Plan to give within a day or two. Include a card telling the recipient to keep the sauce refrigerated and use within one week.

⑤ ⟪⟪ ▦
DILLED GREEN BEANS

A classic pickled vegetable.

Makes four 1-pint jars.

- **2 pounds green beans, trimmed**
- **4 whole pimientos, sliced**
- **1 teaspoon whole mustard seeds**
- **4 cloves garlic**
- **4 large stems dill**
- **2½ cups water**
- **2½ cups vinegar**
- **¼ cup salt**

1. Pack the beans, lengthwise, into 4 hot, sterilized 1-pint jars, leaving ¼-inch headroom. Tuck in the pimiento slices. Add ¼ teaspoon of the mustard seeds, 1 clove of garlic and 1 dill stem to each jar.
2. Bring the water, vinegar and salt to boiling in a medium-size saucepan. Pour over the beans in the jars, leaving ¼-inch headroom. Seal the jars and process for 10 minutes in a Hot Water Bath, following the directions on page 232.

Cook's Tip: For Dilled Carrots, substitute 2 pounds of carrots, cut into 4-inch thin sticks, for the green beans.

⑤
CORN RELISH

This is a super way to use up the last vegetables from your garden.

Makes six 1-pint jars.

- **4 cups fresh or frozen corn off the cob**
- **1 cup chopped green cabbage**
- **½ cup chopped onion**
- **½ cup chopped red pepper**
- **½ cup chopped green pepper**
- **1 cup sugar**
- **3 tablespoons prepared mustard**
- **1 teaspoon salt**
- **½ teaspoon pepper**
- **2 cups cider vinegar**
- **⅓ cup all-purpose flour**
- **2 tablespoons dry mustard**
- **1 teaspon dry turmeric**
- **1 cup cold water**

1. Combine the corn, cabbage, onion, red and green peppers, sugar, prepared mustard, salt and pepper in a large, heavy kettle; stir in the vinegar until well blended.
2. Bring to boiling; lower the heat and simmer for 1 hour, stirring often.
3. Combine the flour, dry mustard and turmeric in a small bowl; stir in the cold water to make a smooth paste.
4. Bring the vegetable mixture back to boiling; stir in the flour mixture with a wooden spoon until the mixture thickens and bubbles for 3 minutes.
5. Ladle into 6 hot, sterilized 1-pint jars. Cover and process for 10 minutes in a Hot Water Bath, following the directions on page 232. Store for 1 month before serving or giving as a gift.

💲 𝕶
HAWAIIAN PEAR MARMALADE

Tangy, with chunks of fruit.

Makes ten ½-pint jars.

> 5 **pounds slightly underripe pears**
> **(about 11 medium-size)**
> 1 **small pineapple**
> 2 **teaspoons grated lemon rind**
> 2 **tablespoons lemon juice**
> ½ **pound crystallized ginger, finely chopped**
> 5 **cups granulated sugar**

1. Pare, quarter and core the pears, then cut the quarters into slices. Pare the pineapple; cut it into quarters, lengthwise; core and chop coarsely.
2. Combine the pears, pineapple, lemon rind, lemon juice, ginger and sugar in a large, heavy kettle. Bring to boiling, stirring constantly, until the sugar dissolves.
3. Lower the heat slightly. Cook, uncovered, stirring occasionally, for 45 minutes, or until the mixture thickens and will sheet from a cold metal spoon.
4. Ladle the hot marmalade into 10 hot, sterilized ½-pint jars. Wipe the rims; seal the jars and cool on a wooden board. Label the jars and store in a cool, dry place.
5. At gift-giving time, decorate the jars with colored plastic wrap and ribbons. Suggest that heated marmalade is delicious over chilled fruits.

𝕶
CELERY RELISH

Serve on hamburgers, hot dogs, fried fish fillets or as an accompaniment to broiled meats.

Makes 4½ cups.

> 4 **cups sliced celery**
> 1 **large onion, cut into sixths**
> 1 **jar (4 ounces) pimientos, drained**
> 1 **envelope unflavored gelatin**
> 1 **bottle (8 ounces) Italian salad dressing**

1. Put the celery, onion and pimientos into an electric-blender container; reserve.
2. Mix the gelatin and salad dressing in a small sauce-pan. Stir over low heat just until gelatin is dissolved.
3. Pour the gelatin mixture on the vegetables in the blender. Cover, then whirl at low speed until the ingredients are coarsely chopped.
4. Pour the mixture into a bowl and chill until thick. Spoon into jars, then seal, label and chill until ready to give as a gift. (This will keep for about a week.)

💲 𝕶
PICKLED PEPPERS

Here is the perfect last-minute gift. Just be sure to attach a label telling the recipient that the jar must be kept in the refrigerator.

Makes four 1-pint jars.

> 1 **jar (32 ounces) pickled yellow peppers**
> 1 **jar (32 ounces) pickled red peppers**
> 1 **can (1 pound) sauerkraut**
> 2 **cups cider vinegar**
> 2 **cups olive or vegetable oil**
> 1 **tablespoon pickling spices**

1. Drain the liquid from the peppers; hollow out the peppers at the bottom with a paring knife. Drain on paper toweling.
2. Rinse the sauerkraut in a strainer under cold running water; drain on paper toweling.
3. Stuff the sauerkraut into the peppers. Pack the peppers, alternating colors, in 4 hot, sterilized 1-pint jars.
4. Combine the vinegar, oil and pickling spices in a small saucepan. Bring to boiling; lower the heat and simmer for 5 minutes. Pour the hot liquid to within ½ inch of the tops of the jars. Seal the jars and cool to room temperature. Refrigerate until ready to give. Be sure that the recipient knows that the peppers *must* be refrigerated.

𝕶
SPICED FRUIT COMPOTE

Make this dried-fruit compote several days before gift-giving time.

Makes six 1-pint jars.

> 2 **packages (12 ounces each) mixed dried**
> **fruit**
> 4 **cups water**
> 1 **cup brandy**
> 2 **3-inch pieces stick cinnamon**
> 3 **whole cloves**

1. Combine the fruit, water, brandy, cinnamon and cloves in a large saucepan.
2. Bring to boiling over moderate heat; cover and reduce the heat. Simmer for 10 minutes. Cool and pack in six 1-pint hot, sterilized jars. Keep refrigerated.

WINTER FRUIT CONSERVE

Team fresh winter fruits with dried fruits for a delicious gourmet treat.

Makes eight 1-pint jars.

> 4 **medium-size pears, cored and chopped (not peeled)**
> 2 **medium-size green apples, cored and chopped (not peeled)**
> 1 **medium-size red apple, cored and chopped (not peeled)**
> 2 **cups fresh cranberries (from a 12-ounce package)**
> 1 **eating orange, thinly sliced**
> 1 **lemon, thinly sliced**
> ½ **cup raisins**
> ½ **cup diced dried apricots**
> 4 **cups sugar**
> 1 **cup honey**
> 1 **cup chopped walnuts**

1. Combine the pears, green and red apples, cranberries, orange, lemon, raisins and apricots in a large, heavy kettle. Stir the sugar and honey into the mixture until well blended.
2. Heat slowly to boiling, stirring often with a wooden spoon; lower the heat and simmer for 2 hours, or until mixture thickens; stir in the walnuts.
3. Ladle into 8 hot, sterilized 1-pint jars to within ½ inch of the top; seal and process for 5 minutes in a Hot Water Bath, following the directions on page 232.

APPLE-ONION CHUTNEY

Pennsylvania Dutch homemakers serve chutney with cold sliced meats or cold cuts.

Makes five 1-pint jars.

> 3 **medium-size tart apples (about 1 pound), peeled, cored and chopped**
> 4 **medium-size onions, peeled and finely chopped**
> 2 **cloves garlic, crushed**
> **Juice of 1 lemon**
> 1 **tablespoon mustard seed**
> 3 **cups cider vinegar (divided into 2 cups and 1 cup)**

> 4 **cups firmly packed brown sugar**
> 1 **box (15 ounces) raisins**
> 1 **tablespoon ground ginger**
> 2 **teaspoons salt**

1. Place the apples, onions, garlic, lemon juice, mustard seed and 2 cups of the vinegar in a large kettle.
2. Bring to boiling; reduce the heat and simmer, stirring occasionally, for 1 hour, 30 minutes, or until the mixture thickens.
3. Add the brown sugar, raisins, ginger, salt and the remaining 1 cup of vinegar. Bring to boiling; lower the heat. Simmer, stirring frequently, for 30 minutes, or until thickened.
4. Ladle into 5 hot, sterilized 1-pint jars, leaving ½-inch headroom, and seal and process for 5 minutes in a Hot Water Bath, following the directions on page 232.

HOT-HOT PEPPER JELLY

Delicious served with crackers and cream cheese or used as a glaze for lamb.

Makes eight ½-pint jars.

> 2 **medium-size green peppers, seeded and chopped**
> ⅓ **cup canned jalapeño peppers, seeded and rinsed in cold water**
> 1½ **cups cider vinegar**
> 6 **cups sugar**
> 1 **bottle (6 ounces) liquid pectin**
> 3 **drops green food coloring (optional)**

1. Place the green peppers and jalapeño peppers in the container of an electric blender or food processor with the vinegar. Cover and process on high speed for 1 minute, or until the mixture is puréed.
2. Pour the mixture into a kettle. Add the sugar; stir. Bring to a full rolling boil. Remove the pan from the heat and allow to stand for 5 minutes; skim off the foam.
3. Add the pectin and food coloring, if using. Ladle into 8 hot, sterilized ½-pint jelly jars, leaving ½-inch headroom, and process for 10 minutes in a Hot Water Bath, following the directions on page 232.

💲 🎜

YANKEE TOMATO KETCHUP

Mustard seed and vinegar make a tangy ketchup.

Makes four ½-pint jars.

> **6 medium-size tomatoes, cored and skinned**
> **1 medium-size onion, quartered**
> **3 stalks celery, quartered**
> **¼ green pepper, seeded**
> **¼ cup sugar**
> **1½ tablespoons mustard seed**
> **½ cup cider vinegar**

1. Cut the tomatoes into pieces; combine with the onion, celery and green pepper in a saucepan. Bring to boiling, then lower the heat and simmer for 15 minutes, or until soft.
2. Run the vegetables through a food mill; return to the saucepan. Add the sugar and mustard seed.
3. Bring to boiling, then lower the heat and boil for 1 minute, stirring often. Add the vinegar. Simmer the ketchup for 10 minutes longer.
4. Ladle into 4 hot, sterilized ½-pint jars to within ½ inch of the top. Seal and process for 10 minutes in a Hot Water Bath, following the directions on page 232. Allow to mellow for at least a week before serving.

💲 🞧 🎜

CRANBERRY DRESSING

Toss fresh fruits and greens with this tangy salad dressing.

Makes four 1-pint bottles.

> **1 bottle (32 ounces) cranberry juice cocktail**
> **1 cup honey**
> **1 cup vegetable oil**
> **1 tablespoon toasted sesame seeds**
> **2 teaspoons salt**
> **¼ teaspoon seasoned pepper**

1. Wash four 1-pint bottles in hot, sudsy water and rinse with hot water; dry on a tray in a cooling oven.
2. Combine the cranberry juice cocktail, honey, vegetable oil, toasted sesame seeds, salt and pepper in a medium-size bowl.
3. Fit a funnel into the top of a bottle and ladle in the cranberry mixture to within ½ inch of the top. Repeat with the remaining bottles and dressing; seal the bottles.
4. Refrigerate for 3 days to blend the flavors. Give with a card suggesting that the dressing be poured on chicken salad.

🎜

CRANBERRY LIQUEUR

Start this delicious ruby-red cordial a few weeks before you plan to give it as a gift.

Makes 5 cups.

> **1 pound fresh cranberries**
> **1 eating orange**
> **1 bottle (750 ml.) vodka**
> **1½ cups sugar**
> **¾ cup water**

1. Chop the cranberries coarsely. Peel the orange with a vegetable parer, using only the thin orange—not the white—part of the rind.
2. Combine the cranberries, orange peel and vodka in a glass or ceramic 1-gallon container. Cover and let stand at room temperature for 3 to 4 weeks.
3. Strain the cranberry-orange liquid into a clean container; filter off the liquid if cloudy.
4. Combine the sugar and water in a medium-size saucepan. Bring to boiling over high heat; boil for 1 minute, then cool.
5. Stir the sugar syrup into the cranberry-orange liquid. Taste; for a sweeter liqueur, prepare and add more sugar syrup.
6. Pour into five 1-cup sterilized bottles and cover. Store for up to 6 months.
7. At gift-giving time, decorate the bottles and include a card suggesting that the liqueur be served over ice cream or pound cake.

💲 🞧 🎜

BASIL BUTTER

Spread on bread or place a pat on grilled steak, grilled chicken or hot vegetables.

Makes ½ cup.

> **1 tablespoon fresh basil, finely chopped**
> **2 teaspoons lemon juice**
> **½ cup unsalted butter, softened**

Stir the basil and lemon juice into the softened butter in a small bowl. Spoon into a serving container. Store, tightly covered, in the refrigerator. Keep refrigerated until just before you give or serve it.

FRENCH HERB BLEND

Use this blend to season meats, poultry, salad dressings and vegetables.

Makes 2⅓ cups.

- ½ **cup tarragon**
- ½ **cup chervil**
- 2 **tablespoons leaf sage**
- ½ **cup thyme**
- 2 **tablespoons rosemary**
- 5 **tablespoons freeze-dried chopped chives**
- 2 **tablespoons dehydrated orange rind**
- 2 **tablespoons ground celery seed**

Combine the tarragon, chervil, sage, thyme, rosemary, chives, orange rind and celery seed in a medium-size bowl and stir until well blended. Pack into crocks or small jars, then seal and label. Store in a cool, dry place. Crumble in your hand when using.

ITALIAN HERB BLEND

This easy-to-make bouquet of flavors can be used to season any food that needs an Italian character—from salad dressings and pasta sauces to meat loaves, roast meats, and eggplant.

Makes 1⅔ cups.

- ½ **cup leaf oregano**
- ½ **leaf basil**
- 2 **tablespoons leaf sage**
- 1 **jar (3¼ ounces) seasoned salt**
- 2 **tablespoons lemon pepper**
- 2 **tablespoons garlic powder**

Combine the oregano, basil, sage, seasoned salt, lemon pepper and garlic powder in a small bowl and stir until well blended. Pack into small crocks, jars or clear plastic containers, then seal and label. Store in a cool, dry place.

ZESTY SALAD DRESSING

This is more than a salad dressing. It's also delightful as a basting sauce for broiled chicken and fish.

Makes 2⅔ cups.

- 2 **cups vegetable oil**
- ⅔ **cup red wine vinegar**
- 2 **cloves garlic, chopped**
- 2 **tablespoons Italian Herb Blend** (see recipe below)
- ¼ **cup grated Parmesan cheese**
- 1 **tablespoon sugar**
- 1 **tablespoon salt**
- 1 **teaspoon cracked pepper**

Combine the oil, vinegar, garlic, herb blend, cheese, sugar, salt and pepper in a large bowl. Beat with a wire whisk until thick and well blended. Pack into three ½-pint jars, then seal and label. Store in the refrigerator. Beat or shake well before using.

HERBED VINEGAR

Herbed vinegars add special flavor to salads and sauces.

Makes four 1-quart jars or eight 1-pint jars.

Whole-stem herbs such as thyme, oregano and rosemary
Garlic cloves, sliced (optional)
Whole peppercorns
4 **quarts cider or wine vinegar**

1. Wash four 1-quart jars or eight 1-pint bottles and lids or tops in hot, sudsy water. Rinse well in hot water; drain well.
2. Place an herb, then the sliced garlic, if using, on a long wooden skewer in each container; add 6 peppercorns to each container. Fill to the top with the vinegar. Cover with lids or caps and close tightly. Let stand at room temperature for at least 1 week.

BREADS AND FRUITCAKES

TRIPLE-TREAT YEAST DOUGH

From one simply delicious yeast dough comes a trio of festive holiday breads. Make ahead and freeze, or bake on Christmas Eve to fill the house with the wonderful fragrances of the season.

Bake at 350° for 30 minutes.
Makes 3 yeast breads.

½ **cup (1 stick) butter or margarine**
¾ **cup sugar**
1 **teaspoon salt**
2 **cups milk**
3 **envelopes active dry yeast**
¾ **cup very warm water**
1 **teaspoon sugar**
4 **eggs**
11 **cups all-purpose flour**
1 **teaspoon ground cinnamon**
½ **teaspoon ground nutmeg**

1. Combine the butter or margarine, sugar, salt and milk in a small saucepan. Heat just until the butter melts; remove the pan from the heat and cool to lukewarm.
2. Sprinkle yeast and 1 teaspoon of sugar into the very warm water in a very large bowl. ("Very warm" water should feel comfortably warm when dropped on the wrist.) Stir until dissolved; allow to stand until the mixture bubbles, for about 10 minutes.
3. Add the cooled milk mixture, eggs, 3 cups of the flour, the cinnamon and nutmeg to the yeast. Beat with a wooden spoon for 300 strokes. Stir in the remaining flour, a part at a time, until the mixture forms a soft dough.
4. Turn the dough out onto a lightly floured pastry cloth or board; knead for 5 minutes, or until smooth and shiny. Turn the dough into a large greased bowl; turn to coat all sides, then cover the bowl with plastic wrap. Let rise in a warm place, away from drafts, for 2 hours, or until doubled in volume.
5. Punch the dough down, then divide and shape, following the individual recipes that follow.
6. Cover the shaped dough with plastic wrap. Allow to rise in a warm place, away from drafts, for 45 minutes, or until doubled in volume.
7. Meanwhile, preheat the oven to moderate (350°).
8. Bake in the preheated moderate oven (350°) for 30 minutes, or until the tops are a rich golden brown. Cool in the pans on wire racks for 5 minutes. Invert the Glazed Apricot Bread onto a large square of heavy-duty aluminum foil and cool on a wooden board. Slide the Giant Raspberry Claw onto a large wire rack with a large spatula; cool completely. Cool the Rum-Raisin Ring in the pan on a wire rack.
9. To freeze: Wrap the cold breads in heavy-duty aluminum foil; label, date and freeze.
10. At gift-giving time: Remove the breads from the foil and thaw.

Baked goodies shown in photo, *top row, left to right:* Rum-Raisin Ring (page 240); Plumb Pudding (page 248). *Middle, left to right:* Golden Fruitcake (page 249); small-version Plumb Pudding; Old-Fashioned Fruitcake (page 251); Boston Brown Bread (page 245). *Bottom:* Candied-Orange Tea Bread (page 246).

GLAZED APRICOT BREAD

Rum can be substituted for the brandy in this recipe.

1 **package (6 ounces) dried apricots**
¼ **cup brandy**
¼ **cup (½ stick) butter or margarine**
½ **cup firmly packed brown sugar**
2 **tablespoons light corn syrup**
2 **tablespoons milk**
¼ **recipe Triple-Treat Yeast Dough (page 238)**

1. Soak the apricots in the brandy in a small cup for 10 minutes. Melt the butter or margarine in a small saucepan; stir in the brown sugar, corn syrup and milk. Heat to bubbling, stirring constantly.
2. Pour the corn syrup mixture into the bottom of an 8-cup tube pan. Arrange the apricot halves in a decorative pattern over the corn syrup.
3. Arrange the Triple-Treat Yeast Dough into a 14-inch rope; shape into a ring, pinching the ends together with the fingers. Press over the fruit and syrup layer in the pan. Let rise and bake, following the basic directions for Triple-Treat Yeast Dough.

GIANT RASPBERRY CLAW

For a flavor variation, substitute the raspberry with apricot preserves.

½ **remaining Triple-Treat Yeast Dough (page 238)**
¼ **cup (½ stick) butter or margarine, melted**
½ **cup raspberry preserves**
    Sliced blanched almonds
    Coarse sugar

1. Roll out the Triple-Treat Yeast Dough to a 16 x 12-inch rectangle on a lightly floured pastry cloth or board.
2. Brush with a part of the melted butter or margarine, then with the raspberry preserves. Roll up from one long end, jelly-roll fashion. Place, seam-side down, on a large cookie sheet. Cut at ½-inch intervals almost to the other side with a knife. Let rise, following the basic directions in Triple-Treat Yeast Dough.
3. Just before baking, brush the loaf with the remaining melted butter, then sprinkle with the sliced almonds and the coarse sugar. Bake, following the basic directions for Triple-Treat Yeast Dough.

BAKING WITH YEAST

● *Substitute one cake (0.6 oz.) of compressed yeast for one envelope of active dry yeast in recipes. Use warm water to dissolve the fresh yeast. (Warm water will feel tepid when a few drops are sprinkled on the inside of your wrist.)*
● *To determine when a dough has doubled in volume, press the dough flat in a greased bowl. Mark the dough's level, then remove it. Fill the bowl with water to double the first mark, then mark this second level. Return your dough to the bowl.*
● *Dough has doubled in volume when a depression made with your fingertip remains.*

RUM-RAISIN RING

Heating the raisins and the rum produces moist, flavorful results.

1 **cup raisins**
3 **tablespoons rum**
    Remaining Triple-Treat Yeast Dough (page 238)
1 **can (12 ounces) almond filling**
    Milk
    Coarse sugar

1. Combine the raisins and the rum in a small saucepan. Heat to bubbling; remove from the heat and cool to room temperature.
2. Roll out the Triple-Treat Yeast Dough to a 16 x 12-inch rectangle on a lightly floured pastry cloth or board.
3. Spread with the canned almond filling. Sprinkle with the soaked raisins. Roll up from one long end, jelly-roll fashion. Shape into a ring, pinching the ends together with the fingers.
4. Place the ring in a well-greased 12-cup shallow, round baking pan. Make the cuts from the top to the side at ½-inch intervals with a sharp knife. Let rise, following the basic directions in Triple-Treat Yeast Dough.
5. Just before baking, brush the ring with the milk and sprinkle with the coarse sugar. Bake, following the basic directions for Triple-Treat Yeast Dough.

CHRISTMAS BRAID

Amaretto-soaked raisins and almonds lend a festive touch to rich yeast dough.

Bake at 350° for 1 hour.
Makes 1 large loaf.

- *2 packages active dry yeast*
- *½ cup very warm water*
- *1 tablespoon sugar*
- *1 cup milk*
- *¾ cup sugar*
- *1 teaspoon salt*
- *½ cup (1 stick) butter or margarine*
- *3 egg yolks, well beaten*
- *5 cups all-purpose flour*
- *1 teaspoon grated lemon rind*
- *⅛ teaspoon ground cardamom*
- *⅛ teaspoon crushed anise seeds*
- *1 cup raisins*
- *½ cup amaretto*
- *1 cup chopped almonds*
- *½ cup all-purpose flour*
- *2 egg yolks, well beaten*
- *1 tablespoon milk*
- *½ cup sliced almonds*
- *Granulated sugar*

1. Sprinkle the yeast over the very warm water and the 1 tablespoon of sugar in a small bowl; stir well and set aside. ("Very warm" water should feel comfortably warm when dropped on the wrist.)
2. Scald the milk in a medium-size saucepan with the ¾ cup of sugar, the salt and butter or margarine until the butter melts; cool.
3. Pour the milk mixture into a large bowl and add the 3 egg yolks, yeast mixture and 2 cups of the flour. Beat with a wooden spoon for 2 minutes, or for 30 seconds with an electric mixer. Add the lemon rind, cardamom, anise seeds and remaining 3 cups of flour to make a fairly stiff dough.
4. Turn out onto a floured pastry cloth or board and knead for at least 7 minutes. (You may have to add a bit more flour to the dough if it is sticky.) Knead the dough until it is smooth and elastic with blisters. Place in a clean, large, well-buttered bowl; cover with plastic wrap and let rise in a warm place, away from drafts, for 1 hour, or until doubled in volume.
5. Soak the raisins in the amaretto in a small bowl while the dough rises. Drain the raisins; place with the chopped almonds in a plastic bag and add the ½ cup flour. Shake well. Add to the dough and

knead well until the raisins and almonds are absorbed.
6. Divide the dough into 6 parts; 3 parts should be larger and 3 smaller. Roll the larger 3 parts into 3 long ropes and braid. Then roll the smaller 3 parts into ropes and braid together. Beat the 2 egg yolks and the tablespoon of milk in a cup with a fork and brush the larger braid with the mixture. Place the smaller braid on top; press down firmly and brush with the egg mixture. Place onto a well-buttered jelly-roll pan. Cover with plastic wrap and let rise, away from drafts, for 35 minutes, or until doubled in volume. Brush the braid with the beaten egg yolks and milk, and sprinkle with the sliced almonds.
7. Meanwhile, preheat the oven to moderate (350°).
8. Bake in the preheated moderate oven (350°) for 1 hour, or until a cake tester comes out clean and the braid is golden brown. Remove from the oven and immediately sprinkle with the sugar. Cool completely. Cover and let stand overnight before slicing, or wrap in heavy-duty aluminum foil; label, date and freeze.

PECAN TWISTS

One batch of dough makes two delectable yeast breads. Keep one for the family and give the other as a gift.

Bake at 350° for 45 minutes.
Makes 2 loaves.

¾ cup milk
¼ cup firmly packed brown sugar
½ cup (1 stick) butter or margarine
2 envelopes active dry yeast
1 teaspoon sugar
½ cup very warm water
3 eggs, beaten
4¼ cups all-purpose flour
1½ teaspoons salt
1 teaspoon ground cinnamon
1 teaspoon ground mace
1 cup chopped pecans
Cinnamon-sugar
Rich Glaze (recipe follows)

1. Scald the milk with the brown sugar and ¼ cup of the butter or margarine in a small saucepan; cool to lukewarm.

2. Sprinkle the yeast and 1 teaspoon of sugar into very warm water in a large bowl. ("Very warm" water should feel comfortably warm when dropped on the wrist.) Stir until the yeast dissolves; allow to stand until the mixture bubbles for about 10 minutes, then stir in the cooled milk mixture and the eggs.

3. Beat in 2 cups of flour, the salt, cinnamon and mace until smooth, then beat in the remaining 2¼ cups of flour to form a soft dough.

4. Turn out the dough onto a lightly floured pastry cloth or board; knead for 5 minutes, or until smooth and elastic, adding only enough flour to keep the dough from sticking. Place in a greased bowl; turn to coat with the shortening.

5. Cover with plastic wrap. Let rise in a warm place, away from drafts, for 1 hour, or until doubled in volume.

6. Punch the dough down, then turn out; divide in half.

7. Roll out half the dough to a rectangle, 12" x 9". Brush with part of the remaining butter or margarine; sprinkle with part of the pecans and generously with the cinnamon-sugar. Cut lengthwise into 3 strips; twist each strip, one at a time, like a rope to cover the pecans, then pinch the 3 strips together at one end to fasten, and braid. Place in a well-greased 9 x 5 x 3-inch loaf pan, tucking the ends under, if necessary; sprinkle with additional pecans. Repeat with the second half of the dough.

8. Cover the breads with a clean towel; let rise in a warm place, away from drafts, for 45 minutes, or until doubled in volume.

9. Meanwhile, preheat the oven to moderate (350°).

10. Bake in the preheated moderate oven (350°) for 45 minutes, or until the breads give a hollow sound when tapped. Remove from the pans; cool on wire racks.

11. Wrap in heavy-duty aluminum foil; label, date and freeze.

12. To serve, remove the foil and place on a cookie sheet. Heat in a moderate preheated oven (350°) for 20 minutes, or until heated through.

13. Prepare Rich Glaze; drizzle over the loaves and garnish with additional pecans, if you wish.

RICH GLAZE: Makes enough to frost 8 squares. Combine 1 cup *sifted* 10X (confectioners' powdered) sugar, 2 tablespoons (¼ stick) of butter or margarine, melted, and 1½ teaspoons of rum or brandy in a small bowl. Beat until very smooth and creamy.

WHOLE-WHEAT PRETZELS

A new twist on an old favorite!

Bake at 400° for 20 minutes.
Makes 30 pretzels.

2 packages active dry yeast
2 tablespoons sugar
2 cups warm water
⅓ cup honey
¼ cup (½ stick) butter or margarine, softened
1 egg
1 tablespoon spicy brown mustard
2¼ teaspoons salt
1 teaspoon caraway seeds
1 cup cornmeal
3 to 3¼ cups whole-wheat flour
3 to 3¼ cups all-purpose flour
1 egg yolk
Coarse (kosher) salt
Caraway seeds

1. Sprinkle the yeast and sugar over the water in a large bowl. Stir until the yeast dissolves.
2. Add the honey, butter or margarine, egg, mustard, salt, caraway seeds, cornmeal and 1 cup each whole-wheat and all-purpose flour. Beat at low speed with an electric mixer until blended, then at medium speed until smooth.
3. Stir in enough additional whole-wheat and all-purpose flour to make a stiff dough. Cover the bowl tightly with plastic wrap and refrigerate for 4 to 6 hours, or until doubled in volume.
4. Punch the dough down. Turn out onto a lightly floured pastry board or cloth and divide the dough in half. Return half of the dough to the refrigerator.
5. Cut the remaining dough into 15 pieces. Form each into sticks about 18 inches long by rolling back and forth between floured hands. Draw the ends together to form a circle. Twist the ends around each other once or twice and press under the circle to form a pretzel shape. Place, 3 inches apart, on well-greased cookie sheets. Repeat with the other half of the dough. Cover with a damp towel. Let the pretzels rise in a warm place, away from drafts, for 30 minutes, or until doubled in volume. Uncover.
6. Meanwhile, preheat the oven to hot (400°).
7. Beat the egg yolk and brush onto the pretzels. Sprinkle with the coarse salt and caraway seeds.
8. Bake in the preheated hot oven (400°) for 20 minutes, or until golden brown. Remove from the cookie sheets and let cool on wire racks. Pack in plastic bags. To freeze: Let cool; wrap in plastic bags or heavy-duty aluminum foil. Label, date and freeze. To heat: Place the frozen pretzels on cookie sheets in a hot oven (400°) and bake for 20 minutes, or until hot and crisp.

PHILADELPHIA STICKY BUNS

Bake two pans, one for the family and one as a gift.

Bake at 375° for 30 minutes.
Makes two 9-inch rounds.

4½ cups all-purpose flour
 1 package fast-rising active dry yeast
 1 cup milk
 ½ cup water
 ⅓ cup sugar
 ¼ cup (½ stick) butter or margarine
 1 teaspoon salt
 1 teaspoon ground cinnamon
 2 eggs
 ½ cup (1 stick) butter or margarine, melted
 2 cups firmly packed brown sugar
 6 tablespoons light corn syrup
 6 tablespoons light cream
 2 cups pecan halves

1. Stir together 1½ cups of the flour and yeast in a large bowl with an electric mixer with a dough hook.

2. Heat the milk, water, sugar, ¼ cup of butter or margarine, salt and cinnamon in a small saucepan over low heat until warm. (The butter need not melt.)

3. Add the liquid ingredients to the flour-yeast mixture and beat at medium speed for 3 minutes. Add the eggs and 1 cup of the remaining flour; continue to beat for 2 minutes. Stir in the remaining flour to make a moderately soft dough. Turn out onto a lightly floured pastry cloth or board. Knead for

5 minutes, or until smooth and shiny. Cover the dough with a bowl and let rest in a warm place, away from drafts, for 20 minutes, or until doubled in volume.

4. Divide the dough in half. Roll out one half to a 12 x 9-inch rectangle on a lightly floured board. Spread with part of the melted butter; sprinkle with ½ cup of the brown sugar. Repeat with the second half of the dough. Roll up, jelly-roll fashion, starting at one of the short sides.

5. Divide the remaining melted butter between two 9-inch layer cake pans. Stir in ½ cup of the brown sugar, 3 tablespoons of light corn syrup and 3 tablespoons of light cream into each pan. Heat over low heat, stirring constantly, until the mixture bubbles. Sprinkle 1 cup of pecan halves in each pan.

6. Cut each yeast roll into 6 slices with a sharp French knife and place, cut-side up, over the nut-syrup layer in each pan. Cover with plastic wrap. Let rise in a warm place, away from drafts, for 20 minutes, or until doubled in volume.

7. Meanwhile, preheat the oven to moderate (375°).

8. Bake in the preheated moderate oven (375°) for 30 minutes or until golden. For the last 5 to 7 minutes, cover with a sheet of aluminum foil to prevent excessive browning. Cool in the pans on wire racks for 5 minutes, then loosen the cakes around the edges. Invert onto a serving plate, or onto sheets of heavy-duty aluminum foil. Serve warm, or cool completely and wrap in foil, then label, date and freeze.

Note: If you use active dry yeast, let rise for 40 minutes in Step 3, and let rise for 40 minutes in Step 6.

BLUEBERRY COFFEE BREAD

Summertime blueberries add a special touch to a honey-and-lemon-flavored batter.

Bake at 350° for 1 hour.
Makes 1 loaf.

- ⅓ **cup vegetable shortening**
- 1 **cup sugar**
- 2 **eggs**
- ⅓ **cup honey**
- **Rind of 1 lemon, grated**
- ½ **cup brewed coffee**
- 2½ **cups all-purpose flour**
- 1 **teaspoon baking powder**
- 1 **teaspoon baking soda**
- ½ **teaspoon salt**
- ½ **teaspoon ground cinnamon**
- 2 **cups frozen dry-pack blueberries**

1. Preheat the oven to moderate (350°). Grease and flour a 9 x 5 x 3-inch loaf pan.
2. Beat the shortening and the sugar until fluffy in a large bowl with an electric mixer at high speed. Beat in the eggs, one at a time. Lower speed; stir in the honey, lemon rind and coffee.
3. Sift in the flour, baking powder, baking soda, salt and cinnamon. Beat until smooth; fold in the blueberries. Pour into the prepared loaf pan.
4. Bake in the preheated moderate oven (350°) for 1 hour, or until a wooden pick inserted into the center comes out clean. Cool in the pan on a wire rack for 10 minutes, then loosen around the edges with a knife. Cool on the rack. Cut into thin slices. Serve with cream cheese, blueberry preserves or peach jam.

BOSTON BROWN BREAD

Brown bread is a traditional part of New England cuisine.

Steam for 3 hours.
Makes 2 loaves.

- 1 **cup all-purpose flour**
- 2 **teaspoons baking soda**
- 1 **teaspoon salt**
- 1 **cup yellow cornmeal**
- 1 **cup whole-wheat flour**
- 1 **cup raisins**
- 2 **cups buttermilk**
- ¾ **cup molasses**

1. Grease two 1-pound coffee cans.
2. Sift the flour, baking soda and salt into a large bowl; stir in the cornmeal, whole-wheat flour and raisins until well blended.
3. Combine the buttermilk and molasses in a 4-cup measure; pour over the dry ingredients and stir with a spoon, just until blended.
4. Spoon the batter, dividing evenly, into the coffee cans. Cover with a double thickness of aluminum foil and tie with string.
5. Place the cans on a trivet in the bottom of a large, deep kettle. Pour boiling water to half the depth of the coffee cans; cover the kettle.
6. Steam, adding more boiling water, if necessary, for 3 hours, or until a wooden skewer inserted near the center comes out clean. Cool in the cans on a wire rack for 10 minutes, then loosen the bread around the edge of the can; invert onto the wire rack. Cool completely. Wrap in aluminum foil and freeze. When ready to serve, heat in the foil in a preheated slow oven (325°) for 40 minutes, or until heated through.

💲 ⚡ 《

CANDIED ORANGE TEA BREAD

Made from orange peel you candy yourself.

Bake at 325° for 1 hour, 20 minutes.
Makes 1 large loaf.

> **2 large eating oranges**
> **½ cup sugar**
> **2 eggs**
> **1 cup sugar**
> **¾ cup milk**
> **½ cup (1 stick) butter or margarine, melted**
> **3 cups all-purpose flour**
> **1 teaspoon baking soda**
> **1 teaspoon baking powder**
> **1 teaspoon salt**
> **½ teaspoon ground ginger**
> **½ cup chopped walnuts**

1. Pare the oranges with a sharp knife and cut the peel into slivers. Cover with cold water and bring to boiling. Pour off the hot water and cover with cold water; bring to boiling and simmer for 5 minutes.
2. Drain off the water and add the ½ cup of sugar. Cook, stirring constantly, for 5 minutes, or until thick and syrupy. Cool completely in the pan.
3. Preheat the oven to slow (325°).
4. Beat the eggs until light with a wire whisk, then beat in the 1 cup of sugar until well blended; beat in the milk. Stir in the candied orange peel, then the melted butter or margarine.
5. Sift the flour, baking soda, baking powder, salt and ground ginger into a medium-size mixing bowl. Mix in with a wooden spoon, just until blended; fold in the nuts. Pour into a greased 9 x 5 x 3-inch loaf pan.
6. Bake in the preheated slow oven (325°) for 1 hour, 20 minutes, or until a wooden skewer inserted in the center comes out clean. Cool in the pan on a wire rack for 10 minutes. Loosen the bread around the edges of the pan and invert onto the wire rack; cool completely. Wrap in a plastic bag and allow to mellow at room temperature for 2 days, or freeze until party time.

A NEAT SLICE

Quick breads slice better if allowed to mellow for at least 24 hours before serving.

💲 ⚡ 《

EASY CURRANT SQUARES

Start with a loaf of frozen dough for this quick sweet bread.

Bake at 425° for 15 minutes.
Makes 2 dozen pieces.

> **1 loaf (1 pound) frozen plain bread dough, thawed overnight in the refrigerator**
> **⅓ cup currants**
> **2 tablespoons melted butter**
> **2 tablespoons sugar**
> **¼ teaspoon ground cinnamon**
> **¼ cup sifted 10X (confectioners' powdered) sugar**
> **2 teaspoons orange juice**

1. Allow the dough to stand at room temperature on a lightly floured surface for 1 hour. Knead the currants into the dough.
2. Push and stretch the dough to fit a well-greased jelly-roll pan (15 x 10 x 1-inch). Brush the dough with the melted butter, then sprinkle with the mixture of sugar and cinnamon.
3. Let the dough rise until doubled in volume (about 30 minutes). Poke holes in the dough with the end of a wooden spoon or your fingers at 1-inch intervals.
4. Meanwhile, preheat the oven to hot (425°).
5. Bake in a hot oven (425°) for 15 minutes. Remove the pan to a wire rack. When cooled, drizzle with a mixture of the 10X sugar and orange juice. Cut into pieces.

Note: These may be frozen. To reheat, place the wrapped frozen bread on a cookie sheet. Heat in a moderate oven (350°) for 10 minutes.

DUNDEE CAKES

This variation of the classic Scottish fruitcake makes several loaves—enough for gift-giving and to have on hand for company.

Bake at 325°, 45 minutes for loaves and 1 hour, 15 minutes for 2-cup cake.
Makes one 2-cup cake and three 1-cup loaves.

> **1 cup raisins**
> **1 cup golden raisins**
> **1 cup currants**
> **2¼ cups all-purpose flour**
> **1 teaspoon ground cinnamon**
> **½ teaspoon ground mace OR: nutmeg**
> **½ teaspoon baking powder**
> **½ teaspoon salt**
> **1 cup (2 sticks) butter or margarine, softened**
> **1¼ cups sugar**
> **4 eggs**
> **   Grated rind of 1 lemon**
> **   Grated rind of 1 orange**
> **   Whole blanched almonds**
> **   Crystal Glaze (recipe follows)**

1. Preheat the oven to slow (325°). Grease very well and flour one 2-cup mold and three 5¹¹⁄₁₆ x 3¼ x 2-inch loaf pans; tap out any excess flour.
2. Toss the raisins and the currants with ¼ cup of the flour. Sift the remaining 2 cups of flour with the cinnamon, mace or nutmeg, baking powder and salt onto wax paper.
3. Beat the butter or margarine and the sugar until light and fluffy in a large bowl with an electric mixer at high speed. Add the eggs, one at a time, beating just until well blended. Beat in the grated lemon and orange rinds. Add the flour mixture, ⅓ at a time, beating just until smooth. Fold in the floured raisins and currants.
4. Spoon the batter into the prepared pans, filling ⅔ full. Arrange the whole almonds in a decorative pattern on top of the loaves.
5. Bake in the preheated slow oven (325°) for 45 minutes for the loaf pans, or for 1 hour, 15 minutes for the 2-cup mold, or until a skewer inserted in the center comes out clean. Cool in pans on wire racks for 10 minutes. Loosen around the edges with a long thin-bladed knife. Invert onto the racks; cool completely. Wrap each cake tightly in heavy-duty aluminum foil. Store in an airtight container for up to one month. Or label, date and freeze.

6. At serving time, brush the cakes with Crystal Glaze, then decorate with additional almonds and angelica strips, if you wish.

Note: You can bake this batter in one 8- or 9-inch-square or -round pan, too. Grease very well. Line with brown paper and grease the paper. Bake in a preheated moderate oven (350°) until the cake shrinks from the sides of the pan. Let cool for 15 minutes. Turn out of the pan onto the cake rack. Peel off the paper. Cool completely.

CRYSTAL GLAZE: Makes ½ cup. Heat ⅓ cup of light corn syrup with 2 tablespoons of brandy or orange juice in a small saucepan until bubbly, stirring often.

PLUMB PUDDING

In Colonial days, raisins were called plumbs—therefore, the name for this raisin-rich dark fruitcake.

Steam for 2 hours.
Makes 1 large mold.

> 1 **package (15 ounces) raisins**
> 1 **package (10 ounces) currants**
> 2 **jars (4 ounces each) diced candied citron**
> ½ **cup brandy**
> 1 **cup vegetable shortening**
> 1 **cup firmly packed brown sugar**
> ¼ **cup molasses**
> 4 **eggs**
> 2½ **cups all-purpose flour**
> 2 **teaspoons ground cinnamon**
> 1 **teaspoon ground cloves**
> 1 **teaspoon ground nutmeg**
> 1 **teaspoon baking soda**
> 2 **teaspoons salt**
> **Unseasoned dry bread crumbs**
> **Blanched whole almonds**

1. Combine the raisins, currants and citron in a large bowl; sprinkle the brandy over and toss to coat evenly. Allow to stand for 10 minutes.
2. Beat the shortening, brown sugar and molasses until creamy-smooth in a large bowl with an electric mixer at high speed. Beat in the eggs, one at a time, until light and fluffy.
3. Sift the flour, cinnamon, cloves, nutmeg, baking soda and salt into a large bowl; stir just until blended. Add the brandied fruits and stir just until blended.
4. Grease a 10-cup tube mold; sprinkle with the bread crumbs. Arrange a ring of almonds on the bottom of the pan, then spoon the batter into the prepared mold. Cover with a double thickness of aluminum foil and tie with string.
5. Place the mold on a trivet in the bottom of a large, deep kettle. Pour boiling water to half the depth of the mold; cover the kettle.
6. Steam, adding more boiling water, if necessary, for 2 hours, or until a wooden skewer inserted near the center comes out clean. Cool in the mold on a wire rack for 15 minutes. Loosen around the edge of the mold. Invert onto the wire rack; cool completely.
7. Drizzle the cake with additional brandy, then wrap in a plastic bag; seal the bag. Store for at least 2 weeks to blend flavors, or wrap in heavy-duty aluminum foil and freeze. Thaw for one day before serving.

Baker's Tip: This recipe can also be baked in two 5-cup molds which have been greased, sprinkled with the unseasoned dry bread crumbs and lined with the almonds. Bake in a preheated slow oven (325°) for 1 hour, or until a skewer inserted into the center comes out clean.

TO FREEZE FRUITCAKES

● *Wrap the cakes first in cheesecloth soaked in Sherry or brandy.*
● *Do not brush the cakes with glaze.*
● *Wrap the cakes in heavy-duty aluminum foil, freezer-weight plastic wrap or large freezer bags.*
● *Seal the wrap around the cakes.*
● *Label, date and freeze for up to 1 year. Thaw before glazing and decorating.*

PAN SUBSTITUTION

● *If you do not have the specific size of baking pan or mold called for in a fruitcake recipe, substitute a pan of equal volume from the list below.*
● *If the pan you are substituting is made of glass, reduce the baking temperature by 25°.*
● *If you are substituting a pan that is shallower than the pan in the recipe, reduce the baking time by about one-quarter.*
● *If you are substituting a pan that is deeper than the pan in the recipe, increase the baking time by one-quarter.*

4-cup mold:
9-inch pie plate
8 x 1¼-inch cake pan
7 x 3 x 2-inch loaf pan

6-cup mold:
10-inch pie plate
9 x 1½-inch cake pan
8 x 3½ x 2½-inch loaf pan

8-cup mold:
8 x 8 x 2-inch-square pan
9 x 5 x 4-inch loaf pan

10-cup mold:
9 x 9 x 2-inch-square pan

GOLDEN FRUITCAKE

Rich with fruits and nuts and yet so easy to make. Bake as two large cakes or a number of smaller cakes to give as gifts.

Bake at 300° for 2 hours.
Makes two 10-inch tube cakes.

- **2 containers (1 pound each) candied mixed fruits**
- **1 package (15 ounces) golden raisins**
- **2 cans (3½ ounces each) sliced almonds**
- **1 can (4 ounces) flaked coconut**
- **5 cups all-purpose flour**
- **2 teaspoons baking powder**
- **1 teaspoon salt**
- **1 teaspoon ground nutmeg**
- **1 cup (2 sticks) butter or margarine**
- **2 cups sugar**
- **6 eggs**
- **½ cup brandy**
- **½ cup orange juice**
- **Apricot Glaze (recipe follows)**

1. Grease two 10-inch tube pans. Preheat the oven to slow (300°).
2. Combine the mixed fruits, raisins, almonds and coconut in a very large bowl. Sift the flour, baking powder, salt and nutmeg over the mixture. Toss until the fruits and nuts are evenly coated.
3. Beat the butter or margarine and the sugar until fluffy in a large bowl with an electric mixer at high speed. Beat in the eggs, one at a time, then stir in the brandy and juice.
4. Pour the mixture over the fruits and nuts, and mix until well blended.
5. Spoon the batter into the prepared pans, dividing evenly. Place the oven rack on the lower third of the oven; arrange the pans at opposite sides of the rack.
6. Bake in the preheated slow oven (300°) for 2 hours, or until a wooden skewer inserted into the center comes out clean. (If cake tops brown too quickly, place a piece of aluminum foil over.) Cool in the pans on wire racks for 15 minutes. Loosen the cakes around the edges and tubes of pans with a long, sharp knife. Invert onto the wire racks; cool completely. Drizzle the cakes with brandy and wrap in plastic bags or store in metal tins with tight-fitting lids. Store at room temperature for at least 2 weeks.
7. Brush the cakes with the Apricot Glaze and garnish with mixed candied fruits, if you wish, just before serving.

Baker's Tip: This batter can also be divided among 12 large muffin-pan cups, one 8-inch flan pan and one 8-inch tube pan. Bake in a preheated slow oven (300°) for 1 hour and then begin to test for doneness. Double the recipe for the Apricot Glaze.

APRICOT GLAZE: Makes enough glaze for two 10-inch tube cakes. Combine 1 jar (10 ounces) of apricot preserves and ⅓ cup of apricot brandy in a small saucepan. Heat, breaking up the large pieces of apricot. Brush on the fruitcakes with a pastry brush.

◀◀◀

FRUIT 'N' NUT CAKES

Dried pears and apricots add a lighter touch to this fruitcake, mixed with whole blanched hazelnuts.

Bake at 300°, 1 hour, 45 minutes for smaller cake and 2 hours, 45 minutes for 9-inch cake.
Makes a 3-cup mold and a 9-inch round.

1   pound dried pears, chopped
1   pound dried apricots, chopped
½   cup Triple Sec OR: orange liqueur
4   cups all-purpose flour
2   teaspoons baking powder
1½ cups (3 sticks) butter or margarine,
     at room temperature
2   cups sugar
6   eggs
1   teaspoon ground cinnamon
1   teaspoon ground mace or nutmeg
     Grated rind of 1 orange
1   pound whole hazelnuts, blanched*
     (see note)
½   pound whole dried pears
¼   pound whole dried apricots
     Whole blanched hazelnuts
     Crystal Glaze (recipe on page 247)

1. Toss the chopped dried pears and apricots with the Triple Sec in a large bowl; cover with foil. Let stand for at least 2 hours, preferably overnight, tossing occasionally.
2. Grease very well and flour a 3-cup mold, tapping out any excess flour. Grease very well a 9-inch (loose-bottom) baking pan and line the bottom with wax paper; grease. Preheat the oven to slow (300°).
3. Sift together 3 cups of the flour and the baking powder onto wax paper.
4. Beat the butter or margarine and the sugar until light and fluffy in a large bowl with an electric mixer at high speed. Add the eggs, one at a time, beating well after each addition. Beat in the cinnamon, mace or nutmeg and the grated orange rind. Drain the chopped fruits; add the drained liqueur to the butter-sugar mixture. Add the sifted flour mixture, beating only until blended.
5. Toss the remaining 1 cup of flour with the chopped fruits and nuts, then fold into the batter. Spoon 2 cups of the mixture into the 3-cup pan; spoon the remainder into the 9-inch pan. Smooth the tops with the spoon. Decorate the top of the 9-inch pan with the whole dried pears, apricots and hazelnuts, pressing in lightly.

6. Bake in the preheated slow oven (300°) for 1 hour, 45 minutes for the small mold and 2 hours, 45 minutes for the large pan, or until a skewer inserted in the center comes out clean. Loosely cover the top of the large pan with aluminum foil after 30 minutes, so the fruit does not burn.
7. Cool in the pans on wire racks for 15 minutes. Loosen around the sides. Invert onto the racks. Cool completely. Wrap tightly with aluminium foil and store in an airtight metal tin.
8. At serving time, brush the Crystal Glaze on top. Decorate with additional dried fruits and nuts, if you wish.

***Note:** To blanch hazelnuts, place the nuts in a single layer in an ungreased pan; bake in a preheated moderate oven (350°) for 10 minutes, stirring once or twice, or until the skins begin to crack and peel away from the nutmeat. Briskly rub the nuts, a handful at a time, in a clean tea towel to remove as much skin as possible.

◀◀◀

HOME-CANDIED FRUITS

For someone who likes holiday fruitcake made completely from scratch.

Makes four ½-pint jars.

2   large California oranges
1   large lemon
1   large pineapple
1   jar (8 ounce) maraschino cherries
2   cups golden raisins
1   cup sugar

1. Peel the rinds from the oranges and the lemon in chunks. Simmer in enough water to cover in a large skillet for 15 minutes; drain. Scrape off the white membrane and cut the rinds into thin strips.
2. Cut the pineapple into ½-inch slices, then peel and core. Simmer in enough water to cover in a large skillet for 10 minutes; drain.
3. Combine the rind strips with the pineapple slices, well-drained cherries, raisins and ½ cup of water in a large skillet; sprinkle evenly with the sugar.
4. Cook, stirring often, for 30 minutes, or until glazed. Let stand in the syrup overnight. Place on a cheesecloth-covered rack; cover. Dry for 2 days, then chop. Spoon into 4 hot, sterilized ½-pint jars and seal.

OLD-FASHIONED FRUITCAKE

Dark and rich, it stores well, so you can serve it all winter long.

Bake at 300° for 2 hours, 30 minutes.
Makes two 7- or 8-inch cakes.

> **2** jars (1 pound each) candied mixed fruits
> **1** package (15 ounces) seedless raisins
> **1** package (15 ounces) currants
> **1** cup chopped pecans
> **2½** cups all-purpose flour
> **1** teaspoon baking powder
> **2** teaspoons ground cinnamon
> **1** teaspoon ground mace
> **½** teaspoon ground cloves
> **½** teaspoon salt
> **1** cup (2 sticks) butter or margarine
> **1½** cups dark brown sugar
> **6** eggs
> **½** cup Port wine
> **½** cup strawberry jelly, melted
> Angelica (optional)

1. Grease two 7-inch springform pans or 8-inch Bundt® pans very well. Preheat the oven to slow (300°).
2. Combine the candied fruits, raisins, currants and pecans in a very large bowl. Sift in 1 cup of the flour; stir to coat the fruits and nuts well.
3. Measure the remaining 1½ cups of flour, the baking powder, cinnamon, mace, cloves and salt into the sifter. Cream the butter or margarine and the sugar until fluffy in a large bowl with an electric mixer at high speed.
4. Beat in the eggs, one at a time. Blend in the wine. Sift in the dry ingredients; stir with a spoon or beat with the mixer at low speed just until well blended.
5. Pour the batter over the fruit-nut mixture; fold and blend until thoroughly mixed. Spoon into the prepared pans, pressing down firmly with a spoon to make the tops even.
6. Bake in the preheated slow oven (300°) for 2 hours, 30 minutes, or until a long wooden skewer inserted near the center comes out clean. Cool in the pans on wire racks for 15 minutes.
7. Loosen around the edges with a knife. Invert onto the racks; cool completely. Sprinkle with the wine. Wrap in a plastic bag or aluminum foil. Allow to mellow for several weeks at room temperature. Brush with the melted jelly and garnish with thin strips of angelica just before serving.

QUICK COOKIE AND CAKE DECORATIONS

- **Lace Topping:** *Place a paper doily in the center of the top of a plain round cake. Dust the top of the cake generously with 10X (confectioners') sugar. Lift the doily straight up, very carefully, so you don't disturb the pattern.*
- **Chocolate Glaze:** *Melt chocolate bars or chocolate-covered peppermints in a heavy saucepan over low heat. Add a little milk or cream if the mixture seems very stiff. Cool slightly and use as a glaze on cookies or cakes.*
- **Fruitcake Glaze:** *Combine 2 cups of honey, ½ cup of lemon juice and 2 teaspoons of grated lemon rind in a small saucepan. Heat to boiling, then lower the heat. Simmer for 5 minutes. Brush on fruitcakes while still warm. (Makes enough to coat 6 cakes.)*
- **Dark Fruitcake Glaze:** *Combine a 1-pound jar of strawberry jam with ½ cup of brandy, sherry or apple juice in a small saucepan. Heat to boiling, then lower the heat. Simmer for 5 minutes. Brush on fruitcakes while still warm. (Makes enough for 6 cakes.)*
- **Frosted Fruit:** *Frosted strawberries, cranberries or grapes can be made quickly. Beat an egg white with a fork until foamy. Brush the fruit with the mixture, then roll in sugar. Let dry on wax paper. Use the fruit to top cakes and garnish cookie platters.*
- **Other Quick Cake Toppers:** *Chopped candied chestnuts; strawberry, blueberry or orange preserves, melted and spooned over the cake; or honey, melted until liquid enough to brush over the cake.*

THE CHRISTMAS COOKIE JAR

For most holiday bakers, Christmas is a time to bake tinfuls of cookies, each more elaborately decorated than the next.

Although "The Christmas Cookie Jar" often features fancy cutout cookies, don't feel pressured to bake this most time-consuming of cookies. Refrigerator, drop and bar cookies are quicker choices and can be simply decorated with frosting, nuts and candied fruit for an extra-festive look. Some cookies (such as the Chocolate Bourbon Balls shown at right) don't require any baking at all!

Another solution for the harried baker: Host a Christmas Cookie Exchange. Invite 11 friends over for an evening and tell each to bring 12 dozen homemade cookies (from a favorite recipe, in packages of one dozen), along with 11 copies of the recipe. One dozen cookies will be for eating, the rest for exchanging.

As hostess, you also bake 12 dozen cookies and prepare a hot wine punch or eggnog. When guests arrive, take a bag of cookies from each one and serve them with the punch or eggnog. Everyone samples the cookies and votes by secret ballot for the best. The winner gets a simple prize, such as a tree ornament, and everyone takes home 11 dozen different cookies with their recipes.

NOËL WREATHS

Buttery little wreaths with fruited centers.

Bake at 350° for 12 minutes.
Makes 4 dozen.

 1 cup (2 sticks) butter or margarine, softened
½ cup sugar
 1 egg
 1 teaspoon vanilla
2½ cups all-purpose flour
 1 cup finely chopped walnuts
¼ cup finely chopped raisins
¼ cup honey
    Red and green candied cherries

1. Preheat the oven to moderate (350°).
2. Beat the butter or margarine, sugar, egg and vanilla until light and fluffy in a medium-size bowl with an electric mixer at high speed. Stir in the flour to make a soft dough.
3. Measure out ⅓ cup of the dough and transfer it to a small bowl. Blend in the walnuts, raisins and honey; reserve.
4. Spoon the remaining dough into a pastry bag fitted with a small star tip. Press out into 1½-inch rings on ungreased cookie sheets. Fill the center of each cookie with about a teaspoonful of the reserved nut mixture. Decorate the wreaths with slivers of the red and green candied cherries.
5. Bake in the preheated moderate oven (350°) for 12 minutes, or until lightly golden at the edges. Remove from the cookie sheets to wire racks; cool completely. Store in tightly covered containers.

Clockwise from bottom right: Holly Wreaths, Viennese Sandwiches, Shortbread Diamonds, Almond Spritz, Maple-Nut Nests, Peppermint Twists, No-Bake Chocolate Bourbon Balls, Pale Pink Stars, Double-Decker Cookies. (See pages 252-269.)

💲 𝄗

PEPPERMINT TWISTS

Pink and white cookie dough ropes twist easily together to make a super holiday cookie.

Bake at 350° for 10 minutes.
Makes 5 dozen.

3¼ cups all-purpose flour
4 teaspoons baking powder
1 teaspoon salt
½ cup (1 stick) butter or margarine
1¼ cups sugar
1 egg
½ teaspoon peppermint extract
¼ cup milk
   Red food coloring

1. Preheat the oven to moderate (350°).
2. Measure the flour, baking powder and salt into a sifter set on wax paper.
3. Beat the butter or margarine and sugar in a large bowl until fluffy with an electric mixer at high speed. Beat in the egg and peppermint extract.
4. Sift in the dry ingredients, a third at a time, adding alternately with the milk; stir until well blended.
5. Spoon half of the dough into a medium-size bowl. Blend in a few drops of red food coloring to tint pink; leave the other half plain.
6. Pinch off about a teaspoonful each of the pink and white doughs at a time and roll each into a pencil-thin strip about 5 inches long on a lightly floured surface. Place the strips side by side, pressing the ends together, then twist into a rope. Place, 1 inch apart, on ungreased cookie sheets.
7. Bake in the preheated moderate (350°) for 10 minutes, or until firm. Remove carefully from the cookie sheets with a pancake turner to wire racks; cool completely. Store with wax paper between the layers in a metal container with a tight-fitting lid.

𝄗

ALMOND SPRITZ

Quick to mix, shape and bake—so versatile.

Bake at 350° for 12 minutes.
Makes 7 dozen.

1 cup (2 sticks) butter or margarine
¾ cup sugar
2 eggs
1 teaspoon almond extract
3½ cups all-purpose flour
½ teaspoon salt
   Green food coloring
   Semisweet chocolate pieces, melted
   Chopped toasted almonds

1. Preheat the oven to moderate (350°).
2. Beat the butter or margarine with the sugar until fluffy in a large bowl with an electric mixer at high speed. Beat in the eggs and almond extract. Stir in the flour and salt to make a soft dough.
3. Tint the dough pale green with the green food coloring.
4. Fit a snowflake or star plate or disk on an electric food gun or manual cookie press. Fill with the dough, a part at a time, and press out onto ungreased cookie sheets.
5. Bake in the preheated moderate (350°) oven for 12 minutes, or until the cookies are firm. Remove from the cookie sheets with a spatula; cool completely on wire racks. Leave some cookies unfrosted. Decorate the remaining cookies with a swirl of the melted chocolate and a sprinkling of the chopped almonds.

Suggested Variations: For Spicy Spritz, substitute 2 teaspoons of vanilla for the almond extract, add 1 teaspoon of ground nutmeg with the flour and omit all coloring. For Rum Spritz, add 1 teaspoon of rum extract and increase the vanilla extract to 2 teaspoons; use red food coloring instead of green to tint the dough pink. Decorate the center of the cookies with Almond Frosting (page 256), tinted green, and red candies.

SHORTBREAD DIAMONDS

A cookie treasure from Scotland that gets even better when allowed to mellow for a few weeks.

Bake at 300° for 45 minutes.
Makes about 4 dozen.

1½ cups all-purpose flour
1½ cups 10X (confectioners' powdered) sugar
1 cup (2 sticks) butter or margarine
   Colored sugars
   Whole blanched almonds

1. Preheat the oven to slow (300°).
2. Sift the flour and 10X sugar into a medium-size bowl; cut in the butter or margarine until the mixture is crumbly. Work the dough into a ball with the hands and knead for about 10 minutes, or until smooth and shiny.
3. Pat the dough into a 14 x 12-inch rectangle on a large ungreased cookie sheet. Cut into 2-inch diamonds or squares with a sharp knife, but do not separate the cookies; sprinkle with the colored sugars and garnish with the almonds.
4. Bake in the preheated slow oven (300°) for 45 minutes, or until firm and delicately golden.
5. Recut the cookies at the marks and separate very carefully; remove from the cookie sheets with a pancake turner. Cool on wire racks. These cookies are very delicate, so handle them carefully. Store with wax paper between layers in a metal container with a tight-fitting lid.

STORING COOKIES AND CAKES

● *To keep your cookies crisp, store in a metal or glass container with a tight-fitting lid between layers of wax paper. Keep in a cool, dry place.*
● *To keep cookies soft, store in a tin with an apple wedge or a piece of soft white bread to add moisture, but be sure to replace it often.*
● *To freshen soft cookies, place them in a casserole, then cover and heat at 300° for 8 to 10 minutes.*
● *To freshen crisp cookies before serving them, place them on a baking sheet and heat at 300° for 3 to 5 minutes.*
● *For cakes with a fluffy frosting, slip a knife under the cake carrier so it won't be airtight.*
● *For cakes with a whipped cream frosting, keep in the refrigerator or freezer, covered with an inverted bowl.*
● *Cakes with butter frostings may be loosely covered with foil or plastic wrap, or stored in a cake carrier. Refrigerate or freeze for long-term storage.*

MAPLE-NUT NESTS

A quick trick turns part of the dough into a nut-filled center.

Bake at 350° for 12 minutes.
Makes 6 dozen.

1 cup (2 sticks) butter or margarine
½ cup sugar
1 egg
1 teaspoon vanilla
2½ cups all-purpose flour
1⅓ cups finely chopped walnuts
¼ cup maple-flavored corn syrup
   Red and green candied cherries

1. Preheat the oven to moderate (350°).
2. Beat the butter or margarine with the sugar until fluffy-light in a large bowl with an electric mixer at high speed. Beat in the egg and vanilla. Stir in the flour, a third at a time, blending well to make a soft dough.
3. Measure out ⅓ cup of the dough and mix with the walnuts and maple syrup in a small bowl until well blended; reserve.
4. Fit a pastry bag with a small star tip and fill the bag with the remaining dough. Press out into 1½-inch rings on large cookie sheets. Fill the center of each cookie with about a teaspoonful of the nut mixture; decorate with slivers of the red and green candied cherries.
5. Bake in the preheated moderate oven (350°) for 12 minutes, or until lightly golden at the edges. Remove carefully from the cookie sheets with a spatula to wire racks; cool completely. Store between sheets of wax paper in a metal tin with a tight-fitting lid.

DOUBLE-DECKER COOKIES

Pressed cookies sit on a butter-rich base.

Bake at 375° for 10 minutes.
Makes 5 dozen cookies.

1½ cups (3 sticks) butter or margarine
1 cup sugar
1 egg
1 teaspoon vanilla
4¼ cups all-purpose flour
1 teaspoon salt
½ teaspoon almond extract
    Red and green food colorings
    Almond Frosting (recipe follows)

1. Beat the butter or margarine with the sugar until fluffy in a large bowl with an electric mixer at high speed; beat in the egg and vanilla. Stir in 4 cups of the flour and the salt, a third at a time, blending well to make a soft dough.
2. Divide the dough in half; stir the remaining ¼ cup of flour into one-half of the dough for making the rounds for the base. Divide the remaining half into two equal parts and place each in a small bowl.
3. Blend ¼ teaspoon of the almond extract and enough red food coloring into the dough in one bowl to tint a delicate pink, and the remaining ¼ teaspoon almond extract and enough green food coloring into the dough in the second bowl to tint light green. Chill the tinted doughs for 30 minutes, or until slightly firm.
4. Preheat the oven to moderate (375°).
5. Roll out the plain dough to a ¼-inch thickness on a lightly floured pastry cloth or board. Cut into 2½-inch rounds with a floured cookie cutter. Place, 1 inch apart, on ungreased cookie sheets.
6. Fit the star plate or disk on a cookie press and fill it with the pink dough; press out onto the ungreased cookie sheets. Fit the press with the sunburst plate or disk; repeat with the green dough.
7. Bake all in the preheated moderate oven (375°) for 10 minutes, or until firm. Remove from the cookie sheets; cool completely on wire racks.
8. Place a swirl of the Almond Frosting in the center of each plain cookie; top with a tinted one. Let stand until the frosting sets. Store between layers of wax paper in a metal tin with a tight-fitting lid.

Cook's Tip: You can also use this dough to make 2 kinds of cookies, omitting the Almond Frosting.

ALMOND FROSTING: Makes ½ cup. In a small bowl, mix ¾ cup of 10X (confectioners' powdered) sugar with 2 teaspoons of water, 1 teaspoon of vanilla and ¼ teaspoon of almond extract until smooth.

VIENNESE SANDWICHES

All the goodness of a Linzer torte in just a few nibbles.

Bake at 350° for 10 minutes.
Makes about 3 dozen.

1 cup (2 sticks) butter or margarine
½ cup 10X (confectioners' powdered) sugar
1½ cups all-purpose flour
1 teaspoon vanilla
½ cup ground almonds or hazelnuts
    Red raspberry preserves
    Almond Frosting (recipe, above)

1. Preheat the oven to moderate (350°).
2. Beat the butter or margarine and 10X sugar until well blended in a large bowl with an electric mixer at high speed. Stir in the flour, vanilla and ground nuts.
3. Roll the dough, a half at a time, to a ¼-inch thickness on a lightly floured pastry cloth. Cut with a floured 2½-inch-round cutter. Place, 1-inch apart, on large ungreased cookie sheets. Repeat with the remaining dough and trims.
4. Bake in the preheated moderate oven (350°) for 10 minutes, or until golden around the edges. Remove carefully from the cookie sheets to wire racks with a spatula; cool completely.
5. Spread the bottoms of half of the cookies with the raspberry preserves; sandwich with the remaining cookies. Store in a metal tin with a tight-fitting lid.
6. When ready to serve, tint the Almond Frosting with yellow food coloring and swirl on top of the cookies, then garnish with red candies.

PALE PINK STARS

Delicate sugar cookies make a lovely decoration for the tree, too.

Bake at 350° for 10 minutes.
Makes 5 dozen.

¾ **cup (1½ sticks) butter or margarine**
1 **cup sugar**
1 **egg**
2 **teaspoons vanilla**
3 **cups all-purpose flour**
1 **teaspoon baking powder**
½ **teaspoon salt**
   Pink Glaze (recipe follows)
   Silver dragées

1. Beat the butter or margarine with the sugar until fluffy in a large bowl with an electric mixer at high speed; beat in the egg and vanilla.
2. Sift in the flour, baking powder and salt, a quarter at a time, blending well to make a stiff dough. Chill for 1 hour, or until firm enough to roll.
3. Preheat the oven to moderate (350°).
4. Roll out the dough, one-third at a time, to a ¼-inch thickness on a lightly floured surface; cut with a 3-inch star cutter. Place on ungreased cookie sheets.
5. Bake in the preheated moderate oven (350°) for 10 minutes, or until firm. Remove from the cookie sheets with a spatula; cool on wire racks.
6. Coat with the Pink Glaze, decorate with silver dragées and allow the frosting to dry before storing between layers of wax paper in a metal tin with a tight-fitting lid.

Suggested Variations: For Holly Wreaths, cut the dough with a 3-inch round cutter, then cut out the centers with a 1-inch cutter. Substitute green food coloring for the red in the Pink Glaze and decorate with red candies. For Golden Stars, substitute yellow food coloring for the red in the Pink Glaze and sprinkle the frosted cookies with colored candies.

PINK GLAZE: Makes about 2 cups. Sift 1 package (1 pound) of 10X (confectioners' powdered) sugar into a medium-size bowl; beat in 6 tablespoons of water until the mixture is smooth. Tint pink with a few drops of red coloring. (If the frosting stiffens as you work, beat in a little more water, a drop or two at a time, until thin enough to pour from a spoon.)

ENGLISH TOFFEE DROPS

Buttery cookies that combine almond brickle with semisweet chocolate.

Bake at 375° for 8 to 10 minutes.
Makes about 8 dozen.

2¼ **cups all-purpose flour**
1 **teaspoon baking soda**
1 **teaspoon salt**
1 **cup (2 sticks) butter or margarine, softened**
¾ **cup granulated sugar**
¾ **cup firmly packed brown sugar**
1 **teaspoon almond extract**
2 **eggs**
1 **package (12 ounces) miniature semisweet chocolate morsels**
1 **package (6 ounces) almond brickle chips candy**

1. Sift the flour, baking soda and salt together on wax paper.
2. Beat the butter or margarine, granulated and brown sugars and almond extract in a large bowl with an electric mixer at high speed until creamy, then beat in the eggs, one at a time. Stir in the flour mixture with a wooden spoon, mixing just until blended. Stir in the chocolate pieces and almond brickle.
3. Drop the dough by rounded teaspoons, 2 inches apart, onto ungreased cookie sheets. (Do not crowd sheets.)
4. Bake in a moderate oven (375°) for 8 to 10 minutes, or until the edges are golden. Transfer to wire racks with a metal spatula. Cool completely.

OATMEAL SANDWICH BARS

Filled with a lemon-date mixture, these bars keep well.

Bake at 400° for 25 minutes.
Makes about 30.

 3 **cups cut-up pitted dates**
1½ **cups water**
 ¼ **cup granulated sugar**
     Grated rind and juice of 1 lemon
 ¾ **cup (1½ sticks) butter or margarine, softened**
 1 **cup firmly packed light brown sugar**
1¾ **cups all-purpose flour**
 1 **teaspoon salt**
 ½ **teaspoon baking soda**
1½ **cups quick-cooking rolled oats**

1. Combine the dates, water, granulated sugar and lemon juice in a small, heavy saucepan. Cook over low heat, stirring often, until the mixture thickens. Remove from the heat and stir in the lemon rind.
2. Beat the butter or margarine and light brown sugar until fluffy in a large bowl with an electric mixer at high speed. Stir the flour, salt and baking soda together. Beat into the butter mixture, then beat in the oats.
3. Press half of the oat mixture with your hands into a greased 9 x 13-inch baking pan, spreading evenly to cover the bottom of the pan. Spread the cooled date mixture in an even layer on top. Sprinkle the remaining oat mixture on top. Pat down lightly.
4. Bake in a hot oven (400°) for 25 minutes, or until the top is golden brown. Cool for 15 minutes in the pan on a wire rack. Cut into 2 x 1½-inch bars. Cool completely in the pan on the wire rack.

FREEZING COOKIES

● *Both cookie dough and baked cookies can be frozen and stored for 9 to 12 months.*
● *Baked cookies should be frozen in a strong box lined with plastic wrap or foil. Separate each layer with more wrap or foil; thaw the cookies at room temperature for 10 minutes.*
● *Cookie dough may be frozen in foil or plastic wrap.*
● *Drop-cookie dough should be thawed until just soft enough to use.*
● *Refrigerator-cookie rolls should be thawed just enough to slice.*
● *Rolled cookies can be frozen already shaped. Place them, still frozen, on cookie sheets.*
● *Freeze bar-cookie dough in the pan in which it is to be baked. Cover it with plastic wrap, then foil.*

PARISIENNES

Meringues are made special with the addition of two kinds of nuts and grated chocolate.

Bake at 275° for 20 minutes.
Makes about 10 dozen.

 3 **egg whites**
 ½ **teaspoon salt**
 ¼ **teaspoon cream of tartar**
 1 **cup superfine granulated sugar**
 4 **squares (1 ounce each) semisweet chocolate, grated**
 1 **cup blanched almonds, ground**
 1 **package (6 ounces) semisweet chocolate morsels**
 1 **tablespoon vegetable shortening**
 ⅓ **cup finely chopped pistachio nuts or almonds**

1. Beat the egg whites with salt and cream of tartar in a small, deep bowl with an electric mixer at high speed, until foamy-white and doubled in volume. Add the sugar, 1 tablespoon at a time, beating well after each addition. Continue beating until the meringue forms firm peaks. Gently fold in the grated chocolate and ground almonds with a wire whip.
2. Drop the meringue mixture by half teaspoonfuls, 1 inch apart, on a greased cookie sheet. Or fit a pastry bag with a #22 star tip and fill with the meringue mixture. Press out into small kisses, 1 inch apart.
3. Bake in a very slow oven (275°) for 20 minutes, or just until set but still creamy in color. Carefully remove from the cookie sheets to a wire rack with a metal spatula. Cool the cookies completely on the racks.
4. Melt the semisweet chocolate morsels with the shortening in the top of a double boiler over hot, not boiling, water. Dip the tops of the cookies into the melted chocolate, then into the chopped pistachios or almonds. Let stand for 30 minutes until the chocolate sets. Store cookies between layers of wax paper in a metal container with a tight lid.

◄◄◄

LEBKUCHEN

Honey and citron are essential ingredients in this classic German cookie.

Bake at 350° for 10 mintues.
Makes about 5 dozen.

¾ **cup honey**
¾ **cup firmly packed brown sugar**
 1 **egg**
 2 **teaspoons grated lemon rind**
 3 **tablespoons lemon juice**
3½ **cups all-purpose flour**
 1 **teaspoon salt**
 1 **teaspoon baking soda**
 2 **teaspoons pumpkin pie spice**
 1 **container (8 ounces) candied citron, finely chopped**
 1 **cup chopped almonds**
   Sugar Glaze (recipe follows)

1. Heat the honey to boiling in a small saucepan and pour it into a large bowl. Cool to room temperature for about 30 minutes.
2. Stir in the brown sugar, egg, lemon rind and lemon juice, blending well.
3. Sift the flour, salt, baking soda and pumpkin pie spice onto wax paper.
4. Stir the flour mixture into the honey mixture, a third at a time. Stir in the citron and almonds. (Dough will be stiff, but sticky.) Wrap in wax paper and refrigerate several hours, or until the dough is firm.
5. Roll out the dough, an eighth at a time, to a 5 x 6-inch rectangle on a lightly floured pastry cloth or board. Cut into 8 rectangles, 2½ x 1½ inches each. Place 1 inch apart on greased cookie sheets.
6. Bake in a moderate oven (350°) for 10 minutes, or until firm. Remove the cookies to wire racks with a spatula.
7. While the cookies are hot, brush with hot Sugar Glaze. Cool completely. Pack in a tightly covered metal container and allow to mellow for at least 2 weeks.

SUGAR GLAZE: Makes 2 cups. Combine 1½ cups of granulated sugar and ¾ cup of water in a medium-size saucepan. Bring to boiling, then lower the heat. Simmer for 3 minutes. Remove from the heat and, with a spoon, stir in ½ cup of 10X (confectioners' powdered) sugar until smooth and creamy.

◄◄◄

HOLIDAY ALMOND MOUNDS

Just two ingredients—almonds and honey—go into this Italian Christmas candy.

Bake at 300° for 20 minutes.
Makes 12 rings.

 4 **cups (1 pound) slivered almonds**
½ **cup honey**

1. Preheat the oven to slow (300°).
2. Spread the almonds in a single layer in a 15 x 10 x 1-inch jelly-roll pan.
3. Bake in the preheated slow oven (300°), shaking the pan several times, for 20 minutes, or just until richly golden.
4. Heat the honey to boiling in a large, heavy skillet. Stir in the toasted almonds with a wooden spoon. Keep stirring over low heat for 2 minutes, or just until the almonds start to stick together. Remove from the heat.
5. Moisten a wooden board. Spoon the nut mixture into 24 mounds on the board, dividing evenly. Sprinkle with multicolored sprinkles, if you wish.
6. Let the mounds stand on the board for at least an hour to cool and harden. Wrap in wax paper or plastic wrap.

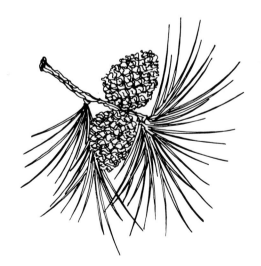

◀◀◀

SPICED DATE BARS

All the flavors of holidays past baked in quick-to-mix bar cookies.

Bake at 400° for 35 minutes.
Makes 36 bars.

1½ cups chopped pitted dates
¾ cup sugar
1 tablespoon grated orange rind
⅓ cup orange juice
¾ cup water
1¾ cups all-purpose flour
1½ teaspoons ground cinnamon
1 teaspoon salt
2 cups quick-cooking rolled oats
1¼ cups firmly packed light brown sugar
1 cup (2 sticks) butter or margarine
1 cup finely chopped walnuts

1. Mix the dates, sugar, orange rind and juice and water in a small saucepan. Cook, stirring often, for 10 minutes, or until mixture thickens. Remove from the heat and cool.
2. Preheat the oven to hot (400°).
3. Sift the flour, cinnamon and salt into a large bowl; stir in the oats and brown sugar. Cut in the butter or margarine with a pastry blender until the mixture is crumbly; stir in the walnuts. Press half of the mixture into the bottom of a greased 13 x 9 x 2-inch baking pan.
4. Bake in the preheated hot oven (400°) for 5 minutes. Spread the date mixture into the pan; sprinkle the remaining crumb mixture over the top, pressing down firmly with your hand.
5. Continue baking for 30 minutes, or until golden. Cool completely in the pan on a wire rack. Cut into 36 bars.

$ ◀◀◀

CHOCO-PEANUT BARS

Peanut butter and brown sugar bars are frosted with semisweet chocolate pieces.

Bake at 350° for 35 minutes.
Makes 3 dozen bars.

1 cup crunchy peanut butter
⅔ cup butter or margarine, softened
1 teaspoon vanilla
2 cups firmly packed light brown sugar
3 eggs
1 cup all-purpose flour
½ teaspoon salt
½ teaspoon ground nutmeg
½ cup semisweet chocolate morsels (from a 6-ounce package)
1 teaspoon vegetable shortening

1. Preheat the oven to moderate (350°).
2. Combine the peanut butter, butter or margarine and vanilla in a large bowl with an electric mixer at medium speed until blended. Beat in the brown sugar until light and fluffy; beat in the eggs, one at a time, until well blended.
3. Stir in the flour, salt and nutmeg just until well blended. Spread the batter in a greased 13 x 9 x 2-inch baking pan.
4. Bake in the preheated moderate oven (350°) for 35 minutes, or until the center springs back when lightly touched with a fingertip. Remove the pan from the oven to a wire rack; cool slightly.
5. Melt the chocolate with the shortening in a metal cup over simmering water. Drizzle the chocolate over the top of the cookies to cover thinly. When cool, use a sharp knife to cut 4 strips lengthwise and 9 strips crosswise to make 36 bars. Carefully lift the cookies out of the pan with a wide spatula and store in a metal tin with a tight-fitting lid.

🔀
TROPICAL BERRY BARS

Nut-rich meringue tops a raspberry and coconut layer. Just right for a party.

Bake at 350° for 40 minues.
Makes 32 bars.

- ¾ **cup (1½ sticks) butter or margarine**
- ¾ **cup sugar**
- 2 **eggs, separated**
- 1½ **cups all-purpose flour**
- 1 **cup chopped walnuts**
- 1 **cup raspberry preserves**
- ½ **cup flaked coconut**

1. Preheat the oven to moderate (350°).
2. Beat the butter or margarine with ¼ cup of the sugar in a medium-size bowl with an electric mixer at high speed, until the mixture is fluffy; beat in the egg yolks.
3. Stir in the flour until blended. Spread evenly in a greased 13 x 9 x 2-inch baking pan with a spatula.
4. Bake in the preheated moderate oven (350°) for 15 minutes, or until golden; remove from the oven.
5. While the layer bakes, beat the egg whites in a small bowl with the electric mixer at high speed until foamy white and doubled in volume. Gradually beat in the remaining ½ cup of sugar until the meringue stands in firm peaks; fold the walnuts into the meringue.
6. Spread the raspberry preserves over the layer in the pan; sprinkle with the coconut. Spread the meringue over the raspberry-coconut layer.
7. Bake in the preheated moderate (350°) oven for 25 minutes, or until lightly golden. Cool completely in the pan on a wire rack. Cut 4 strips lengthwise and 8 strips crosswise to make 32 bars. Carefully lift the cookies out of the pan with a wide spatula. Store in an airtight container between layers of wax paper.

Suggested Variation: For Strawberry Bars, substitute sliced almonds for the walnuts and use strawberry preserves for the raspberry.

💲 🔀
BEST-EVER BROWNIES

Try these, and you'll know why we call them the best ever!

Bake at 350° for 30 minutes.
Makes 16 brownies.

- 2 **squares (1 ounce each) unsweetened chocolate**
- ½ **cup (1 stick) butter or margarine**
- 2 **eggs**
- 1 **cup sugar**
- 1 **teaspoon vanilla**
- ½ **cup all-purpose flour**
- ⅛ **teaspoon salt**
- ¾ **cup chopped walnuts**

1. Preheat the oven to moderate (350°).
2. Melt the chocolate and butter or margarine in a small saucepan over low heat; cool to lukewarm.
3. Beat the eggs in a small bowl with an electric mixer at high speed; gradually beat in the sugar until the mixture is fluffy and thick. Stir in the chocolate mixture and the vanilla.
4. Fold in the flour and salt until well blended; stir in the walnuts. Spread in a greased 8 x 8 x 2-inch baking pan.
5. Bake in the preheated moderate oven (350°) for 30 minutes, or until shiny and firm on top. Cool in the pan on a wire rack. Cut 4 strips each way to make 16 bars.

SPICY FRUIT BARS

Molasses is a traditional flavor of the Christmas season. These molasses bars are a good substitute for fruitcake.

Bake at 350° for 20 minutes.
Makes 2 dozen bars.

    1   cup all-purpose flour
    ¼   teaspoon baking powder
    ⅛   teaspoon baking soda
    ½   teaspoon salt
    ½   teaspoon ground cinnamon
    ¼   teaspoon ground ginger
    ¼   teaspoon ground allspice
    2   eggs
    ⅔   cup sugar
    ¼   cup dark molasses
    ½   cup (1 stick) melted butter or margarine,
        cooled
    ½   cup diced candied cherries
    ½   cup chopped pecans or walnuts
    1   tablespoon grated orange rind

1. Preheat the oven to moderate (350°).
2. Sift the flour, baking powder, soda, salt, ground cinnamon, ginger and allspice onto wax paper.
3. Beat the eggs until light in a large bowl with an electric mixer at high speed. Add the sugar and molasses; beat well. Stir in the cooled butter or margarine. Add the flour mixture and stir with a wooden spoon just until blended.
4. Fold in the cherries, nuts and orange rind. Spread the batter into a greased 9 x 9 x 2-inch baking pan.
5. Bake in the preheated moderate oven (350°) for 20 minutes, or until the top springs back when lightly touched with a fingertip. Cool in the pan on a wire rack. Cut into 4 strips one way and 6 strips the other way to make 24 bars. Store in a metal tin with a tight-fitting lid.

CANDIED FRUIT COOKIES

So rich, so fruity. They're even better when allowed to mellow for several weeks.

Bake at 375° for 10 minutes.
Makes 4 dozen.

    1   cup (2 sticks) butter or margarine
    ½   cup firmly packed light brown sugar
    ½   cup light corn syrup
    2   eggs, separated
    2½   cups all-purpose flour
         Candied-Fruit Filling (recipe follows)

1. Beat the butter or margarine and the brown sugar until fluffy in a large bowl with an electric mixer at medium speed.
2. Add the corn syrup and the egg yolks, beating until well mixed. Stir in the flour until blended. Cover the bowl with plastic wrap; refrigerate for several hours or overnight.
3. Beat the egg whites with a fork until foamy in a small bowl. Shape the dough into small balls, using 1 tablespoon of the dough for each. Place, 2 inches apart, on a greased cookie sheet. Brush with the egg white.
4. Bake in the preheated moderate oven (375°) for 5 minutes. Remove from the oven. Make a hollow in the center of each cookie with the back of a wooden spoon. Spoon ½ teaspoon of the Fruit Filling into each hollow.
5. Return the cookie sheet to the oven and bake 5 minutes longer, or until the cookies are brown around the edges. Let cool for 5 minutes in the pan on wire racks. Remove with a spatula to the wire racks; cool completely. Store in a metal tin with a tight-fitting lid.

CANDIED-FRUIT FILLING: Makes 1 cup. Stir ½ cup of 10X (confectioners' powdered) sugar, ¼ cup (½ stick) of butter or margarine and 2 tablespoons of light corn syrup in a small saucepan. Bring to boiling, stirring constantly. Remove from the heat. Stir in ½ cup of finely chopped mixed candied fruit and 1 tablespoon of brandy. Cool for 1 hour.

MOLASSES JACKS

These chewy cookies are studded with multicolored candies.

Bake at 350° for 12 minutes.
Makes 7 dozen.

¾ cup (1½ sticks) butter or margarine
2½ cups firmly packed brown sugar
1 cup molasses
3 cups all-purpose flour
1½ teaspoons baking soda
¼ teaspoon salt
½ cup flaked coconut
½ cup chopped walnuts
Multicolored milk-chocolate candies

1. Beat the butter or margarine and the brown sugar in a large bowl with an electric mixer at high speed until light and fluffy. Beat in the molasses until well blended.
2. Sift the flour, baking soda and salt onto a sheet of wax paper; slowly beat into the creamed mixture until blended. Stir in the coconut and nuts. Cover with plastic wrap and refrigerate overnight.
3. Preheat the oven to moderate (350°).
4. Drop dough by teaspoonfuls, 2 inches apart, on greased cookie sheets. Press 4 or 5 candies into each mound of dough.
5. Bake in the preheated moderate oven (350°) for 12 minutes. Cool for 1 minute on the cookie sheets on wire racks. Remove the cookies with a spatula and cool on the wire racks.

Baker's Tip: Semisweet chocolate pieces may be used instead of the candies.

WALNUT CLUSTERS

For a flavor switch, use pecans instead of walnuts.

Bake at 350° for 10 to 12 minutes.
Makes about 36 cookies.

½ cup sifted all-purpose flour
½ teaspoon salt
¼ teaspoon baking powder
¼ cup (½ stick) unsalted butter, softened
½ cup sugar
1 egg
1 teaspoon vanilla
1½ squares (1 ounce each) unsweetened chocolate, melted
1½ cups walnut pieces
1 egg white
1 teaspoon water

1. Preheat the oven to moderate (350°). Lightly grease cookie sheets with shortening.
2. Sift together the flour, salt and baking powder onto a sheet of wax paper.
3. Beat together the butter, sugar, egg and vanilla in a small bowl until fluffy, for about 3 minutes. Fold in the flour mixture and the melted chocolate. Fold in the walnuts.
4. Drop the dough by heaping teaspoonfuls, 2 inches apart, onto the prepared cookie sheets.
5. Beat the egg white with the water in a small cup just until combined. Brush over the cookies.
6. Bake in the preheated moderate oven (350°) for 10 to 12 minutes, or until firm. Transfer the cookies to wire racks to cool.

MARIE'S TATUS

Enlivened with orange and spice, these chocolate fudge cookies are easy to form.

Bake at 375° for 12 minutes.
Makes about 6 dozen.

3½ cups all-purpose flour
½ cup cocoa powder (not a mix)
2 teaspoons baking powder
2 teaspoons ground cinnamon
1 teaspoon ground allspice
½ teaspoon ground nutmeg
½ cup vegetable shortening
¾ cup sugar
2 eggs
1 teaspoon vanilla
Grated rind and juice of 1 orange
¼ cup milk
½ cup finely chopped walnuts
Cocoa Glaze (recipe follows)
White prepared icing (from a 4¼-ounce tube)

1. Sift together the flour, cocoa, baking powder, cinnamon, allspice and nutmeg onto wax paper.
2. Beat the shortening and the sugar until light and fluffy in a large bowl with an electric mixer at high speed. Beat in the eggs until well blended; beat in the vanilla, orange rind and juice and milk.
3. Gradually add the sifted flour mixture. Blend in the chopped nuts. Wrap in wax paper and refrigerate the dough, if necessary, until easy to handle.
4. Preheat the oven to moderate (375°).
5. Shape the dough into 1-inch balls and place, 2 inches apart, on lightly greased cookie sheets.
6. Bake in the preheated moderate oven (375°) for 12 minutes, or until firm. Remove from the cookie sheets to wire racks. Cool completely before glazing.
7. Top the cookies with the Cocoa Glaze; let the glaze dry. Decorate with the icing.

COCOA GLAZE: Makes enough for 1 batch of cookies. Combine 1 package (1 pound) of 10X (confectioners' powdered) sugar, sifted, with ½ cup of cocoa powder and 1 tablespoon of softened butter or margarine in a large bowl. Stir with a wooden spoon until well blended. Beat in ¼ to ½ cup of milk to make a glaze that is the right consistency for spooning over the cookies.

GREEK WALNUT CAKES

These rich, moist orange-nut cakes keep well.

Bake at 350° for 30 minutes.
Makes 2 dozen.

Honey Syrup (recipe follows)
1½ cups all-purpose flour
2 teaspoons baking powder
1 teaspoon ground cinnamon
¼ teaspoon salt
1 cup (2 sticks) butter or margarine, softened
1 cup sugar
4 eggs
1 tablespoon grated orange rind
⅓ cup orange juice
2 cups finely chopped walnuts
Walnut halves

1. Prepare and cool Honey Syrup.
2. Sift the flour, baking powder, cinnamon and salt onto wax paper.
3. Beat the butter or margarine with the sugar until light and fluffy in a large bowl with an electric mixer at high speed. Beat in the eggs, 1 at a time, beating well after each addition. Stir in the orange rind.
4. Stir in the flour mixture alternately with the orange juice, beginning and ending with the flour and mixing just until blended. Stir in the walnuts. Pour the batter into a 9 x 13-inch greased pan.
5. Bake in a moderate oven (350°) for 30 minutes, or until the center springs back when lightly pressed with a fingertip.
6. Cool the cake in the pan on a wire rack for 10 minutes. Gradually pour the cool Honey Syrup over the cake, letting the syrup soak in before adding more. Let the cake cool completely. Cover the pan with aluminum foil. Refrigerate for up to 1 week, or wrap the pan in aluminum foil, label, date and freeze it for up to 3 months.
7. At gift-giving time, cut the cake into 3 lengthwise strips, then cut each strip into eighths to make 24 cakes. Place each cake in a fluted paper baking cup and garnish with a walnut half.

HONEY SYRUP: Makes about 1 cup. Combine ½ cup of sugar, ½ cup of water, one 2-inch piece of orange rind (no white) and one 1-inch piece of stick cinnamon in a small saucepan. Bring to boiling, then lower the heat. Simmer for 5 minutes, or until the temperature reaches 230° on a candy thermometer. Stir in ½ cup of honey. Cool. Remove the orange rind and cinnamon stick.

MEXICAN WEDDING CAKES

Place these in tiny paper cups before packing or serving at Christmastime.

Bake at 350° for 30 minutes.
Makes 2 dozen.

> *2 cups all-purpose flour.*
> *1 cup pecans, finely chopped*
> *½ cup sifted 10X (confectioners' powdered) sugar*
> **Pinch of salt**
> *1 teaspoon vanilla*
> *1 cup (2 sticks)* unsalted *butter, softened*
> *10X (confectioners' powdered) sugar*

1. Preheat the oven to moderate (350°).
2. Combine the flour, nuts, sugar and salt in a medium-size bowl. Stir in the vanilla. Cut in the butter with a pastry blender. Stir until the mixture forms a ball.
3. Divide the dough into 24 even pieces. Shape into patties between your hands. Place on an ungreased cookie sheet.
4. Bake in the preheated moderate oven (350°) for 30 minutes, or until the cookies are delicately browned. Remove from the cookie sheet to wire racks; cool slightly. Dust thickly with the 10X sugar.

Baker's Tip: Butter really does give better flavor to these cookies. However, if you choose to use margarine, omit the pinch of salt.

KYSKAGER

Hazelnuts add a special flavor to these meringues.

Bake at 250° for 10 minutes.
Makes 3 dozen.

> *6 egg whites*
> *2¼ cups 10X (confectioners' powdered) sugar*
> *1 tablespoon mild white vinegar*
> *1 cup finely chopped hazelnuts*

1. Preheat the oven to slow (250°). Grease cookie sheets and sprinkle with flour to coat lightly.
2. Beat the egg whites until soft peaks form in a medium-size deep bowl with an electric mixer at high speed.

3. Add the 10X sugar, a part at a time, beating well after each addition, until the meringue is stiff. Beat in the vinegar and fold in the chopped hazelnuts.
4. Drop the meringue mixture by teaspoonfuls, 2 inches apart, on the prepared cookie sheets.
5. Bake in the preheated slow oven (250°) for 10 minutes, or until the cookies are light brown. Transfer to wire racks with a spatula and cool completely. Store between sheets of wax paper in a metal tin.

OATMEAL LACE WAFERS

Delicate cookies that get their lacy look in baking.

Bake at 350° for 10 to 12 minutes.
Makes 48 cookies.

> *¼ cup sifted all-purpose flour*
> *½ teaspoon ground allspice*
> *½ teaspoon ground cinnamon*
> *½ teaspoon ground cloves*
> *½ teaspoon ground ginger*
> *½ teaspoon salt*
> *¼ teaspoon baking powder*
> *½ cup (1 stick)* unsalted *butter, softened*
> *⅓ cup granulated sugar*
> *⅓ cup firmly packed light brown sugar*
> *1 egg*
> *1 teaspoon vanilla*
> *1 cup old-fashioned rolled oats*
> *⅓ cup chopped walnuts*

1. Preheat the oven to moderate (350°). Lightly grease cookie sheets with shortening.
2. Sift together the flour, allspice, cinnamon, cloves, ginger, salt and baking powder onto a piece of wax paper.
3. Beat together the butter, granulated and light brown sugars, egg and vanilla in a large bowl until fluffy, for about 3 minutes.
4. Stir in the flour mixture, oats and nuts until thoroughly blended.
5. Drop the mixture by heaping teaspoonfuls, 3 inches apart, onto the prepared cookie sheets. Flatten slightly with the moistened tines of a fork.
6. Bake in the preheated moderate oven (350°) for 10 to 12 minutes, or until the edges are golden. Remove immediately from the cookie sheets to wire racks to cool.

RASPBERRY-NUT PINWHEELS

The rolls may be frozen and then cut and baked as needed.

Bake at 375° for 9 minutes.
Makes 3 dozen cookies.

> **2 cups all-purpose flour**
> **1 teaspoon baking powder**
> **½ cup (1 stick) butter or margarine, softened**
> **1 cup sugar**
> **1 egg**
> **1 teaspoon vanilla**
> **¼ cup seedless raspberry jam**
> **1 cup finely chopped walnuts**

1. Sift together the flour and baking powder onto wax paper.
2. Beat together the butter or margarine, sugar and egg in a large bowl with an electric mixer until fluffy. Stir in the vanilla. Gradually add the flour mixture, stirring until well combined.
3. Roll out the dough between two pieces of wax paper to a 12 x 10-inch rectangle. Remove the top piece of wax paper. Spread the jam evenly over the entire surface of the dough. Sprinkle evenly with the nuts.
4. Firmly roll up the dough from a long side, jelly-roll style, removing the wax paper as you roll. Wrap the roll in wax paper and refrigerate for several hours, or overnight.
5. Preheat the oven to moderate (375°).
6. Cut the roll into generous ¼-inch-thick slices with a thin sharp knife. Transfer the slices to ungreased cookie sheets, spacing them 2 inches apart.
7. Bake in the preheated moderate oven (375°) for 9 minutes, or until golden around the edges. Cool on wire racks.

GRANOLA

Bake at 300° for 20 minutes.
Makes 6 cups.

> **3 cups rolled oats**
> **⅓ cup firmly packed brown sugar**
> **½ teaspoon salt**
> **½ cup vegetable oil**
> **1 cup dried apples, cut in half**
> **1 cup raisins**
> **½ cup walnuts**
> **⅓ cup shelled sunflower seeds**
> **⅓ cup shelled pumpkin seeds**
> **2 tablespoons sesame seeds**

1. Combine the rolled oats, brown sugar, salt and oil in a large bowl.
2. Add the apples, raisins, walnuts, sunflower seeds, pumpkin seeds and sesame seeds to the oat mixture, stirring thoroughly. Spread the mixture in a 15 x 10 x 1-inch jelly-roll pan.
3. Bake in a slow oven (300°) for 20 minutes, turning once. Remove to a wire rack. Let cool thoroughly. Store in a tightly covered container.

CRISP REFRIGERATOR COOKIES

Pack the dough into juice cans and refrigerate for at least four hours. When ready to bake, slice the chilled dough, using the edge of the can as a guide.

Bake at 350° for 10 minutes.
Makes about 9 dozen.

> **4 cups all-purpose flour**
> **1 teaspoon baking powder**
> **1 teaspoon salt**
> **¼ teaspoon baking soda**
> **1¼ cups (2½ sticks) butter or margarine, softened**
> **1 cup firmly packed brown sugar**
> **½ cup granulated sugar**
> **2 eggs**
> **2 teaspoons vanilla**

1. Measure the flour, baking powder, salt and baking soda into a sifter; sift onto wax paper.
2. Beat the butter or margarine with the brown and granulated sugars until fluffly in a large bowl with an electric mixer at high speed. Beat in the eggs and the vanilla until well blended. Stir in the flour mixture, a third at a time, to make a soft dough.
3. Divide the dough among 3 clean, empty 6-ounce juice cans. Cover with aluminum foil. Refrigerate overnight, or until ready to bake.
4. Preheat the oven to moderate (350°).
5. To slice, remove the bottom of each can and use as a pusher to push the dough to the top of the can. Cut the dough to a ¼-inch thickness with a sharp knife, using the edge of the can as a guide. Place the slices, 1 inch apart, on ungreased cookie sheets.
6. Bake in the preheated moderate oven (350°) for 10 minutes, or until golden. Cool on wire racks. Store in a metal tin.

NO-BAKE COOKIES AND CONFECTIONS

CHOCOLATE BOURBON BALLS

Not every cookie has to be baked. You can use vanilla as a substitute for the bourbon.

Makes 3 dozen.

- 1 **package (6 ounces) semisweet chocolate pieces**
- ¼ **cup brewed coffee**
- ¼ **cup light corn syrup**
- 2 **tablespoons bourbon OR: vanilla**
- 2 **cups finely crushed chocolate cookie crumbs**
- 1 **cup 10X (confectioners' powdered) sugar**
- 1 **cup chopped pecans or walnuts**
  Chocolate sprinkles
  Bourbon Frosting (recipe follows)
  Candied cherries

1. Heat the semisweet chocolate pieces, coffee, corn syrup and bourbon or vanilla in a large saucepan over low heat, stirring occasionally, until the chocolate melts. Beat with a wire whisk until smooth. Remove the saucepan from the heat to a wooden board.
2. Stir in the cookie crumbs, 10X sugar and nuts, and mix with a wooden spoon until well blended; let stand for 10 minutes, or until cool enough to handle.
3. Shape the mixture, a tablespoon at a time, between the palms of your hands to make 1-inch balls. Sprinkle the chocolate sprinkles on wax paper and roll the cookie balls in the chocolate sprinkles to coat. Layer between sheets of wax paper in a metal tin with a tight-fitting lid. Garnish with the Bourbon Frosting and the candied cherries, just before serving.

BOURBON FROSTING: Makes about 1 cup. Combine 3 cups of 10X (confectioners' powdered) sugar, dash of salt, 3 tablespoons of butter or margarine, ¼ cup of bourbon whiskey, 1 teaspoon of vanilla and a dash of ground nutmeg in a medium-size bowl. Beat until creamy-smooth with an electric mixer at high speed.

ROCKY ROAD BROWNIES

Packaged tea cookies provide the shortcut in creating these confection-like cookies.

Makes about 2 dozen cookies.

- 6 **tablespoons (¾ stick) butter or margarine, cut up**
- 3 **squares (1 ounce each) unsweetened chocolate**
- 1 **teaspoon vanilla**
- 3 **egg yolks**
- ⅓ **cup sugar**
- 1 **egg white**
- 1 **package (11 ounces) tea cookies, each broken into 12 pieces (5 cups)**
- 1 **cup miniature marshmallows**
- ¾ **cup coarsely chopped walnuts**

1. Melt the butter and chocolate in a heavy medium-size saucepan over moderate heat. Remove from the heat; stir in the vanilla. Reserve.
2. Beat the egg yolks with the sugar in a large bowl with an electric mixer until thick and light. Gradually stir in the chocolate mixture.
3. Beat the egg white in a small bowl with the electric mixer until soft peaks form; fold into the chocolate mixture until no streaks of white remain. Stir in the cookie pieces, marshmallows and walnuts until thoroughly combined.
4. Spread evenly into a greased 8 x 8 x 2-inch pan. Refrigerate, covered, for at least 1 hour. Cut into bars, approximately 2 x 1½ inches.

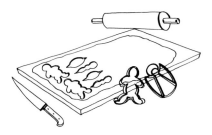

GOLDEN FIG NUGGETS

Makes 20 cookies.

¼ cup (½ stick) butter or margarine, softened
¼ cup firmly packed brown sugar
1 teaspoon grated lemon rind
1 cup graham cracker crumbs
    (7 double crackers, crushed)
1 cup finely chopped dried figs, stems
    removed
¼ cup honey
2 tablespoons grated orange rind
¼ cup orange juice

1. Generously grease 20 miniature (1¾ inches) muffin pan cups. Press a 3-inch square of wax paper into each.
2. Beat the butter or margarine, sugar and lemon rind in a large bowl with an electric mixer until creamy, blending thoroughly. Stir in the graham cracker crumbs until well combined.
3. Press a rounded tablespoon of the crumb mixture firmly over the bottom and partly up the side of each lined muffin pan cup. Refrigerate until firm, about 1 hour.
4. Combine the figs, honey, orange rind and orange juice in a small saucepan. Bring to boiling, then lower the heat. Cook, stirring constantly, until thickened, about 2 minutes. Cool.
5. Spoon a rounded teaspoon of the fig mixture into the graham cracker shells. Remove the cookies from the muffin pan cups by pulling up the wax paper. Serve in the miniature muffin pan liners. Store, covered, in the refrigerator.

PEANUT BUTTER MUNCHIES

No cooking and only one mixing bowl!

Makes about 3 dozen cookies.

1¼ cups graham cracker crumbs
1 cup 10X (confectioners' powdered) sugar
1 cup creamy peanut butter
¼ cup (½ stick) butter or margarine, softened
½ cup chopped walnuts
½ cup flaked coconut

1. Mix the graham cracker crumbs, 10X sugar, peanut butter and butter or margarine in a medium-size bowl, using a wooden spoon.
2. Roll between the palms to shape into small balls. Roll half in nuts and half in coconut. Refrigerate.

GINGER SNAPPY TURTLES

Whimsical cookies the kids will love to help decorate.

Makes 2 dozen cookies.

1½ cups pecan halves
¾ cup vegetable shortening
2 egg whites
1 teaspoon vanilla
3 cups 10X (confectioners' powdered) sugar
1 package (16 ounces) gingersnaps
1 package (6¼ ounces) caramels
1 tablespoon water

1. Reserve 24 whole pecan halves, then cut the remaining pecans in half lengthwise.
2. Beat the shortening, egg whites and vanilla in a medium-size bowl with an electric mixer until smooth. Beat in the 10X sugar until thick and creamy.
3. Spread a generous tablespoon of frosting on the bottom of one gingersnap. Press another cookie on top so that the frosting oozes out slightly. Press in the cut pecan pieces to resemble legs and one whole pecan half to resemble the head of a turtle. Repeat to make 23 more sandwich cookies.
4. Melt 14 caramels with the water in a small saucepan over low heat; stir until smooth. Drizzle about ½ teaspoon of the melted caramel on the back (top of gingersnap) of each turtle. Let stand until firm.
5. Store with wax paper between the layers in a container with a tight-fitting lid.

MINCEMEAT BALLS

A no-bake cookie-candy the kids can make by themselves.

Makes 6 dozen balls.

  1 package (13½ ounces) graham cracker crumbs
  1 package (9 ounces) condensed mincemeat, finely crumbled
  1 can (14 ounces) sweetened condensed milk (not evaporated milk)
  1 cup finely chopped walnuts
  1 tablespoon rum extract
  1 teaspoon ground cinnamon
  1 teaspoon ground cloves
     10X (confectioners' powdered) sugar
     Candied cherries, halved

1. Combine the graham cracker crumbs, condensed mincemeat, sweetened condensed milk, walnuts, rum extract, cinnamon and cloves in a large bowl until well blended.

2. Shape the mixture into 1-inch balls with lightly buttered hands on wax paper; roll the balls in the 10X sugar spread on additional wax paper. Press a cherry half into each. Store at room temperature in a tightly covered container.

DOUBLE CHOCOLATE CHUNKS

This snack was developed with chocoholics in mind!

Makes 36 squares.

  1 package (6 ounces) semisweet chocolate pieces
  ½ cup crunchy peanut butter
  3 cups ready-sweetened chocolate-flavored rice cereal
     Chopped peanuts (optional)
     Chocolate drink mix (optional)

1. Melt the chocolate pieces and peanut butter in a saucepan, stirring until smooth. Remove from the heat.

2. Stir in the cereal until well coated. Press the mixture evenly into a 9-inch-square pan. Scatter the top with the chopped peanuts and a few tablespoons of the dry chocolate drink mix, if you wish.

3. Refrigerate for 3 hours, or until firm. Let stand at room temperature for 10 minutes before cutting into 1½-inch squares with a sharp knife. Pack into decorative boxes to give as gifts.

CHINESE CHOCOLATE DROPS

Makes 1½ dozen cookies.

  ¼ cup (½ stick) butter or margarine
  6 squares (1 ounce each) semisweet chocolate
  1 tablespoon light corn syrup
  ¼ teaspoon almond extract
  1 can (3 ounces) chow mein noodles, crumbled
  ¾ cup sliced blanched almonds
 18 whole blanched almonds

1. Melt the butter or margarine and chocolate in a medium-size heavy saucepan over low heat. Remove from the heat and stir in the corn syrup and almond extract.

2. Combine the chow mein noodles and the sliced almonds in a large bowl. Add the chocolate mixture and stir until thoroughly combined.

3. Drop by rounded tablespoonfuls onto a wax paper-lined cookie sheet. Press a whole almond into the top. Refrigerate for about 30 minutes, or until firm.

KRISPIES TREAT

Breakfast cereal is the backbone of this chewy snack.

Makes 24 squares.

  ¼ cup (½ stick) butter or margarine
  1 bag (10 ounces) marshmallows
  ⅓ cup smooth peanut butter
  ½ cup raisins
  5 cups oven-toasted rice cereal

1. Melt the butter or margarine in a large saucepan. Stir in the marshmallows and peanut butter. Cook over low heat for 3 minutes, until melted and well combined.

2. Remove from the heat. Add the raisins and cereal, stirring until well coated.

3. Turn the mixture into a greased 13 x 9 x 2-inch pan. Using a wad of folded wax paper, quickly press the mixture evenly into the pan. Cool completely, then cut into 2-inch squares with a sharp knife. Pack into decorative boxes to give as gifts.

SAVORY DELIGHTS

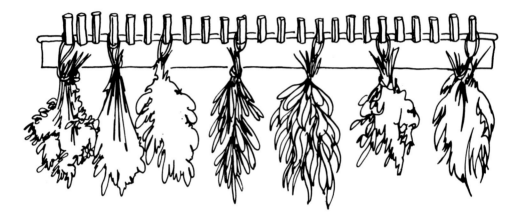

BACON & CHEESE LOAVES

The perfect accompaniment to salads or a sausage and cheese tray.

Bake at 375° for 30 minutes.
Makes 4 small loaves.

 6 **slices bacon**
 3 **cups all-purpose flour**
 1 **tablespoon baking powder**
 ½ **teaspoon salt**
 1 **cup shredded Cheddar cheese (4 ounces)**
 2 **eggs**
1½ **cups milk**
 1 **tablespoon melted butter or margarine**
 1 **tablespoon prepared mustard**

1. Preheat the oven to moderate (375°). Grease 4 miniature loaf pans.
2. Cut the bacon into 1-inch pieces and fry until crisp in a medium-size skillet, stirring often; drain on paper toweling.
3. Sift the flour, baking powder and salt into a large bowl; stir in the crisp bacon and the shredded cheese until well blended.
4. Beat the eggs until well blended in a medium-size bowl with a wire whisk. Beat in the milk, melted butter or margarine and mustard.
5. Pour the egg mixture over the dry ingredients and stir, just until blended, with a wooden spoon. Do not overmix.
6. Divide the batter evenly between the prepared loaf pans. Run a spatula across the tops until smooth.
7. Bake in the preheated moderate oven (375°) for 30 minutes, or until a wooden skewer inserted near the center comes out clean. Cool in the pans on wire racks for 10 minutes. Loosen the bread around the edges of the pan. Invert onto the wire racks; cool completely.
8. Wrap the loaves in plastic wrap or aluminum foil. Give within 2 days or freeze.

WINE AND CHEESE SPREAD

White Port wine gives a gourmet flavor to sharp Cheddar cheese.

Makes one large crock, or four 1-cup crocks.

> 1 **pound sharp Cheddar cheese**
> ½ **cup (1 stick) butter or margarine, softened**
> ⅓ **cup white Port wine**
> 2 **tablespoons sharp prepared mustard**

1. Shred the cheese into a large bowl. (A food processor will do this job in seconds.) Bring to room temperature.
2. Work in the butter or margarine, wine and mustard with a wooden spoon to make a very smooth mixture.
3. Cover the bowl with plastic wrap and refrigerate for 45 minutes, or until the mixture firms up.
4. Pack the mixture into one large crock or four 1-cup crocks, dividing evenly. Cover with plastic wrap and refrigerate until gift-giving time. Plan to give within two weeks.

GARLIC CHEESE BALL

A pungent blend of cream cheese, garlic, pepper and herb-blended salt.

Makes 12 servings.

> 2 **packages (8 ounces each) cream cheese, softened**
> ¼ **cup dairy sour cream**
> 1 **clove garlic, mashed**
> 1 **tablespoon herb-blended salt**
> ¼ **teaspoon seasoned pepper**
> ½ **cup finely chopped walnuts**

1. Beat the cream cheese until very smooth in a medium-size bowl. Mix in the sour cream, garlic, herb-blended salt and pepper until well blended. Refrigerate for at least 1 hour, or until firm.
2. Shape the mixture into a 4-inch ball on a flat plate. Cover with the chopped walnuts and wrap tightly in plastic wrap. Refrigerate for up to one week.

Cook's Tip: To make an Herbed Cheese Ball, substitute 1 tablespoon of chopped fresh basil, or 1 teaspoon of leaf basil, crumbled, for the herb-blended salt.

GREEN PEPPERCORN CHEESE

Green peppercorns, garlic and cracked pepper enhance this creamy spread. Try it on dark pumpernickel.

Makes one 7-inch mold.

> 2 **packages (8 ounces each) cream cheese, softened**
> 1 **pound cottage cheese**
> 1 **cup heavy cream**
> 1 **can (1¾ ounces) green peppercorns in brine, drained**
> 2 **green onions, thinly sliced**
> 1 **clove garlic, minced**
> ½ **teaspoon cracked pepper**

1. Combine the cream cheese and the cottage cheese until well blended in a medium-size bowl with an electric mixer at medium speed. Lower the speed to slow.
2. Gradually beat in the cream until the mixture is smooth. Stir in all but 1 tablespoon of the drained peppercorns, the green onions, garlic and cracked pepper.
3. Spoon the mixture into a sieve lined with a double layer of cheesecloth; place over a deep bowl. Refrigerate for 8 hours, stirring often.
4. Rinse a 7-inch porcelain coeur à la crème mold. Line with a double layer of cheesecloth (or line a wicker mold with a moistened cheesecloth). Spread the mixture into the mold. Cover lightly with plastic wrap. Place on a large, deep platter. Refrigerate for 8 hours, or overnight, discarding any liquid that accumulates.
5. Unmold the cheese, then remove the cheesecloth and return to the mold. Garnish with unsprayed leaves and the reserved peppercorns.

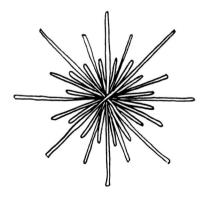

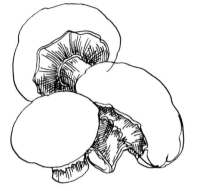

GOURMET MUSHROOMS

Tempting as an appetizer or when served in a spinach salad.

Makes five ½-pints.

 2 **cups water**
 ¾ **cup vegetable oil**
 ½ **cup lemon juice**
 3 **stalks celery, cut into 3-inch pieces**
 1 **clove garlic, halved**
 ½ **teaspoon ground coriander**
 ¼ **teaspoon leaf thyme, crumbled**
 ½ **teaspoon salt**
 8 **peppercorns**
1½ **pounds small mushrooms, trimmed**
 1 **jar (4 ounces) pimiento, drained and sliced**

1. Combine the water, oil, lemon juice, celery, garlic, coriander, thyme, salt and peppercorns in a large saucepan. Bring to boiling; lower the heat.
2. Add the mushrooms; simmer for 5 minutes. Remove from the heat and let cool.
3. Add the sliced pimiento. Pack the mushrooms, celery and pimiento into five ½-pint sterilized jars; pour the liquid over the mushrooms to within ¼ inch of the jar tops. Cover and refrigerate overnight, or for up to 1 week, to blend the flavors.
4. At gift-giving time, decorate the jars and add a card suggesting that the mushrooms be served with cold cuts or in an antipasto.

BRANDY PÂTÉ

So simple to make.

Makes 4 cups.

1½ **pounds liverwurst**
 1 **cup (2 sticks) butter or margarine**
 1 **small onion, grated**
 ¼ **cup brandy**
    Chopped parsley
    Chopped pimiento

1. Fit the container of an electric food processor with the chopping blade. Slice the liverwurst and the butter or margarine into the container; add the onion.
2. Process on high until very smooth, then remove the tube cover and slowly add the brandy until well blended.
3. Spoon the mixture into a glass or ceramic bowl. Cover with plastic wrap and refrigerate for at least 2 days to develop flavors.
4. Pack in 4 small crocks and decorate with the tines of a fork, then with the parsley and chopped pimiento. Give with a card suggesting that the pâté be kept in the refrigerator and used within one week.

POPCORN & PRETZEL NIBBLES

Cheese and garlic add to delicious munching!

Makes 16 cups.

10 **cups freshly popped popcorn**
 6 **cups stick pretzels**
 ½ **cup (1 stick) butter or margarine, melted**
 ¼ **cup Parmesan cheese**
 1 **tablespoon garlic salt**

1. Toss the popcorn, pretzels, melted butter or margarine, Parmesan cheese and garlic salt in a very large bowl. (If you don't have a bowl large enough, divide all amounts in half and make two batches.)
2. Spoon the mixture into hot, sterilized 1-quart jars and seal. Store at room temperature until ready to give away or serve.

Suggested Variation: For Corn Chip & Pretzel Nibbles, use a 1-pound bag of tortilla corn chips, a 12-ounce bag of pretzels and a 12-ounce can of peanuts for the popcorn and pretzels in the recipe above. Toss with ½ cup (1 stick) of butter or margarine, melted, with 1 to 3 teaspoons of curry powder.

CREAMY CURRY FONDUE SAUCE

Serve as a dipping sauce for beef fondue, shrimp, fruit, chips or crackers; as a salad dressing for fruit; or as an accompaniment to chicken salad.

Makes 2½ cups.

- **1 cup mayonnaise or salad dressing**
- **1 cup dairy sour cream**
- **½ cup chopped chutney**
- **1 teaspoon curry powder**
- **1 teaspoon grated orange rind**
- **½ cup finely chopped pecans**

Combine the mayonnaise or salad dressing, sour cream, chutney, curry powder, orange rind and pecans in a medium-size bowl. Stir until well blended. Pack into glass jars or fancy containers. Seal, label and chill until ready to give as a gift. (This will keep for about a week.)

SPICY TOMATO FONDUE SAUCE

Good as a dipping sauce for beef, chicken or shrimp fondue; on hamburgers and hot dogs; or to heat and serve over spaghetti or veal parmigiana.

Makes 3 cups.

- **1 jar (21 ounces) red cooking sauce**
  OR: 2½ cups of prepared spaghetti sauce with mushrooms
- **1 can (4 ounces) sweet green chilies, drained**
- **2 cloves garlic**
- **½ cup drained pitted ripe olives**

Combine the cooking sauce, green chilies, garlic and olives in an electric-blender container. Whirl at top speed until smooth and well blended. Pack in glass containers, then seal, label and chill until ready to give. (This will keep for about a week.)

SUPER-QUICK GOODIES

Here are some delectable gifts you can whip up in your kitchen in very little time.

1. Quick Apricot Conserve: Combine a 10-ounce jar of apricot preserves, ½ cup of chopped golden raisins and ½ cup of toasted slivered almonds with 1 tablespoon of amaretto in a bowl. Spoon into a jar.

2. Stuffed Fruit: Stuff pitted dates or prunes with almond paste, chopped toasted almonds and enough rum to make the mixture pliable. Roll the stuffed fruit in 10X (confectioners' powdered) sugar.

3. Chocolate-Dipped Fruit: Melt a 12-ounce package of semisweet chocolate pieces with 1 tablespoon of vegetable shortening. Use to dip unhulled strawberries, orange sections and banana chunks. Keep refrigerated and plan to give within several hours.

4. Lime-Peppercorn Mustard: Mix 2 cups of Dijon-style mustard with ¼ cup of drained and crushed green peppercorns and 1 tablespoon of lime juice. Pour into clean, dry jars with tight-fitting lids and store in the refrigerator.

5. Quick Cheese Straws: Add ½ cup (2 ounces) of shredded sharp Cheddar cheese and ½ teaspoon of dry mustard powder to your favorite single piecrust recipe. Roll it out to a ¼-inch thickness on a lightly floured surface, then cut into 4-inch strips. Brush with beaten egg and sprinkle with paprika and caraway seeds. Bake in a preheated hot oven (400°) for 8 to 10 minutes, or until golden. Store between paper-towel layers in an airtight container.

6. Honey Butter: Blend equal parts of honey and soft butter. Flavor with cinnamon, if you wish. Pack in crocks, cover with plastic wrap and chill.

7. Herbed Olives: Drain a can of pitted ripe olives and place them in a jar. Add 2 minced cloves of garlic, ½ teaspoon of crumbled leaf oregano and 3 whole peppercorns. Pour olive oil over this mixture, then cover. Let stand overnight.

8. Herb and Garlic Cheese: Place a softened 8-ounce package of cream cheese, a ½-pint container of dairy sour cream or plain yogurt, ¼ cup (½ stick) of softened butter, 2 mashed cloves of garlic, 1 chopped green onion and a few drops of liquid red-pepper seasoning in an electric food processor fitted with the metal blade. Cover and process on high speed until well blended. Transfer to crocks. Cover and refrigerate overnight to allow the flavors to blend.

9. Raisin Spread: Combine 1½ cups of raisins, ¾ cup of orange juice, 1 tablespoon of sugar, 2 teaspoons of grated orange rind and ¼ teaspoon of ground ginger in a small saucepan. Bring to boiling, then lower heat. Simmer, uncovered, for 10 minutes. Cool slightly. Pour into an electric blender or food processor fitted with metal blade and process until smooth. Transfer to jars.

10. Chunky Peanut Butter: Mix natural-style peanut butter with coconut and granola.

11. Cider Mix: Wrap the ingredients for mulled cider or wine in cheesecloth bags, then wrap again with some calico and ribbon. Attach these pouches to mugs or jugs, with the recipes attached. Great to give with a bottle of wine or cider.

CHOCOLATE FUDGE SAUCE

Smooth and delicious! You'll want to make this topping over and over.

Makes 2 cups.

 1 *package (6 ounces) semisweet chocolate
      pieces*
 1 *can (14 ounces) sweetened condensed milk*
 1 *teaspoon vanilla*
    Pinch salt
 ⅓ *cup hot water*

1. Melt the chocolate pieces in the top of a double boiler over simmering water. Add the condensed milk, vanilla and salt, stirring constantly until the mixture is slightly thickened. Then stir in the hot water.
2. Let cool, then cover and refrigerate. This sauce can be thinned more by adding hot water, 1 tablespoon at a time, before serving.

PINEAPPLE TOPPING

This makes plain cake or ice cream extra fancy.

Makes 3 cups.

 ½ *cup firmly packed brown sugar*
 1 *tablespoon cornstarch*
 1 *can (20 ounces) crushed pineapple in syrup*
 4 *tablespoons (½ stick) butter or margarine*

1. Mix the brown sugar and cornstarch in a medium-size saucepan. Stir in the pineapple.
2. Cook, stirring constantly, until the mixture thickens and boils for 3 minutes. Remove from the heat. Stir in the butter just until melted.
3. Serve warm or cold over ice cream or plain cake.

HOLIDAY FRUIT SAUCE

Spoon this sweet sauce over cake squares, vanilla ice cream and fresh fruit, or use as a filling between cake layers.

Makes about 6 cups.

 1 *can (1 pound, 5 ounces) apple-pie filling*
 1 *can (1 pound, 4 ounces) crushed pineapple,
      drained*
 1 *jar (12 ounces) orange marmalade*
 1 *cup chopped maraschino cherries
      (from an 8-ounce jar)*
 ⅓ *cup chopped crystallized ginger*

Combine the apple-pie filling, pineapple, marmalade, cherries and ginger in a large bowl. Stir until well blended. Pour into glass containers, then seal, label and chill until ready to give as a gift.

HOT MOCHA MIX

Just add boiling water to this mix and serve it in coffee mugs. (The milk and cream are already included!)

Makes 6½ cups.

 1 *cup unsweetened cocoa*
 2 *cups sugar*
 2 *cups nonfat dry milk powder*
 2 *cups dry nondairy coffee creamer*
 ½ *cup instant coffee*
 1 *vanilla bean, cut into quarters*

1. Combine the cocoa, sugar, milk powder, coffee creamer, instant coffee and vanilla bean in a large dry bowl. Stir until well blended.
2. Pack into jars, making sure a piece of vanilla bean is in each jar. Seal and label. Store in the refrigerator for at least a week before using to allow the vanilla flavor to be absorbed into the mix.
3. For drinking, use 3 level tablespoonfuls for every 6 ounces of boiling water. Top with a marshmallow or whipped cream.

Colorful ways to wrap your food gifts using ribbon, cloth swatches and decorative baskets and jars.

FOOD WRAP-UPS

Once you've baked your cookies, glazed the fruitcakes and prepared the snack mix, it's time to wrap your food attractively and *safely*.

• Look for attractive bottles and decanters to hold flavored vinegars, oils and homemade liqueurs.
• For jams and jellies, look for decorative jars with tight-fitting lids. If desired, top with a Decorative Jar Cover (shown with Pickled Peppers on page 230 and explained below), a doily or a round piece of fabric cut with pinking shears and tied around the top with ribbon or yarn. For thick spreads, try attaching a small wooden spoon or spreader to the lid.
• *Decorative Jar Cover:* Cut a circle one-inch wider than the top of your jar out of a piece of lightweight fabric using pinking shears. Sew some lace trim around the edge of the round. Sew ¼-inch elastic ½ inch from the outer edge.
• For both jars and bottles, you can tie a piece of one of the ingredients (such as a whole chili pepper or a knob of fresh gingerroot) around the lid, using a piece of yarn or ribbon.
• Use large mugs to hold snack mixes and hors

d'oeuvre straws. Tie with ribbon and wrap in heavy cellophane.
• Place fruitcakes and breads on top of a breadboard that is big enough to hold the food. Then wrap your creation in heavy cellophane and tie it with a ribbon.
• Give cookies in baskets lined with doilies and threaded with grosgrain ribbon. Wrap it all up with heavy cellophane.
• Present cakes and cupcakes in the pans in which they were baked. This way, it's a double gift.
• Use fragrant herbs and greens to decorate the tops of jars and baskets.
• Wrap cookies and confections in colored tissue and twist the ends. Pile wrapped nibbles in a decorative tin or basket.
• Make homemade jams extra special by giving them in crystal jars.
• Small, plastic-wrapped loaves of bread look even more tantalizing when wrapped in colorful fabric. Try adding some ribbon, too.
• Sew sacks from fabric that are large enough to hold jars or bottles, then thread the tops with some decorative ribbon.

PACKING AND SHIPPING FOOD

Be sure to choose the right cakes, breads and cookies for mailing. Foods to be mailed must be sturdy and should keep well. Soft drop, bar and fruit cookies are good travelers, as are fruit- and pound cakes, and all kinds of breads. Give your crisper cookies and tender pies to neighbors and family nearby.
For Cookies: Use empty metal coffee or shortening tins for packing. Wrap two drop cookies back to back, but wrap bar cookies individually with foil, and then seal using cellophane tape.
For Breads and Cakes: These should be sent in strong cardboard boxes, after you've wrapped your delicacies first in plastic wrap or strong plastic bags, and then again in aluminum foil.
To Pack:
• Line your containers with waterproof plastic wrap, wax paper or aluminum foil. As filler, use crumpled foil, tissue paper or wax paper but *not* unsalted

popcorn, which can become moldy, especially if the package is sent overseas.
• Pack cookies close together in order to leave as little empty space as possible. Shifting will cause them to break. If you're sending a variety of cookies, place the heaviest ones on the bottom. Place wrapped cakes and breads in a filler-lined box.
• Add more filler to the container, packing it down to minimize shifting and breakage. The box should be so full that you have to use pressure to tape it shut.
• If you can, wrap your package in corrugated cardboard, then a double layer of brown paper.
• Label only the top with the address of your friend or family member. Write "Fragile—Handle with Care" and "Perishable—Keep from Heat" on the top and on the sides of your package.
• Send overseas packages by air whenever possible to avoid spoilage.

CRAFTS BASICS
AND
ABBREVIATIONS

It doesn't matter if you've never picked up a knitting needle or crochet hook before. This primer will show you the basics of knitting and crocheting and embroidery stitches. With these skills, you can create virtually all our projects. We also explain the abbreviations used for the crafts in this book, as well as how to enlarge our designs.

So learn these basics, and get crafting. You'll be surprised how simple our projects really are when you go back through your Christmas Treasury and begin making all the wonderful gifts that are as much a joy to give as they are to receive.

HOW TO KNIT

KNITTING ABBREVIATIONS AND SYMBOLS

Knitting directions are always written in standard abbreviations. They look mysterious at first, but you'll soon know them: **beg** — beginning; **bet** — between; **bl** —block; **ch** —chain; **CC** — contrasting color; **dec(s)** — decrease(s); **dp** — double-pointed; **"** or **in(s)** — inch(es); **incl** — inclusive; **inc(s)** — increase(s); **k**— knit; **lp(s)** —loop(s); **MC** —main color; **oz(s)** — ounce(s); **psso** — pass slipped stitch over last stitch worked; **pat(s)** — pattern(s); **p** — purl; **rem** — remaining; **rpt** — repeat; **rnd(s)** — round(s); **sc** — single crochet; **sk** — skip; **sl** — slip; **sl st** — slip stitch; **sp(s)**, —space(s); **st(s)** — stitch(es); **st st** — stockinette stitch; **tog** — together; **yo** — yarn over; **pc** — popcorn stitch.

* (asterisk) — directions immediately following * are to be repeated the specified number of times indicated in addition to the first time — i.e., "repeat from * 3 times more" means 4 times in all.

( ) (parentheses) — directions should be worked as often as specified — i.e., "(k 1, k 2 tog, k 3) 5 times" means to work what is in ( ) 5 times in all.

THE BASIC STITCHES

Get out your needles and yarn, and slowly read your way through this special section—practicing the basic stitches illustrated here as you go along. Once you know them, you're ready to start knitting.

CASTING ON: This puts the first row of stitches on the needle. Measure off about two yards of yarn (or about an inch for each stitch you are going to cast on). Make a slip knot at this point by making a medium-size loop of yarn; then pull another small loop through it. Place the slip knot on one needle and pull one end gently to tighten (FIG. 1).

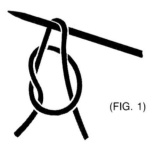

(FIG. 1)

● Hold the needle in your right hand. Hold both strands of yarn in the palm of your left hand securely but not rigidly. Slide your left thumb and forefinger between the two strands and spread these two fingers out so that you have formed a triangle of yarn.

Your left thumb should hold the free end of yarn, your forefinger the yarn from the ball, while the needle in your right hand holds the first stitch (FIG. 2).

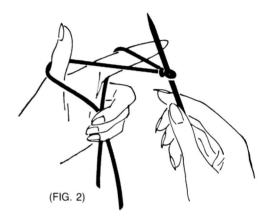

(FIG. 2)

You are now in position to cast on. See ABBREVIATIONS for explanation of asterisk (*).

● * Bring the needle in your right hand toward you; slip the tip of the needle under the front strand of the loop on left thumb (FIG. 3).

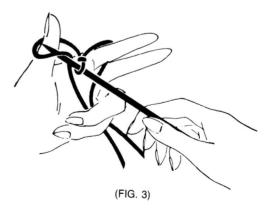

(FIG. 3)

- Now, with the needle, catch the strand of yarn that is on your left forefinger (FIG. 4).

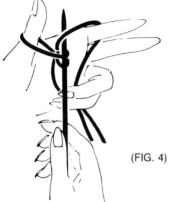

(FIG. 4)

- Draw it through the thumb loop to form a stitch on the needle (FIG. 5).

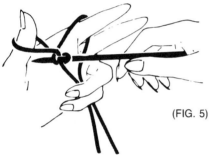

(FIG. 5)

- Holding the stitch on the needle with the right index finger, slip loop off your left thumb (FIG. 6). Tighten up the stitch on the needle by pulling the freed strand back with your left thumb, bringing the yarn back into position for casting on more stitches (FIG. 2 again).

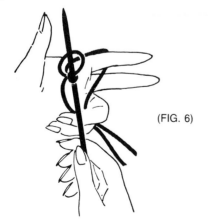

(FIG. 6)

- **Do not cast on too tightly.** Stitches should slide easily on the needle. Repeat from * until you have cast on the number of stitches specified in your instructions.

KNIT STITCH (k): Hold the needle with the cast-on stitches in your left hand (FIG. 7).

(FIG. 7)

- Pick up the other needle in your right hand. With yarn from the ball in **back** of the work, insert the tip of the right-hand needle from **left to right** through the front loop of the first stitch on the left-hand needle (FIG. 8).

(FIG. 8)

- Holding both needles in this position with your left hand, wrap the yarn over your little finger, under your two middle fingers and over the forefingers of your right hand. Hold the yarn firmly, but loosely enough so that it will slide through your fingers as you knit. Return the right-hand needle to your right hand.
- With your right forefinger, pass the yarn under (from right to left) and then over (from left to right) the tip of the right-hand needle, forming a loop on the needle (FIG. 9).

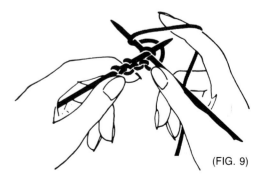

(FIG. 9)

● Now draw this loop through the stitch on the left-hand needle (FIG. 10).

(FIG. 10)

● Slip the original stitch off the left-hand needle, leaving the new stitch on right-hand needle (FIG. 11).

(FIG. 11)

Keep stitches loose enough so that you can slide them along the needles, but firm enough so they do not slide when you don't want them to. Continue until you have knitted all the stitches from the left-hand needle onto the right-hand needle.

● To start the next row, pass the needle with stitches on it to the left hand, reversing it, so that it now becomes the left-hand needle.

PURL STITCH (p): Purling is the reverse of knitting. Again, keep the stitches loose enough to slide, but firm enough to work with. To purl, hold the needle with the stitches in your left hand, with the yarn in **front** of your work. Insert the tip of the right-hand needle from **right to left** through the front loop of the first stitch on the left-hand needle (FIG. 12).

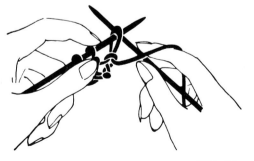

(FIG. 12)

● With your right hand holding the yarn in the same manner as to knit, but in **front** of the needles, pass the yarn over the tip of the right-hand needle, then under it, forming a loop on the needle (FIG. 13).

(FIG. 13)

● Holding the yarn firmly so that it won't slip off, draw this loop through the stitch on the left-hand needle (FIG. 14).

(FIG. 14)

● Slip the original stitch off the left-hand needle, leaving the new stitch on the right-hand needle (FIG. 15).

(FIG. 15)

SLIP STITCH (sl st): Insert the tip of the right-hand needle into the next stitch on the left-hand needle, as if to purl, unless otherwise directed. Slip this stitch off the left-hand needle onto the right, **without working it** (FIG. 16).

(FIG. 16)

BINDING OFF: This makes a finished edge and locks the stitches securely in place. Knit (or purl) two stitches. Then, with the tip of the left-hand needle, lift the first of these two stitches over the second stitch and drop it off the tip of the right-hand needle (FIG. 17).

(FIG. 17)

One stitch remains on the right-hand needle, and one stitch has been bound off.
● Knit (or purl) the next stitch; lift the first stitch over the last stitch and off the tip of the needle. Again, one stitch remains on the right-hand needle, and another stitch has been bound off. Repeat from * until the required number of stitches has been bound off.
● Remember that you work **two** stitches to bind off one stitch. If, for example, the directions read, "k 6, bind off the next 4 sts, k 6 ..." you must knit six stitches, then knit **two more** stitches before starting to bind off. Bind off four times. After the four stitches have been bound off, count the last stitch remaining on the right-hand needle as the first stitch of the next six stitches. When binding off, always knit the knitted stitches and purl the purled stitches.

● Be careful not to bind off too tightly or too loosely. The tension should be the same as the rest of the knitting.
● To end off the last stitch on the bound-off edge, if you are ending this piece of work here, cut the yarn leaving a six-inch end; pass the cut end through the remaining loop on the right-hand needle and pull snugly (FIG. 18).

(FIG. 18)

SHAPING TECHNIQUES
Now that you know the basics, all that's left to learn are a few techniques which will help shape whatever it is you are making.
Increasing (inc): This means adding stitches in a given area to shape your work. There are several ways to increase.
1. To increase by knitting twice into the same stitch: Knit the stitch in the usual way through the front loop (FIG. 19), but

(FIG. 19)

before dropping the stitch from the left-hand needle, knit **another** stitch on the same loop by placing the needle into the back of the stitch (FIG. 20).

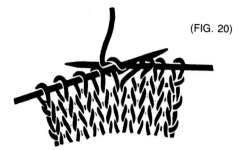

(FIG. 20)

(FIG. 23)

Slip the original stitch off your left-hand needle. You have made two stitches from one stitch.

2. To increase by knitting between stitches: Insert the tip of the right-hand needle under the strand of yarn **between** the stitch you've just worked and the following stitch; slip it onto the tip of the left-hand needle (FIG. 21).

Decreasing (dec): This means reducing the number of stitches in a given area to shape your work. Two methods for decreasing are:

1. To decrease by knitting (FIG. 24) or purling (FIG. 25) two stitches together:

(FIG. 21)

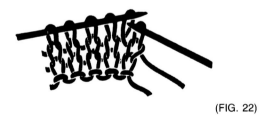

(FIG. 22)

(FIG. 24)

(FIG. 25)

Now knit into the back of this new loop (FIG. 22).

3. To increase by "yarn-over" (yo): Pass the yarn over the right-hand needle after finishing one stitch and before starting the next stitch, **making an extra stitch (arrow in FIG. 23). If you are knitting,** bring the yarn under the needle to the back. **If you are purling,** wind the yarn around the needle once. On the next row, work all yarn-overs as stitches.

Insert the right-hand needle through the loops of two stitches on the left-hand needle at the same time; complete the stitch. This is written as "k 2 tog" or "p 2 tog."

● If you work through the **front** loops of the stitches in the usual way, your decreasing stitch will slant to the right. If you work through the **back** loops of the stitches, your decreasing stitch will slant to the left.

2. Slip 1 stitch, knit 1 and psso: Insert the right-hand needle through the stitch on the left-hand needle, but instead of working it, just slip if off onto the right-hand needle (go back to FIG. 16). Work the next stitch in the usual way. With the tip of the left-hand needle, lift the slipped stitch over the last stitch worked and off the tip of the right-hand needle (FIG. 26).

(FIG. 26)

Your decreasing stitch will slant to the left. This is written as "sl 1, k 1, psso."

Pass Slipped Stitch Over (psso): Slip one stitch from the left-hand needle to the right-hand needle and, being careful to keep it in position, work the next stitch. Then, with the tip of the left-hand needle, lift the slipped stitch over the last stitch and off the tip of the needle (FIG. 26 again).

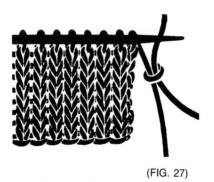

(FIG. 27)

ATTACHING THE YARN
When you end one ball of yarn or wish to change colors, begin at the start of a row and tie new yarn with the previous yarn, making a secure joining. Continue to knit or purl (FIG. 27).

HOW TO CROCHET

CROCHET ABBREVIATIONS

Following is a crochet abbreviations listing, with definitions of the terms given. To help you become accustomed to abbreviations used, we have repeated them through our stitch instructions.

beg — begin, beginning; **ch** — chain; **dc** — double crochet; **dec** — decrease; **dtr** — double treble crochet; **hdc** — half double crochet; **in(s)** or ″ — inch(es); **inc** — increase; **oz(s)** — ounce(s); **pat** — pattern; **pc** — picot; **rem** — remaining; **rnd** — round; **rpt** — repeat; **sc** — single crochet; **skn(s)** — skein(s); **sk** — skip; **sl st** — slip stitch; **sp** — space; **st(s)** — stitch(es); **tog** — together; **tr** — triple crochet; **work even** — continue without further increase or decrease; **yo** — yarn over; ***** — repeat whatever follows * as many times as indicated; **( )** — do what is in parentheses as many times as indicated.

Directions for right-handed and left-handed crocheters
Most crochet stitches are started from a base of chain stitches. However, our stitches are started from a row of single crochet stitches which gives body to the sample swatches and makes practice work easier to handle. When making a specific item, follow the stitch directions as given.

Holding the crochet hook properly (see FIG.1), start by practicing the slip knot (see FIG. 2) and base chain (see FIG. 3, page 287).

FIG. 1 HOLDING THE HOOK

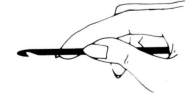

**FIG. 2 THE SLIP KNOT
(BASIS FOR CHAIN STITCH)**

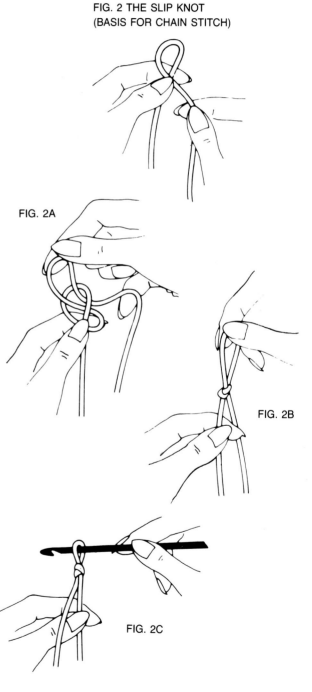

FIG. 2A

FIG. 2B

FIG. 2C

For Left-handed Crocheters

FIGS. 1 to 3 are for right-handed crocheters and are repeated in FIGS. 1 Left to 3 Left for left-handed crocheters.

From here on, we won't be showing hands—just the hook and stitches. Left-handed crocheters can use all the following right-handed illustrations by simply turning the book upside down and using a mirror (with backstand) that will reflect the left-handed version.

LEFT-HANDED CROCHETERS
FIGS. 1 LEFT TO 3 LEFT

CHAIN STITCH (CH)

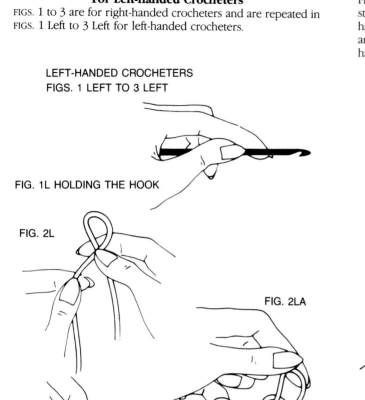

FIG. 1L HOLDING THE HOOK

FIG. 2L

FIG. 2LA

FIG. 2LB

FIG. 2LC

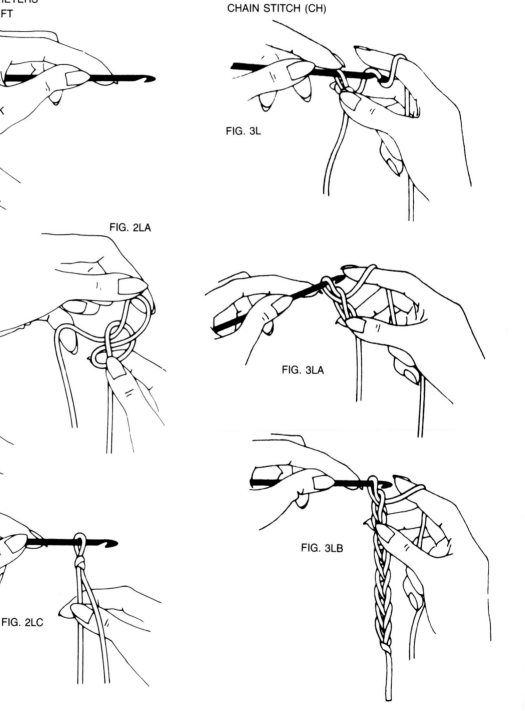

FIG. 3L

FIG. 3LA

FIG. 3LB

Chain Stitch (ch): Follow the steps in FIG. 3. As you make the chain stitch loops, the yarn should slide easily between your index and middle fingers. Make about 15 loops. If they are all the same size, you have maintained even tension. If uneven, rip them out by pulling on the long end of the yarn. Practice making chains and ripping out until you have a perfect chain.

Single Crochet (sc): Follow the steps in FIG. 4. To practice, make a 20-loop chain (this means 20 loops in addition to the slip knot). Turn the chain, as shown, and insert the hook in the second chain from the hook (see arrow) to make the first sc stitch. Yarn over (yo); for the second stitch, see the next arrow. Repeat to the end of the chain. Because you started in the second chain from the hook, you end up with only 19 sc. To add the 20th stitch, chain one (called a turning chain) and pull the yarn through. Now turn your work around (the "back" is now facing you) and start the second row of sc in the first stitch of the previous row (at the arrow). Make sure your hook goes under both of the strands at the top of the stitch. Don't forget to make a ch 1 turning chain at the end before turning your work. Keep practicing until your rows are perfect.

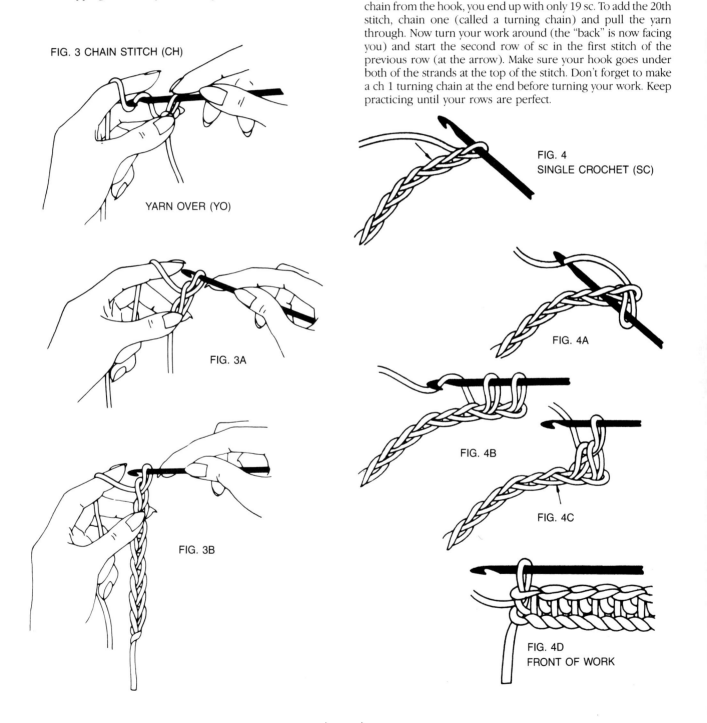

FIG. 3 CHAIN STITCH (CH)

YARN OVER (YO)

FIG. 3A

FIG. 3B

FIG. 4
SINGLE CROCHET (SC)

FIG. 4A

FIG. 4B

FIG. 4C

FIG. 4D
FRONT OF WORK

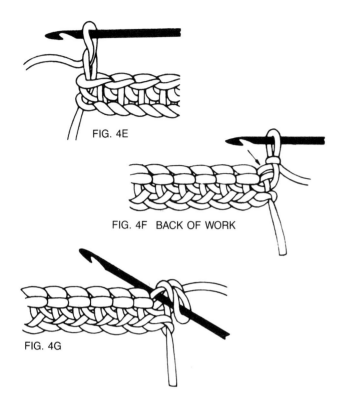

FIG. 4E

FIG. 4F   BACK OF WORK

FIG. 4G

Ending Off: Follow the steps in FIG. 5. To finish off your crochet, cut off all but 6″ of yarn and end off as shown. (To "break off and fasten," follow the same procedure.)

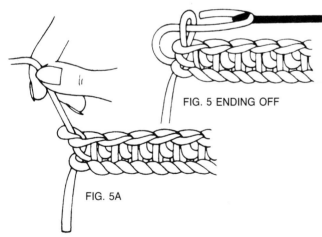

FIG. 5 ENDING OFF

FIG. 5A

Double Crochet (dc): Follow the steps in FIG.6. To practice, ch 20, then make a row of 20 sc. Now, instead of a ch 1, you will make a ch 3. Turn your work, yo and insert the hook in the second stitch of the previous row (at the arrow), going under both strands at the top of the stitch. Pull the yarn through. You now have three loops on the hook. Yo and pull through the first two, then yo and pull through the remaining two—one double

crochet (dc) made. Continue across the row, making a dc in each stitch (st) across. Dc in the top of the turning chain (see arrow in FIG. 7). Ch 3. Turn work. Dc in second stitch on the previous row and continue as before.

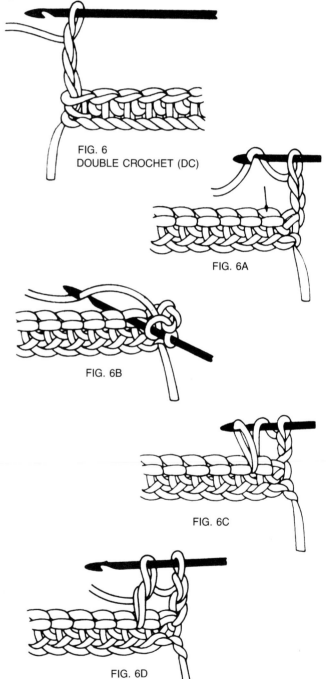

FIG. 6
DOUBLE CROCHET (DC)

FIG. 6A

FIG. 6B

FIG. 6C

FIG. 6D

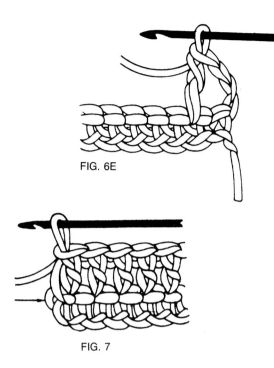

FIG. 6E

FIG. 7

Slip Stitch (sl st): Follow the steps in FIG. 9. This is a utility stitch you will use for joining, shaping and ending off. After you chain and turn, *do not yo*. Just insert the hook into the *first* stitch of the previous row (see FIG. 9A), and pull the yarn through the stitch, then right through the loop on the hook—sl st made.

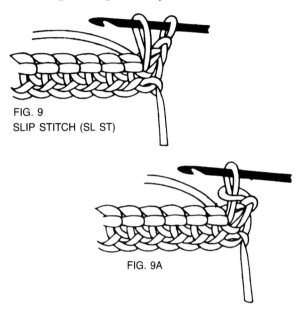

FIG. 9
SLIP STITCH (SL ST)

FIG. 9A

Note: You may also start a row of dc on a base chain (omitting the sc row). In this case, insert the hook in the fourth chain from the hook, instead of the second (see FIG. 8).

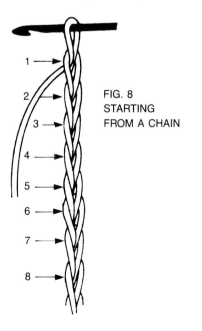

FIG. 8
STARTING
FROM A CHAIN

Half Double Crochet (hdc): Follow the steps in FIG. 10 and 10A. To practice, make a chain and a row of sc. Ch 2 and turn; yo. Insert the hook in the second stitch, as shown; yo and pull through to make three loops on the hook. Yo and pull the yarn through *all* three loops at the same time—hdc made. This stitch is used primarily as a transitional stitch from an sc to a dc. Try it and see—starting with sc's, then an hdc and then dc's.

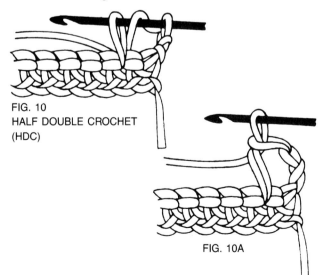

FIG. 10
HALF DOUBLE CROCHET
(HDC)

FIG. 10A

Techniques of Crocheting: Now that you have practiced and made sample squares of all the basic stitches, you are ready to learn about adding and subtracting stitches to change the length of a row whenever it's called for. This is achieved by increasing (inc) and decreasing (dec).

To increase (inc): Just make two stitches in the same stitch in the previous row (see arrow in FIG. 11). The technique is the same for any kind of stitch.

FIG. 12 DECREASING (DEC) FOR SINGLE CROCHET

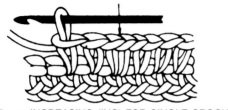

FIG. 11 INCREASING (INC) FOR SINGLE CROCHET

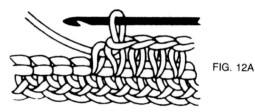

FIG. 12A

To decrease (dec) for single crochet (sc): Yo and pull the yarn through two stitches to make three loops on the hook (see steps in FIG. 12). Pull the yarn through all the loops at once—dec made. Continue in regular stitches.

To decrease for double crochet (dc): In a dc row, make the next stitch and stop when you have two loops on the hook. Now yo and make a dc in the next stitch. At the point where you have three loops on the hook, pull yarn through all loops at the same time. Finish the row with regular dc.

EMBROIDERY STITCH GUIDE

BACK STITCH

CHAIN STITCH

FEATHER STITCH

FRENCH KNOT

WHIPPED STEM STITCH

COUCHING STITCH

STRAIGHT STITCH

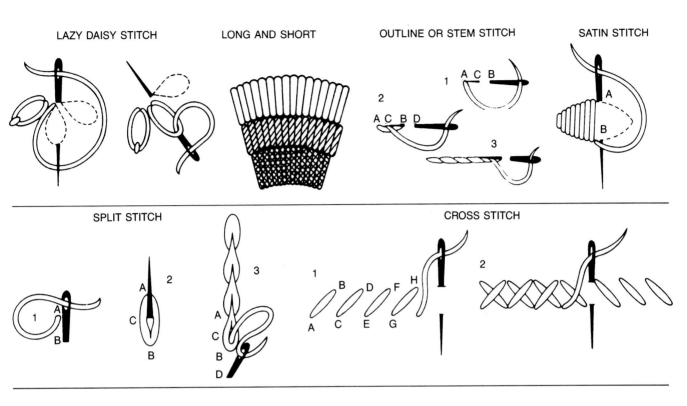

LAZY DAISY STITCH   LONG AND SHORT   OUTLINE OR STEM STITCH   SATIN STITCH

SPLIT STITCH   CROSS STITCH

Blanket Stitch

Work from left to right, with the point of the needle and the edge of the work toward you. The edge of the fabric can be folded under or left raw. Secure the thread and bring out below the edge. For the first and each succeeding stitch, insert the needle through the fabric from the right side and bring it out at the edge. Keeping the thread from the previous stitch *under* the point of the needle, draw the needle and thread through, forming a stitch over the edge. The stitch size and spacing can be the same or varied.

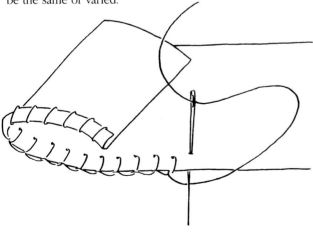

HOW TO ENLARGE DESIGNS

If the design is not already marked off in squares, make a tracing of it. Mark the tracing off in squares: For a small design, make squares ¼"; for larger designs, use ½" or 2" squares, or the size indicated in the directions. Decide the size of enlargement. On another sheet of tracing paper, mark off the same number of squares that are on the design or original tracing. For example, to make your design, each new square must be 6 times larger than the orignal. Copy the outline from your original tracing to the new one, square by square. Use dressmaker's carbon and a tracing wheel to transfer the design onto the material that you are decorating.

MATERIALS SHOPPING GUIDE

T*he following page lists the projects that suggest using specific manufacturer's products. Next, you'll find an alphabetized list of these manufacturers, along with their mailing addresses. All items were available at press time.*

PROJECTS AND PRODUCTS

Boy and Girl Dolls (page 89)— Clothes, "Memories of Christmas Past" (style #459-Rand) and "Christmas Present" (style #319-T), by VIP Fabrics; fiberfill, Poly-fil®, by Fairfield Processing Corp.; faces and feet, Polyform Modeling Compound, by PolyForm Products, Inc.; hair, "Feel O'Fleece," by Plaid Enterprises.

Candlewick Hearts and Bells (page 90)—Candlewicking thread, candlewick yarn (Art. 514, 100% cotton, 4 strands, 3-ply, color 862 natural) by Lily Craft Products/B. Blumenthal Inc.; fiberfill, Poly-fil®, by Fairfield Processing Corp; lace (style #181 8211, ¾" wide) by William E. Wright Co.

Decorated Satin Balls (page 69)—Satin balls (style #1330 3"-diameter, shocking pink) by Holiday Handicrafts, Inc.; grosgrain ribbon (style #550, ⅜" wide, apple green) and double-face ribbon (style #2203, ⅛" wide, red 250) by C.M. Offray and Son.

Fantasy Fashion Trims (page 122)— Pailettes and mixed color sequins by Walbead.

Lace Tree Garland (page 79)—White lace is Lion Ribbon lace.

Mr. and Mrs. Claus (page 24)— Contact® self-adhesive coverings in 9955 Solid-White, 9925 Solid-Red, 9945 Solid-Blue, 9975 Solid-Yellow, 9935 Solid-Black, 2512 Solid-Chrome, 2513 Solid-Brass, 9585 Strawberries-Green, 9755 Candy Stripes and 9505 Gridworks-Red by Rubbermaid Specialty Products, Inc.

Orange Tweed Cardigan and Hat (page 133 and 134)—Plymouth Persian Yarn in orange #406 and yellow #416.

Origami Wreath (page 44)—Ribbon by C.M. Offray and Son.

Padded Hangers (page 149)—Love My Carpet™ Soft-Scent Rug and Room Deodorizer in 20-oz. container by Lehn and Fink.

Piano Key Scarf (page 118)—Lion Brand Sayelle 4-ply worsted-wt. yarn (3½-oz. skein) in white and black.

Poinsettias (page 47)—Fabric, "Bridal Slipper Satin" (style #800, 100% East man Estron® acetate, in color mortar, 45" wide), by Pago Fabrics Corp.; clear acrylic spray, Krylon®, by Borden Chemical Inc.; felt-tip pen, Flair's Ultra-Fine, by Paper-Mate®; watercolor, alizarin crimson (available at art supply stores); velvet floral ribbon (style #6066 in apple green, 2⅝" wide) by WFR Ribbon Corp; green floral tape by Lion Ribbon Co.; covered wire (#24 gauge) from Lee Wards.

Quick and Easy Fabric Gifts (page 152)—#2 and #4: Fabric by Liberty. #6: Quilted fabric by VIP. #7: Appliquéd pot-holder fabric by Springs Industries; interfacing by Pellon Corp. #8: Fabric for Christmas tree coasters by Springs Industries.

Split-Second Hair Ornaments (page 154)—All ribbons by C.M. Offray and Son; appliqués by William E. Wright Co.; buttons by JHB International, Inc.; adhesive is Elmer's "Stix-All" by Borden Chemical Inc.

Twisted-Rib Pullover (page 117)—Caron "Wintuk" Bone #3003.

Rice-Paper Jars (page 150)— Mod-Podge® mat by Plaid Enterprises available at craft and hobby stores.

Rose Vest (page 137)—Brunswick "Germantown" Knitting Worsted 482 Burgundy Heather; DMC Tapestry Wool 7370 Soft Green, 7204 Med. Rose and 7202 Lt. Rose.

Strip Quilting (page 99)—Runner batting: "Cotton Classic" by Fairfield Processing Corp. Fabrics: "Joan Kessler" by Concord Fabrics, Inc.; VIP Fabrics.

White Crocheted Dove (page 70)— "Knit-Cro-Sheen" by Coats & Clark, Inc.

MANUFACTURERS AND ADDRESSES

Borden Chemical, Inc., Consumer Products, 180 Broad St., Columbus, OH 43215

Brunswick, Worsted Mills, Inc., P.O. Box 276, Pickens, SC 29671

Caron International, Ave. E and First St., Rochelle, IL 61068

Coats & Clark, Inc., Dept. CS, P.O. Box 1010, Toccoa, GA 30577

Columbia Minerva, 295 Fifth Ave., New York, NY 10001

Concord Fabrics, 1359 Broadway, New York, NY 10018

DMC Corporation, 107 Trumbull St., Elizabeth, NJ 07206

Fairfield Processing Corp., 88 Rose Hill Ave., Danbury, CT 06810

Holiday Handicrafts, Inc., P.O. Box 470, Winsted, CT 06098

JHB International Inc., 1955 South Quince, Denver, CO 80231

Lee Wards (Retail Division), 1210 St. Charles St. Elgin, IL 60120

Lehn and Fink, 225 Summit Ave., Montvale, NJ 07645

Liberty Fabrics of New York, Inc., 2 Park Ave., New York, NY 10016

Lily Craft Products/ B. Blumenthal Inc., 140 Kero Rd., Carlstadt, NJ 07072

Lion Ribbon Co., 100 Metro Way, Secaucus, NJ 07094

C.M. Offray and Son, 261 Madison Ave., New York, NY 10016

Pago Fabrics Corp., 48 W. 38th St., New York, NY 10018

Paper-Mate, Division of the Gillette Co., P.O. Box 61, Boston MA 02199

Pellon Corp., 119 W. 40th St., New York, NY 10018

Plaid Enterprises, 1649 International Blvd., P.O. Box 7600, Norcross, GA 30091-7600

Plymouth Yarn Co., Inc., Box 28, 500 Lafayette St., Bristol, PA 19007

PolyForm Products, Inc., 9420 Byron St., Schiller Park, IL 60176

Rubbermaid Specialty Products, Inc., Taylorsville Rd., Box 5050, Statesville, NC 28677

Springs Industries, Inc., Retail and Specialty Fabrics Division Customer Service Center, P.O. Box 111, Lancaster, SC 29720

VIP Fabrics, 1412 Broadway, New York, NY 10018

Walbead Inc., 29-76 Northern Blvd., Long Island City, NY 11101

WFR Ribbon Corp., 115 W. 18th St., New York, NY 10011

William E. Wright Co., One Penn Plaza, New York, NY 10001

INDEX

ITALICIZED PAGE NUMBERS REFER
TO ILLUSTRATIONS AND PATTERNS.

CRAFTS

A

Advent, Lollipop Calender, *104*-105
Angel
    Cornhusk Tree-Top, 65-67
    Satin Ornament, *61*, 62
    Tree, *58*, 69-70
Apple, Candy, 74
Apple Pot-Holder Set, 123-124
Appliqued and Quilted Pot Holder, 153
Apron, Set-to-Cook, 154

B

Baby Booties, 135
Balls, Decorated Satin, *68*, 69
Basic Artificial Wreath, 44
Basic Bow and Streamers Wreath, 44
Basic Evergreen Wreath, 44
Bazaar. *See* Gift Bazaar
Belt, Tie/Rack, 117
Birds (Quick Outdoor Tricks), 25
Birds 'N' Berries Window Box, *26*, 27
Blotter, Desk, 157
Booties, Baby, 135
Bottle Bag, 152
Boxes
    Keepsake, 121-122
    Knife, 125
Boy and Girl Dolls, *84, 86, 88,* 89
Button and Bow Wreath, *86,* 91

C

Calendar, Lollipop Advent, *104,* 105
Candles
    care and usage, 168, 169
    entryway, 38
    outdoor lantern, 25
    Scented, 156
Candlewick Heart and Bells, *84, 86,* 90

Candy Apple, 74
Canisters, 123
Cardigan, Orange Tweed, and Hat, *133,* 134
Cards. *See* Christmas cards
Case, Lingerie, 150, *151*
Centerpieces, 38, 50-57
    Gingerbread House, *54,* 55-56, *57*
    Glass Bowl, 50
    Gold and Silver Balls, 50
    Jiffy Decorations, 38
    Twig Creche, *51,* 52-53
Chenille Tree Garland, 76, 77
Christmas cards
    decorating with (entryway), 38
    Heart Christmas Card Holder, 98
    list, 11
Christmas Pudding Mouse, 72-74
Christmas Stockings, *40,*41
Christmas tree
    in a Basket, *96,* 97
    buying tips, 60
    care, 60
    coasters, 153
    garlands, 75-79
    Kiddy, 101, 102
    lights, 60, 70
    Natural, *92*
    ornaments. *See* Ornaments, Christmas tree
    safety, 60
    Skirts, 80-83, 104
    Toppers, *61,* 62-67
    Victorian-style, *84, 86,* 88-91

Cinnamon Garland, 35
Cinnamon Wreath, *34,* 35
Clown, Holiday, 62, *63*
Coasters, Christmas Tree, 153
Cocktail napkins, 153
Cornhusk
    Tree-Top Angel, 65-67
    Wreath, 94
Coupon organizer, 128
Cow, Stuffed, *111,* 112, *113*
Crafts materials list, 14
Creche, Twig, *51,* 52-53
Crochet
    Baby Booties, 135
    How to, 285-291
Curtains, Ruffled, and Valance, 36

D

Decorated Satin Balls, *68,* 69
Desk Set, 157
Dolls
    Boy and Girl, *84, 86, 88,* 89
    Santa Stocking-Stuffer, 30-33
    Twig Doll Furniture, *130, 131,* 132
    Twin Stuffed, 138-142
Door decorations
    Door Tree, *28,* 29-30
    Santa Door Wreath, 30-33
Dried flowers and leaves, 94-95

E

Earmuffs, Scarf, Tam, *120,* 121
Entryway decorations
    Jiffy, 38
    other ideas for, 38
    scents, 38
    Silver Foil Mirror and Fan, *37,* 38
Evergreen
    entryway decorations, 38
    Garland Tips, 48
    Instant Yuletide Windows, 36
    Pine-branch Tree, 25
    Basic Wreath, 44
    See also Christmas tree
Eyeglass Case, 150, *151*

F

Fabric-Covered Frames, 153
Fantasy Fashion Trims, 122

Felt Santa, *100,* 102, 103
Flowers and Leaves, Dried, 94-95
Foil Mirror And Fan Entryway, *37,* 38
Fragrant Keepsake Wreaths, 94-95
Frames, 110, 112
    Fabric-Covered, 153
    Gathered, *108,* 109
    Padded, *108,* 109
Furniture, Twig Doll, *130, 131,* 132

G

Garlands
    Chenille, 76, 77
    Christmas Tree, 75-79
    Cinnamon, 35
    evergreen, 36, 48
    Lace, *78,* 79
    Pasta, 79
    Pine Branch, 25
    Simple Tree, 76
    Snowman, Elf and Candy-Cane
        Tree, 75-76
    tips, 48
Gathered Frame, *108,* 109
Gift bazaar, 148-153
    gifts for, 149, 153
    list for, 13
    tips, 148
Gift Boxes Wreath, 35-36
Gift certificates
    charitable, 146
    personal, 115, 129, 132, 150
Gift list, 12
Gingerbread House, *54,* 55-56,
    57
Gingham
    Stocking, 103
    Tree Skirt, 104
Glass Bowl Centerpiece, 50
Gold and Silver Balls (centerpiece),
    50
Goose Planter, 126, *127*
Graphics, Stick-On, 147
Gauge, Spaghetti, 115

H

Hair, Split-Second ornaments, 154,
    155
Hand Towels, 153
Hangers, Padded, 149
Hats
    Orange Tweed Cardigan and,
        133, 134
    Scarf, Tam, Earmuffs, *120,*
        121
Heart and Bells, Candlewick, *84,*
    86, 90

Heart Christmas Card Holder, 98
Hot Pad (Apple), 124
Holiday Clown, 62, *63*

J

Jars, Rice-Paper, 150, *151*
Jiffy Decorations, 38

K

Keepsake Box, 121-122
Keepsake, Fragrant Wreath, 94-95
Kentucky Mountain Chain Quilt,
    106, 110
Kiddy Christmas tree, 102
Knife Box, 125
Knitting
    directions, 279-284
    Orange Tweed Cardigan and Hat,
        133, 134
    Piano Key Scarf, 118, *119*
    Rose Vest, *136,* 137-138
    Twisted-Rib Pullover, 116, 117

L

Lace
    Panel Pillow, 152
    Star, *58,* 70
    Tree Garland, *78,* 79
Lanterns, outdoor, 25
Lawn decorations
    Mr. and Mrs. Claus, *22, 23,* 24-25
    quick tricks, 25, 27
Lights, Christmas tree, 60, 70
Lingerie Case, 150, *151*
Lists
    Christmas card, 11
    crafts materials, 14
    gift, 12
    gift bazaar, 13
Lollipop Advent Calendar, *104, 105*

M

Mailing packages, 160-161, 277
Mantel decorations
    Santa Wreath, 30-33
    See also Stockings; Wreaths
Merry Old England Stocking, 41
Mitt (Apple), 124
Mouse, Christmas Pudding, 72-74
Mr. and Mrs. Claus, *22, 23,* 24-25
Musical Austria Stocking, 41
Muslin Star, *86,* 91

N

Napkins
    Cocktail, 153

Strip Quilting for, 99
Native American Stocking, *39,* 41
Nativity scene (Twig Creche), *51,*
    52-53
Natural Christmas Tree, *92*
Nesting Trays, *127,* 128
Noel Panel, 153
Notebook, Three-Ring, 157
Note Paper, Wallpaper, *145,* 146

O

Orange Tweed Cardigan and Hat,
    133, 134
Origami Wreath, *43, 44, 45*
Ornaments, Christmas tree
    Boy and Girl Dolls, *84, 86,*
        88, 89
    Candlewick Heart and Bells,
        84, 86, 90
    Candy Apple, 74
    Christmas Pudding Mouse, 72-74
    Decorated Satin Balls, *68,* 69
    Felt Santa, *100,* 102, *103*
    Lace Star, *58,* 70
    Muslin Star, *86,* 91
    natural, *92*
    Pasta Ornaments, 69
    quick paper, 60
    storing, 60
    Tree Angel, *58,* 69-70
    White Dove, 70-72
Ornaments, Split Second Hair,
    154, *155*

P

Packages, mailing, 160-161, 277
Padded
    Frame, *108,* 109
    Hangers, 149
Pasta
    Ornaments, 69
    Tree Garland, 79
Patchwork Tree Skirt, 81
Pencil Holder, 157
Peppermint Candy Wreath, 48, *49*
Photographs, 110, 165
Piano Key Scarf, 118, *119*
Pillow, Lace-Panel, 152
Pine-branch Garland, 25
Pine-branch Tree, 25
Pinecone Wreath, 95
Placemats, Strip Quilting for, 99
Planning, 6-19
Planter, Goose, 126, *127*
Plants
    poisonous, 102
    See also Evergreens; Poinsettias

Pocket Tissue Case, 150, *151*
Poinsettias
    care of, 29
    Wreath, *46,* 47
Poisonous holiday plants, 102
Pot Handle Cover, 124
Pot Holders
    Apple Pot Holder Set, 123-124
    Appliqued and quilted, 153
Pullover, Twisted-Rib, *116,* 117
Pull-toys, 129, *130*

Q

Quilts and quilting
    Appliqued and Quilted Pot
      Holders, 153
    Kentucky Mountain Chain Quilt,
      106, 110
    Strip Quilting for Runner and
      Napkins, 99
    Trip Around the World Quilt,
      106, 110, *111*

R

Rack
    Tie/Belt, 117
    Wine, *114, 115*
Raffia and Calico Star Finial, *64,* 65
Recipe Stand, 125
Ribbon, 36
Rice-Paper Jars, 150, *151*
Rose Vest, *136,* 137-138
Ruffled Curtains and Valance, 36
Runners, table, 99
Rustic Wreath, 98

S

Santa
    Door Wreath, 30-33
    Felt, *100,* 102, *103*
    Mantel Decoration, 30-33
    Stocking-Stuffer Doll, 30-33
Satin
    Angel Ornament, *61,* 62
    Balls, Decorated, *68,* 69
Scarves
    Piano Key, 118, *119*
    Tam, Earmuffs and, *120,* 121
Scents, 38, 219
    Fragrant Keepsake Wreaths,
      94-95
    Scented Candles, 156
Scrapbook, 141
Set-to-Cook Apron, 154
Shipping packages, 160-161, 277
Silver Foil Mirror and Fan Entryway,
    37, 38

Skirts, Christmas Tree
    Gingham, 104
    Patchwork, 81
    Snowman, 80
    Snowman, Elf and Candy-Cane
      Tree Garland, 75-76
    Teddy Bear, 82, 83
    Tree Skirt, 80
Spaghetti Gauge, 115
Split-Second Ornaments (hair), 154,
    155
Stand, Recipe, 125
Star
    Lace, *58,* 70
    Muslin, *86,* 91
    Raffia and Calico Finial, *64,* 65
Stenciled Sweatshirts, *143,* 144
Stick-On Graphics, 147
Stocking, *40,* 41-42
    Christmas, *40,* 41
    Gingham, 103
    Merry Old England, 41
    Musical Austria, 41
    Native American, *39,* 41
    Stocking stuffers, 42, 150-156
    Santa Doll, 30-33
    Santa Door Wreath, 30-33
Strip Quilting for Runner and
    Napkins, 99
Stuffed Cow, *111,* 112, *113*
Stuffed, Twin Dolls, 138-142
Sweaters
    Orange Tweed Cardigan and Hat,
      133, 134
    Rose Vest, *136,* 137-138
    Twisted-Rib Pullover, *116,* 117
Sweatshirts, Stenciled, *143,* 144

T

Table decorations, 99
Tam, Scarf, Earmuffs, *120,* 121
Tape Recordings, 109
Teddy Bear Tree Skirt, 82, *83*
Three-Ring Notebook, 157
Tie/Belt Rack, 117
Tied Trays, 109
Tissue Case, Pocket, 150, *151*
Toppers, Christmas tree, *61,* 62-67
    Cornhusk Tree-Top Angel, 65-67
    Holiday Clown, *62,* 63
    Raffia and Calico Star Finial, *64,*
      65
    Satin Angel Ornament, *61,* 62
Towels, Hand, 153
Toys
    buying tips, 132
    Pull-, 129, *130*

Twig Doll Furniture, *130, 131,*
    132
Twin Stuffed Dolls, 138-142
Trays, *114,* 115
    Three Nesting, *127,* 128
    Tied, 109
Tree. *See* Christmas tree
Tree Angel, *58,* 69-70
Tree-Top, Cornhusk Angel, 65-67
Trims, Fantasy Fashion, 122
Trip Around the World Quilt, *106,*
    110, *111*
Twig
    Creche, *51,* 52-53
    Doll Furniture, *130, 131,* 132
Twin Stuffed Dolls, 138-142
Twisted-Rib Pullover, *116,* 117

V

Valance, Ruffled Curtains and, 36
Vest, Rose, *136,* 137-138
Victorian-style Christmas tree, *84, 86,*
    88-91

W

Wallpaper Note Paper, *145,* 146
White Dove, 70-72
Window boxes, 25
    Birds 'N' Berries, *26,* 27
Window decorations, 35-36, 38
    Birds 'N' Berries Window Box,
      26, 27
    Cinnamon Garland, 35
    Cinnamon Wreath, *34,* 35
    Gift Boxes Wreath, 35-36
    instant, 36
    Ruffled Curtains and Valance, 36
Wine Rack, 114, *115*
Wrapping tips, 158-161
    basic, 158
    clever ideas, 159
    food, *276,* 277
    for shipping, 160-161, 277
Wreaths, 44-49
    Basic Artificial, 44
    Basic Bow and Streamers, 44
    Basic Evergreen, 44
    Button and Bow, *86,* 91
    Cinnamon, *34,* 35
    Cornhusk, 94
    Fragrant Keepsake, 94-95
    Gift Boxes, 35-36
    Origami, *43,* 44, *45*
    Peppermint Candy, 48, *49*
    Pinecone, 95
    Poinsettia, *46,* 47
    Rustic, 98
    Santa Door, 30-33

FOOD AND ENTERTAINMENT

A

Almond
    Frosting, 256
    Holiday Almond Mounds, 259
    Spritz, *253, 254*
Apple-Onion Chutney, 235
Appliances, 216, 217
Apricot
    Aprikosenflek, 189
    Glazed Apricot Bread, 240
    Glaze, 249
    Quick Conserve, 274
Artichokes, California Platter, 195

B

Bacon
    Baked Sausage and, 187
    Cheese Loaves and, 270
    Striped Oriental Salad, 196-197
Bagna Cauda, Fondue Pot, 217
Basil Butter, 236
Best-Ever Brownies, 261
Beverages
    Café au Lait, 191
    Cocoa with Créme de Menthe, 191
    Gløgg, 176
    Golden Punch, 207
    holiday party bar, 177
    Hot Mocha Mix, 275
    Instant Coffee, 223
    Mulled Cider, 165, 181, 217, 274
    Rosé Spritzers, 207
    Sangria, 195
    Spiced Cappuccino, 203
Bisque, Butternut Squash, 166
Blueberry Coffee Bread, 245
Boiled New Potatoes and Onions, 210
Boston Brown Bread, *239,* 245
Bourbon Balls, Chocolate, *253,* 267
Brandy Pâté, 272
Bread, 223, 238-246
    Bacon and Cheese Loaves, 270
    Blueberry Coffee, 245
    Boston Brown, *239,* 245
    Candied Orange Tea, *239,* 246
    Christmas Braid, 241
    Easy Currant Squares, 246
    freezing tips, 191
    Giant Raspberry Claw, 240
    Glazed Apricot, 240
    Kugelhopf Coffee Cake, 190

Pecan Twists, 242
    Philadelphia Sticky Buns, 244
    Pizza, 199
    Rum-Raisin Ring, *239,* 240
    Toaster Oven Cheddar Loaves, 217
    Triple-Treat Yeast Dough, 238
    Whole Wheat Pretzels, 243
    See also Muffins
Broiled Breakfast Steaks, 187
Brownies
    Best-Ever, 261
    Rocky Road, 267
Brussels Sprouts, Buttered, 168
Bûche de Noël, 200, *201*
Buns, Philadelphia Sticky, 244
Butter
    Basil, 236
    Brussels Sprouts with, 168
    Honey, 274
    Vegetables Broiled in, 188
Buttermilk
    Dressing, 211
    powder, cultured, 222
Butternut Squash Bisque, 166
Butterscotch Sauce, Rich, 172

C

Café au Lait, 191
Cake, 218
    Aprikosenflek, 189
    Bûche de Noël, 200, *201*
    freezing tips, 191
    Kransekage, 182, *183*
    Kugelhopf Coffee Cake, 190
    quick decorations, 251
    storage tips, 255
    Velvety Creme Chocolate, 212, *213*
    See also Fruitcake
California Artichoke Platter, 195
Candied
    Fruit Cookies, 262
    Home-Candied Fruits, 250
    Orange Tea Bread, *239,* 246
Candles
    Candlelight, 169
    Care and usage, 168
    light fantastic, 169
Candy
    Chocolate Bourbon Balls, *253,* 267
    Holiday Almond Mounds, 259
    Mincemeat Balls, 269
Canned fruits, 222
Canned Meat and Seafood, 222
Canning tips, 232
Cappuccino, Spiced, 203
Carrots, Dilled, 233

Celery Relish, 234
Cereal, 222
Cheese, 218, 222
    Bacon and Cheese Loaves, 270
    Cheese and Ham Sandwiches, 178
    Cheese Guide, 226-227
    Garlic Cheese Ball, 271
    Gouda Muffins, 199
    Green Peppercorn, *230,* 271
    Herb and Garlic, 274
    Products, 222
    Quick Cheese Straws, 274
    Toaster Oven Cheddar Loaves, 217
    Wine and Cheese Spread, 271
Chicken
    Chicken and Peanut Kabobs, 196
    Curried Chicken Liver Pâté, 207
China, care of, 167
Chinese Chocolate Drops, 269
Chocolate
    Beverages
        Cocoa with Créme de Menthe, 191
        Hot Mocha Mix, 275
    Chutney, Apple-Onion, 235
    Cake
        Bûche de Noël, 200, *201*
        Velvety Creme Chocolate, 212, *213*
    Cookies
        Best-Ever Brownies, 261
        Bourbon Balls, *253,* 267
        Chinese Chocolate Drops, 269
        Choco-Peanut Bars, 260
        Double Chocolate Chunks, 269
        Marie's Tatus, 264
        Parisiennes, 258
        Rocky Road Brownies, 267
        Walnut Clusters, 263
    Dipped Fruit, 274
    Fudge Sauce, 275
    Glaze, 251, 264
Christmas Braid, 241
Chunky Peanut Butter, 274
Chunky Tomato Sauce, *230,* 233
Chutney, Apple-Onion, 235
Cider, Mulled, 165, 181, 217, 274
Cocoa
    with Créme de Menthe, 191
    Glaze, 264
Coffee
    Café au Lait, 191
    Cream Filling, 200
    Hot Mocha Mix, 275
    Instant Coffee Beverages, 223
    Spiced Cappuccino, 203
Cold Cuts, 222

Colonial Cranberry Pie, 171
Compote
    Continental Fruit, 186
    Spiced Fruit, *230, 234*
Conserve
    Quick Apricot, 274
    Winter Fruit, 235
Continental Fruit Compote, 186
Cookies, 252-269
    Almond Spritz, *253, 254*
    Best-Ever Brownies, 261
    Candied,-Fruit, 262
    Chinese Chocolate Drops, 269
    Chocolate Bourbon Balls, *253,* 267
    Choco-Peanut Bars, 260
    Crisp Refrigerator, 266
    Double Chocolate Chunks, 269
    Double-Decker, *253, 256*
    freezing tips, 258
    Ginger Snappy Turtles, 268
    Greek Walnut Cakes, 264
    Jødekager, 182
    Krispies Treat, 269
    Kyskager, 265
    Lebkuchen, 259
    Maple-Nut Nests, *253, 255*
    Marie's Tatus, 264
    Mexican Wedding Cakes, 265
    Mincemeat Balls, 269
    Molasses Jacks, 263
    Noël Wreaths, 252
    Oatmeal Lace Wafers, 265
    Oatmeal Sandwich Bars, 258
    Parisiennes, 258
    Peanut Butter Munchies, 268
    Peppermint Twists, *253, 254*
    quick decorations, 251
    Raspberry-Nut Pinwheels, 266
    Rocky Road Brownies, 267
    Shortbread Diamonds, *253, 255*
    Spiced Date Bars, 260
    Spicy Fruit Bars, 262
    Sprutter (Pressed Cookies), 181
    storage tips, 255
    Tropical Berry Bars, 261
    Viennese Sandwiches, *253, 256*
    Walnut Clusters, 263
Corn Relish, 233
Cranberry
    Colonial Pie, 171
    Dressing, 236
    Liqueur, 236
Creamed dishes
    Beans and Onions, 169
    Curry Fondue Sauce, 273
    Creamy Scrambled Eggs, 187
Crisp Refrigerator Cookies, 266

Crystal, care of, 167
Cuban-Style Pork, 197
Cultured Buttermilk Powder, 222
Currants, Easy Squares, 246
Curried dishes
    Chicken Liver Pâté, 207
    Creamy Fondue Sauce, 273

D

Date Bars, Spiced, 260
Dilled Green Beans, *230, 233*
Dip
    for dieters, 208
    Fondue Pot Bagna Cauda, 217
    Pimiento-Sour Cream, 195
    Tangy Tomato, 196
    Tzatziki, 208
Double Chocolate Chunks, 269
Double-Decker Cookies, *253, 256*
Doughnuts, Pineapple, 167
Dressing, salad
    Buttermilk, 11
    Cranberry, 236
    Oriental, 197
    Zesty Salad, 237
Dundee Cakes, 247

E

Easy Currant Squares, 246
Eggs, 218
    beating, 187
    Creamy Scrambled, 187
    hard-cooked, 179
    Salmon and Scrambled Egg
        Sandwiches, 178
Electric Frypan Rice Ball, 217
Entertaining Guide, 214-229

F

Figs, Golden Nuggets, 268
First Aid for Food, 218
Fish. *See* Seafood
Fluffy Mashed Potatoes, 168
Flatware, care of, 167
Flavored Wafers, 223
Fondue
    Bagna Cauda, 217
    Creamy Curry Fondue Sauce, 273
    Spicy Tomato Fondue Sauce, 273
Freezing tips, 191, 219, 248
French Herb Blend, 237
Frikadeller (Danish Meatballs), 180
Frosting
    Almond, 256
    Bourbon, 267
    Chocolate butter, 200
    Ornamental (Kransekage), 182, *183*

Royal (Gingerbread House), *54,* 56
Fruit
    Apple-Onion Chutney, 235
    Apricot Glaze, 249
    Candied Fruit Cookies w/filling,
        262
    Canned, 222
    Chocolate-Dipped, 274
    Continental Compote, 186
    Cranberry Dressing, 236
    Frosted, 251
    Fruit 'N' Nut Cakes, 250
    Hawaiian Pear Marmalade, 234
    Holiday Fruit Sauce, 275
    Home-Candied, 250
    Pineapple Doughnuts, 167
    Pineapple Toppings, 275
    Quick Apricot Conserve, 274
    Raisin Spread, 274
    Spiced Date Bars, 260
    Spiced Fruit Compote, 234
    Spicy Fruit Bars, 262
    Stuffed, 274
    Winter Fruit Conserve, 235
Fruitcake, 247-251
    Dundee Cakes, 247
    freezing tips, 248
    Fruit 'N' Nut Cakes, 250
    Glazes, 247, 251
    Golden, *239,* 249
    Home-Candied Fruits for, 250
    Old-Fashioned, *239,* 251
    pan substitution, 248
    Plumb Pudding, *239,* 248

G

Garlic Cheese Ball, 271
Giant Raspberry Claw, 240
Gingerbread house, *54,* 55-56, *57*
    Dough, 56
    Royal Frosting, 56
Ginger Snappy Turtles, 268
Glaze
    Apricot, 249
    Chocolate, 251, 264
    Cocoa, 264
    Crystal, 247
    Dark Fruitcake, 251
    Fruitcake, 251
    Lemon, 170
    Pink, 257
    Rich, 242
    Sugar, 259
Glazed Apricot Bread, 240
Gløgg, 176
Golden Fruitcake, *239,* 249
Golden Punch, 207

Gouda Muffins, 199
Gourmet Mushrooms, 272
Granola, 266
Greek Walnut Cakes, 264
Green Beans
    Creamed Beans and Onions, 169
    Dilled, *230,* 233
Green Peppercorn Cheese, *230,* 271

H

Ham
    Cheese and Ham Sandwiches, 178
    Maple-Glazed, 166
    Savory Ham Sandwiches, 178
    tips, 167
    See also Pork
Hawaiian Pear Marmalade, 234
Herb(ed)
    French blend, 237
    Herb and Garlic Cheese, 274
    Italian Blend, 237
    Olives, 274
    Vinegar, *230,* 237
Herring Salad, 179
Holiday Almond Mounds, 259
Holiday Fruit Sauce, 275
Home-Candied Fruits, 250
Honey
    Butter, 274
    Syrup, 264
Hot-Hot Pepper Jelly, 235
Hot Mocha Mix, 275

I

Italian Herb Blend, 237

J

Jelly, Hot-Hot Pepper, 235
Jødekager, 182

K

Kabobs, Chicken and Peanut, 196
Ketchup, Yankee Tomato, 236
Kransekage, 182, *183*
Krispies Treat, 269
Kugelhopf Coffee Cake, 190
Kyskager, 265

L

Lebkuchen, 259
Lemon-Caraway Muffins, 170
Leverpostej (Liver Pâté), 179
Lime-Peppercorn Mustard, 274
Liqueur, Cranberry, 236
Lists
    chore, 17
    fix-up, 19

food and beverage, 16
gift, 12
gift bazaar, 13
guest, 15
inventory, 19
party shopping, 18
Liver. *See* Pâté
Low-Cal Switch Chart, 180

M

Maple
    Glazed Ham, 166
    Nut Nests, *253,* 255
Marbled Waffles, 188
Marie's Tatus, 264
Marlborough Pie, 203
Marmalade, Hawaiian Pear, 234
Meatballs, 218
    Frikadeller (Danish Meatballs), 180
    Party, 209
Menus, 164, 174, 184, 192, 204
Meringues
    Kyskager, 265
    Mushroom, 202
    Parisiennes, 258
    tips, 202
    Tropical Berry Bars, 261
Mexican Wedding Cakes, 265
Mincemeat Balls, 269
Mixers, nonalcholic, 223
Mocha Mix, 275
Molasses, 223
    Molasses Jacks, 263
Muffins
    freezing tips, 191
    Gouda, 199
    Lemon-Caraway, 170
    Pumpkin, 189
    tips, 170
Mulled cider, 165, 181, 217, 274
Mushrooms
    Butter-Broiled Vegetables, 188
    Gourmet, 272
    Tomatoes and, 180
Mustard, Lime Peppercorn, 274

N

Napkins, 214, *215*
Navy Bean Picadillo, 198
Nibbles, Popcorn and Pretzel, 272
Noël Wreaths, 252
Nonalcoholic Mixers, 223
Noodles and Sauce Products, 223

O

Oatmeal
    Granola, 266

Lace Wafers, 265
    Sandwich Bars, 258
Olives, Herbed, 274
Onions, Creamed Beans and, 169
Oriental
    Spinach Rolls, 208
    Striped Salad, 196-197

P

Packing hints, 277
Parisiennes, 258
Party Meatballs, 209
Party Mix (Cereal), 222
Party tips, 181, 214-221
Pastry
    filling, 223
    lattice, 171
    Rich, 171
Pâté
    Brandy, 272
    Curried Chicken Liver, 207
    Leverpostej (Liver Pâté), 179
Peanuts
    Chicken and Peanut Kabobs, 196
    Choco-Peanut Bars, 260
    Chunky Peanut Butter, 274
Peanut Butter Munchies, 268
Pears
    Fruit 'N' Nut Cakes, 250
    Hawaiian Marmalade with, 234
Peas à la Française, 198
Pecan Twists, 242
Peppermint Twists, *253,* 254
Peppers
    Hot-Hot Pepper Jelly, 235
Philadelphia Sticky Buns, 244
Pickled Peppers, *230,* 234
Pie(s), 223
    Colonial Cranberry, 171
    Marlborough, 203
    perfect piecrusts, 171
    prepared shells, 223
Pilaf
    Rice, 197
    Zucchini Boats with Bulgur, 211
Pimiento-Sour Cream Dip, 195
Pineapple
    Doughnuts, 167
    Topping, 275
Pizza Bread, 199
Planning, 6-19
    holiday party, 9, 15-19, 214-229
    lists, 9-19
    meal, 165, 176, 186, 194, 206
    timetables, 7-9
Plumb Pudding, *239,* 248
Popcorn and Pretzel Nibbles, 272

Pork
    Cuban-Style, 197
    Leverpostej (Liver Pâté), 179
    See also Ham
Potatoes
    Boiled New, 210
    Fluffy Mashed, 168
Pretzels
    Popcorn and Pretzel Nibbles, 272
    Whole Wheat, 243
Pudding
    Plumb, *239*, 248
    Pumpkin Steamed, 172, *173*
Pumpkin
    Muffins, 189
    Steamed Pudding, 172, *173*
Punch, Golden, 207

Q

Quick Apricot Conserve, 274
Quick Cheese Straws, 274

R

Raisin Spread, 274
Raspberries
    Giant Claw, 240
    Raspberry-Nut Pinwheels, 266
Refrigerator Cookies, Crisp, 266
Rejer (Tiny Shrimp) Sandwiches, 178
Relish
    Celery, 234
    Corn, 233
Rice
    Pilaf, 197
    Balls, 217
Rocky Road Brownies, 267
Rosé Spritzers, 207
Rum-Raisin Ring, *239,* 240

S

Safety tips, 180
Salad
    dressings for. *See* Dressing, salad
    Herring, 179
    Striped Oriental, 196-197
    Winter, of Julienne Vegetables,
        210-211
Salmon and Scrambled Egg
    Sandwiches, 178
Sandwiches, Buffet, 178
Sangria, 195
Sauce
    Chocolate Fudge, 275
    Chunky Tomato, *230,* 233
    Creamy Curry Fondue, 273
    Holiday Fruit, 275
    Rich Butterscotch, 172

Spicy Tomato Fondue, 273
Sausage, Baked with Bacon, 187
Savory Ham Sandwiches, 178
Seafood
    Herring Salad, 179
    Rejer (Tiny Shrimp) Sandwiches,
        178
    Salmon and Scrambled Egg
        Sandwiches, 178
Serving pieces, 216
Shipping hints, 277
Shortbread Diamonds, *253,* 255
Shrimp Sandwiches (Rejer), 178
Smoked Turkey Sandwiches, 178
Smørrebrod buffet, 178
Spiced(y)
    Cappuccino, 203
    Date Bars, 260
    Fruit Bars, 262
    Fruit Copmpote, *230,* 234
    Tomato Fondue Sauce, 273
Spinach Rolls, Oriental, 208
Spritz, Almond (cookies), 254
Sprutter (Pressed Cookies), 181
Squash
    Butternut Squash Bisque, 166
    buying tips, 166
    Zucchini Boats with Bulgur Pilaf,
        211
Steaks, Broiled Breakfast, 187
Striped Oriental Salad, 196-197
Stuffed
    Fruit, 274
    Turkey Breast, *205,* 210
Succotash, Yankee, 167
Sugar Glaze, 259

T

Table decorations, 99, 214-*215*
Toaster Oven Cheddar Loaves, 217
Tomatoes
    Butter-Broiled Vegetables, 188
    Chunky Tomato Sauce, *230,* 233
    Mushrooms and, 180
    Spicy Tomato Fondue Sauce, 273
    Tangy Dip, 196
    Yankee Ketchup, 236
Topping, Pineapple, 275
Triple-Treat Yeast Dough, 238
Tropical Berry Bars, 261
Turkey
    Smoked Turkey Sandwiches, 178
    Stuffed Turkey Breast, *205,* 210
Tzatziki, 208

V

Vegetables

Butter-Broiled, 188
Buttered Brussels Sprouts, 168
Butternut Squash Bisque, 166
California Artichoke Platter, 195
Creamed Beans and Onions,
    169
Dilled Green Beans, *230,* 233
Fluffy Mashed Potatoes, 168
Mushrooms and Tomatoes, 180
Navy Bean Picadillo, 198
Oriental Spinach Rolls, 208
Peas á la Française, 198
Pickled Peppers, 234
Relish
    Celery, 234
    Corn, 233
Salad
    Striped Oriental, 196-197
    Winter of Julienne Vegetables,
        210-211
Tzatziki, 208
Zucchini Boats with Bulgur Pilaf,
    211
Velvety Creme Chocolate, 212, *213*
Viennese Sandwiches, *253,* 256
Vinegar, Herbed *230,* 237

W

Wafers, flavored, 223
Waffles, Marbled, 188
Walnut Clusters, 263
Whole Wheat Pretzels, 243
Wine, 177
    buying guide, 224-225
    Gløgg, 176
    Rosé Spritzers, 207
    Sangria, 195
    Wine and Cheese Spread, 271
Winter Fruit Conserve, 235
Winter Salad of Julienne Vegetables,
    210-211
Wok Mulled Cider, 217
Wrapping hints, 277

Y

Yankee
    Succotash, 167
    Tomato Ketchup, 236
Yeast, 190, 223
    baking with, 240
    breads, 238-244
    Triple-Treat Dough, 238

Z

Zesty Salad Dressing, 237
Zucchini Boats with Bulgur Pilaf,
    211